FIELD GUIDE FOR
PRACTICAL
APARTMENT
MANAGEMENT

IREM Institute of Real Estate Management

ACKNOWLEDGEMENTS

The Institute of Real Estate Management® is thankful for the people listed below for taking time from their personal and professional schedules to serve as Review Team Members on this book. Their dedication and support of IREM® education is greatly appreciated!

REVIEW TEAM CHAIR

Michael McCreary, CPM®
[Marietta, GA]

REVIEW TEAM MEMBERS

Sheila Austin, CPM®
[Franklin, MI]

Kathy Harmon, CPM®, ARM®
[Minnetonka, MN]

Dr. Debbie Phillips, CPM®
[Stockbridge, GA]

Steven Rea, CPM®
[Austin, TX]

Robin Stinson, CPM®
[Altamonte Springs, FL]

Mollie Wood, CPM®
[Indianapolis, IN]

ADDITIONAL REVIEWERS

Audrey Demson, CPM®
[Phoenix, AZ]

Carolyn Emery-Brunk, CPM®
[Wichita, KS]

Vickie Gaskill, CPM®, ARM®
[Kent, WA]

Enis Hartz, CPM®
[Anaheim, CA]

Larry Johnson, CPM®
[South Dennis, MA]

Ed Zehfuss, CPM®
[Pittsburgh, PA]

IREM DEVELOPMENT

Rebecca Niday
Content and Curriculum Development
Mindy Wallis
Content and Curriculum Development

Library of Congress Cataloging-in-Publication Data

Field guide for practical apartment management. -- Third edition.
     pages cm
  Reviewed by Michael McCreary, CPM, Marietta, GA, and others.
  ISBN 978-1-57203-224-8 (softcover) -- ISBN 1-57203-224-3 (softcover) 1. Real estate management-
-Handbooks, manuals, etc. 2. Apartment houses--Management--Handbooks, manuals, etc. 3. Rental
housing--Management--Handbooks, manuals, etc. I. Institute of Real Estate Management.
  HD1394.F48 2015
  333.33'8--dc23
                                    2014046750

FIELD GUIDE FOR
PRACTICAL
APARTMENT
MANAGEMENT

TABLE OF CONTENTS

TABLE OF CONTENTS

ICON GUIDE

 RESOURCES

 TIPS

 LEGAL NOTES

 NOTES

 SUSTAINABILITY

 AFFORDABLE HOUSING IMPACT

 SINGLE FAMILY HOUSING IMPACT

 STUDENT HOUSING IMPACT

 CONDOMINIUM IMPACT

INTRODUCTION

There is never a dull moment in the life of a residential site manager. From hiring new employees and balancing the budget, to overseeing construction projects and keeping the apartments leased, every day brings a new challenge and a problem to solve. There is no doubt that residential site management is a complex and rewarding field.

The goal of this book is to provide site managers with the tools and expertise necessary to professionally manage the day-to-day aspects of residential properties. It is a comprehensive guide book that will serve as an ongoing reference tool, and provides many forms and checklists for immediate, on-the-job application.

The contents of this book are organized into four parts.

Part 1: Human Resources and Relationship Management covers the fundamental components of the human resources function, including developing job descriptions, performing performance appraisals, recruiting, retention, and disciplinary action. Legal issues that pertain to the hiring process are also addressed. This section also reviews varying management styles and intergenerational differences that affect the workplace, and shares tips and best practices regarding effective communication techniques and conflict management strategies.

Part 2: Finance introduces the accounting and budgeting skills needed to meet the owner's goals and objectives and to provide a foundation for making day-to-day operating decisions. The components of cash flow are covered, along with a discussion on how site staff impact the property's net operating income. Finally, the finance section addresses budgeting capital for major expenditures, and highlights capitalization techniques used to project the market value of a property.

Part 3: Maintenance and Risk Management reviews the benefits and components of a maintenance and risk management plan, as well as the tools and techniques for conducting inspections to protect residents, guests, and the owner's asset. This section also covers how to implement effective inventory and purchasing control procedures, select and oversee contract workers, and identify conservation techniques to improve sustainability.

Part 4: Marketing and Leasing describes how to conduct market, property, and comparison analyses which are critical to setting optimal rents and meeting the owner's goals and objectives. Additionally, this section covers how to determine appropriate marketing and leasing practices, including key legal considerations, in order to successfully lease apartments to potential residents and increase resident retention.

PART I:
HUMAN RESOURCES AND
RELATIONSHIP MANAGEMENT

The following topics are covered:

- **Management Styles**

- **Intergenerational Dynamics**

- **Employee Motivation**

- **Recruiting and Hiring**

- **Employment Laws**

- **Communication**

- **Performance Evaluations**

- **Fostering Productive Relationships with Owners**

CHAPTER 1:
ABOUT SITE MANAGEMENT

Knowledge of property-specific considerations and key site management themes will position the site manager for success. The manager needs to understand management considerations for the different specialty residential property types as well as the key site management themes that apply to all competency areas.

In this chapter:

> • **Specialty Residential Property Types**
>
> • **Site Management Themes**

SPECIALTY RESIDENTIAL PROPERTY TYPES

While the fundamental principles of management apply to all property types, including our focus on conventional properties, there are some unique considerations for the following specialty property types that will be explored at a high-level throughout this book:

- Affordable Housing
- Condominium
- Single Family Houses & Other Small Residential Housing
- Student Housing

Exposure to a variety of property types is important as you never know where your career will take you. Refer to the following table for a brief overview of each property type.

Property Type	Description
Affordable Housing 	When the U.S. Government provides subsidies to make housing more affordable • Subsidy programs vary, and may be administered via the resident, the owner of the property, or through Public Housing, which is housing owned and administered through the government • Programs may include Section 8, Section 236, Section 202, Low-Income Housing Tax Credit (LIHTC), and many others both on a federal and state level. • Income qualifications for prospects may include government rent-controlled vouchers or other forms of project-based assistance • Unique marketing and leasing requirements—some regulatory, some due to the nature of the property type • Marketing directly to subsidized housing renters is not widely practiced; managers of subsidized housing market to the PHA, if it maintains wait lists of prospective renters • Tax credit properties may compete with market rate properties. • Additional challenges include extensive paperwork, working with both owners and regulatory bodies, tight budgets, maintaining compliance, and resident screening criteria

Property Type	Description
Condominium	Joint ownership of real property by individual investors • Unit ownership is usually comprised of the interior air space inside the walls of the dwelling and an undivided interest in the common areas, which are for the use of owners and maintained by the association • Governed by a board of directors responsible for decisions regarding CID policy. Board members are volunteer owners. • Detailed governance procedures must be followed (e.g., Covenants, Conditions, and Restrictions (CC&Rs), bylaws, board meetings and voting, etc.) • As a non-income producing property, budgeting and finance tasks differ significantly from conventional properties • Marketing and leasing activities typical of conventional properties do not apply to condominium management • One of the primary challenges is navigating the roles and responsibilities between management, the Board of Directors, and owners
Single Family Houses & Other Small Residential Housing	Majority are Detached Single-Family Houses, others are 2-4 family attached units or converted large houses • 6-16 unit buildings are also often managed by managers of Single-Family Houses • Managing single-family homes is common in areas with resorts and second homes, but is also increasing in other areas • As many as one-fifth of single-family houses in the top U.S. markets are rentals • Many owners are "accidental investors or investors by circumstance" due to inability to sell or other reasons. Working with individual owners is typically 1 property=1 owner. • Every rental home is unique and spread out over a wide area, making marketing efforts, routine maintenance, working with contractors, and management inspections more challenging to schedule • Often, budgets for major repairs are limited
Student Housing	Student housing encompasses both on-campus and off-campus housing for university or college students. Often, on-campus housing is owned and operated by the university and off-campus housing is owned and operated by outside entities • Students and parents have high expectations for amenities, services, maintenance, and programming • Managing residents may be complicated by roommate issues and the fact that most students are living away from home for the first time • Strong focus on elevating student lifestyle and experiences, establishing personal relationships, and offering a concierge approach to services • Additional challenges include the seasonal nature of lease-up, the higher turnover from year-to-year, and managing expectations of students, parents, and university staff

SITE MANAGEMENT THEMES

Site managers are responsible for the day-to-day operations at the property, often juggling multiple responsibilities and priorities at once. From hiring and coaching employees, managing budgets, dealing with unexpected maintenance issues, screening residents, and collecting rent, there is no question that the role of site manager is critical to the success of the property.

The variety of activities and broad range of skills used on a daily basis make site management a challenging and rewarding career. While no two days are ever the same, the site manager should keep the following themes in mind in order to be prepared for whatever the day brings.

Owner's Goals and Objectives

Every decision a site manager makes affects the bottom line and the value of the building. For example:

- Following up on a package delivery may help a resident feel cared for, prompting them to renew their lease
- Hiring a qualified maintenance supervisor will ensure work orders are handled appropriately and efficiently in order to minimize major repairs and deferred maintenance
- Developing an emergency and disaster plan will help protect the lives of residents, guests, and employees and minimize damage to the owner's investment
- Ignoring a pavement issue may cause a resident to slip and fall, resulting in a costly lawsuit

While most investment property owners seek to make a profit from their investment, each owner will have specific goals they wish to attain during the term of his or her investment. For example, an owner who wants to sell quickly and make a profit will not be as likely to invest in a new roof or a new energy-efficient HVAC system as the owner who is looking for periodic cash flow over a long holding period.

TIPS:
Knowing that the site manager's daily decisions impact the bottom line, it is important to understand the specific goals and objectives of the owner in order to align key decisions with the desired outcomes.

Agency Relationships and Management Agreements

The relationship between the management company and the property owner is an agency relationship. An *agency relationship* exists when a principal, in this case the property owner, authorizes another person (the agent) to act on his/her behalf. This relationship is usually formalized in writing. In real estate management, this legally recognized relationship is based on management's fiduciary responsibility to the owner. As an agent, the management company is entrusted to act in the owner's best interests to safeguard the investment. These responsibilities extend to the manager and the entire on-site staff.

In real estate management, the document that formalizes the agency relationship between the property owner and the management company is a management agreement. The *management agreement* is a contract that authorizes the site manager to perform the specific functions, duties, and obligations of the property owner (the principal) as an agent. The agreement establishes a fiduciary relationship in which the agent is expected to:

- Demonstrate loyalty to the principal and to keep him or her informed about the status and operations of the property
- Follow the principal's instructions, provided they are legal and ethical, and to perform his or her duties diligently
- Represent the principal in dealings with third parties and to create new contractual obligations for the owner in the book of business
- Be included as an additional named insured party on the owner's property insurance and potentially be indemnified against liability for incidents that occur on the property
- Be protected from acts or omissions of the owner if the management agreement contains hold harmless clauses. Note that this does not protect the agent from liability for personal acts of gross negligence or malfeasance

The manager is expected to disclose to prospective residents that he or she is an agent of the owner. This is important because, while the manager does have certain responsibilities to residents under landlord-tenant law, the specific fiduciary responsibilities of agency apply only to his or her relationship with the property owner—the manager is an agent of the owner, not of the residents.

Customer Service

At the end of the day, real estate management is all about service. Residents can expect trimmed landscaping, online rent payments, and recycling programs anywhere they go. But, exceptional customer service is harder to come by.

The service industry has set a new standard for customer service, and residents expect a similar "above and beyond" model from their management team. Every aspect of a site manager's role encompasses an element of customer service. For example:

- Training site staff to be responsive and proactive
- Providing accurate and timely financial reports to the owner
- Anticipating potential maintenance issues and responding immediately to resident requests
- Planning resident appreciation events, soliciting feedback, and responding to resident complaints

As the eyes and ears of the property, site managers are uniquely positioned to offer exceptional customer service on a daily basis. The single most important thing that will distinguish your property from others is a commitment to providing an incomparable customer service experience for your residents.

TIPS:
Customer service can be implemented regardless of budget.

RESOURCES:
Best practices on customer service can be found in the Institute's publication Marketing Residential Properties The Science and the Magic by Laurence C. Harmon CPM®, CRE and Kathleen M. Harmon, CPM®, ARM®.
Visit **www.irem.org** for additional information.

Problem Solving

One of the hallmarks of a successful site manager is a proactive management approach and a "manage by plan" philosophy. However, despite the best laid maintenance and risk management plans, marketing and leasing plans, and emergency and disaster plans, things happen.

The reality is that site managers spend the majority of their time responding to unexpected situations and resolving issues. Effective site managers must understand effective problem solving techniques, and practice them daily.

CHAPTER 2:
MANAGEMENT STYLES AND MOTIVATION

An effective manager is one that can understand employee needs and create a motivational environment to encourage employees to do their best work. A manager must understand the different styles needed to coach, motivate, and reward team members.

What Is Covered in this chapter:

- **Management Styles**
- **Intergenerational Dynamics**
- **Employee Motivation**
- **Rewarding Employees**
- **Self-Management**

MANAGEMENT STYLES

In his book, *The Human Side of Enterprise,* Douglas McGregor examines the behavior of individuals at work. He has formulated two management styles that he calls Theory X and Theory Y. In addition, a number of other management theories are in circulation today, from Management by Objectives (MBO), to Six Sigma.

Autocratic (Theory X)

Autocratic, or *Theory X,* managers assume that employees inherently dislike work and prefer to be directed. These managers believe that because of their dislike for work, most people must be controlled and threatened before they will work hard enough and that the average human desires security above all else.

Autocratic environments have the following characteristics:

- Management has great responsibility but lower-level team members have virtually none.
- Decisions are imposed upon direct reports.
- Little communication or teamwork takes place.

McGregor states that assumptions made by autocratic managers can be incorrect because employees need more than financial rewards at work, they also needs some deeper motivation—the opportunity for fulfillment and satisfaction on the job. Theory X managers do not give their team this opportunity, so employees behave in the manner expected of them.

Participatory (Theory Y)

Participatory, or *Theory Y*, managers assume that employees are inherently trustworthy and can be self-directed. They motivate their team with rewards and involvement in making decisions. Participatory managers believe that, under proper conditions, the average employee learns not only to accept but also to seek responsibility.

Participatory environments have the following characteristics:

- The creativity of all team members is used to solve work problems.
- Team members feel responsible for achieving organizational goals.
- Communication (both vertical and horizontal) and teamwork are common.

Theory Y may sometimes be difficult to put into practice (e.g., on the shop floor in a large mass production plant). Exercising authority is part of the manager's job, and in some cases that is the only method of achieving the desired results due to short timelines or team disagreement with goals.

However, in situations in which commitment to objectives can be obtained, explaining the purpose of a task and what it means to the property is a better approach. Under such circumstances, employees will exert self-direction to do better work—quite possibly by better methods than they might have used if they were simply carrying out an order they did not fully understand. Team members will contribute more to the organization if managers treat them as responsible, valued employees. Theory Y also contributes to the development of effective managers. Managers will find that the participative approach to problem solving leads to greatly improved results compared with the alternative approach of giving authoritarian orders.

Theory Z

In 1981, William Ouchi examined both American and Japanese management styles and combined them to form what he called *Theory Z*.

Traditionally, Japanese workers believe in lifetime employment with the same company. They also believe that an employee should not be promoted until he or she has served at least 10 years with the company. During those 10 years, the employee is taught everything about the company, so he or she knows every aspect involved in running it. In Japan, managers commonly work side by side with their employees. This is a holistic approach, in which all decisions are made collectively and all employees take responsibility for the company's performance.

Conversely, in today's world, Americans typically move from company to company trying to advance their careers more rapidly. American employees tend to specialize in one area, and they do not learn about the other facets of the organization. This is a much more individualistic approach in which instant, rather than gradual, evaluation and promotion are sought and the philosophy is "everyone for himself."

American Style	Japanese Style	Theory Z (Combination)
Short-term employment	Lifetime employment	Long-term employment
Individual decision making	Collective decision making	Collective decision making
Individual responsibility	Collective responsibility	Individual responsibility
Rapid evaluation & promotion	Slow evaluation & promotion	Slow evaluation & promotion
Specialized career path	Generalists through job rotation	Moderately specialized career paths

Theory Z combines aspects from American and Japanese management styles to propose a style in which employees are committed to the organization, yet still maintain individual responsibilities. Management encourages employees to expand their skills through job rotation or job broadening, so they are familiar with other aspects of the organization. Thus, promotion is much slower.

Management by Objectives (MBO)

In 1954, Peter Drucker introduced the concept of *Management by Objectives* (MBO) in his book, *The Practice of Management*. MBO relies on employees having strong input when identifying their objectives and timelines for completion. Their performance is then compared against the objectives and timelines. MBO involves ongoing tracking and feedback throughout the process of reaching objectives.

Characteristics of MBO:

- Specific objectives for each employee
- Participative decision making
- Explicit timelines
- Performance evaluation and feedback

Total Quality Management (TQM)

Total Quality Management (TQM) is a management style based upon producing quality products and services as defined by the customer. Dr. W. Edwards Deming introduced this concept in the 1940s, but it gained little support from American business people. Deming introduced his theory in Japan, where many Japanese manufacturing companies quickly adopted it. In the decades to follow, American companies focused on producing large quantities of products, while Japanese companies focused on producing high quality products using TQM.

The result was a huge gain in American market share for the Japanese companies. Today, many American companies have adopted TQM as well. The word "total" in Total Quality Management means that everyone in the organization must be involved in the continuous improvement effort. The word "quality" shows a concern for customer satisfaction, and the word "management" refers to the people and processes needed to achieve the quality.

Characteristics of TQM:

- Quality-centered
- Customer-focused
- Fact-based
- Team-driven
- Senior-management-led
- Goal of continuous process improvement

Six Sigma

The Six Sigma model is an approach that helps companies focus on developing and delivering near-perfect products and services. It is based on the work of Joseph Juran, a Japanese pioneer of quality management. General Electric (GE) has used this approach heavily, and it claims $700 million in documented benefits due to increased productivity and decreased waste.

Sigma is a Greek letter used for a statistical term that measures how close a given process is to perfection. The higher the sigma number, the closer to perfection. One sigma is poor; six sigma means only 3.4 defects per million, or 99.99% accuracy. A *defect* can mean anything from a faulty part to an error on a customer's bill.

The central idea behind Six Sigma is that if you can measure the number of defects, or failures to deliver what the customer wants, you can systematically figure out how to eliminate them and get as close to "zero defects" as possible.

In a nutshell, the steps to achieve Six Sigma follow:

1. Define a process where results are subpar.
2. Measure the process to determine current performance.
3. Analyze this information to pinpoint where things are going wrong.
4. Improve the process and eliminate the error.
5. Set up controls to prevent future errors.

RESOURCES:
More information on quality management is available at the American Society for Quality (ASQ) website: **www.asq.org**

Regardless of the management style used, a variety of management skills are required to be an effective manager. Reference the table below for a list of skills and the application to real estate management:

Management Skill	Examples
Be Nimble	• Adjust priorities daily (e.g., emergency situation, giving a tour, resident complaint) • Accept interruptions—go with the flow! • Respond positively to new situations and expectations
Respond to Technology	• Evaluate opportunities to automate processes • Offer plenty of training and support • Develop a blog and a presence on social media sites
Focus on Customer	• Stress customer satisfaction, not just customer service • Empower team to make decisions up to certain dollar threshold to satisfy a customer
Build Relationships	• Make time to chat with residents • Get to know local agencies (e.g., fire department, police department, city representatives) • Seek to understand owner and owner's goals
Engage the Team	• Ask team for input (e.g. solicit opinions on new marketing brand, brainstorming session to identify resident retention tips, rotating contribution to newsletter or community service event) • Acknowledge strong performance and effort • Plan team lunches and other celebrations
Plan and Execute the Work	• Use tracking and prioritization system • Factor in time for project planning • Delegate where possible
Communicate Effectively	• Keep e-mails simple • Follow-up to check understanding (e.g., reports to the owner, service requests) • Use multiple vehicles (e.g., fliers, e-mail, and face-to-face reminders to promote resident party)
Initiate Learning	• Pursue ARM® Certification • Read the *Journal of Property Management (JPM®)* magazine • Establish training goals for self and team • Host knowledge sharing sessions (e.g., low-cost green initiatives, accounting and budgeting 101)

INTERGENERATIONAL DYNAMICS

The current U.S. workforce belongs to four distinct generations: Traditionalists, Baby Boomers, Generation X, and Generation Y, also known as Millennials. Generally speaking, each generation has its own sets of priorities, divergent views about life and work, and unique goals. They also have different work styles and communication approaches, causing an increased potential for conflict and misunderstanding in the workplace. Managers need to understand where their team is coming from in order to assess their skills and provide relevant training for success, growth, and retention. The following table identifies key workplace dimensions, and each generation's perspective.

Workplace Dimension	Traditionalist 1925-1945	Baby Boomers 1946-1964	Generation X 1965-1982	Generation Y Born after 1982
Work Style	By the book. How is as important as what gets done.	Get it done. Whatever it takes (including overtime).	Take fastest route to results. Protocol is secondary.	Work to deadlines and goals – not necessarily to schedules.
Authority/ Leadership	Command and control. Rarely question authority.	Respect for power and	Egalitarian. Rules are flexible. Team work is vital.	Value freedom. Less inclined to pursue leadership positions.
Communication	Formal yet personal. Through proper channels	Quite formal through structured network. Mix of electronic and face-to-face.	Casual, direct, and electronic. Sometimes skeptical.	Fast, casual, direct, and high-tech. Eager to please.
Recognition and Reward	Personal acknowledge-ment and satisfaction for work done well.	Public acknowl-edgement and career advance-ment	A balance of fair compensation and ample time off.	Individual and public praise. Opportunities to broaden skills.
Work/Family	Work and family should be kept separate.	Work comes first.	Value a work/ life balance.	Value blending personal life into work.
Loyalty	To the organization.	To the importance and meaning of work. To the function or profession.	To individual career goals.	To the people involved with the project.
Technology	Complex and challenging. "If it ain't broke, don't fix it."	Necessary for progress and achievement.	Practical tools for getting things done.	What else is there?

EMPLOYEE MOTIVATION

An equation commonly used to understand employee performance follows:

$$\textbf{Ability} \times \textbf{Motivation} = \textbf{Performance}$$

Ability will be determined through the recruiting, hiring, and training processes. However, discovering what motivates individual workers is important. This is something that a manager can learn by simply asking, "Tell me about a time when you performed well on the job. What motivated you to do so?" Another way to learn about employee motivation is by observing your team members' performance to determine their motivating factors. Does the employee perform well when a bonus is awarded for achieving a certain goal? Does the employee perform well when rewarded with formal recognition? Effective managers use different types of motivation and rewards to encourage employees to perform to their fullest potential.

Maslow's Hierarchy of Needs

Motivating employees means to stimulate dedication to an organization and interest in their work. According to Abraham Maslow, people work to satisfy a series of needs. Maslow described those needs as a hierarchy that resembles a pyramid. Employees start out satisfying the needs at the bottom of the pyramid. Once an employee's needs are met at that stage, he or she begins to think about satisfying needs at the next stage.

Maslow's five stages:

1. **Physiological/Basic.** First are the basic needs of shelter, food, drink, and sleep. In the workplace, this means hygienic working conditions, as well as sufficient salary and benefits.

2. **Safety/Security.** People normally seek out safe, predictable, and orderly environments. In the workplace, safety is being free from the fear of workplace violence, having a good health insurance plan, and having job security.

3. **Belonging/Social.** This stage includes such needs as group membership, friendships, family, and a sense of belonging. These needs can be met at work by being part of a team. People in this stage may enjoy passing out paychecks or organizing the company softball team because it's a chance to connect with coworkers.

4. **Esteem/Ego/Status.** At the fourth stage, a person needs to be regarded as competent or important, both in terms of self-respect (Ego A) and group respect (Ego B). Self-respect is what you think of yourself and group respect is what others think of you. An employee may measure his or her esteem by salary level (often an important status symbol) or recognition for a job well done. An individual might meet these needs by teaching a book or training session or by seeking more responsibility at work.

5. **Self-Actualization or Self-Fulfillment.** In the last stage, a person attains his or her personal goals. At this stage employees realize their full potential and nothing stands between the employee and his or her work. Self-actualization exists when employees feel a genuine joy and satisfaction from doing their very best work. People at this level are the easiest to manage because they are self-motivated and produce consistent, high-quality work.

When the economy slows, and companies are in turmoil or conduct lay-offs, employees may regress back to a previous stage out of necessity.

Goal Setting

Goal-setting theory asserts that people with specific challenging goals (often called "stretch" goals) perform better than those with vague goals such as "do your best" or specific easy goals. A benefit of goal setting, which will be discussed further in the chapter on performance evaluations, is that it often motivates employees to perform better. This is because a goal is the object or aim of an action—for example, to attain a specific occupancy rate within a specified time limit.

Goal setting instills purpose, challenge, and meaning into what may typically be perceived as a tedious or tiresome task. The psychological outcomes of setting and attaining high goals include enhanced task interest, pride in performance, and a heightened sense of personal effectiveness. In addition, goal setting has shown to improve employee attendance.

What is wrong with urging people to "do their best"? This type of direction is vague and is defined differently by different managers. Setting a specific high goal, on the other hand, makes explicit for people what needs to be attained.

REWARDING EMPLOYEES

Based on the stage at which each employee functions, managers can tailor rewards to effectively motivate each individual. Time off for rest and relaxation might address basic physiological needs. Increased health benefits might be a reward for someone at the Safety/Security stage. Being included in meetings and decision making might motivate an employee who values belonging and social needs. Ego-driven employees can be rewarded with an "employee of the month" award or some other form of formal recognition. Finally, those seeking self-actualization will feel rewarded with fulfilling and challenging work.

LEGAL ISSUE:
Be sure to follow federal wage and hour laws regarding change in schedule policies. Note the key points in the following chart.

Key Point	Examples
The employer/employee can change a work schedule anytime	• Employee wants to leave early on Wednesday and work longer on Thursday—this is a change in schedule • For a non-exempt (hourly) employee this must take place within the work week, not pay period if overtime relevance does not want to be taken into consideration • For an exempt employee (salary), this is simply a change to the time he or he is in the office
The employer has the right to change a schedule to prevent overtime pay	• Employee works 10 hours one day because of snow removal and employer wants them to work 6 hours the next day so there will not be overtime. • In most jurisdictions this is legal • However, it may not be the best employee retention/morale decision

Important! Remember to check state and local laws to see if there are more stringent laws for your state than federal wage and hour laws. When approving a change in schedule, be sure that you understand if the change will have overtime consequences and follow the law.

Guidelines for Praise

Praise is a free, effective way for managers to motivate and reward their team. Praise can come in a number of forms, from an e-mail complimenting the employee to verbal recognition in front of the employee's peers, such as at a team meeting. Managers should follow a few guidelines when praising their team:

1. **Be specific.** Instead of saying, "Good job!" try, "I really appreciate your extra efforts to finish the leasing report by 5:00 p.m. yesterday." This allows the employee to know exactly why you are recognizing him or her and will most likely encourage that employee to perform that task well again in the future.

2. **Link the performance to the accomplishment of overall goals.** Praise can be especially effective when the employee sees a link between his or her performance and the success of the entire property. Here are some examples:

   "By coming in early each day this week, you helped us handle the usual resident service requests, even while the new HVAC system was being installed. This achieved one of our most important property goals—keeping the residents satisfied."

   "Your recommendation to use a different contractor for landscaping services really helped us meet the budget and achieve our major financial goal for the property this year."

3. **Express confidence that the employee can duplicate the behavior.** The employee is more likely to repeat the achievement when the manager emphasizes that the individual can do it again.

"I'm confident that you will keep up the good work in this area."

"I'm looking forward to seeing next month's report as well."

SELF-MANAGEMENT

It is a well-known axiom that good management of others begins with managing yourself. As Jed Yueh, CEO of Delphix, a software company, said, "If you don't manage yourself very well, it's hard for you to maximize the performance of a team. And managers can either increase or decrease motivation for their teams. They can either increase or decrease clarity for their teams. They can either build cultures that are highly collaborative and capable of solving problems quickly, or they can create cultures where you have a lot of paralysis and it's very difficult to make decisions." The following table lists some self-management skills.

Skill	Actions
Time Management	• Use "to do" lists. Think about what you need to accomplish each day and plan accordingly. • Prioritize. Make sure the important things get done first. • Don't get distracted from other tasks by always looking at e-mail. • Plan errands so that you can complete them all at once, rather than coming and going.
Record Keeping	• Document as much as you can to ensure that there is no confusion about the actions you've taken. • Use apps and software that allow you to capture information as quickly and easily as possible.
Improve Yourself	• Participate in professional development activities to learn to skills. • Read books and articles about the industry or management in general. • Identify areas of weakness and work to improve them.
Take a Break	• Schedule a period each day when you don't take calls or answer email. • Find time to do the things you enjoy. Too much work leads to stress and ill-health. • Take your vacation time.

CHAPTER 3:
PLANNING AND RECRUITING

The required knowledge, skills, and abilities identified in the job analysis enable a manager to create more effective job descriptions and to recruit more successfully, both internally and externally. The manager must understand the components of human resource activity, including developing a job analysis, recruiting, and conducting performance appraisals.

In this chapter:

> • **Job Descriptions**
>
> • **Recruiting**

 Single Family House Impact: Note that managers of single family house properties often deal with contractors and not employees. However, it is still important to understand the type of skills required for the work.

A *job analysis* is the systematic gathering of information about a job to identify its responsibilities. These essential job functions determine the knowledge, skills, and abilities (KSAs) the jobholder needs to perform the job.

> • **Knowledge:** information necessary to perform the job
>
> • **Skills:** level of competency or proficiency needed to perform the job
>
> • **Abilities:** traits or capabilities necessary to perform the job

The job analysis also answers questions such as the following: How much supervision is necessary? What are the performance expectations for this job? With whom does the jobholder interact? ***Note that the analysis is conducted of the job, not of the person who does the job.***

The job analysis forms the basis of all subsequent human resource activity. It is used in many capacities throughout the employee life cycle:

> • **Recruitment:** the job analysis helps generate a higher-quality pool of applicants by more effectively describing the job tasks, duties, and responsibilities as well as the knowledge, skills, and abilities needed from the applicant
>
> • **Selection:** the job analysis helps determine the tools an interviewer should use when hiring for the position (e.g., a personality test may be administered if the job analysis determines that "extroversion" is a necessary quality)

- **Performance appraisal:** the standards used to judge employee performance should be job-related as determined by the job analysis
- **Compensation:** job analysis information can be used to compare the relative worth of each job's contributions to the company's overall performance, thus determining pay level
- **Training and career development:** employee skill gaps can be identified and training programs can be put into place to increase necessary knowledge, skills, and abilities and to improve job performance

LEGAL ISSUE:
When conducting job analyses, all processes and findings should be documented. This information helps companies defend their actions against alleged unfairness or discrimination. Job analyses can also prove the job-relatedness of criteria used in the hiring process or in performance appraisals. Consult a human resources professional or attorney for guidance and additional information.

Job analyses may be conducted by the company at large, or they can be conducted at the property site through interviews, observations, and questionnaires. Refer to Figure 3-1 for a guide to conducting a job analysis.

FIGURE 3-1: JOB ANALYSIS GUIDE

Job Title:
Department:
Date:

Purpose
1. Summarize the major reason that the job exists. What is its main purpose?

Supervision Received
2. What is the job title of the supervisor of this position?

3. Does this position report to any additional supervisors? What percent of the time?

Title	Percent of Time

Supervision Exercised
4. What are the job titles of those who report to this position?

5. How many people does this position supervise?

6. What percent of the time is spent directing or overseeing the work of others?

Tools/Equipment
7. List any tools or equipment this position frequently uses.

Duties
8. What work activities does this position perform? How often or frequently is each activity done? List the duties in the order of importance.

Duty	Percentage of Time/Frequency

Education
9. What kind of education is essential, at a bare minimum, to begin this job?

Experience
10. What type of certification is essential, at a bare minimum, to begin this job?

11. What kind of experience is essential, at a bare minimum, to begin this job?

Personal Qualities
12. What personal qualities are essential, at a bare minimum, to begin this job?

JOB DESCRIPTIONS

A *job description* summarizes the information collected in the job analysis. It defines the job in terms of its responsibilities, required knowledge, skills, abilities, and reporting structure.

Every job should have a written job description. Having written job descriptions provides current employees with clear guidelines and provides potential employees with comprehensive information about the job for which they are applying.

A job description typically consists of the following elements:

- Title, location, wage category
- Job summary
- Job duties and responsibilities
- Job requirements (knowledge, skills, and abilities)
- Minimum qualifications, including education, experience, licenses, and professional affiliations

Ensure that job titles and information do not refer to a specific gender (e.g., sales*man*). Carefully consider job titles, as they have a strong impact on candidate and employee perception. For example, trends are showing more general titles such as director, associate, and consultant. Build flexibility into the job description; include the line "other duties as assigned" in the list of responsibilities.

LEGAL ISSUE:
Federal law requires that job descriptions document only the essential aspects of the job. Otherwise, the descriptions might inadvertently discriminate against qualified women, minorities, and persons with disabilities for not meeting specified job requirements.

The U.S. Department of Labor's *Dictionary of Occupational Titles* (DOT) may be a helpful *starting point* for writing job descriptions. The DOT describes more than 10,000 occupations. The following is the DOT summary for the job title of Leasing Agent:

TITLE(s): **LEASING AGENT, RESIDENCE**
ALTERNATE TITLE(s): Rental Agent

Shows and leases apartments, condominiums, homes, or mobile home lots to prospective tenants. Interviews prospective tenants and records information to ascertain needs and qualifications. Accompanies prospects to model homes and apartments and discusses size and layout of rooms, available facilities, such as swimming pool and saunas, location of shopping centers, services available, and terms of lease. Completes lease form or agreement and collects rental deposit. May inspect condition of premises periodically and arrange for necessary maintenance. May compile listings of available rental property. May compose newspaper advertisements. May be required to have real estate agent's license. May contact credit bureau to obtain credit report on prospective tenant.

Source: U.S. Department of Labor's Dictionary of Occupational Titles (DOT)

RESOURCES:
This occupational information is available on the Occupational Information Network (O*NET) website: **www.onetcenter.org**. This Web site provides a comprehensive database of worker attributes and job characteristics. As the replacement for the *Dictionary of Occupational Titles* (DOT), O*NET is the nation's primary source of occupational information. In addition, the U.S. Department of Labor publishes the *Occupational Outlook Handbook*, which provides detailed job information for virtually every profession.

Affordable Housing Impact: Be sure to identify additional job description requirements unique to affordable housing properties such as tax credit certified, section 8 experience, etc.

Student Housing Impact: Be sure to identify additional job description requirements unique to student housing properties such as ability to develop student programming, serve as liaison to Housing Office, etc.

Single Family House Impact: Be sure to identify additional job description requirements unique to single family house properties such as travel from site to site to perform leasing and maintenance activities, and familiarity with the unique features of each single family house.

RESOURCES:

Human Resources information and forms can be found under Resources > Forms & Checklists at **www.irem.org** and are free for members. These sample forms and agreements are not endorsed by the Institute of Real Estate Management. They are presented for informational purposes only.

RECRUITING

Recruiting is the process of identifying and attracting qualified job candidates. Attracting unqualified applicants can be costly and waste time, thus the job description you use for recruiting should be accurate and up-to-date so it will target the right pool of candidates. When recruiting, you have essentially two choices: to look within the organization or to seek candidates externally from the general labor pool.

Internal Recruiting

Recruiting from within fills open jobs through internal promotions and transfers. This method is cost-effective because the organization capitalizes on the investment it has already made in its current employees. Internal recruiting rewards the good work of current employees and may improve morale within the organization. A disadvantage of recruiting internally is that competition for the position or infighting may occur within the company. In addition, the company may have to fill the position of the person who was promoted.

Job posting gives employees the chance to respond to announcements of positions open at the property. The posting should consist of the job description based on the job analysis. Job posting allows qualified employees to compete for positions and helps prevent supervisors from showing favoritism in the promotion process. Job posting may also help discover talent within the organization that was previously unknown. A good job posting can even prevent a bored or dissatisfied but competent employee from quitting by allowing the employee to move into a different role.

Employee Referrals

Current employees can be valuable resources when filling job openings. They may be more knowledgeable about the job specifications, and they typically pre-qualify referrals and identify people who will fit well into the position and the organization. Studies show that employees hired through referrals from current employees tend to stay with the organization longer and display greater loyalty than employees recruited by other means.

Employee referrals are cost-effective, and some companies even pay workers a bonus if their referral is hired and achieves the performance goals for the position. Some companies provide employees with business card size recruitment cards, so employees can distribute to individuals who have demonstrated customer service or technical skills that would be an asset to their company. However, current employees tend to recommend people who are demographically similar to themselves, which can perpetuate any existing patterns of discrimination and create equal employment opportunity (EEO) problems. Thus, employee referral programs are generally most effective when used in conjunction with other recruiting techniques.

External Recruiting

External recruiting involves advertising the job to the labor market at large. Advantages of external recruiting include bringing new ideas and talent to the property and potentially helping the property meet diversity goals. Disadvantages include increased recruitment costs, a longer orientation time for the new hire, and potential morale problems for internal candidates.

When the unemployment rate is high, the organization will have an easier time finding qualified candidates from the external labor supply. When unemployment is low, the company may need to recruit more heavily. Recruiting methods may include the Internet, media advertisements, career fairs, employee referrals, and employment agencies.

Internet

The Internet is the primary source of employee recruitment. Online job advertisements are inexpensive and far-reaching. They can often produce faster results than other recruiting methods. Thousands of career websites exist and most are free to those searching for jobs. Monster.com, one of the best-known sites, lists over a million positions. Job seekers can search for jobs by location, job category, and keywords. For a reasonable fee, employers can post open positions and search candidate resumes on the site.

While a benefit of using the Internet is that applicants can easily submit resumes, a disadvantage is that volumes of resumes may inundate a company that posts a job. Human resources must screen out the mismatches. After identification of desirable potential employees, personal contact becomes especially important. An interviewer should contact the job applicant quickly (preferably within 24 hours) to establish a rapport and potentially move forward with the selection process.

RESOURCES:
Designed specifically for those seeking and posting jobs in real estate management, **www.IREMJobs.org** displays jobs across the country in fields such as residential property management, leasing, maintenance, finance, administration, and other categories. Refer to Figure 3-2 for a sample.

FIGURE 3-2: IREMJOBS SAMPLE

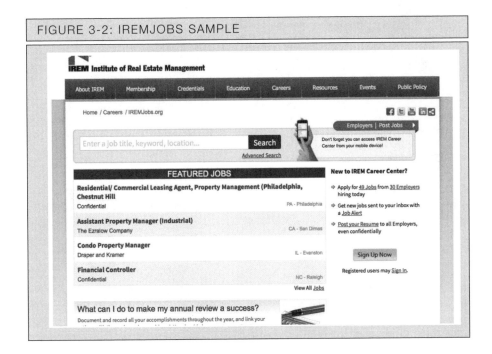

Media Advertisements

Advertising in newspapers and trade journals is another way to reach large audiences. The advertisement should focus both on the open position and the company image. Include a summary of the job description and desired qualifications. Always state that the organization is an equal opportunity employer (EEO). Compensation information may or may not be included, depending on the position and the company's desire to reveal that information at that stage in the hiring process.

Career Fairs

Job fairs and educational recruiting can occur at the high school and college levels. Candidates from those sources are educated but usually have minimal full-time work experience. To conduct an effective college recruitment program, establish a relationship with the college placement office, faculty members, and corporate alumni. Have recruiters discuss your career opportunities and requirements and share equal employment opportunity (EEO) policies with the students. Offer the students the opportunity to tour your company's facilities and speak with current employees in similar positions. Career fairs may take place on the school campus or as an "open house" on the company premises. Companies that have a large number of positions to fill might wish to consider holding their own career fair.

Student Housing Impact: Campus recruiting is also an effective method for recruiting employees. Consider the following opportunities available through campus recruiting:
- Campus organizations
- University job center
- Student union
- Career placement offices
- Work study/financial aid office

Employment Agencies

Some organizations use external sources to recruit and screen applicants for a position. Typically, the employment agency earns a fee based on the salary or hourly wage offered to the new employee. An advantage of employment agencies is that they often seek out candidates who currently have jobs, which indicates that their current employer is satisfied with their performance. You should research these agencies carefully, as their costs and services vary.

Professional Associations

Networking is consistently cited as the best way to get a new job. Employers are more inclined to meet with someone who comes recommended, as there is already a level of knowledge about both the candidate and employer. Involvement in a professional association such as IREM®, The National Apartment Association (NAA), local apartment associations, National Association of Residential Property Managers (NARPM®), National Association of Home Builders (NAHB®), or Community Associations Institute (CAI) is a great way to stay connected to the industry and network on an ongoing basis. Attending IREM® chapter meetings at the local level is a great way to get connected, maximize membership value, and pursue added networking opportunities.

Affordable Housing Impact: There are many professional associations targeted toward affordable housing such as the National Affordable Housing Management Association (NAHMA), National Association of Housing and Redevelopment Officials (NAHRO), state and local associations, and so forth.

Student Housing Impact: The Association of College & University Housing Officers–International is a professional association geared toward student housing.

RESOURCES:
Information on the compensation and properties managed by those who hold the IREM® ARM® Certification can be found in the Institute publication *Profile and Compensation Study, ARM Edition 2014.* It is available for download at **www.irem.org**.

CHAPTER 4:
LEGAL ISSUES AND HIRING

Understanding and abiding by employment laws ensures ethical behavior at the property and minimizes any potential liability. An effective employee orientation presents important company policies and successfully integrates the employee into the property. A manager must identify the legal issues that impact the employee life cycle, from hiring to employee orientation.

In this chapter:

- **Legal Issues**

- **Hiring Employees**

- **Employee Orientation**

LEGAL ISSUES

In the past four decades, Congress has passed a multitude of legislation in an attempt to end workplace discrimination and uphold employee rights. Complying with these laws ensures the property is acting ethically and minimizes the organization's potential liability. **In addition to federal legislation, managers should know their state and local laws as they relate to workplace practices.**

Law	Year	Key Provisions
National Labor Relations Act (NLRA)	1935	Establishes union representation and identifies unfair labor practices
Title VII (Civil Rights Act) *Applies to employers with 15+ employees*	1964	Prohibits discrimination in employment on basis of race, color, religion, sex, national origin (also prohibits harassment)
Age Discrimination in Employment Act (ADEA) *Applies to employers with 20+ employees*	1967	Prohibits discrimination against persons over age 40
Occupational Safety and Health Act (OSHA) *Applies to employers with 10+ employees*	1970	Establishes standards and regulations for workplace safety
Fair Credit Reporting Act (FCRA), Fair and Accurate Credit Transactions Act (FACTA)	1970, 2003	Protect job applicants' privacy and ensure that information collected by credit agencies is accurate

Law	Year	Key Provisions
Vietnam-Era Veterans Readjustment Act (VEVRAA)	1974	Prohibits discrimination against Vietnam-era veterans by federal contractors The Jobs for Veterans Act (JVA) amended VEVRAA by raising the dollar amount of the contract from $25,000 to $100,000, and changing the categories of protected veterans. The JVA amendments to VEVRAA apply to contracts entered on or after December 1, 2003.
Pregnancy Discrimination Act	1978	Prohibits discrimination on the basis of pregnancy or childbirth
Fair Labor Standards Act (FLSA)	1986	Establishes minimum wages, hours worked, overtime pay, and equal pay for equal work
Immigration Reform and Control Act	1986	Establishes penalties for employers who knowingly hire illegal aliens; prohibits discrimination based on national origin or citizenship
Americans with Disabilities Act (ADA) *Applies to employers with 15+ employees*	1990	Requires employer to make reasonable accommodations for disabled individuals
Family and Medical Leave Act (FMLA) *Applies to employers with 50+ employees* **National Defense Authorization Act for FY2008 (NDAA)**	1993, 2008	Requires employers to allow employees time off to handle family and medical problems. NDAA amends the FMLA to provide a new entitlement to leave in two situations related to military service: caregiver leave for an injured servicemember and family leave due to a call to active duty.
Personal Responsibility and Work Opportunity Reconciliation Act (PRWORA)	1996	Requires employers to report all new hires; established as part of welfare reform legislation
Health Insurance Portability and Accountability Act (HIPAA)	1996	Mandates privacy standards and protections regarding health information. Every employer that offers health benefits or health services to its employees is affected by the HIPAA rules.
Lilly Ledbetter Fair Pay Act of 2009	2009	The 180-day statute of limitations for filing an equal-pay lawsuit regarding pay discrimination resets with each new paycheck affected by that discriminatory action.

National Labor Relations Act (NLRA)

What is it?

Congress enacted the National Labor Relations Act (NLRA) in 1935. Previously, employers were free to spy on, interrogate, discipline, terminate, and blacklist union members. But in the 1930s workers began to organize militantly. A great strike wave in 1933 and 1934 included citywide general strikes and factory takeovers. Violent confrontations occurred between workers trying to form unions and the police and private security forces defending the interests of antiunion employers. Some historians believe that Congress adopted the NLRA primarily in the hopes of averting greater, possible revolutionary, labor unrest.

The NLRA guaranteed workers the right to join unions without fear of management reprisal. It created the National Labor Relations Board (NLRB) to enforce this right and prohibited employers from committing unfair labor practices that might discourage organizing or prevent workers from negotiating a union contract.

Section 7, the heart of the NLRA, defines protected activity:

> Employees shall have the right to self-organization, to form, join, or assist labor organizations, to bargain collectively through representatives of their own choosing, and to engage in other concerted activities for the purpose of collective bargaining or other mutual aid and protection.

Section 8 defines five types of employer conduct that is illegal under the NLRA:

1. Employer interference, restraint, or coercion directed against union or collective activity
2. Employer domination of unions
3. Employer discrimination against employees who take part in union or collective activities
4. Employer retaliation for filing unfair-labor-practice charges or cooperating with the NLRB
5. Employer refusal to bargain in good faith with union representatives

Title VII (Civil Rights Act)

What is it?

The cornerstone of antidiscrimination legislation is Title VII of the Civil Rights Act of 1964. The heart of this law, Section 703(a), reads as follows:

> It shall be an unlawful employment practice for an employer:

> (1) to fail or refuse to hire or to terminate any individual, or otherwise discriminate against any individual with respect to his compensation, term, conditions, or privileges of employment, because of such

individual's membership in a protected class:

- race
- color
- religion
- sex
- national origin

(2) to limit, segregate, or classify his employees or applicants for employment in any way which would deprive or tend to deprive any individual of employment opportunities or otherwise adversely affect his status as an employee, because of such individual's membership in a protected class

The Equal Employment Opportunity Commission (EEOC) is the regulatory agency that enforces antidiscrimination laws (**www.eeoc.gov**).

What are the Key Terms?

Recognizing discrimination in the workplace can be difficult. However, managers should be aware of two primary types of discrimination:

- **Disparate treatment** occurs when individuals are treated differently because of their membership in a protected class. Examples include a manager automatically rejecting Latino job applicants, using a different hiring process for woman than for men, or disciplining African-American but not Caucasian workers for violating the same policy.

- **Adverse impact**, which may be less intentional, occurs when the equal application of an employment standard has an unequal effect on a protected class. For example, requiring nonessential education for a job may impact a minority group that has been limited in access to educational opportunities. Managers should be careful not to perpetuate past policies that may have discriminatory results.

Disparate Treatment	Adverse Impact
• Direct discrimination	• Indirect discrimination
• Intentional	• Unintentional
• Unequal treatment	• Unequal consequences or results
• Different standards for different groups	• Same standards but different consequences

What are the Exceptions?

Employers can defend potentially discriminatory human resource practices in a few exceptions:

- **Job relatedness**: Employers may be able to defend a practice if it is job-related and required by business necessity. For example, some occupations require the ability to lift a certain amount of weight; this may discriminate against women, but if it were a business necessity, it would be permitted.

- **Bona fide occupational qualification (BFOQ)**: A BFOQ is a characteristic that must be present in all employees for a particular job. For example, a film director is permitted to consider only females for the part of an actress. In this case, being female is a BFOQ.

- **Seniority**: Employment decisions made in the context of a formal seniority system that was not designed to discriminate are permitted, even if they inadvertently discriminate against certain protected classes.

Although Title VII does not currently cover sexual orientation as a protected class, some state and local laws do prohibit discrimination based on sexual orientation. In the absence of federal laws, employers can take steps to provide a fair workplace: revising nondiscrimination policies to include sexual orientation, enforcing discipline against harassment of gay and lesbian employees, and extending employment benefits to domestic partners of gay and lesbian workers.

Harassment

What is it?

Title VII also prohibits sexual harassment and harassment based on a protected class. The Equal Employment Opportunity Commission (EEOC) defines sexual harassment and harassment as follows:

Definition of Harassment

Unlawful harassment is verbal or physical conduct that denigrates or shows hostility or aversion toward an individual because of his or her race, color, religion, gender, national origin, age or disability, or that of his/her relatives, friends, or associates, and that:

1. has the purpose or effect of creating an intimidating, hostile, or offensive working environment;

2. has the purpose or effect of unreasonably interfering with an individual's work performance; or

3. otherwise adversely affects an individual's employment opportunities.

Definition of Sexual Harassment

Unwelcome sexual advances, requests for sexual favors, and other verbal or physical conduct of a sexual nature constitute sexual harassment when:

1. submission to such conduct is made either explicitly or implicitly a term or condition of an individual's employment;

2. submission to or rejection of such conduct by an individual is viewed as a basis for employment decisions affecting such individual; or

3. such conduct has the purpose or effect of unreasonably interfering with an individual's work performance or creating an intimidating, hostile, or offensive working environment.

What are the Key Terms?

There are two categories of sexual harassment:

- **Quid pro quo**, meaning "this for that," harassment occurs when sexual activity is required in return for getting or keeping a job or job-related benefits such as a promotion or pay increase.

- **Hostile environment** harassment occurs when the behavior of anyone in the work setting is sexual in nature and is perceived by an employee as offensive and undesirable. Hostile environment can be created by supervisors, coworkers, and even nonemployees such as tenants.

Age Discrimination in Employment Act (ADEA)

What is it?

The Age Discrimination in Employment Act (ADEA) of 1967 prohibits discrimination in employment against individuals age 40 and over. The ADEA forbids mandatory retirement at any age and limiting employees in any way that adversely affects their status due to age. The ADEA also allows for jury trials. Instead of punitive or compensatory damages, the ADEA provides for the doubling of damages awarded by the jury for a "willful" violation.

LEGAL ISSUE:
In 2011, the U.S. Equal Employment Opportunity Commission (EEOC) received over 23,465 charges files under the ADEA, a 40% increase over 2006. Recently, the EEOC brought suit on behalf of an office manager at a health care company because her manager said she "sounded old on the phone," and looked "like a bag of bones." The U.S. District Court of Hawaii awarded nearly $200,000 in damages.

Occupational Safety and Health Act (OSHA)

What is it?

In addition to obeying antidiscrimination laws, organizations have a legal responsibility to protect the physical well-being of their employees. Companies have a vested interest in maintaining safe and secure work environments due to the personal and economic impact that accidents and breaches of security can cause.

The Occupational Safety and Health Act (OSHA) of 1970 (**www.osha.gov**) encourages employers and employees to reduce safety and health hazards and implement programs that will improve the safety and security of the working environment. Specifically, OSHA gives employees the right to:

- Demand safety and health on the job without fear of punishment
- Request and accompany inspections by an OSHA officer
- File a complaint to an employer, OSHA, or other government agency
- Be informed of workplace hazards and precautions that should be taken
- Receive training on workplace safety and health issues

To promote safe and healthy work environments, employers should become aware of and remove any hazards in the workplace. They should use safeguards and warning signs where appropriate and instruct employees on how to avoid or deal with potential health or safety risks. Emergency exits and routes should be clear.

Employers should also take security measures to protect employees and property. They should install adequate lighting, surveillance, and alarms and supply key cards and other access systems. Security guards can also reduce or prevent loss.

What are the Key Terms?
Providing a healthful and safe working environment has three components:

1. **Health**: state of well-being, freedom from illness and disease
2. **Safety**: freedom from hazard, risk, or injury
3. **Security**: reduction or elimination of loss of assets (property, employees, intellectual capital)

Fair Credit Reporting Act (FCRA), Fair and Accurate Credit Transactions Act (FACTA)
What is it?
The Fair Credit Reporting Act (FCRA) of 1970 deals with employers' use of credit reports and other background information to determine an applicant's suitability for employment. The FCRA is designed to protect applicants' privacy and ensure that information collected is accurate. Under the FCRA, employers must obtain a signed authorization to collect background or credit information. If the employer rejects an applicant based on the report, a rejection letter to the applicant must:

1. Provide the name, address, and telephone number of all consumer credit reporting agencies that provided information.

2. Make clear that the credit agencies only provided information about the applicant's credit history, took no part in the decision process, and cannot explain why the decision was made.

3. Explain the applicant's rights to obtain a free copy of the credit report from the agency, dispute the accuracy of the report, and provide a consumer statement describing his or her position.

Employers can also use this report to examine the applicant's past employers and verify whether the information matches what the employee lists on the application or resume.

In 2003, Congress passed the Fair and Accurate Credit Transactions Act (FACTA). This bill contains a number of new provisions, including notice of negative credit score treatment caused by credit inquiries; prompt reinvestigation and correction of inaccurate information; and a study of the effects of credit scoring on insurance and other financial products. The bill also permanently extends expiring FCRA provisions that preempt many state consumer-protection laws. More information on the FCRA and the FACTA is available on the Federal Trade Commission website: **www.ftc.gov**.

Vietnam-Era Veterans Readjustment Act (VEVRAA)
What is it?
The Vietnam Era Veterans' Readjustment Assistance Act of 1974 requires that contractors and subcontractors with a federal contract or subcontract in the amount of $100,000 or more, entered into on or after December 1, 2003, for the purchase, sale, or use of personal property or non-personal services (including construction), take affirmative action to employ and advance in employment qualified covered veterans. Disabled veterans, recently separated veterans (veterans within 3 years of their discharge or release from active duty), veterans who served on active duty during a war or in a campaign or expedition for which a campaign badge has been authorized (referred to as "other protected veterans"), and Armed Forces service medal veterans are covered veterans under VEVRAA.

Prior to amendments made by the Jobs for Veterans Act (JVA), VEVRAA applied to contracts in the amount of $25,000 or more, and covered other categories of veterans. The JVA amendments apply only to contracts entered into on after December 1, 2003. For contracts or subcontracts of $25,000 or more, entered into before December 1, 2003, VEVRAA requires contractors to employ and advance in employment qualified disabled veterans, veterans of the Vietnam era, recently separated veterans (veterans within 1 year of their discharge or release from active duty), and other protected veterans.

Source: **www.dol.gov**

Pregnancy Discrimination Act

What is it?

In 1978, the Pregnancy Discrimination Act was added to Title VII to prohibit discrimination on the following bases:

- likelihood to become pregnant
- actual pregnancy
- childbirth
- related conditions

Under this act, it is illegal for employers to refuse to hire or to terminate a woman, force a woman to leave work, or stop the accrued seniority of a woman because she is pregnant, has given birth, or has had an abortion. Employers are required to treat pregnancy as a temporary disability. They cannot deny sick leave for pregnancy-related illnesses such as morning sickness if they allow sick leave for other similar nausea-related illnesses. This law also states that benefit plans must provide coverage for pregnancy.

Fair Labor Standards Act (FLSA)

What is it?

The Fair Labor Standards Act (FLSA) establishes the minimum wage, overtime pay, record keeping, and child labor standards that affect full-time and part-time workers in the private sector and in federal, state, and local governments. Covered nonexempt workers and exempt workers whose annual salary is less than a certain dollar amount ($23,660 in 2005) are entitled to a minimum wage no less than that set by the government. Overtime pay at a rate of not less than one and one-half times their regular rates of pay is required after 40 hours of work in a workweek.

What are the Key Terms?

Employees whose jobs are governed by the FLSA are either exempt or nonexempt employees. Nonexempt employees are entitled to overtime pay, while exempt employees are not. With few exceptions, most exempt employees are paid on a salary basis, in which the employee receives a full salary for the workweek, regardless of the actual number of hours worked.

- **Exempt-Executive**: These employees perform exempt tasks such as: regularly supervising two or more other employees, having management as the primary duty of the position, or having some input into the job status of other employees (such as hiring, firing, promotions, or assignments). In small communities, the Service Manager may not be exempt if there are no other staff or if he manages only one employee.

- **Exempt-Professional**: These employees perform work that is predominantly intellectual, requires specialized education, and involves the exercise of discretion and judgment. Professionally exempt workers must have education beyond high school, sometimes beyond college, in fields that are distinguished from the mechanical arts or a skilled trade.

- **Exempt-Administrative**: The most elusive and imprecise of the definitions of exempt job duties is for exempt administrative job duties. The Regulatory definition provides that exempt administrative job duties are office or non-manual work that is directly related to the management or general business operations of the employer or the employer's customers, and a primary component of which involves the exercise of independent judgment and discretion about matters of significance.

- **Nonexempt**: Nonexempt employees are not exempt from the provisions of the Fair Labor Standards Act. An employee who is nonexempt must have his or her hours counted so that he or she can be paid overtime pay if he or she works more than 40 hours per week. Individuals are compensated for all hours worked as detailed on the employee's timesheet and signed off by the supervisor. Employees are considered nonexempt and entitled to overtime unless they are determined to be exempt as provided in one of the definitions of exempt status, listed above.

Immigration Reform and Control Act

What is it?

The Immigration Reform and Control Act (IRCA) was designed to deal with issues arising from the influx of immigrants into the United States. The purpose of this Act is two-fold: to prohibit discrimination against job applicants based on national origin, and at the same time, to penalize employers for hiring illegal aliens. Employers who hire individuals who are not authorized to work in this country are subject to both civil and criminal charges.

Verifying that an individual is eligible to work in the United States is the burden of the employer. Generally, within three days of hiring, the new employee and the employer must fill out Form I-9 *(Employment Eligibility Verification form)*, which verifies the employee's identity and right to work in the United States. Employers should retain I-9 forms in the employee's personnel file for at least three years. Employees can present a number of documents to verify their identity and right to work. Employers cannot specify which documents an employee can present.

The following is a list of possible documents (this list is not all-inclusive):

Identity + Right to Work	Identity Only	Right to Work Only
• U.S. passport • Unexpired permanent resident card • Unexpired employment authorization card • Unexpired reentry permit	• Driver's license with photo • U.S. military card • Voter's registration card • School identification card with photo	• Social Security card • U.S. citizen ID card • Resident citizen ID card • Native American tribal documents

Americans with Disabilities Act (ADA)

What is it?

This law prohibits discrimination against a qualified individual with a disability because of that individual's disability. A qualified individual is one who can perform the essential functions of a job with or without reasonable accommodation.

Temporary disabilities are not included in the ADA, but a wide range of medical conditions, are covered, including alcoholism, cancer, cerebral palsy, diabetes, drug addiction, emotional illness, epilepsy, hearing and speech disorders, HIV and AIDS, mental retardation, multiple sclerosis, and learning disabilities.

What are the Key Terms?

It is important to define the terms used in this act:

- **Disability**: physical or mental impairment that substantially limits one or more major life activities such as walking, speaking, seeing, hearing, caring for oneself, etc.
- **Essential Functions**: primary job duties that a qualified individual must be able to perform
- **Reasonable Accommodation**: modifying or adjusting a job application process, work environment, or the circumstances under which the job is performed to enable a qualified individual with a disability to be considered for the job and perform its essential functions

Examples of providing reasonable accommodations would be installing ramps, lowering counters or drinking fountains, designing alternative training formats, using Braille labels for a blind employee, or providing a telephone device for a deaf employee. However, the ADA does not require employers to take action that involves undue hardship. The reasonableness of a particular accommodation is decided on a case-by-case basis.

Family and Medical Leave Act (FMLA)

What is it?

Covered employers must grant an eligible employee up to a total of 12 workweeks of unpaid leave during any 12-month period for one or more of the following reasons:

- birth and care of the newborn child of the employee
- adoption or foster care of a child by the employee
- care for an immediate family member (spouse, child, or parent) with a serious health condition
- medical leave when the employee is unable to work because of a serious health condition

An employer covered by FMLA is any person engaged in commerce or in any industry or activity affecting commerce, who employs 50 or more employees for each working day during each of 20 or more calendar work weeks in the current or preceding calendar year. The FMLA only requires unpaid leave. However, the law permits an employee to elect, or the employer to require the employee, to use accrued paid leave, such as vacation or sick leave, for some or all of the FMLA leave period. When paid leave is substituted for unpaid FMLA leave, it may be counted against the 12-week FMLA leave entitlement if the employee is properly notified of the designation when the leave begins. Employers may select one of four options for determining the 12-month period:

- the calendar year
- any fixed 12-month period such as a fiscal year, a year required by state law, or a year starting on the employee's anniversary date
- the 12-month period measured forward from the date any employee's first FMLA leave begins
- a rolling 12-month period measured backward from the date an employee uses FMLA leave

National Defense Authorization Act for FY2008 (NDAA), Public Law 110-181.

What is it?

On January 28, 2008, President Bush signed into law the National Defense Authorization Act for FY2008 (NDAA), Public Law 110-181. Section 585(a) of the NDAA amended the FMLA to provide eligible employees working for covered employers two important new leave rights related to military service:

- **New Qualifying Reason for Leave**. Eligible employees are entitled to up to 12 weeks of leave because of "any qualifying exigency" arising out of the fact that the spouse, son, daughter, or parent of the employee is on active duty, or has been notified of an impending call to active duty status, in support of a contingency operation. By the terms of the statute, this provision requires the Secretary of Labor to issue regulations defining "any qualifying exigency." In the interim, employers are encouraged to provide this type of leave to qualifying employees.

- **New Leave Entitlement**. An eligible employee who is the spouse, son, daughter, parent, or next of kin of a covered servicemember who is recovering from a serious illness or injury sustained in the line of duty on active duty is entitled to up to 26 weeks of leave in a single 12-month period to care for the servicemember. This provision became effective immediately upon enactment. This military caregiver leave is available during "a single 12-month period" during which an eligible employee is entitled to a combined total of 26 weeks of all types of FMLA leave.

Source: U.S. Department of Labor

Personal Responsibility and Work Opportunity Reconciliation Act (PRWORA)

What is it?

President Clinton signed into law the Personal Responsibility and Work Opportunity Reconciliation Act (PRWORA) in 1996 to reform the nation's welfare system into one that requires work in exchange for time-limited assistance. The bill contains strong work requirements, a performance bonus that rewards states for moving welfare recipients into jobs, state maintenance of effort requirements, comprehensive child support enforcement, and support for families moving from welfare to work, including increased funding for childcare and guaranteed medical coverage.

This bill also created a national new hire reporting system in which employers must report all new hires to state agencies for transmittal of new hire information to the National Directory of New Hires. This expands and streamlines the procedures for direct withholding of child support from wages.

Health Insurance Portability and Accountability Act (HIPAA)
What is it?
The Health Insurance Portability and Accountability Act of 1996 was passed by congress to provide consumers with greater access to health care insurance, to protect the privacy of health care data, and to promote more standardization and efficiency in the health care industry. Every employer that offers health benefits or health services to its employees will be affected by the HIPAA rules. This is because the Rules directly regulate most employer group health plans and certain health care providers.

From a property management perspective, HIPPA ensures that insurance and health information on employees and residents is not divulged. While this has always been good practice, it is now essential to control the way this information is released, collected, and stored.

HIRING EMPLOYEES
After recruiting efforts have identified a pool of candidates, it is time to begin the hiring, or selection, process. *Employee selection* is the process of hiring the most suitable candidate for a vacant position. Hiring practices will affect many aspects of the organization. Hiring people who are above-average performers can have a sizeable economic impact, especially if the organization hires many workers. On the other hand, selecting the wrong person for the job can decrease performance outcomes, cause problems among team members, and lead to negative economic ramifications. This section examines the most commonly used methods of hiring employees.

Application Forms and Resumes
Properties may use standard or custom job application forms during their hiring process. Application forms and resumes serve as pre-screening devices to determine if the candidate meets the minimum selection criteria for the job.

LEGAL ISSUE:
Job application questions should be job-related and the applicant's privacy should not be violated. The EEOC and courts have found that questions regarding height, weight, arrest records, and marital status may have a disproportionate impact on certain groups of applicants. The application should request only information that is critical to job success. The company's legal department or outside counsel should analyze application forms for their EEO impact.

An application form or resume should include the following information:

Personal Information

- Name
- Address
- Social Security number

Education and Training

- Schools attended (name, address, and degrees earned)
- Apprenticeships, licenses, training programs, and professional affiliations

History

- **Work experience** (company names, addresses, brief description of responsibilities, pay rates, names of supervisors, and reasons for leaving)
- **Military service** (may ask for dates of military service, branch of service, experience, and skills gained, but not the type of discharge)
- **Criminal records** (may inquire about convictions, but any inquiry regarding criminal arrest records will have to be justified as job-related and a business necessity—if the job vacancy requires significant customer contact or contact with the public, requires carrying a weapon, or gives access to significant amounts of money or valuables, employers have a right and a responsibility to ask more detailed questions about the applicant's criminal record)

The Equal Employment Opportunity Commission (EEOC) has suggested that the application include the following statement near the inquiry about a criminal record:

"Conviction of a crime will not necessarily be a bar to employment. Factors such as age at the time of the offense, type of offense, remoteness of the offense in time, and rehabilitation will be taken into account in determining effect on suitability for employment."

LEGAL ISSUE:
Due to the proportionally larger number of African-Americans and Hispanics who have had contact with the criminal justice system, employers may be liable to charges of racial discrimination if they are not careful about how they use an applicant's criminal records.. The EEOC recently published guidelines for employers regarding the use of arrest or conviction records in employment decisions under the Civil Rights Act of 1964 (Title VII).

References

- Business contacts (names and current addresses and contact information)

Availability

- If the job requires working irregular hours, the employer may ask if the applicant can work the night shift, overtime, transfers, holidays. Applicants who indicate a need for Saturdays, Sundays, or holidays off for religious reasons may not be discriminated against.

Additional Statements and Information

- Authorization/release (to allow the organization to check references)

- "At-will" employment (the employee will not have a contract for a specific duration and employment can be terminated at any time by either party for any reason, with or without cause; not all states are "at-will" states–check your state laws before adding an at-will clause)

- Verification–(the applicant should verify that the information provided is true; also state that providing false information may result in rejection or dismissal)

- EEO (state that the organization is an equal opportunity employer)

Identify the most critical factors for success in the position. Use the information in the applications and these criteria to develop a potential candidate pool. When reviewing applications and resumes, be aware of the following red flags:

- Insufficient education or experience to fulfill minimum job requirements

- Significant unexplained gaps in employment history

- Frequent job changes

Applications should be kept on file for a period (usually 1 to 2 years) determined by federal and state regulations. Although the application will be kept on file for the required period, it may be prudent to include in the application form language that indicates the application will remain in the selection pool for open positions for a limited time (30 to 90 days), after which the job seeker must reapply to remain in consideration.

Interviews

Organizations rely heavily upon interviews to determine how well the applicant meets the needs of the property. Interviews can range from short (20 minutes or less) prescreening discussions to long (1 hour or more) in-depth meetings.

When preparing for an interview, consider the following guidelines:

- Choose a quiet, private space for the interview

- Hold all telephone calls and interruptions

- Offer refreshments such as coffee, tea, or water to ease tension

- Have the candidate sit in chair positioned in a way that avoids imbalance of power

- Explain up front what the interview process will entail
- Thank the candidate and explain any next steps in the selection process

An interviewer can increase the effectiveness of interviews by establishing a structured set of questions to ask each candidate. A *structured* interview asks a series of job-related questions based on the findings of the job analysis. The interviewer asks the same questions of each applicant and establishes predetermined desirable and undesirable answers. Although the structured interview may reduce spontaneity, it ensures that similar information is gathered from each candidate.

Structured interview questions typically fall into three categories:

- **Behavioral** questions ask candidates to describe their past behavior in particular work situations. Behavioral questions typically begin as follows: "Tell me about a time when..." For example, "Tell me about a time when you had to deal with ambiguity on the job." Or, "Tell me about a time when you acted as a team player on the job."

- **Job knowledge** questions assess whether the applicant has the knowledge necessary to perform the job. A job knowledge question may be, "What is the procedure for repairing a cooling system that has stopped blowing cold air?"

- **Worker requirements** questions assess the candidate's willingness to perform under certain job conditions. For example, "Weekends are an extremely busy time for our business. What are your feelings about working on weekends?"

While interviewing, be sure to establish and maintain a rapport with the candidate, listen carefully to responses, and ask *open-ended* questions. Open-ended questions are those such as "Describe for me a time when...," "What were your responsibilities in your last position?" or "What career goals do you have for the future?"

Avoid *closed or* "yes or no" questions unless you need to confirm a specific question: "You were with Pinnacle Properties from 2008 to 2011, correct?" Use follow-up questions to elicit additional information: "Tell me more about that." "Why was that?" "I'm not sure I understand. Can you elaborate on that?" Always take notes throughout the interview, preferably on a separate piece of paper from the application form or resume.

LEGAL ISSUE:
Refer to Figure 4-1 for a list of interview questions that are potentially discriminatory.

FIGURE 4-1: INTERVIEW QUESTIONS AND DISCRIMINATION

Category	Nondiscriminatory	Potentially Discriminatory
Gender and Family	Whether applicant has relatives employed by the organization	• Gender of applicant • Marital status • Number of children • Spouse's occupation • Childcare arrangements • Healthcare coverage through spouse
Race	No questions may be asked	• Noting applicant's race or skin color • Photo to be affixed to the application form
National Origin	• Whether applicant has legal right to be employed in the U.S. • Ability to speak/write English fluently (if job-related) • Other languages spoken (if job-related)	• Ethnic association of surname • Birthplace of applicant or parents • Nationality, lineage, national origin • Nationality of spouse • Whether applicant is a citizen of another country • Applicant's native language • Maiden name
Religion	No questions may be asked	• Religious affiliation • Religious holidays observed
Age	• If applicant is over age 18 • If applicant is over age 21 (if job-related)	• Date of birth • Date of graduation • Age
Disability	Whether applicant can perform essential job-related functions	• If applicant has disability • Nature or severity of disability • Whether applicant has ever filed a worker's compensation claim • Recent or past surgeries • Past medical problems or conditions

Source: © 2005 *Society for Human Resource Management.* Reprinted with permission.

Hiring Employees—Additional Tools

Testing

- **Ability tests** can measure anything from physical strength to typing skills. General cognitive ability, typically measured by summing scores on verbal and math tests, has been shown to be a predictor of job performance.

- **Work sample tests** ask candidates to perform the exact tasks they would be performing on the job. For example, a service technician applicant might be asked to troubleshoot a faulty HVAC system. Always be sure that the test items are job-related and are predictors of performance on the job.

- **Personality tests** assess traits, or personality characteristics that tend to be consistent and enduring. In the past, many have argued that these traits are subjective, unreliable, unrelated to job performance, and not legally acceptable. However, recent research has demonstrated that personality is composed of five dimensions that can be reliably measured.

- **Work Ethics Surveys** determine candidate's motivational alignment with the company standards.

Realistic Job Preview (RJP)

A *realistic job preview (RJP)* is part of the entire selection process and provides the candidate with honest and complete information about the position and work environment. The purpose of the RJP is to give applicants as much information as possible so they can make informed decisions about their suitability for the job. This means that the RJP should share both favorable and unfavorable information. The following are types of information that organizations should share as part of the selection process:

- Description of a typical day on the job
- Organization's mission, vision, and values
- Succinct description of the organization's properties and services
- Aspects of the job that have been difficult for other employees
- Aspects of the job that have been rewarding for other employees
- Compensation and benefits realities
- Unique aspects of the job
- Pending organization layoffs, reorganizations, mergers, etc.
- Steps in the selection process

RJPs help organizations accurately represent themselves, encourage self-selection on the part of the candidate, increase job satisfaction, prevent disappointments, reduce post-entry stress, and reduce employee turnover.

References and Background Checks

Employers may conduct several types of background checks on applicants for a position. Each type of background check is subject to federal and state laws that govern when and how an employer may conduct a check. Some general guidelines follow:

- Establish and document a standard policy for conducting background checks on applicants and employees. Be sure to document if checks will only be conducted in certain instances or for particular positions.

- Only conduct the background checks that are necessary for the particular position. For example, if a position does not require handling money or expensive equipment, running a credit check to screen applicants may not be necessary. On the other hand, if the position requires access to tenants' units, a criminal background check may be prudent.

- If conducting background checks without the use of a third party, documenting all steps taken and the results during the background and reference check process is prudent. Include details about who was contacted, what information was provided, and what information (if any) was requested but not received.

- Inform applicants in writing of the background checks that will be performed. Get their permission in writing when required by law.

- Civil rights laws may apply when using background checks in hiring or promotion decisions. Certain types of checks may have adverse impacts on protected groups. It is wise to consult a specialist in employment law when instituting a background check policy.

References

Many organizations verify application information and check references after they decide that the applicant is a good match for the job. Some general guidelines follow:

- Obtain a signed release from the candidate indicating that the employer may seek confidential information from former employers and other sources.

- Verify that the individual was employed during the periods listed on his or her application or resume.

- The most useful information will be that received from former direct supervisors and colleagues.

- Start by verifying the basics: employment dates, title, job duties, reason for leaving, and salary.

- If the reference seems receptive, ask about the candidate's strengths and weaknesses, about the candidate's ability to work with others, and about the candidate's work ethics.

Criminal Background Checks

The laws regarding the use of criminal background checks vary from state to state. Restrictions may govern inquiries about arrests, convictions from the past, juvenile crimes, sealed records, relevancy to the job, or specific positions. Justification for obtaining conviction records may be based on the type of position being filled or information obtained from other steps in the screening and background check process. Obtaining arrest records is rarely permitted. A number of states have laws that grant applicants and employees certain protections against criminal disclosure based on privacy concerns.

A business should consider doing criminal checks on applicants who will have the following responsibilities:

- Have access to money or valuables
- Carry a weapon
- Drive a company vehicle
- Have access to hazardous materials (explosives, chemicals)
- Have a lot of contact with the public, patients, or children

In addition to privacy and antidiscrimination laws, a business faces liability for not conducting adequate checks. Some positions require a criminal background check under state law. In order to obtain conviction records, a business may contact the appropriate state, county, and/or local agencies directly, hire a private agency to conduct the checks, or order reports from a private service provider online. Engage a company that specializes in performing background checks on job applicants is advisable. Ensure that the company is licensed if required in your state. Primary responsibility for the accuracy of reports and compliance with the law lies with the company performing the check.

TIPS:
A **fidelity bond** is no-cost insurance coverage protects employers against employee dishonesty, theft or embezzlement. Employers may consider fidelity bonding if job applicants have:
- limited work history
- poor credit history
- a record of arrest, conviction or imprisonment
- a dishonorable military discharge

Credit Checks

An organization may want to run a credit check if the position for which they are hiring requires handling large sums of money or exercising financial discretion. In addition to identification information such as the applicant's name, address, and Social Security number, a credit report will include the following information:

- Bankruptcies
- Tax liens

- Judgments
- Child support obligations
- Loans

Drug Testing

The majority of employers across the United States are not required to conduct drug testing and many state and local governments have statutes that limit or prohibit workplace testing, unless required by state or federal regulations for certain jobs. On the other hand, most private employers have the right to test for a wide variety of substances. Some general guidelines follow:

- The current law in the private sector generally permits nonunion companies to require applicants and/or employees to take drug tests.
- Employers can test for a variety of substances, although only a few have established testing protocols.
- All employers should consult with legal advisors to ensure that they comply with any applicable state or local laws and design their testing programs to withstand legal challenges.
- In unionized workforces, the implementation of testing programs must be negotiated. Even when federal regulations require testing, the disciplinary consequences of testing positive need to be determined and are subject to collective bargaining.

Perhaps the most important component in implementing a drug-testing program is employee education. Organizations should educate their employees about the problems associated with alcohol and drug abuse, the reasons for testing, and the nature of the testing programs. These education programs should be designed through a cooperative effort with employee representatives.

RESOURCES:
More detailed information is available through the Drug and Alcohol Testing Industry Association (**www.datia.org**) and the Substance Abuse Program Administrators Association (**www.sapaa.com**).

Making an Offer

An *employment offer* makes the hiring decision final and should immediately follow the final decision to hire an applicant. All signatures and authorizations should be in place prior to making an offer. An employment offer can take the form of a letter, and the employer should word it carefully. Follow these guidelines when using employment letters:

Do's	Don'ts
• Use a standard letter or customized version that has been cleared with legal counsel • Clearly state the terms of the offer • Clarify any contingencies (reference checking, drug testing) • Clarify acceptance details (requiring a signature returned on a copy of the letter) • Use the transition period to help the new employee feel welcome (send informational brochures)	• Back down on any promises made • Set an excessively short acceptance time • Lose touch with the candidate once the offer is accepted • Quote salary terms in an annual format; use hourly or monthly figures (in the event of termination, an annual figure could become binding)

Source: © 2005 *Society for Human Resource Management*. Reprinted with Permission.

EMPLOYEE ORIENTATION

Orientation is the process of informing new employees what is expected of them on the job as well as making the new team member feel welcome and comfortable. Employers must realize that orientation isn't just a nice gesture put on by the organization. It serves as an important element of the recruitment and retention process. Some key benefits of orientation follow:

- **Reduced Startup Costs**: Proper orientation can help the employee get "up to speed" much more quickly, thereby reducing the costs associated with learning the job.

- **Reduced Anxiety**: Any employee, when put into a new, strange situation, will experience anxiety that can impede his or her ability to learn to do the job. Proper orientation helps reduce the anxiety that results from entering into an unknown situation, and helps provide guidelines for behavior and conduct so the employee doesn't have to experience the stress of guessing.

- **Reduced Employee Turnover**: Employee turnover increases when employees feel they are not valued or are put in positions where they can't possibly do their jobs. Orientation shows that the organization values the employee, and helps provide the tools necessary for succeeding in the job.

- **Time Savings for the Supervisor**: The better the initial orientation, the less time supervisors and coworkers have to spend teaching the employee.

- **Development of Realistic Job Expectations and Job Satisfaction**: It is important that employees learn as soon as possible what is expected of them, what to expect from others, and what the values and attitudes of the organization are.

Some common mistakes that employers make hinder the integration of the employee and reduce the effectiveness of the orientation. Follow these guidelines for a successful employee orientation:

- Begin the orientation process before the new person starts work. Send an orientation agenda with the offer letter so the employee knows what to expect.
- Make sure a work area has been created or assigned. (Do not have the employee sit in a hall or share a cube.)
- Do not schedule the new employee to start work while his or her supervisor is on vacation.
- Introduce the employee to coworkers and assign him or her a positive mentor.
- Tour the entire facility, including other departments, restrooms, and break areas.
- Provide the employee a copy of his or her job description.
- Review the job description and set up a training schedule.
- Provide a glossary of company acronyms, buzzwords, and FAQs.
- Do not leave the new employee at the work station to manage on his or her own, while coworkers pair up and head out to lunch.
- Do not assign the employee "busy work" that has nothing to do with his or her core job description, because you are having a busy week.
- Evaluate the effectiveness of the orientation with a survey. Tweak the orientation based on employee feedback.

Employee handbooks are generally the most common format to communicate company policies. The handbook should be updated as necessary over time. It should be professional looking and clearly written. Have the employee sign and date that they have read the handbook and policies.

Affordable Housing Impact: Employee orientation for those working at affordable housing properties should also include an overview of the ownership entities and funding programs, including both federal program funding sources and state specific funding sources as requirements may vary.

Single Family House Impact: Orientation programs for those managing single family house properties may be tailored towards contractors instead of employees. As single family house properties will be scattered across multiple sites, orientation programs should address the need to travel from site to site, as well as any specific requirements or procedures for each property.

An employee handbook may include, but is not limited to, the following:

Category	Sample Items to Include
Introduction	• Letter of welcome from the president or CEO • Equal Employment Opportunity (EEO) statements • Fair housing compliance statement • Organizational mission, vision, and values • Company history • Ethics statements
Terms of Employment	• Terms of introductory period • At-will employment • Employment categories (exempt, nonexempt, part-time) • Hours of work including lunch and rest periods • Absenteeism • Telecommuting
Compensation	• Performance management • Transfers and promotions • Salary administration
Time Off	• Vacation • Sick days • Holidays • Leave under the Family and Medical Leave Act (FLMA) • Leave of absence without pay • Funeral leave • Jury duty • Military leave
Benefits	• Health insurance • Dental insurance • Life insurance • Disability benefits • Retirement plan • 401(k) plan • Worker's compensation • Tuition reimbursement
Policies and Codes of Conduct	• Grievance procedures • Harassment • Discipline • Technology policy • Rules of conduct • Conflicts of interest • Employee referral program • Smoking policy • Dress code • Confidentiality • Romantic relationships in the workplace
Employee Separation	• Voluntary and involuntary separation • Separation procedures

CHAPTER 5:
COMMUNICATION AND CONFLICT RESOLUTION

Managing employees involves an understanding of communication skills as well as the various styles of conflict resolution. A manager must develop active listening and nonverbal communication skills to break down communication barriers and enable more effective problem solving among employees.

In this chapter:

- **Communication Barriers**
- **Active Listening**
- **Nonverbal Communication**
- **Conflict Resolution**
- **Problem Solving**

COMMUNICATION BARRIERS

Property management requires communication with many individuals: employees, contractors, property owners, residents, vendors, government authorities, and others. For a site manager to communicate effectively to these various parties is essential. Thus, understanding the potential for error in communications and constantly counteracting those tendencies by making a conscientious effort to ensure a minimal loss of meaning in your conversations is critical.

The following are potential barriers to effective communication:

- Poor choice of words
- Misreading of body language
- Only hearing what you want to hear
- Cultural differences (e.g., language and ethnicities)
- Making assumptions
- Lack of active listening

Affordable Housing Impact: To ensure effective communication, it is extremely important for all team members to understand the various players involved in managing affordable housing properties (e.g., regulatory authorities, HUD, management, residents, ownership entities, non-profit boards, tenant council organizations) as well as the specific assistance program requirements and funding source information. Specifically, everyone should be aware of the relationship between the ownership entity and the various regulatory bodies, such as HUD. While the real estate manager ultimately serves as the owner's representative and fiduciary, it is important to also recognize the different perspectives of the regulatory bodies and residents. At times, the owner's goals and those of HUD may differ. As the first line of defense for the day-to-day operations at the property, the site team should take care to capture relevant information appropriately, and should have a clear understanding of how to disseminate that information in accordance with company policy.

Single Family House Impact: Those managing single family house properties face a unique set of communication challenges. With multiple owners and residences to manage, it is critical to establish clear processes and mechanisms for regular communication.

Condominium Impact: Communication can be a sensitive area for those managing condominiums. Not only must you maintain communication with association members, but you must also communicate with the Board. It may be helpful to have a Designated Board Liaison, perhaps the board chair or president, to streamline communication. Avoid sending emails to all board members which may inadvertently result in the convening of an official meeting.

Senior Housing Impact: In nursing homes and boarding facilities, Federal law requires residential councils, so that residents have a voice in maintaining or improving the quality of care and to make recommendations regarding the facilities. A staff member who has good rapport with both residents and other staff members should be designated as a liaison to that group

Student Housing Impact: Note that student housing managers also interact with parents, student organizations, campus officials, adding additional complexities to the communication process. Additional considerations that may impact communications are the unique circumstances inherent in having students as residents, as listed on the "Communication Issues Unique to Student Housing" slide.

Communication Vehicles

In real estate management, communication is a critical success factor. Effective communication involves both what and how various messages are transmitted. Selecting the right communication vehicle is often overlooked in today's fast-paced business environment where e-mail is the standard go-to tool. While e-mail is certainly a quick and efficient communication method, it may not always be the best solution. Various communication vehicles follow:

- **Face-to-face meeting**: Best for situations that involve discussion and collaborative decision-making, sensitive topics, and employee feedback and coaching.
- **Telephone**: When face-to-face meetings aren't feasible due to geographic proximity and cost, or when subject matter is ambiguous or might involve clarification, questions, or background information.
- **Webcasts/Conference Calls**: Best for balancing the requirement for face-to-face meetings while limiting cost.
- **Letter or memo**: Best for confidential or legal documents, or when communicating formal decisions and information from the company. Can be a great opportunity to show appreciation and importance.
- **E-mail**: Quick, efficient, and can reach a wide audience simultaneously.
- **Fax**: Best for general announcements or sharing signed documents

Keep the following considerations in mind when selecting a communication vehicle:

- **Culture**: The company's culture may dictate appropriate forms of communication both internally and externally.
- **Goal**: Consider the goal of the communication event. Is it a transfer of information, or is additional information needed? What do you want the other person to do? How sensitive is the message? Is discussion needed? How complex is the subject matter? What is the tone of the message? Are you assigning a task or giving feedback on performance?
- **Audience**: How many people are involved? Are you communicating to an owner or client, or to a colleague?
- **Urgency**: What other events are dependent on your message? Is resident safety a consideration?
- **Intergenerational differences**: How will your audience best understand the message? Are multiple communication channels required?

E-mail Guidelines

When using e-mail in the business environment, follow these guidelines:

- Use complete sentences and appropriate punctuation and grammar
- Use spell-check, as correct spelling is a sign of professionalism
- Ensure the subject line is meaningful, concise, and relevant to the message
- Use a standard signature containing contact information
- Use the cc: field to keep appropriate parties in the loop
- Use caution when "replying to all". Only copy everyone if truly necessary.
- Never write something in e-mail that you wouldn't say in person
- Never write something in e-mail that you would be embarrassed about if seen by your boss or other co-workers. Remember that you have no control over the e-mail once it is sent – it can be forwarded.

- Avoid writing e-mail when you are upset or angry. Remember that e-mail cannot be retrieved once sent.

- Re-read e-mail prior to sending to see if the tone can be misconstrued

- Avoid e-mail for sensitive or personnel related issues

- Acknowledge receipt of e-mails you receive

- Keep messages brief, organized, concise, and straight to the point as it allows recipients to give quicker responses

- Consider the time of the person reading your e-mail

- Do not write in capital letters, as you appear to be screaming at your recipient

- Use "please" and "thank you" where appropriate

- Consolidate items that take place throughout the day to avoid sending multiple messages

- Limit graphics and emoticons to maintain professional image

- Always refer to company policy

ACTIVE LISTENING

One way to overcome communication barriers is active listening. How do you feel when someone does not listen to you? Perhaps you feel unimportant, or dismissed. You may even view the other as rude or insensitive. Alternatively, how often have you listened to another, but in the end, not really heard what he or she said?

The term *active listening* describes communication in which the listener is as active in the process as the speaker. The goal of active listening is for you to hear and understand other people, and to let them know you've heard and understood them. Acknowledge their motivations, feelings, and point of view, even when you do not agree with what they are saying. Your goal is to understand the message, not to judge what they are saying.

If you practice active listening, you should be able to repeat the main points and communicate an understanding of what he or she said back to the speaker. We cannot retain all that someone else says to us. However, if we summarize and restate what was said, we can improve the lines of communication and retain more information. Asking questions can also help, as can taking notes. In fact, studies have shown that effective managers spend *60-70 percent* of their time listening!

Good listeners:

- Do not interrupt, especially to correct mistakes or make points

- Do not judge

- Think before answering

- Face the speaker

- Are close enough to hear

- Watch nonverbal behavior
- Are aware of personal biases or values that distort what they hear
- Look for the feelings and basic assumptions underlying remarks
- Concentrate on what is being said
- Avoid rehearsing answers while the other person is talking
- Do not insist on having the last word

Affordable Housing Impact: As mentioned earlier, the site manager plays a critical role in gathering and communicating information appropriately. The concept of active listening can help in this area. For example, if the site manager receives a call from the equity partner announcing a visit to the property the next day, there is some basic information that needs to be obtained and communicated to the regional manager or other appropriate authority, including:

- What is the nature of the visit/what do you want to see?
- What time will you be arriving?
- Do you intend to go into occupied units? (if yes, need to provide 48 hours notice to residents)
- What is your phone number in case I need to call you back?

Throughout this dialogue, it is important for the manager to summarize and restate what is said to ensure effective communication. This ensures that you are accurately receiving the information so that you can communicate it appropriately.

NONVERBAL COMMUNICATION

Multiple studies indicate that when we communicate in person:

- Around **55 percent** of what others hear us say is a direct result of what we communicate visually: dress, posture, movements, facial expressions, and eye contact.
- The next **38 percent** of the message we send comes from the sound of the communication: tone of voice, accent, rate of speech, volume, and timbre.
- Only the last **7 percent** of your message comes from the words used, and the way they are put together. Mastering the art of nonverbal communications is an obvious advantage and can help overcome barriers to effective communication.

How can you improve the nonverbal components of communication?

- **Body orientation**: to indicate you like and respect people, face them when interacting
- **Posture**: good posture is associated with confidence and enthusiasm, it indicates our degree of tenseness or relaxation; open arms are more inviting that crossed arms
- **Facial expressions**: notice facial expressions—some people mask emotions by not using facial expression; others exaggerate facial expression to belie their real feelings
- **Gestures**: hand and arm motions can be very telling

- **Eye contact:** frequent eye contact communicates interest and confidence; avoidance communicates the opposite
- **Use of space:** the less distance, the more intimate and informal the relationship; staying behind your desk when someone comes to visit gives the impression that you are unapproachable
- **Personal appearance:** people tend to show more respect and respond more positively to individuals who are well dressed, but not overdressed
- **Cultural differences:** remember that what might be appropriate in one culture, might not be appropriate in another; for example, eye contact, hand gestures, approaches to teamwork.

CONFLICT RESOLUTION

Inevitably, conflicts arise in the workplace. Conflict situations offer an opportunity for us to choose the manner in which we respond and to take responsibility for our actions. We all have different ways of resolving conflict. Often, some ways are viewed as desirable and others as undesirable, yet each style is appropriate for different situations. With knowledge of the styles of conflict resolution, you can expand your repertoire of techniques and tailor your response for the best outcome. The following are the five conflict resolution styles:

- Adversarial
- Avoiding
- Compromising
- Accommodating
- Collaborative

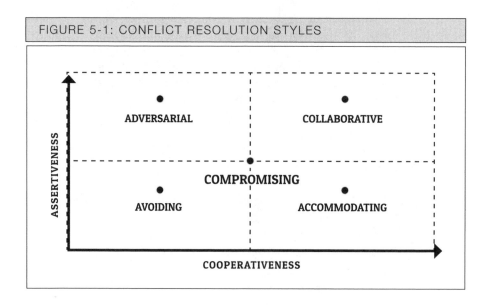

FIGURE 5-1: CONFLICT RESOLUTION STYLES

Adversarial (High Assertiveness, Low Cooperativeness)

The adversarial style of conflict resolution involves taking an assertive and aggressive approach. This is a "win-lose" situation in which one party gets his or her way and the other party does not. People who use an adversarial style feel that their view is better than that of others, and they do not want their authority questioned.

This person might believe:
"Only the strong survive."
"I know better than you"

Advantages	Disadvantages	Appropriate Uses
• Assuming the enforcer is correct, the best ideas win out • Leaders will emerge from the pack	• May result in hostility and resentment on the part of the "loser" • If enforcer is not correct, poor ideas may win out	• Resolution is urgent • Stakes are high • Your relationship with the other party is not a factor

Avoiding (Low Assertiveness, Low Cooperativeness)

The avoidance style involves withdrawing from the issue or sidestepping the conflict. A person who is avoiding conflict would rather let the matter pass than confront it. This person will remain neutral, become passive over disagreements, and may even deny that a problem exists at all.

This person might believe:
"Don't make a mountain out of a molehill."
"Live and let live."

Advantages	Disadvantages	Appropriate Uses
• Relationships are maintained • A greater problem might have resulted by confronting one another	• Areas that need further discussion do not get discussed • Minor problems can escalate to major problems	• Confrontation will damage the relationship • To buy time • Stakes are low

Compromising

Compromising involves finding a middle ground by searching for a mutually agreeable solution. A person who uses a compromising style will take a little of everyone's ideas to synthesize a solution.

This person might believe:
"You must give a little to get a little."
"Something is better than nothing."

Advantages	Disadvantages	Appropriate Uses
• Relationships are maintained • Conflict may be resolved quickly	• If the effort to keep everyone happy is greater than the effort to find the best solution, quality may suffer	• To ensure both parties win • To maintain relationships • To get something instead of risking everything

Accommodating (Low Assertiveness, High Cooperativeness)

The accommodation style involves giving in to someone else's wishes without standing up for your own position. People who use this style may state their opinions at first, but they quickly abandon the idea if someone else offers a different approach. They consider their opinions inferior to others' opinions.

This person might believe:
"The boss knows best."
"My opinion isn't good enough."

Advantages	Disadvantages	Appropriate Uses
• Relationships are maintained	• Poor-quality solutions might be implemented since alternatives were not fully discussed • Accommodator may be taken advantage of	• To get out of a bad situation • To create goodwill • When others know better • If reciprocity is needed down the road

Collaborative (High Assertiveness, High Cooperativeness)

With a collaborative approach, parties work together to solve the problem. Mutual support is a hallmark of this style. Individuals' ideas may be used, abandoned, or modified as appropriate.

This person might believe:
"Two heads are better than one."
"Let the team decide what is best."

Advantages	Disadvantages	Appropriate Uses
• The highest priority is finding the best solution • The problem and solution belong to everyone	• Dominant or more experienced members may control the discussion • Much time and effort may be required	• The group members view one another as partners and are confident in each other • The group has complementary skills • Sufficient time is available

Conflict Resolution Steps

You can take a number of actions to reach a resolution more quickly and effectively. Consider the following steps for successful conflict resolution:

1. Acknowledge the conflict and the feelings that surround it. Describe what you see happening and how you feel about the conflict. Empathize with the other party's viewpoint as well.
   - "I realize we don't agree on this issue."
   - "I know there has been frustration for both of us."
   - "I understand your apprehension about the new leasing goals—they are substantially different from our former goals."

2. Set your expectation that the conflict can be resolved and invite participation by all parties. Commit to working toward resolving the conflict. Respect all parties involved, even when they behave disagreeably.
   - "I am hopeful that we can resolve this situation and establish clearer communication between our groups."

3. Clarify the facts of the case: any issues, points of contention, situations, preferences, expectations, and objectives. Stay objective and neutral; avoid becoming defensive of your position or finding fault with others. Give the other party ample opportunity to share his or her view as well.
   - "From our viewpoint, we feel that resources are allocated unfairly to areas with greater exposure to client contact. We believe each department should have equal access to the resources it needs. What is your perception?"

4. Listen actively and reflectively. Adopt nonaggressive body language and eliminate communication barriers.
   - "What I understand you are saying is that the funds we see allocated to your commercial division cover direct and indirect costs; whereas funds to us in the industrial division cover only direct costs. So we are treated differently in accounting, and that difference is what appears on this report?"

5. Negotiate an agreement or resolution using the appropriate conflict resolution style, as described earlier. Put the agreement in writing if fitting. Spend your energies on resolution of the conflict, not on score keeping or getting even.
   - "In the future, to prevent similar misunderstandings, can we do the following...?"

Consider these two examples of conflict resolution.

Example 1:

Service Technician:	"This new maintenance schedule stinks! It's slowing down our response time. Do you know how many repairs I made today?"
Site manager:	"I don't know, maybe five."
Service Technician:	"Well aren't you concerned about that? That's only half as many as I usually do!"
Site manager:	"I know it's only half as many. You'll just have to work faster."
Service Technician:	"I can't. You've got to do something about the schedule."
Site manager:	"Our new policy is to stick to the schedule. There isn't anything I can do." "Well I can!" (Leaves, angry.)
Service Technician:	"Well I can!" (Leaves, angry.)

Example 2:

Service Technician:	"The new maintenance schedule stinks! It's slowing down our response time. Do you know how many repairs I made today?"
Site manager:	"I know it must be very frustrating to stick to the new schedule. I can understand why you are upset."
Service Technician:	"I'm only doing half as many repairs as I usually do!"
Site manager:	"I'm concerned about that. Let's talk about what we can do to fix this problem."
Service Technician:	"Well, I have a few ideas..."
Site manager:	"What do you think we could do differently?"

In the second instance, the manager's ability to address this conflict effectively allowed the pair to move on to problem solving.

Affordable Housing Impact: Working with union employees or contractors is often a requirement when managing affordable housing properties. As such, it may be necessary to deal with the union on various communication and conflict resolution situations. Professional arbitrators should always be used when negotiating with the union. Remember to budget appropriately for services such as arbitrators, lawyers, and other professionals.

PROBLEM SOLVING

In real estate management, managers deal with problems on a daily basis. From addressing resident complaints to implementing new software in the office—there is never a shortage of challenges. Problem-solving skills are critical to effectively working together as a team, and ultimately serving the residents of the property. While there are many approaches to problem solving, here are some basic guidelines:

CHECKLIST: PROBLEM SOLVING TIPS

- ☐ Clearly define the problem.
- ☐ Gather as much information about the situation as possible.
- ☐ Document communication (follow-up verbal discussions with written documentation to confirm).
- ☐ Accept the situation and focus on moving forward to a solution (i.e., don't dwell on or resist the reality of an issue).
- ☐ Evaluate the information in order to identify the primary issue as well as any secondary issues. Breaking the problem down can help it seem more manageable.
- ☐ Show respect to all involved by actively listening and asking questions.
- ☐ Consider several possible solutions and their associated impacts.
- ☐ Work with everyone involved and accept their help (as necessary).
- ☐ Determine the type of solution that is most appropriate to the situation.
- ☐ Communicate the action plan or next steps clearly to all involved.
- ☐ Follow-up to ensure that the action steps are working.
- ☐ Don't be afraid to adjust if additional information becomes available or a change in approach is warranted.

Often, a collaborative approach to problem solving yields the greatest results. The following techniques foster an open and collaborative environment:

- Avoid blame
- Focus on effective communication
- Define processes and procedures
- Meet as a team regularly
- Encourage cross-functional team assignments
- Challenge group to think beyond task at hand

CHAPTER 6:
PERFORMANCE EVALUATION AND RETENTION

It is important for managers to fairly assess performance and to avoid potential errors in these practices, especially when disciplining or terminating an employee. A manager has to evaluate performance to determine employee effectiveness and control employee turnover.

In this chapter:

- **Performance Evaluations**
- **Performance Coaching**
- **Disciplinary Action**
- **Retention and Turnover**

PERFORMANCE EVALUATIONS

The performance management process involves identifying goals, setting performance standards, and then measuring results and providing feedback via performance evaluations (also called performance appraisals).

Employee goals should align with the property's strategies. By comparing goals defined in the job description with the level of achievement, supervisors can get an accurate idea of how the employee is progressing.

Goals should follow the *SMART* acronym:

S	SPECIFIC
M	MEASURABLE
A	AGREED UPON
R	REALISTIC
T	TIME-BASED

For example, "to increase occupancy" is not an appropriate goal. A more effective goal would be, "to increase occupancy by 8 percent within 6 months."

Supervisors measure the achievement of those goals and provide feedback to their employees through performance evaluations. *Performance evaluations* accomplish three purposes:

1. providing feedback
2. allocating rewards
3. determining employees' training and developmental needs

In self-reviews, employees may also include areas in which they would like to receive additional training or development. Supervisors should read self-reviews carefully and take employees' judgments and goals into account.

The performance evaluation involves a discussion between the employee and his or her supervisor. This feedback session provides the supervisor an opportunity to discuss the rating, rationale, and future development of the employee. Consider holding this performance evaluation meeting separately from the compensation adjustment meeting.

Also, consider conducting quarterly reviews as this supports a consistent and ongoing coaching process.

Managers should keep the following guidelines in mind when providing performance appraisals:

- **Describe the behavior; do not judge it**. If the evaluation is negative and accusatory, the employee may react defensively. Instead, describe the issue in an impersonal way. Instead of saying, "Carol, you've got to stop coming to work late," try, "We are still having a problem reducing tardiness."

- **Assume an attitude of helpfulness rather than power**. Convey respect for the employee's ability to work on a problem and arrive at an effective solution. Rather than saying, "James, I'd like you to send a letter of apology to the resident," ask, "James, what do you think we could do to improve this situation?"

- **Give specific examples of good and substandard performance**. Generalizations are not helpful to the employee. Instead of saying, "Paula, you're doing a great job," say, "Paula, your numbers are above standard by 8 percent and your vacancy rate continues to decline."

- **Begin and end the conversation positively**. Use the "positive-negative-positive" rule. Start the discussion with a positive statement regarding the employee's performance. Then discuss any areas for development. Finally, end on a positive note.

After discussing performance, the employee and the supervisor should work together to determine an action plan that will guide the employee in achieving property and individual goals. Agree upon the evaluation ratings and discuss what the employee must accomplish before the next review meeting.

LEGAL ISSUE:
Performance documentation is one of the most important items to keep in an employee's personnel file. Up-to-date information will help the supervisor justify comments in the performance appraisal. Documentation of performance can support the reasoning behind disciplining, terminating, or failing to promote an employee.

Potential Errors

Supervisors can fall victim to a number of common errors when giving performance evaluation ratings. They must be aware of the following common errors:

- **Halo/Horn**: The halo error can occur when an employee is extremely competent in one area and therefore rates highly in all areas. For example, if an assistant manager is very customer-service oriented and is well liked by residents, his or her supervisor might give the assistant manager high ratings in all other areas as well. The horn effect occurs when an employee receives low scores in all categories because of one performance area that is below standard.

- **Recency**: The recency error occurs when the supervisor gives more weight to recent performance and discounts incidents from early in the performance period. This may occur because it is difficult for the supervisor to remember performance from so long ago. In addition, employees' performance may actually improve as time goes by or employees may perform better closer to the review in anticipation of a higher evaluation.

- **Severity/Leniency**: Supervisors may believe that performance standards are too low, or they may be reluctant to give high ratings. This is the severity error. These raters have higher expectations than supervisors of other departments or properties. Thus, they rate their employees inconsistently. Conversely, supervisors who do not want to give low scores are committing the leniency error.

- **Central Tendency**: The error of central tendency occurs when a supervisor rates all employees within a very narrow range, regardless of the differences in their actual performance.

- **Contrast**: The contrast error occurs when a supervisor bases a rating on how the employee's performance compares to that of another employee and not on an objective rating standard.

- **Bias**: The bias error refers to a supervisor's beliefs or prejudices distorting ratings. National origin, age, religion, gender, appearance, and seniority can all influence the supervisor's appraisal. In addition, "liking" can cause errors in performance appraisals when supervisors allow like or dislike of a person to influence their assessment of that person's performance. Liking is emotional and often subconscious, while formal ratings should be non-emotional. Research has shown that rater liking and performance ratings are highly correlated. This may be the result of a "liking bias" or it may be that supervisors just like higher performers and dislike poor performers.

LEGAL ISSUE:
Performance appraisals are subject to the same guidelines as all other employment practices. They should meet legal requirements that include absence of evidence that might imply discrimination, evidence that proves validity of the appraisal (e.g., job analysis), formal evaluation criteria, personal interaction with the rated employee, a review process that prevents one manager from over-influencing an employee's career, and equitable treatment of all employees.

PERFORMANCE COACHING

Performance coaching is an ongoing process in which you monitor the performance of your team and reward outstanding work while communicating any need for adjustments. It addresses problems while they are manageable.

Managers who are good at coaching do it in such a way that employees may not even know they had a coaching session. The manager will talk about things the employee is doing well, suggest possible ways to improve, and be open to the employees' ideas and comments.

Performance Coaching Steps

The following steps can be used in a performance coaching session.

Step	Description
1. Start on a positive or conversational note	• Ensure relaxed environment • Recognize work in other areas • Ask for help in solving problem • Example: "You always put forth a great deal of effort. I would like your help in solving a problem that I have been noticing lately."
2. Describe the problem.	• Be clear and straightforward • Cite specific performance examples • Compare performance with what you expect • Avoid finding fault or making accusations • Focus on problem, not the person
3. Discuss solutions to the problem.	• Ask for help solving the problem • Try not to offer your solution too quickly • Example: "I need your help in getting the work volume back up to where it should be. What do you think we can do?"
4. Agree on actions.	• End with a clear understanding of next steps • Summarize actions in writing
5. Arrange follow-up.	• Set time to revisit performance problem
6. Express confidence in the employee.	• Let employees know you believe in them • Be genuine • Example: "I know you can get your work volume up. You have done it before and I know you can do it again."

Training and Development

Often, performance coaching reveals a need for training—either to address a performance gap or to position for growth and new responsibilities. The goal is to choose the right opportunity for each team member.

Overall, it is important to understand how adults learn best. Training, whether attended off-site or developed in-house should address the unique needs of adult learners. Adults:

- Want to focus on "real world" issues
- Have goals and expectations
- Enjoy debating and challenging ideas
- Expect their ideas to be heard and respected
- Want to be resources to each other
- Need to understand "What's in it for me?"

Learning styles must be considered as well. Learning styles describe the way students prefer to learn and how they process ideas. There are three distinct learning styles: visual, auditory, and kinesthetic (tactile). The most effective training addresses multiple learning styles.

- **Visual:** Visual learners learn best through seeing. They need to see body language and facial expressions to understand content fully.
- **Auditory Learners:** Auditory learners learn best through hearing. Lectures, discussions, and listening to what others have to say are their preferred methods of learning.
- **Kinesthetic Learners:** Kinesthetic or tactile learners learn best through a hands-on approach. They prefer to explore the physical world around them.

Training methods can be thought of as the way the information is conveyed to the participants. Examples include instructor-led classroom books, e-learning, books, articles, podcasts, on-the-job training, computer-based training, professional conferences, networking, job broadening or stretch assignments, and so forth.

LEGAL ISSUE:
Legal regulations affect training just as they affect all other human resource management functions. Specifically, the law requires that employees have access to training and development programs in a nondiscriminatory fashion. All employees must have equal opportunity to participate in training programs and equal opportunity for advancement.

DISCIPLINARY ACTION

While most employees will perform at or above standards, some, unfortunately, will not. Potential reasons for disciplinary action include performance issues, absenteeism and tardiness, insubordination, and drug and alcohol abuse.

Poor Performance

Poor performance should be addressed in performance evaluations and remedied through performance coaching and training and development activities. However, poor performance sometimes calls for immediate attention. For example, if a site manager receives daily complaints from prospective residents regarding the behavior of a leasing consultant, the manager should discipline the agent immediately. If poor performance is a result of factors beyond the employee's control, managers should identify and address the root of the problem. Discipline for poor performance should follow these guidelines:

- Performance standards should be reasonable and communicated to all employees

- Poor performance should be documented and poor performers should be informed that they are not meeting standards

- Managers should make a good-faith attempt to give employees an opportunity to improve their performance

Poor Attendance

Poor attendance involves employee absenteeism and tardiness. Poor attendance leads to decreased productivity and can lower the morale of those who have good attendance and are forced to take on additional responsibilities. Poor attendance can be a sign of work avoidance—employees might be avoiding work due to issues with coworkers or supervisors, unchallenging work, family demands, or another reason. These reasons should be addressed if appropriate. Supervisors should distinguish between those who miss work due to legitimate reasons and those who are chronically absent or tardy.

Insubordination

Insubordination refers to an employee's refusal to obey a direct order from a supervisor or to an employee's verbal abuse of a supervisor. Employees' willingness to carry out management directives is critical to the company's success. A supervisor should document insubordinate employee behavior by recording the direct order given to the direct report and the employee's refusal to obey the order—whether verbally or by not doing what was asked. Discipline for insubordination will vary based on the severity of the situation, the employee's subordination history, and whether the supervisor provoked the employee. Exceptions that allow an employee to disobey a direct order are if the activity is illegal, or if safety is a consideration.

Alcohol or Drug Abuse

Using alcohol or drugs on the job are serious misconduct that can lead to harsh discipline. These situations present great challenges to managers. Individuals who are alcoholics should be treated in a different manner that those who were under the influence on the job. Alcoholics are generally viewed more sympathetically because alcoholism is an illness that may be treated. If an appropriate program or counseling for alcohol or drug abusers is part of the employee's benefits, the employee should have the opportunity to take advantage of this counseling. Sometimes, other symptoms such as poor attendance or poor performance can be indicators of alcohol or drug abuse. There is a major difference between the use of alcohol and the use of drugs. While the use of alcohol in moderation while not on the job is socially acceptable, illegal drug use of any sort is not tolerable.

Progressive Discipline

Specific policies to handle disciplinary issues must be developed and communicated. *Progressive discipline* is a common method of dealing with these issues. This method involves a series of interventions that gives employees opportunities to correct their behavior before being dismissed. Each warning step is more severe than the last, and failure to correct behavior results in justifiably discharging the employee.

Progressive discipline can be used for the same rule violation, similar rule violations, a serious rule violation, or a series of frequent but dissimilar rule violations. Minor violations of company policies will use all of the steps in the system, while severe violations, sometimes called *gross misconduct,* may call for skipping some of the steps, or even jumping to the last step, termination.

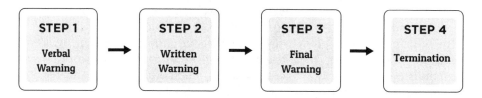

Step 1. Verbal Warning

A verbal warning should be given and the employee should be informed that if the problem continues within a specific timeframe, further action will be taken. This warning should be given in private. The objective of the meeting should be to devise a solution to the problem, not to criticize the employee. The supervisor should also provide clear expectations for improvement. The verbal warning should be recorded in the employee's personnel file.

Step 2. Written Warning

If the employee violates the same rule within the specified period, the supervisor then gives a written warning to the individual. This warning should be filed in the employee's records. The employee should be told again that failure to correct the problem will lead to further disciplinary action.

Step 3. Final Warning

If the employee continues to violate the same rule, the employee is given a final warning. This final warning can take the form of a second written warning or the employee can even be suspended without pay for a specific time, if company policies allow. The final warning should indicate that the employee will be let go if the documented issue continues.

Step 4. Termination

If the employee does not correct the problem within the stated period, he or she is terminated. Note that termination is the immediate response to severe violations such as violence, theft, or falsification of records.

Positive Discipline

Sometimes, punishment does not motivate an employee to change behavior and can actually cause the person to fear or resent the supervisor. To avoid this outcome, some companies use *positive discipline*, which encourages employees to monitor their own behavior and assume responsibility for their actions.

Positive discipline also uses a series of steps ending in the termination of the employee; however, counseling sessions between the employee and the supervisor replace the punishment used in progressive discipline. The focus of these sessions is getting the employee to learn from his or her mistakes and to initiate positive behavior. In positive discipline, the steps are as follows:

1. The employee suggests solutions to the problem and enters into a verbal agreement with the supervisor.

2. If the solution does not work, the pair examines the reasons for failure and develops a different solution.

3. If the problem continues, the employee receives a final warning that he or she is at risk of being terminated.

4. Finally, the employee is dismissed if the problem persists.

With positive discipline, the supervisor motivates and encourages the employee, rather than enforcing punishment. This causes the supervisor to be seen as a counselor, rather than as an adversary. Of book, this method calls for the appropriate training of supervisors—they must be equipped with the skills to problem solve and guide their employees as they deal with these issues.

Hot Stove Rule

Regardless of the type of discipline administered, managers should adhere to the "hot-stove rule." This rule suggests that the disciplinary process is similar to touching a hot stove:

Hot Stove	Discipline
A hot stove provides a warning that one will be burned if one touches it	Disciplinary policies should inform employees of the consequences of breaking the rules
Touching a hot stove results in an immediate consequence, which is a burn	Discipline should also be an immediate consequence following a rule infraction
A hot stove is consistent in administering pain to anyone who touches it	Discipline should be applied consistently to all

LEGAL ISSUE:
The *Weingarten case* states that a union employee has the right to have a coworker present during an investigatory interview, that is, when an employee is questioned to obtain information that could be used as a basis for discipline, or when an employee is asked to defend his or her conduct. The Supreme Court ruled that the employee has the right to select which coworker will be present; management must inform the coworker of the subject of the interview; the coworker can interrupt for clarification; and the coworker can advise the employee on how to respond to a question. In addition, at the end of the interview, the coworker can add information to support the employee's case. As of January 1, 2006, nonunion employees are *not* entitled to this right.

RETENTION AND TURNOVER

Turnover describes the process in which employees leave the property's employ. Workers leave their employing organization for a number of reasons. Poor performers often remove themselves from the property before being terminated involuntarily. Other employees may see opportunities when market conditions are good. Employees sometimes leave due to dissatisfaction with their current position. Some turnover is unavoidable, such as when an employee's spouse is transferred to another location.

A number of costs are associated with employee turnover:

- loss of training investments
- need to recruit, hire, and train a replacement
- severance pay
- need for other employees to cover work
- interruption of procedural flow
- loss of organization-specific knowledge (the loss of which may also make training others more difficult)

However, a departure may also create benefits:

- opportunity to replace a senior person with a lower-wage, less-senior new hire or promotion
- chance for the property to acquire new thoughts, skills, and perspectives that are essential to business adaptation and innovation

Aiming for 100 percent retention is the wrong goal for any company. Effective retention means keeping the right or best people. Retention efforts should be less focused on the number of people leaving and more focused on who is leaving and why. The costs of retention should also be balanced with the benefits of new ideas, perspectives, and skills. A company should develop some sense of a healthy turnover rate. If this rate is exceeded (too many people are staying) or is not met (too many people are leaving) then selection, compensation, and other human resource practices may require reevaluation.

Retention Strategies

Following are some retention strategies to consider implementing:

- Give retention bonus on various employment anniversaries
- Provide extra vacation if you stay for a certain amount of time
- Develop a bonus rewards program where points are accumulated for tenure or established accomplishments, and employees can select gifts from website or catalog
- Provide recognition letters or plaques
- Give Starbucks gift card after 90-day period is over
- Conduct team member engagement surveys as a way to consider team member input on day to day company business operations
- Pay expenses for job related professional development, such as IREM®

Voluntary Turnover

Voluntary turnover occurs when an employee decides, for personal or professional reasons, to leave the organization. Voluntary separations include resignations (quits) and retirements.

Resignations can be a result of the employee's dissatisfaction with one or many aspects of the job or of an attractive alternative outside the organization. While a resignation can occur at any time, a *retirement* happens at the end of an employee's career. Retirement usually involves the employee receiving retirement benefits, such as Social Security. Retirement can be planned for by grooming other employees to fill open positions.

Prior to a voluntary departure, an *exit interview* should be conducted to find out the reasons the employee is leaving. The interviewer should not assume that honest answers will be easy to obtain; employees are often afraid of being truthful and "burning bridges." The interviewer should ask open-ended questions and assure confidentiality. The interview should also cover administrative issues such as when benefits will cease. Other topics might include:

- Hiring practices
- Orientation practices
- Degree to which job met expectations
- Training and development
- Organization culture
- Compensation and benefits
- Direct supervision
- Ideas for improvement
- Positive aspects of the department or organization
- Negative aspects of the department or organization

Involuntary Turnover

Involuntary turnover occurs when an employee's relationship with a company is terminated due to economic necessity or a poor fit between employer and employee. Involuntary turnover is the result of serious deliberation and can have a profound effect on the departing employee as well as the rest of the property. Involuntary turnover includes terminations and layoffs.

Terminations are a result of poor performance or refusal to correct disciplinary issues. *Layoffs* differ from terminations in that they are not typically the result of employee behavior, but rather, of economic conditions or a change in the company's strategy. Layoffs may occur after a reduction in demand, an introduction of new technology, or a merger or acquisition. A layoff implies that the employee may be called back to work. Therefore, laid-off employees should be told to consider themselves terminated if they are not called to work within a specific period. Employers should be cautious not to guarantee that employees will be rehired.

To protect the company from litigation, it is important to handle disciplinary terminations as carefully as possible. Follow the "Cardinal Rules of Termination," as developed by the Society for Human Resource Management (SHRM):

- **Never immediately terminate.** It is never prudent to terminate an employee on the spot. If necessary, the employee should be "suspended subject to termination pending further investigation."
- **Ensure the investigation is thorough and well documented.** Unbiased evidence should be collected and managers or human resource personnel should not assume the role of prosecutor.
- **Conduct all interviews with care.** The approach should be investigative, not adversarial. Weingarten rights must be upheld.
- **Investigate promptly.** Any misconduct should be investigated within 48 to 72 hours after the event. The employee should be advised of a decision within 24 to 48 hours thereafter.
- **Always conduct a "final" review.** Analyze all findings and recommendations before making a final decision. Be sure that other employees have been treated the same way in similar situations.
- **Pinpoint the basis of the termination.** Carefully identify and articulate the reasons for termination. Whenever possible, cite the specific work policy or rule violated.
- **Inform the employee in person of the decision to terminate.** Also, explain the reasons for termination and have one other management or human resource person present when the employee is told.
- **Follow disciplinary procedures and keep documentation.** Documentation of progressive discipline can help substantiate the cause for termination in a legal environment.
- **Go for it (but do your homework).** Continuing to employ someone whose performance is unacceptable can be even more costly than termination. Team morale problems, productivity losses, and endangerment of other employees are all potential outcomes of retaining poor performers.
- **Beware of a setup.** As progressive discipline steps unfold, employees often see that termination is looming. It is possible that they will prepare for a lawsuit. If this is detected, legal counsel should become involved immediately.

LEGAL ISSUE:

In cases of wrongful termination, U.S. courts require the employer to prove that the employee was terminated for just cause. This standard is determined by seven questions that the employer must answer affirmatively for just cause to exist:

1. Was the employee forewarned of the disciplinary consequences of his or her conduct? (Notification)
2. Was the rule the employee violated reasonably related to safe and efficient operations? (Reasonable Rule)
3. Did managers conduct an investigation into the misconduct before administering discipline? (Investigation before Discipline)
4. Was the investigation fair and impartial? (Fair Investigation)
5 Did the investigation provide substantial evidence or proof of guilt? (Proof of Guilt)
6. Were the rules, orders, and penalties of the disciplinary action applied evenhandedly and without discrimination? (Absence of Discrimination)
7. Was the disciplinary penalty reasonably related to the seriousness of the rule violation? (Reasonable Penalty)

Student Housing Impact: Note that student employees are subject to evaluation, and based upon academic performance may be required to discontinue employment.

DIG DEEPER WITH IREM RESOURCES

Publications

IREM White Paper Package on Leadership Development. Chicago: Institute of Real Estate Management, 2013.

These IREM White Papers cover important leadership competencies for real estate management professionals.

Principles of Real Estate Management, Sixteenth Edition. Chicago: Institute of Real Estate Management, 2011.

This book provides key considerations for managing real estate today, and includes specific insights and guidance by property type.

Profile and Compensation Study, ARM Edition 2014.
Chicago: Institute of Real Estate Management, 2014.

Detailed comparative data including compensation; years of management experience; education; region; portfolio size.

Websites

www.irem.org
The IREM website is your first-stop for information on real estate management. With resources organized by topic and property type, you will find the forms, tools, publications, webinars, and tutorials you need to help you manage your business and keep up with the industry.

Note that the IREM® Code of Professional Ethics can be found on the IREM® website at **www.irem.org/ethics**

IREM On-Demand Learning (www.irem.org)
• Assessing Your Leadership Skills (Tutorial)
• Attracting Talent: Employing a Diverse Workforce (Tutorial)
• Generational Preferences: A Glimpse into the Future Office (Video)
• Interviewing, Hiring and Retention (Recorded Webinar)

Articles
Published bi-monthly by IREM, the *Journal of Property Management* offers comprehensive coverage of the real estate management industry, including frequent features and columns on human resource topics.

Income/Expense Analysis® Reports
The IREM Income/Expense Analysis® Reports are the industry standard in relaying precise property data to owners, investors and tenants. Valuable operating data is collected for Conventional Apartments; Office Buildings; Federally Assisted Apartments; Condos, Co-ops, and Planned Unit Developments; and Shopping Centers. But we can't do it without your help.

Submit your data by April 1 of each year at http://IE.IREM.ORG to receive a FREE Income/Expense Analysis® book (a $485 value) and a FREE Individual Building Report. (Available once published by September.)

The Income/Expense Analysis® Reports are available for purchase in softcover books, downloadable .pdf or Excel, and Interactive online Labs.

PART II:
FINANCE

The following topics are covered:

- Accounting
- Budgeting
- Operating expenses
- Capital expenses
- Financial reports

CHAPTER 1:
INTRODUCTION TO ACCOUNTING

Overseeing and executing accurate and efficient accounting procedures ensures the financial health of the property. A property manager must be able to identify and understand accounting skills needed to meet the owner's objectives for the property's performance and to provide a foundation for making day to day operating decisions.

In this chapter:

- **Owner's Goals and Objectives**
- **Central Role of the Real Estate Manager**
- **Accounting Terms**
- **Types of Accounting**
- **Chart of Accounts**
- **Assets and Liabilities**
- **Purchasing**
- **Accounting Software**

OWNER'S GOALS AND OBJECTIVES

Investors purchase income-producing real estate for two primary reasons:

1. Speculation
2. Investment

Speculation offers investors an opportunity to take a high risk and potentially receive a high reward from a relatively short-term holding period. Their return is typically achieved at the time of sale and is realized from the profit made on the sale of the property.

Investment in real estate, on the other hand, typically extends for a longer holding period and offers investors five fundamental opportunities:

- Periodic return
- Capital preservation
- Capital appreciation
- Leverage
- Income tax advantage

In addition to the five fundamental financial reasons for investment, investors also enjoy the benefit of the pride of ownership that comes from owning income-producing property.

While all investors have these financial goals, the goal of an effective real estate manager is to understand the mix of the various elements in relationship to the individual investor's risk tolerance.

Sustainability Impact: Some owners will incorporate sustainability goals such as waste reduction and use of environmentally preferable materials. Goals should be in line with the budget outlined by ownership.

CENTRAL ROLE OF THE REAL ESTATE MANAGER

The central role of a real estate manager is to maintain or increase the value of the asset for the owner. To accomplish this goal, a real estate manager generates and uses financial information as part of his or her daily job responsibilities. They deal with the following areas of financial and managerial information:

1. The real estate manager collects rents and verifies the receipt of goods and services for payment of expenses. In other words, the manager gathers basic financial information about rents, residents, and cash outlays. A real estate manager should therefore be actively engaged in assessing information and creating reports about the basic financial activities of the business.

2. The real estate manager uses the information gathered about leases and expenses in preparing the annual operating budget. For example, the real estate manager's monitoring of the purchasing process means that information about expenses can be made available for budgeting and for making decisions about costs and vendors.

3. The real estate manager gathers information and maintains records on trends in marketing and leasing, delinquency rates, resident turnover, and competing properties. The information the real estate manager gathers is often included in reports to the owner. Because accuracy is paramount in reporting, the information the real estate manager collects must be reliable.

ACCOUNTING TERMS

Accounting and bookkeeping are ways of maintaining records. Accounting makes several important distinctions. This chapter highlights three of those distinctions: income and expenses, assets and liabilities, and receivables and payables. A chart of accounts is important in organizing how a business handles money. Businesses use purchase orders to monitor expenses.

Accounting is largely concerned with monitoring the flow of income and expenses in a business. To monitor this flow better, categories of debts and credits are used to clarify how money should flow into or out of the business. In a further refinement, short-term movements in accounts are monitored through accounts payable and accounts receivable.

An account is a detailed statement of receipts and payments of money that have taken place between two or more parties. Examples of accounts that monitor the flow of money into a business are revenue accounts and accounts receivable. Examples of accounts that track the flow of money from a business are expense accounts and accounts payable. Revenue accounts may track categories such as rents, sales, and miscellaneous income. Expense accounts may include salaries, supplies, materials, and utilities.

This section is devoted to managing and monitoring money, to making financial decisions, and to reporting financial "vital signs" to interested persons within a company and to property owners. The following terms are used throughout this book:

- **Accounting:** the practice of classifying, recording, and summarizing financial transactions
- **Cash:** money in the form of currency (dollar bills), negotiable money orders, checks, and demand deposits
- **Invoice:** an itemized bill presented to a buyer by a seller that specifies the price of goods sold or services delivered and the terms of the sale
- **Income:** money or value received
- **Revenue:** income of various kinds coming into a business as cash receipts, yield, tax credits, and other forms of income
- **Expense:** any business-specific cost incurred in operating a business or investment real estate. In accounting, an expense can sometimes be divided over more than one accounting period; in that case, the cost is said to be expensed.
- **Cost:** any expenditure of money, goods, or services for the purpose of acquiring goods or services
  - ○ **Fixed Cost:** price remains the same regardless the number of units leased. Examples include insurance and real estate taxes. Seasonal services can be arranged as a fixed cost, for example, retaining the services of a landscaping company for a fixed monthly cost.
  - ○ **Variable Cost:** price changes with usage. Electricity and water are typical variable costs. Paying for snow removal each time it snowed, rather than on a fixed cost contract, is an example of variable cost.
- **Asset:** one of a company's economic resources. They include real property, cash, land, stocks, bonds, or equipment.
- **Liability:** a debt owed by an individual or a business
- **Accounts Payable:** monies due to others for services rendered or goods ordered and received
- **Accounts Receivable:** monies due from others for services rendered or goods ordered and delivered
- **Pro-rating:** To divide or assess the rent proportionally when a resident moves in or moves out mid-month

Example 1.1: Pro-Rating Methods

There are two ways to pro-rate. The method that you should use is determined by your management company or the housing agency you are dealing with.

For example, assume a resident moves in on May 6 and the rent is $500 per month.

Method 1
Divide the rent by 30 and multiply that amount by the actual number of days the resident will live in the apartment that month:

$$\$500 / 30 = \$16.67 \times 26 = \$433.42$$

Method 2
Divide the rent by the actual days in that particular month and multiply that amount by the actual number of days the resident will live in the apartment that month:

$$\$500 / 31 = \$16.13 \times 26 = \$419.38$$

RESOURCES:

The Institute of Real Estate Management publishes the *Glossary of Real Estate Management Terms* which is a compilation of terms used and encountered in real estate management. Because real estate managers must be familiar with terminologies from other disciplines, terms related to accounting, finance, contracting, and insurance and risk management have also been included along with descriptions of many of the laws that impact real estate operations. The book includes definitions of more than 2,000 terms plus acronyms and abbreviations and mathematical formulas. Any term in the glossary can also be found using the Search function at **www.irem.org**.

TYPES OF ACCOUNTING

Several kinds of accounting exist. Real estate managers should be aware of the three basic ways that income and expenses are recorded in accounting. The differences center on when income and expenses are declared.

Cash Basis

Some companies use *cash basis accounting,* which reports the real-time cash flow of income and expenses. The advantage of that system is that it simplifies bookkeeping requirements. With this method, you record income when payment is actually received. Similarly, expenses are declared at the time when cash is paid out. For example, let's say that a resident was not able to pay his rent in July. He wrote you in advance and promised to send a payment of two month's rent with late fees to be received August 1 to cover July and August. He sent the payment as promised. In cash basis accounting, you would not report the July rent as July income. The late payment for July would be recorded when it was actually received—in August.

Full Accrual Basis

In *full accrual basis* accounting, income is declared in the accounting period in which it is earned, rather than when the cash is received. Expenses are declared in the accounting period in which the expense is incurred, rather than when the cash is paid out. For example, if a company uses full accrual basis accounting, rents are posted when they are earned, even if the actual cash is received later. (In the previous example, the July rent would be recorded in July.) Likewise, expenses are declared when they are incurred, even if they are paid out later. A company would record the expense for a large quantity of lighting fixtures when it places the order in July, even though it will not actually pay the money out until after receiving the invoice in August.

Modified Accrual

In *modified accrual* accounting (also called modified cash accounting), some income categories and expense categories are declared on a cash basis and some are declared on an accrual basis. For example, taxes and insurance may be separated out and treated as accrual expenses rather than as cash expenses.

Here is a recap:

Type of Accounting	Income	Expenses
Cash *Examples:* Yearly income; small business; self-employed person	Declared when cash is received *Example:* Rent payments are declared in the accounting period in which they are actually received	Declared when cash is paid out *Example:* Utilities are recorded as expenses when they are actually paid
Full Accrual *Examples:* Real estate firm with rentals; mid-sized and larger corporations	Declared when income is earned *Example:* Rent payments are declared in the accounting period in which they are due	Declared when expenses are incurred *Example:* Supplies are recorded when they are ordered
Modified Accrual	Mixed	Mixed

CHART OF ACCOUNTS

A *chart of accounts* is a classification or arrangement of account items by type of income or expense as well as by accounts receivable and accounts payable and by assets and liabilities. (This section discusses income, expenses, accounts receivable, and accounts payable. Assets and liabilities are discussed later in this chapter.) The property management firm typically designs a standard chart of accounts based on Generally Accepted Accounting Principles (GAAP). Properties with different amenities may track income or expenses for that amenity, making the chart of accounts vary slightly by property.

Income and Expenses

The chart of accounts is an important system for classifying income and expenses, which are the two major categories. Getting high-quality information requires planning, and the chart of accounts is a good place to begin. Because all income and expenses will flow through the accounts listed there, the chart of accounts is central to record keeping. The classifications should reflect all sources of income and expenses. A well-designed chart of accounts enhances accuracy, produces useful information, and reflects the organization of the business.

Refining Categories

Refining the kinds of information collected is important. For example, setting up a single category called "Landscape" that covers normal maintenance, seasonal repairs, landscaping contracts, and the capital budget for a new courtyard almost guarantees poor information because the category is too broad. Each of the components should be separate since each has a different function and involves different expenses.

Much of accounting is about placing money into proper categories. Figure 1-1 shows a sample chart of accounts for a real estate management company that rents apartments. Note the basic division of the chart of accounts into income and expenses.

Categorizing Expenses

Because expenses involve many different functions, separate line items are set up under various classifications. For example, landscape services appear under the larger category called "Operating & Maintenance," and "Management Fee" shows up under the category named "Administrative."

FIGURE 1-1: SAMPLE CHART OF ACCOUNTS

Chart of Accounts

Income (Revenues)	Acct. No.
Apartment rental	1010
Garage and parking space	1070
Miscellaneous income	1080
Vacancies and collection loss	1090

Expenses (Disbursements)

Marketing	Acct. No.	Operating & Maintenance	Acct.No.
Internet	2010	Maintenance payroll	5010
Website	2020	Supplies	5020
Collateral materials	2030	HVAC repairs	5030
Print advertising	2040	Trash removal	5040
Promotions	2050	Electrical repairs	5050
		Plumbing repairs	5055
Administrative		Elevator repairs/contracts	5060
Other administrative costs	3020	Exterior repairs	5061
Administrative payroll	3030	Interior repairs	5062
Office supplies	3040	Common area repairs	5065
Management fee	3050	Painting/decorating	5070
Bookkeeping fees	3060	Landscape repairs	5075
		Irrigation	5080
Utilities		Security and traffic control	5085
Electricity	4010	Parking	5090
Water	4020	Lighting	5095
Sewer	4030	Snow removal	5100
HVAC/fuel	4040	Miscellaneous services	5110
Combination electricity	4050		
Self-contained energy plant	4060	**Capital Improvements/Repairs**	
		Building	7010
Taxes and Insurance		Building equipment	7020
Real estate taxes	6010	Building equipment – portable	7030
Other taxes, fees, permits	6020	Furnishings	7040
Real estate insurance	6030	Maintenance equipment	7050
Other insurance	6040	Other major repl./repair	7060

Example 1-2: Account Code Breakdown

In the sample chart of accounts in Figure 1.1, "Utilities" are a major subdivision of expenses and a regular part of doing business. Forecasts will be needed, and plans should also be made for controlling the costs of utilities. In addition, "Water" is a specific kind of utility that also comes from a specific supplier (usually, the municipal water treatment plant). Note that the account has been given its own number, in this case, 4020. In budgeting planning, a forecast can be "plugged in" to each established account.

In addition to classifying and arranging account items according to income and expenses, the chart of accounts classifies and arranges them according to accounts receivable and accounts payable.

Accounts Receivable	*Definition:* Accounts waiting to receive money for goods or services that the company has sold; revenues to be collected. Monthly rent is a good example of a receivable; residents owe the rent indicated in their leases. Rent that has not yet been paid is therefore an account receivable. Close management of receivables helps keep a constant and even flow of cash into a company. Receivables should be collected as quickly as possible and should be deposited in the bank promptly. At a rental property, close attention to receivables means keeping track of rent payments, noting late payments, and quickly contacting tenants who have not paid on time. Depositing all receipts daily is a good control measure that can help management more quickly determine which accounts are suffering from "nonsufficient funds." Working hard to collect receivables and making disbursements judiciously can allow for greater control of cash. Proper collection of receivables and control of disbursements have a major impact on the budget in general, as will be seen in following chapters.
Accounts Payable	*Definition:* Payments that a company will make from its various accounts (e.g., plumbing repairs, janitorial supplies, and pest control to vendors, suppliers, and providers of services); debts owed to another party. If a real estate manager contracts with painters to repair the walls and paint an apartment, the invoice from the painters goes to accounts payable.

Accounts payable and accounts receivable are short-term debt, which means that they are expected to be settled during the current accounting period.

ASSETS AND LIABILITIES

One of the most important aspects of understanding the value of a property is to analyze the stability of the rental income stream. To do so, a real estate manager often needs to review a property's assets and liabilities. Like income and expenses, assets and liabilities are a basic division in accounting.

- An **asset** is an economic resource that produces future benefits.
- A **liability** is a debt or obligation.

In general, income (or revenue) of various kinds is an *asset*, and expenses are *liabilities.* This means that accounts receivable are assets, and accounts payable are liabilities. An account receivable increases the value of the property, and an account payable decreases its value. Apartment buildings also are assets since they can provide income either through rentals or sale of the property. *Fixed assets* are properties, goods, or other things of value that cannot be readily sold or otherwise converted on short notice at their true and fair value. They include tangible assets of a long-term nature such as land, buildings, machinery, and equipment that are not intended for resale within the regular operation of a business.

In accounting, assets and liabilities are separated into short-term (or current) and long-term assets.

- **Short-term assets:** expected to be converted to cash or be used up during the year.
- **Long-term assets:** resources that are held for any period longer than one year. Real estate is a prime example of a long-term asset.
- **Current liabilities:** due within the coming year.
- **Long-term liabilities:** will be paid off over some extended time span. A mortgage is a good example of a long-term liability in real estate.

General Ledger

A *general ledger* is a formal record of all the financial transactions of a business. Ownership dictates how often the real estate manager should provide general ledgers (monthly, yearly, etc.). Accounts are transferred as final entries from the various journals to the general ledger, where they are posted as debits and credits and thus show the accumulated effects of transactions. Financial statements are built from the general ledger.

- A **journal** is a book or page on which accounting entries are made.
- A **debit** is one of two values in a double-entry accounting system entry. For every debit, there is an equal and offsetting credit. At least one component of every accounting transaction (journal entry) is a debit amount. Debits increase assets and decrease liabilities and equity.
- A **credit** is the other of the two values in a double-entry accounting system entry. At least one component of every accounting transaction (journal entry) is a credit amount. For every credit, there is an equal and offsetting debit. Credits increase liabilities and equity and decrease assets. The sum of all general ledger debit balances should always equal the sum of all general ledger credit balances.

The general ledger provides a tracking tool for all financial transactions. All funds received and all funds paid out are accounted for in the general ledger. For this tracking system to work properly, it is vitally important to ensure that each financial transaction is originally assigned the correct account number from the property's chart of accounts. Cash, Accounts Receivable, Accounts Payable, Sales, Purchases, Telephone Expenses, and Owners' Equity are all examples of general ledger accounts.

PURCHASING

Purchasing is a way for a company to monitor the many expenses it incurs for supplies, services, and materials. Various forms are used to ensure the control of purchases made and money going out to pay for those purchases.

- **Purchase order:** A *purchase order* is a written authorization to an outside vendor to provide certain goods or services in a given amount, at a given price, to be delivered at a certain time and place.
- **Statement:** A *statement* is a periodic summary of account activity with a beginning date and an ending date. Payment should never be paid from statements.
- **Invoice:** An *invoice*, or bill, is a request for payment. Accounts payable are only paid on an invoice. To monitor how money flows from a business, it is important to make sure that the invoice itself is accurate, that the payment is made on time, and that the payment goes to the right company or person.

Purchase Orders

Purchase orders are used to track expenses at the time the expense is incurred instead of exclusively at the time of billing. Most companies use paperless systems or purchase orders through their software. Often, approval limits are

TIPS:
Site managers use purchase orders as a tool to:
- Help manage cash
- Track a delivery
- Confirm billing
- Ensure billing is for the correct amount and for something that was actually received

Purchasing Procedures

In order to keep better records and provide solid information for budgeting, always use purchase orders for supplies and equipment. Purchase orders create a record of how many items are ordered and how often. They are useful in monitoring inventory levels to ensure that adequate supplies or replacement parts are available. Tracking inventory through purchase orders can prevent purchasing too many or too few parts and supplies, both of which can be costly. An overstock of inventory represents cash that is not available for other uses, while inadequate inventory increases the expense if a single part must be ordered, or if a repair must be delayed.

Purchase Order Form

A purchase order form should contain the following information:

- Vendor name
- Item name and/or description
- Price (per unit and for the quantity being ordered)

- Quantity
- Model number and/or trade number
- Method of payment; any penalty for delay
- Applicable discounts
- Delivery information: location, date, method of transport, special instructions, billing information if different
- Indication of whether purchase is for general stock, the common area, or a specific unit
- Purpose of purchase, if appropriate (e.g., new roll holder for toilet paper in half-bath in unit 123)
- Signature of person making request and authorization by appropriate person (A manager must generally obtain approval to make expensive purchases.)

Purchasing Guidelines

A company's employee manual typically includes purchasing guidelines that explain the process of ordering goods and services for a property. In small management firms the manager may perform all purchasing functions, but in a larger organization a central purchasing authority typically buys all materials and handles all contracts for the property. In addition to instructions for completing a service request form and maintaining a purchase order log, general purchasing guidelines typically include the following:

- Provide vendors with names of authorized staff and any dollar limits. Update as appropriate.
- Create a system to trace the purchase order from original issue to payment of the invoice. Consider using software to track this process automatically.
- Set up a system to verify that the item received is the item ordered, that the item received is in good condition, and that quantity received is correct. The person who issued the purchase order should check the merchandise and review the invoice against the purchase order when it arrives and before approving payment.
- Pay bills for goods and services (operating expenses) only after ascertaining that the correct materials have been delivered and the work has been completed to specifications. By inventorying materials as they are received and inspecting all labor performed, the real estate manager can maintain better control over operating expenses.

FIGURE 1-2: SAMPLE PURCHASE ORDER FORM

Purchase Order #:
This number must appear on all invoices, packages, shipping papers, and service request forms.

Vendor:
Prepay all delivery charges
Deliver by _____

B
I
L
L

S
H
I
P

Date of Order	Shipping Instructions	Terms

Quantity	Unit No.	Description		Acct. No.	Unit Price	Total Price

Purchasing Approvals		Receiving/Payment Approvals	Total	
Requisitioned by		Name/Title	**Discount**	
Date		Date Received		
Approved by		Payment Approval		
Date		Date		
Special Instructions:			**Subtotal**	
			____% Total	
			Net Total	

Purchasing Costly Items

Certain items and situations require the owner's authorization before a purchase is made. Some of these items and situations might include: capital items, items above a set dollar amount, remodeling or renovation, and major maintenance items. The procedure for purchasing costly equipment and supplies is very similar to the procedure for bidding a service contract. In some cases, the manager will be purchasing both a service and a capital item. For example, in bidding a roofing contract, the manager is negotiating a contract to have a roofing contractor perform a service (install a new roof) as well as purchasing the roof materials. However, in this case, the manager would follow instructions for bidding a service contract, because the bulk of the contract is for service. In the case of purchasing a new computer system, however, the manager would bid out for the capital equipment, even though some training or service might be included in the purchase price.

ACCOUNTING SOFTWARE

Many real estate managers use accounting software to track and manage income and expenses. The following are some of the functions that are available in software packages:

- Tracking cash and accrual transactions for a given property
- Maintaining multiple charts of accounts
- Automating recurring journal entries
- Forecasting and tracking multiple versions of a budget
- Tracking purchase orders by department, delivery status, and vendor/buyer communication
- Generating recurring invoices
- Displaying trends from one accounting period to the next

While accounting software provides an automated, efficient way to manage assets and liabilities, it cannot provide the discernment and critical thinking that is required as part of the fiduciary responsibilities of the property management company. Any tool, software included, is only as good as the person using it. Proper training and procedures must be put in place so that the software enhances the accounting function's efficiency and accuracy. Staff must be responsible for ensuring that ethical accounting procedures are being followed and sound accounting practices are being implemented.

CHAPTER 2:
INTRODUCTION TO BUDGETING

Establishing and monitoring budgets is the road map to achieving the owner's goals and objectives for the property. A property manager needs the skills to prepare budgets, forecast, and analyze of variance to help meet the owner's objectives for the property.

What Is covered in this chapter:

- **About Budgeting**
- **Types of Budgets**
- **Forecasting**
- **Budgeting Variances**

ABOUT BUDGETING

Real estate managers use budgets as one of the main sources of information for making decisions about profitability. A budget gives a picture of a property's financial activity. Specialized budgets are used for decision making about financial areas and risks.

Budgeting and decision making use information from several areas. Note how the financial and managerial issues intertwine:

- The annual operating budget is prepared using the information gathered about leases and expenses—an area administered by the real estate manager.
- Because the real estate manager collects rents and verifies the receipt of goods and services for payments of expenses, information gathered by the real estate manager is a basis for examining and forecasting expenses.
- The real estate manager compares actual income and expenses to budget projections and produces reports on the differences, called variances, between what was forecast and what actually happened financially. Variance analysis is important in spotting trends and in assessing why financial performance may differ from expectations.

A *budget* is an itemized projection of income and expenses over a specific period for a particular property, project, or institution. A budget is a tool the manager uses to plan and control a property's operations. A budget report compares the projection to the actual results during the specified period.

Note some of the language of the definition:

- A budget covers a defined period of time (not necessarily a year)
- A budget estimates income and expenses
- Finally, a budget is a forecasting tool and financial measure that offers information that the manager can report to the owner about performance

The budget is the basis for setting measurable goals, planning to accomplish those goals, and assessing how well goals have been achieved.

Budgeting involves several basic management responsibilities. Site managers can use a budget to direct the property's daily operations and to control costs and expenditures. This is normally the purpose of the operating budget and the cash budget, both of which will be examined later in this chapter. Keep in mind that a budget represents plans for the future. The capital budget, which will be described in detail later in the book, deals with setting aside and managing funds to assure the future of a business.

TIPS:
A good site manager can control expenses, a great manager creates more income.

Budgeting expenses are fairly straightforward. The more challenging component, and therefore the most neglected component, is projecting income. One way to budget income is to look at the historical numbers and apply a percentage. Another way is to look at committed income for the next year while keeping in mind other places where you can increase the gross income of your property. For example:

- Miscellaneous income
- Pet rent
- Parking space rental
- Utility income
- Billing fees
- Reduction in vacancy

These are all things you can do as a site manager to help your property make more money and ultimately that is what this business is about.

TIPS:
Be sure to complete thorough research when preparing your budgets, such as calling your utility providers for estimated rate increases.

Affordable Housing Impact: There are special considerations to keep in mind when completing budgets for affordable housing such as Section 8. In order to receive an increase in rents from HUD, it is important to complete the OCAS form appropriately by thoroughly researching projected utility rates and providing documentation (e.g., online notices or articles from utility companies) as well as a comprehensive analysis. Knowledge of this information is paramount to being able to increase what you're able to do from a revenue standpoint each year. The OCAS form can be found on HUD's website at **www.hud.gov/hudclips**.

Top 5 Purposes Of A Budget

Budgets often are customized to represent the diverse needs and activities of a business. As this chapter points out, distinct budgets usually cover certain distinct needs. Let's look at the basic purposes of budgets:

1. Budgets serve as guidelines for operating a property. Because they can help compare actual amounts from previous years' experience or from a similar property, they indicate whether operations are efficient or can be streamlined.
2. Budgets form the foundation of the overall management plan, which should be in writing. This plan can be called an action plan, a workout plan, or some other name.
3. Budgets can help measure the performance of the real estate manager and the management company. Most other indicators, such as increases in occupancy or new sources of miscellaneous income, only roughly show how well the property is doing financially at a certain time. A budget is a more exact measure, a clearer snapshot.
4. Budgets measure the achievement of the owner's cash flow requirements by setting a schedule for before-tax cash flow.
5. Budgets project future income and expenses. While they do not see into the future, they can enable managers to make fairly accurate projections. These projections become the basis for decision making.

Elements of a Budget

Not all budgets place similar emphasis on the same data. For example, operating budgets focus on normal yearly expenses, rather than capital.

Cash flow budgets often have a narrower focus—and cover less time than an operating budget. Nevertheless, the following elements are necessary parts of a budget:

- **Income:** includes rent, fees, and other sources of revenue
- **Expenses:** includes operating expenses such as maintenance, utilities, payroll, advertising, and taxes
- **Financing Expenses:** includes property loan(s), loans for equipment, rehab, or furniture

- **Cash Flow Requirements:** includes the rate of return on the investment, equity, and the owner's other specific financial objectives

Process for Creating a Budget

Budgeting is not a clerical task; it is a process for managing a property or business. It is best thought of as a cycle. The process of preparing budgets and monitoring financial and budgetary performance usually consists of the following steps:

1. Check to ensure that the fiscal period is appropriate for the budget. The fiscal period for operating budgets is one year. Capital budgets may project multiple years.

2. Compare budgeted income and expense items with actual income and expenses, working account by account.

3. Take corrective measures, if needed. This may include consolidating accounts or creating new accounts to reflect new activity.

4. Adjust the projections for various accounts, based on past performance and actual figures for the most recent fiscal period.

5. Prepare reports for the property owner that describe the relationship of actual performance to budget goals. The reports should detail the reasons for variations. Take advantage of software to prepare budget reports.

6. Prepare to repeat the process at the end of the chosen budget period by maintaining accurate records during the budget period.

Single Family House Impact: Ownership may request a budget for each property or may request a cumulative report on all single family homes in the portfolio. The value of budgeting for each single family home is that a baseline budget is developed. This eliminates any element of surprise for the owner.

Affordable Housing Impact: Budget due dates may vary based upon the fiscal year, affordable housing program requirements, and contractual obligations. Typically, federal budgets are due between October and November. This allows enough time to communicate rent increases to residents for the following year.

Student Housing Impact: Note that there is a several year planning horizon when preparing student housing budgets, often up to two years in advance in order to meet student demand projections.

TYPES OF BUDGETS

Different budgets serve different purposes and monitor different types of finances. They are described briefly here, divided into short-term and long-term categories.

Short-Term	Long-Term
• **Operating Budget (Annual Budget):** a one-year, detailed plan for managing an existing property. • **Pro Forma Budget:** used to estimate the revenues and expenses of a new acquisition or future project under normal, stable market conditions. It is also used to analyze the effects major changes might have on a property. Such budgets are used to analyze the merits and drawbacks of real estate investments. • **Cash Flow Budget:** a monthly or other projection of the cash position of a business. It accounts for all sources of income and expected expenditures over the next budget period, which often is as short as a month.	• **Capital Budget:** a projection that describes the sources of funds for building up capital reserves. The capital budget also describes how and when those reserves will be used. Because capital and capital budgets are distinct concepts, they are discussed in detail later in the book. • **Long-Range Budget:** a long-term projection that estimates future expenditures and the return period. It involves methods for forecasting income and expenses more than one year into the future. A typical long-range budget forecasts three to five years into the future.

One of the main differences among cash, operating, long-range, and capital budgets is the span of time considered: a cash budget is usually set up month by month, an operating budget encompasses a year, and a long-range budget covers from three to five years.

Annual Operating Budget

Perhaps the most comprehensive budget, the annual operating budget is a one-year, detailed plan for managing a property. It can be created for a fiscal year or a calendar year. Fiscal years and calendar years do not have to coincide.

The purpose of the operating budget is to forecast annual net operating income (NOI). This makes the annual operating budget especially important. A sample operating budget is shown in the following figure.

FIGURE 2-1: SAMPLE OPERATING BUDGET (YEAR 1)

	Monthly	Annual
Income		
Gross Potential Income	$66,405	$796,860
Vacancy & Collection Loss	3,347	40,164
Net Rent Revenue	63,058	756,696
Other Income	526	6,312
Effective Gross Income	63,584	763,008
Expenses		
Payroll Mgmt.	$6,833	$81,996
Decorating	1,250	15,000
Maintenance	833	9,996
Supplies	833	9,996
Trash Removal	425	5,100
Electricity	2,083	24,996
Gas	2,917	35,004
Water & Sewer	2,500	30,000
Legal and Accounting	792	9,504
Miscellaneous	666	7,992
Administrative	333	3,996
Insurance	917	11,004
Property Taxes	10,000	120,000
Total Operating Expenses	**30,382**	**364,584**
NOI	33,202	398,424
Annual Debt Service	26,616	319,392
Before-Tax Cash Flow	$6,586	$79,032

Above is an annualized budget. Monthly, non-annualized operating budgets would project expenses and income for the actual months that they will occur (such as snow plowing or heating expenses for the winter months), rather than take the total for the year for each account and annualize it over twelve months equally.

The operating budget lists planned income and expense amounts for each month and for each account.

The *IREM® Financial Analysis Spreadsheet* is a tool used to perform financial analysis on a property. It includes 12-Month Operating Budget tab as shown below in Figure 2-2.

FIGURE 2-2: 12-MONTH OPERATING BUDGET SPREADSHEET

12 Month Operating Budget

Site:		For:			By:					Date: 1/8/2015			
				<----- Pro Forma Data ----->									
Income	Month 1	Month 2	Month 3	Month 4	Month 5	Month 6	Month 7	Month 8	Month 9	Month 10	Month 11	Month 12	Total Year
Gross Potential Income (GPI)	$35,000	$35,000	$35,000	$35,000	$35,000	$35,000	$35,000	$35,000	$35,000	$35,000	$35,000	$35,000	$420,000
- Loss to Lease													$0
- Vacancy and Collection Loss													$0
= Net Rent Revenue	$35,000	$35,000	$35,000	$35,000	$35,000	$35,000	$35,000	$35,000	$35,000	$35,000	$35,000	$35,000	$420,000
+ Miscellaneous Income													$0
+ Property Tax Reimbursement													$0
+ Utility Reimbursement													$0
+ CAM Reimbursement													$0
+ Other Reimbursements													$0
= Effective Gross Income (EGI)	$35,000	$35,000	$35,000	$35,000	$35,000	$35,000	$35,000	$35,000	$35,000	$35,000	$35,000	$35,000	$420,000

Operating Expenses

Utilities

	Month 1	Month 2	Month 3	Month 4	Month 5	Month 6	Month 7	Month 8	Month 9	Month 10	Month 11	Month 12	Total Year
Heat	$30,000	$30,000	$30,000	$30,000	$30,000	$30,000	$30,000	$30,000	$30,000	$30,000	$30,000	$30,000	$360,000
Water and Sewer													$0
Total Utilities	$30,000	$30,000	$30,000	$30,000	$30,000	$30,000	$30,000	$30,000	$30,000	$30,000	$30,000	$30,000	$360,000

Maintenance

													Total Year
Landscaping													$0
Janitorial													$0
Painting and Decorating													$0
Maintenance Labor													$0
Maintenance Contract													$0
HVAC													$0
Plumbing													$0
Electrical													$0
Security													$0
Total Maintenance	$0	$0	$0	$0	$0	$0	$0	$0	$0	$0	$0	$0	$0

Administration

Management Fee													$0
Personnel Expense													$0
Office Supplies													$0
Telephone													$0
Marketing													$0
Total Administration	$0	$0	$0	$0	$0	$0	$0	$0	$0	$0	$0	$0	$0

Fixed Expenses

Insurance													$0
Real Estate Taxes													$0
													$0
													$0
													$0
													$0
Total Fixed Expenses	$0	$0	$0	$0	$0	$0	$0	$0	$0	$0	$0	$0	$0

- Total Operating Expenses	$30,000	$30,000	$30,000	$30,000	$30,000	$30,000	$30,000	$30,000	$30,000	$30,000	$30,000	$30,000	$360,000
= Net Operating Income (NOI)	$5,000	$5,000	$5,000	$5,000	$5,000	$5,000	$5,000	$5,000	$5,000	$5,000	$5,000	$5,000	$60,000

Capital Expenditures (Not included in Net Operating Income)

Month 1	Month 2	Month 3	Month 4	Month 5	Month 6	Month 7	Month 8	Month 9	Month 10	Month 11	Month 12	Total Year
												$0

RESOURCES:

The Institute of Real Estate Management publishes the *IREM® Financial Analysis Spreadsheet* which performs cash flow analyses based on property performance and owners' goals and objectives. The spreadsheet is free to IREM members. To download the spreadsheet, go to **www.irem.org**.

Operating Expenses

Operating expenses are the normal, day-to-day expenses of running a property. They include maintenance, utilities, salaries, insurance, replacement reserve deposits, and property taxes.

Some major cash outlays are NOT operating expenses: Loan payments, capital expenditures, depreciation for tax purposes, and income tax are not included among operating expenses. These types of expenses are long-term, specialized expenses that involve separate kinds of budgets.

Expense Budgeting Methodologies

Methodologies that can help estimate a property's expenses include the following:

- Historical average or trends—information on past expenses can help estimate future expenses
- Predicted behavior
- Research/public information
- Industry norms
- Contract/fixed pricing

FORECASTING

Forecasting income and expenses is an essential step in creating a budget. Forecasting techniques help to produce accurate figures for a budget. Forecasting expenses involves thinking about how costs arise and classifying them accordingly.

- **Fixed costs** do not change as occupancy rates change and are generally stable during the budget period. Insurance and real estate taxes can be considered fixed costs.
- **Variable costs** change with usage. Electricity and water are typical variable costs.

Fixed and variable costs are concepts commonly used in accounting. They may be further separated into *controllable* and *noncontrollable* expenses.

Historical Data

Forecasting future expenses usually begins with information about past expenses. Information about past expenses is helpful for budget items that change by predictable amounts from year to year. While the budget items the real estate manager controls are usually fairly predictable, he or she should not assume that a budget item will change predictably.

TIPS:
When putting together an operating budget, managers prepare forecasts that sometimes rely on the previous year's figures. When forecasting future expenses, the manager should use past actual expenses rather than past budgeted expenses as the basis for the forecast.

Working backward through three years of expense statements gives a good basis for a forecast. *Averaging* is a common technique for arriving at realistic numbers for a forecast. However, be aware that for some expenses you will want to average consumption, not simply cost. For example, if you average your heating bill for the last three years, you can get an average of cost (how much you paid for energy at your property in a given year, but not how much you consumed). In the case of energy (as well as some other goods and services for which prices fluctuate), average the previous three year's consumption and then apply the anticipated rate.

Real estate managers commonly use averages to forecast budget figures. Averaging past years' figures usually gives a reasonable estimate of future years' performance. However, no one should follow figures blindly. Averages are sensitive to unusual numbers and are easy to distort.

Zero-Based Budgeting

Instead of using past expenses when preparing a forecast, real estate managers can use a second forecasting technique called *zero-based budgeting* that avoids using past budget figures to determine current figures. Zero-based budgeting de-emphasizes past budgets or past actual figures in creating the current budget. It is primarily used for new buildings that have no budgeting history or in cases in which a property is taken over by a new manager and the previous budgeting was inaccurate or simply does not reflect the current economic situation.

Zero-based budgeting prevents expenses from being inserted automatically (and unthinkingly) into budgets year after year. Normally, when using zero-based budgeting, a real estate manager incorporates current information from sources such as contractors, vendors, utility companies, and *IREM® Income/Expense Analysis Reports®* instead of plugging in historical expenses.

Four factors indicate that zero-based budgeting may be the best choice:

1. If historical information is not available, such as for new buildings or new accounts, zero-based budgeting provides a basis for the budget.
2. When projections from past expenses are likely to be unreliable, for example, when expenses are highly variable from period to period, zero-based budgeting smoothes out the variation and consequent uncertainty.
3. When records are inaccurate or nonexistent, zero-based budgeting avoids bringing mistakes into the budget cycle.
4. As a check to ensure that expenses forecast by another method are not out of line, zero-based budgeting removes financial preconceptions from the budget cycle.

RESOURCES:
The Institute of Real Estate Management publishes the *IREM® Income/Expense Analysis® Reports* which provide detailed, nationwide research results offering financial information on the following residential topics:
• Conventional apartments
• Federally assisted apartments
• Condominiums, cooperatives, and Planned Unit Developments (PUDs)
The reports are grouped as trend reports, regional reports, national reports, age group reports, and special reports. They are constantly used in budgeting and making operating comparisons for individual properties.

BUDGET VARIANCES

Budget variance analysis is another important technique in monitoring existing budgets and preparing new budgets. Variance analysis is used to compare differences between projected and actual amounts of income and expenses. It is used most often in working with the operating and cash flow budgets.

Variance Analysis

A *budget variance* is the difference between the amount forecast for an account in a budget and the actual amount spent or earned in the account.

Budget variances can be used in the following ways:
• Determine the causes of differences between actual and forecast amounts
• Revise budgets, goals, and plans
• Check on forecasting techniques used
• Evaluate and refine the information incorporated into budgets, especially for new buildings

Budget variances can be favorable or unfavorable.
• A **favorable** variance increases NOI.
• An **unfavorable** variance decreases NOI.

FIGURE 2-3: VARIANCES AND NOI

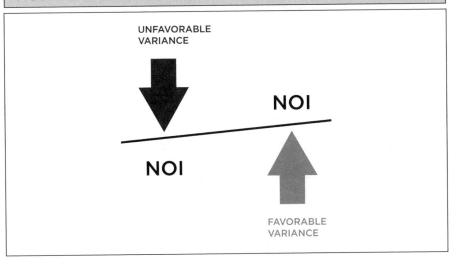

Favorable and unfavorable variances have different meanings depending on whether the variance is in income or expenses. If you project that the electric bill next month will be $2,100 and the actual bill is $2,450, the variance is $350, or 17% ($350/$2,100). Since the actual bill (expense) is $350 over what was forecast, the variance is *unfavorable*. It has decreased NOI.

If monthly rental income is projected at $104,000, and the actual figure for the month is $120,000, the variance of $16,000 or 15%, is *favorable*. The variance has increased NOI.

To determine the total variance, find the difference between the total unfavorable variances and the total favorable variances. This is called the *net total variance*.

Total unfavorable variances < Total favorable variances ➔
favorable net total variances

Total unfavorable variances > Total favorable variances ➔
unfavorable net total variances

Consider the following example:

Amount Projected	Annual Income Earned	Variance	Description
$40,000	$50,000	$10,000 (+25%)	Favorable

The variance for this example is favorable because of the $10,000 over, or 25% more than, the amount from projected to actual income.

Amount Projected	Amount spent on electric bill	Variance	Description
$2,000	$3,000	$1,000 (+50%)	Unfavorable

The variances in this electric bill are unfavorable because the actual expenses were $1,000 over, or 50% more than, the projected budgeted amount.

The net total variance is *favorable:* $10,000 - $1,000 = $9,000.

Reporting Budget Variances

Budget variance reports may be needed regularly as part of the reports that a real estate manager prepares for the building's owners. A budget variance report lists budgeted amounts, actual amounts, and budget variances (in dollars and as percentages of the estimated budget amount) for each line item in the operating budget. All variances should be marked as favorable (F) or unfavorable (U).

When discussing budget variances, whether a "positive" or a "negative" is the intended result can sometimes be confusing. Not all computer programs treat the minus/plus sign in the same manner. Consider the abbreviated statement shown here:

	Budget (B)	Actual (A)	Variance (A – B)	Variance %	F vs. U
Gross Potential Income	$796,000	$799,000	$3,000	.38%	F
Vacancy/ Coll. Loss	38,000	40,000	2,000	5.26%	U
Effective Gross Income	758,000	759,000	1,000	.13%	F
Total Expenses	365,000	375,000	10,000	2.74%	U
NOI	393,000	384,000	-9,000	-2.29%	U
Debt Service	320,000	320,000	0	0%	–
Before-Tax Cash Flow	73,000	64,000	-9,000	-12.33%	U

- **Variance (A-B)** subtracts the *Budget* column from the *Actual* column, producing positive numbers for income line items (except vacancy, where a negative is really a positive). Positive numbers for expenses that are higher than budgeted generally indicate a negative result.
- **Variance %** presents the variance as a percentage [Variance $ ÷ Budget × 100 = Variance %].
- **F vs. U Variance Description** boils down the variance to its impact on NOI.

Many companies use accounting software to create budget variance reports. Depending on the software capabilities being applied, a manager needs to understand when a number is being referred to as "positive" or "negative" as a numerical value, or as the desired outcome. Use of "F" and "U" is preferable to show clearly whether the outcome is desired or not. Note also that some programs may show income loss items (i.e., vacancy and collection) as negative numbers in both the Budget and Actual columns.

Other Reporting Considerations

Figure 2-4 shows a variance report with the variances given in dollars and percentages. By looking at the dollar and percentage changes over three to five years, a real estate manager can gain an accurate reading of trends.

FIGURE 2-4: SAMPLE PROPERTY BUDGET VARIANCE
REPORT (YEAR 1)

	1 Budget	2 Actual	3 Variance (2) - (1)	4 % Change (3) ÷ (1) x 100	5 F/U
Income					
1. Gross Potential Income	$796,860	$796,860	$0	0.00	-
2. Vacancy & Collection Loss	40,164	36,143	4,021	10.01	F
3. Net Rent Revenue	756,695	760,717	4,021	0.53	F
4. Other Income	6,312	6,312	0	0.00	-
5. EFFECTIVE GROSS INCOME	763,008	767,029	4,021	0.53	F
Expenses					
6. Payroll Mgmt.	81,996	83,450	-1,454	-1.77	U
7. Decorating	15,000	15,300	-300	-2.00	U
8. Maintenance	9,996	10,260	-264	-2.64	U
9. Supplies	9,996	9,400	596	5.96	F
10. Trash Removal	5,100	5,250	-150	-2.94	U
11. Electricity	24,996	24,700	296	1.18	F
12. Gas	35,004	37,625	-2,621	-7.49	U
13. Water & Sewer	30,000	33,300	-3,300	-11.00	U
14. Legal & Acct.	9,504	9,450	54	0.57	F
15. Miscellaneous	7,992	7,360	632	7.91	F
16. Administrative	3,996	3,980	16	0.40	F
17. Insurance	11,004	10,490	514	4.67	F
18. Property Taxes	120,000	120,000	0	0.00	-
19. TOTAL OPERATING EXP.	364,584	370,565	-5,981	-1.64	U
20. NOI	398,424	396,464	-1,960	-0.49	U
21. Annual Debt Service	319,392	319,392	0	0.00	-
22. BEFORE-TAX CASH FLOW	79,032	77,072	-1,960	-2.48	U

The variance report may include a narrative. In explaining the variances, the real estate manager should give a rationale for any variances that exceed predetermined standards. For example, explanations may be required for any variances that are 10% greater or less than the budgeted amount. The narrative should also describe any corrective actions taken.

Because budgets are foundations for decision making, corrective actions based on variances should be considered a normal part of budgeting and management.

Finally, reports should have a column for approved budget variances. Sometimes budgets allow some midyear adjustments to reflect changes in circumstances, new information, or changing market conditions.

CHAPTER 3:
MEASURING CASH FLOW

Making sound decisions about a property that positively impact the property's cash flow and stay within the owner's objectives is a core requirement of the site manager and staff. A property manager must be able to identify the components of cash flow and understand how site managers and staff impact the property's net operating income, and produce accurate and meaningful financial reports for the owner.

What Is covered in this chapter:

- **Statement of Cash Flow**

- **Reporting to the Owner**

- **Financial Reports**

STATEMENT OF CASH FLOW

In order to calculate the figures that measure a property's financial performance, it is important to understand the components of the cash flow statement. The *statement of cash flow* is an annual statement that lists income and expenses for the property. It includes revenue and operating expenses through net operating income and before-tax cash flow. A *pro forma statement of cash flow* is typically used for a property that is newly built, about to be acquired, or is in a lease-up mode due to renovations.

Cash flow is the amount of spendable income from a real estate investment; it is the amount of cash available after all expenses and debts have been paid. It is an indicator of overall financial health of a property. By striving to achieve the maximum cash flow for the owner, the real estate manager can benefit through rewards and recognition.

The pro forma statement of cash flow below illustrates the components for computing before-tax cash flow.

FIGURE 3-1: PRO FORMA STATEMENT OF CASH FLOW

Gross Potential Income (GPI)
- Loss to Lease
- Vacancy and Collection Loss

= Net Rent Revenue
+ Miscellaneous Income
+ Expense Reimbursements

= Effective Gross Income (EGI)
- Operating Expenses

= Net Operating Income (NOI)
- Annual Debt Service (ADS)

- BLANK (CapEx, etc.)

= Before-Tax Cash Flow (BTCF)

The cash flow statement illustrates some important financial measurements used in real estate. It shows that gross potential income (GPI) is adjusted to give effective gross income (EGI), which in turn is adjusted by operating expenses to produce net operating income (NOI). NOI is a commonly used measure of financial health in real estate. The residential site manager directly controls the NOI for the owner's property and managing it is a core function of their job. This chapter details how these measurements lead to the bottom line in real estate: before-tax cash flow.

Gross Potential Income

Cash flow is not just money in movement. It involves planning and a bit of calculation. The first step in computing cash flow is determining the *gross potential income.*

Gross potential income (GPI) is the maximum market rent that can be derived from 100% occupancy and 100% collection of rents over the course of a financial period (normally, a year).

TIPS:
In common enterprise software, such as Yardi, the term "gross potential rent" (GPR) is used instead of "gross potential income" (GPI).

To compute gross potential income, assume that all units are occupied, all rents are paid in full, and all payments are received on time.

Silver Creek Case Study:
GPI

Silver Creek is a residential property with 180 units.

The breakdown for Silver Creek is as follows:

Apartments:
100 two-bedroom units at $1,250 per month
80 one-bedroom units at $918 per month

Calculate GPI:

Apartments:

100 units	x	$1,250/month	x	12 =	1,500,000
80 units	x	$918/month	x	12 =	881,280
				GPI:	$2,381,280

Rent Roll

A *rent roll* is a tool used to identify sources of income. It provides a good picture of a property's GPI. In a residential property, a rent roll is a listing of each rental unit described by size and type, rental rates and other payments received.

Loss to lease is the amount of money lost due to rents being less than the maximum market rents, or GPI. This measurement is most important when evaluating a property in a rising market in order to project future rent increases. The term *addition to lease* may also be used as it may be possible to exceed projections during a market upturn.

For example, consider an apartment building that has 10 leases. In 2013 they all rented at $750. At the start of the 2014, the market rent (GPI) rose to $1,000. However, only six of the leases were up for renewal at the start of 2014. Those six rented for $1,000. The other four under the old lease continued to rent at $750. As a result, the loss to lease comes out to $250 per month for each of these four leases.

TIPS:
A loss to lease at many communities represents opportunity. As residents move out and new leases are signed, the new leases will close the gap. At a thriving property, loss to lease will trend down until you raise rents and then it will trend up as shown in Figure 3-2.

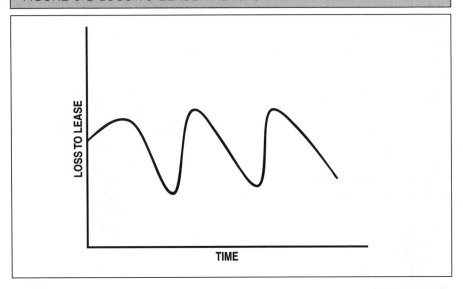

FIGURE 3-2 LOSS TO LEASE TREND GRAPH

LOSS TO LEASE

TIME

Silver Creek Case Study:
Loss to Lease

The loss to lease for Silver Creek is $28,800.

Vacancy and Collection Loss

In the real world, not all units are rented all of the time. GPI must be adjusted down to reflect market conditions. Determining an accurate adjustment for *vacancy* and *collection loss* will depend in part on the real estate manager's attention to these figures, that is, good record keeping.

Vacancy

Two types of vacancies exist:

- **Physical vacancy** consists of any unoccupied units that are available for rent.
- **Economic vacancy** includes the physical vacancies plus any space that is leased but not producing rent, such as the following:
  o Apartments used as offices, as models, or for storage
  o Apartments provided to staff as part of their compensation
  o Space that cannot be rented as is

Student Housing Impact: With student housing, high vacancy during summer months significantly affects cash flow.

Collection Loss

Collection loss consists of several categories:

- **Delinquent rents** or **bad debts** are rents that may be collected late or not at all.
- **Concessions** are rent reductions given to attract residents. Concessions reduce the amount of collectable rent.

Silver Creek Case Study:
Vacancy and Collection Loss

In general, apartment vacancies at Silver Creek are low. The market is good and turnover is minimal. On average, approximately three one-bedroom units and two two-bedroom units are vacant for the whole year due to market conditions or turnover. Leasing staff uses a two-bedroom unit. The bad debt ratio is 2% of GPI. Ten leases have received rent concessions of $500 each.

To calculate vacancy loss (annual):

Vacant one-bedrooms: $918 x 3 x 12 =	$33,048
Vacant two-bedrooms: $1,250 x 2 x 12 =	30,000
Leasing staff apartment:	15,000
Subtotal:	78,048

To calculate collection loss (annual):

Bad debt:	0.02 x GPI = 0.02 x $2,381,280 = 47,626
Rent concessions:	500 x 10 = 5,000
Subtotal:	52,626

Vacancy and collection loss total $130,674 at Silver Creek.

Net Rent Revenue

At this point, subtract the vacancy and collection loss figure from the GPI to determine the *net rent revenue*.

Net Rent Revenue =
GPI – Loss to Lease – Vacancy and Collection Losses

Silver Creek Case Study:
Net Rent Revenue

At Silver Creek, net rent revenue would be calculated as follows:

Net Rent Revenue = $2,381,280 (GPI) – $28,800 (Loss to Lease) – $78,048 (Vacancy) – $52,626 (Collection Loss) = $2,221,806.

Miscellaneous Income

The next step in working toward NOI and calculating before-tax cash flow (BTCF) is to add miscellaneous income and expense reimbursements to the GPI.

Property managers are responsible for identifying and recommending ways to boost revenue and reduce expenses. At times, this requires thinking beyond the most common ways to increase income, such as charging residents for amenities or services. Be mindful of opportunities to create value for the property and recapture costs. For example:

- Preferred parking
- Covered parking
- Pet rent
- Pet fees
- Cell towers
- Gym memberships
- Valet trash service

Silver Creek Case Study:
Miscellaneous Income

For Silver Creek, 250 parking spots are rented to residents at $75 per month. Five parking spots are for employees and visitors. Additional miscellaneous income comes from laundry facilities that bring in $1,400 per month.

Miscellaneous income is calculated as follows:

Parking:	250 x $75 x 12	=	$225,000
Laundry:	$1,400 x 12	=	16,800

The total miscellaneous income is $241,800.

Expense Reimbursements

In addition to miscellaneous income, expense reimbursements are added to the net rent revenue. This revenue consists of amounts collected from the residents in addition to rent. In the residential environment, utilities (e.g., water, sewer, and garbage) are examples of expense reimbursements that management may charge to residents.

TIPS:

RUBS (Ratio Utility Billing System) is a billing method used to recover water, gas, electricity, trash or any other cost involved in the operation of a property. The calculation is based upon one or more factors such as square footage or number of occupants, along with the total utility bill for the property. The charges to the residents will fluctuate as the total property bill changes each month. An added benefit of this method is that usage normally decreases when residents become responsible for their utility bills.

Silver Creek Case Study:
Expense Reimbursements

For Silver Creek, sources of expense reimbursements are utilities. The annual total is $50,000.

Effective Gross Income

Effective gross income (EGI) is the net rent revenue combined with miscellaneous income and expense reimbursements. EGI is the actual amount of income collected. Because EGI represents the actual receipts, this figure becomes the source of funds used for the property's operating expenses.

Silver Creek Case Study:
EGI

For Silver Creek, EGI is calculated as follows:

	$2,381,280	GPI
−	28,800	Loss to Lease
−	130,674	Vacancy and Collection Loss
=	2,221,806	Net Rent Revenue
+	241,800	Miscellaneous Income
+	50,000	Expense Reimbursements
=	$2,513,606	EGI

Operating Expenses

The next major adjustment towards calculating the before-tax cash flow figure is operating expenses. Operating expenses are all the costs of operating and maintaining a property. These expenses include real estate taxes, insurance premiums, utilities, salaries, payroll taxes, maintenance costs, repairs, refurbishing of units or other rental spaces, contracted services, professional services, and administrative expenses. Administrative expenses may include the management fee and office supplies. The categories of operating expenses can be customized to reflect the property's needs and plans.

The categories of operating expenses should be reflected in the chart of accounts. Contracted services may include landscaping, swimming pool maintenance, and extermination of pests. Professional services may include legal fees and auditors' fees.

Silver Creek Case Study:
Operating Expenses

Operating expenses at the Silver Creek property total $1,613,500.

Net Operating Income

Net operating income (NOI), the next component of the cash flow statement, is an important gauge of a property's financial strength.

NOI is:

- The income from operations that goes to lenders (in the form of debt service) and to owners (in the form of return on investment)
- A basis for estimating the value of a property (an important consideration for both lenders and owners)
- A widely used measure of financial health in real estate, even though it is not the same as profit

The formula for calculating NOI follows:

EGI – Operating Expenses = NOI

Silver Creek Case Study:
NOI

For Silver Creek, NOI would be calculated as follows:

$2,513,606 (EGI) – $1,613,500 (Operating Expenses)
= $900,106 (NOI)

NOI shows how well a property meets its day-to-day operating expenses and how much cash is left over to pay on the loan and the costs of major improvements. NOI thus is a strong indicator that enough money is flowing through the business to meet its obligations. On the other hand, because real estate involves many involuntary expenses and high indebtedness, "bottom-line profit" would not be the best measure of performance.

NOI also highlights management effectiveness. NOI can be a gauge of how well a real estate manager is doing. If the owner's goal is to raise NOI (and thus, the property's value), the real estate manager's goal may be to lower operating expenses and increase effective gross income. The manager may have to focus both on how to control expenses and how to gain new sources of income.

Annual Debt Service

Annual debt service (ADS) is payments of principal and interest on a loan made annually. ADS is not considered an operating expense in determining NOI. NOI is what is used to pay the debt service. Debt service can be quite high, depending on the size of a property's mortgage.

Silver Creek Case Study:
ADS

Annual debt service for Silver Creek is fixed and totals $411,000.

BLANK (CapEx, Etc.)

The property may be required to add reserves for replacement or capital improvements expenses above the cash flow line.

The owner's accountant usually makes the determination of the how to handle the capital improvements expenses in regards to BTCF. Some lenders, however, require that an amount be expensed above the NOI for routine replacements (e.g., carpets and appliances). The definition of what is a capital expense may vary according to the owners' goals and the accounting practice for the property. When large payouts of capital expenses are being planned over a multiyear period, a line here may capture expenses incurred.

Before-Tax Cash Flow (BTCF)

Annual debt service was the last adjustment needed to calculate before-tax cash flow (BTCF). Some points to keep in mind about before-tax cash flow are the following:

- Unlike earlier uses of the term cash flow to mean money simply as income or outlay, before-tax cash flow is an indicator of financial health.
- The before-tax cash flow shows that the property successfully meets its major obligations (operating expenses, debt service).
- The before-tax cash-flow figure is the owner's income before taxes are considered. Once the BTCF is known, the owner can decide whether to reallocate part of cash flow to the property.

In many instances, raising cash flow will be a goal of the real estate manager. Because annual debt service is not likely to be altered easily, real estate managers are better off monitoring and controlling operating expenses, minimizing vacancy and collection loss, and carefully budgeting reserves for replacement and capital to meet owners' financial goals and show management effectiveness.

Silver Creek Case Study:
BTCF

At Silver Creek, NOI was $899,054 last year. Annual debt service is $411,000. Since there are no reserves for replacement, NOI can be adjusted by the required debt service:

$$\$900,106 \ (NOI) - \$411,000 \ (ADS) = \$489,106 \ (BTCF)$$

The before-tax cash flow at Silver Creek is $489,106.

To recap how the financial measures relate: GPI is a calculation of the maximum that a property can produce. Adjustments to it produce NOI, which shows how much money is available after basic expenses to pay ADS (and to set aside reserves for major improvements). This major expense is then subtracted from NOI to give BTCF.

Ultimately, the cash flow statement is as follows for Silver Creek:

	Gross Potential Income (GPI)	$2,381,280
−	Loss to Lease	28,800
−	Vacancy and Collection Loss	-130,674
=	Net Rent Revenue	2,221,806
+	Miscellaneous Income	241,800
+	Expense Reimbursements	50,000
=	Effective Gross Income (EGI)	2,513,606
−	Operating Expenses	-1,613,500
=	Net Operating Income (NOI)	900,106
−	Annual Debt Service (ADS)	-411,000
−	BLANK (CapEx, Etc.)	0
=	Before-Tax Cash Flow (BTCF)	489,106

TIPS:
Further financial analysis requires property managers to use more advanced tools, such as a financial calculator and financial analysis spreadsheet. IREM provides webinars on how to use a financial calculator as well as the *IREM® Financial Analysis Spreadsheet* at **www.irem.org.**

REPORTING TO THE OWNER

A *report* is a recap of events. The purpose of a report is to portray past events accurately in an accessible format that communicates information readily to persons inside and outside the organization. Financial reports capture information about the income, expenditures, assets, and liabilities of a property. Accurate information is the foundation of decision making, and reports to the owner should be comprehensive and accurate.

This chapter focuses on the proper information to include in reports and how to interpret reports. These two issues are central to creating an effective report.

Reports should be concise, useful, and informative. Reporting is a cumulative process. For example, budgets are a necessary part of reporting, since a budget shows activity for the month (cash budgets) or the year (annual operating budgets). Comparing several budgets highlights trends at a property. Likewise, rent rolls, delinquency reports, and vacancy reports reflect continuing financial activity and are crucial parts of any report. The accumulation of all this information through reports adds up to a comprehensive picture of a property's financial health.

This chapter emphasizes periodic financial reports to clients or owners of properties, since the owner is ultimately responsible for the property. The owner makes major decisions about the property and sets the property's financial goals. Reporting to the owner is critical in ensuring that the owner's goals and objectives are met.

Normally, the report to the owner includes a narrative portion with a summary and a discussion of the extent to which the owner's goals and objectives for the period have been achieved. The narrative should appear as the first page of the report or in a cover letter. The narrative should be supported by any necessary financial reports, including a summary of cash receipts and disbursements, a variance report, a capital improvements recap, and an income statement. The capital improvements recap describes capital expenditures. The monthly cash-flow budget often summarizes inflows and outlays of cash.

The report to the owner is usually accompanied by a rent roll that provides details of lease arrangements with all residents to date as well as vacancies. Vacancy reports and delinquency reports clarify the information in the rent roll.

The following reports must be updated and distributed to ownership periodically—as often as monthly.

FINANCIAL REPORTS

Monthly Reports

Income Statement

The *income statement* is for internal use; it shows income and expenses for a certain time span. Unlike a budget, it shows actual figures. The year-end income statement is discussed later in this chapter.

Rent Roll/Collections Report

The *rent roll/collections report* is updated monthly and included in the report to the owner. Rentals normally are a property's main source of income, and an up-to-date rent roll is crucial.

Two basic reports can be derived from the rent roll: vacancy reports and delinquency reports.

FIGURE 3-3: RENT ROLL/COLLECTIONS REPORT

Building: Eastwood Property No. 1000-1234
Owner: ABC Inc.   Month/Year: September, 20XX   Receipts as of _____

Suite No.	Resident	Previous Balance	Charges				Collections	New Balance	Remarks
			Rent	Escls.	Pkg.	Other			
101	S. Smith	1600	800				800	800	
102	J. Adams	950	950				950	0	
103	M. Allan	1800	600				600	1200	
104	H. Wu	2000	500				500	1500	
105	(vacant)								
	Totals:	6350					2,850	3,500	

Vacancy Report

The *vacancy report* monitors vacancies; it is updated monthly and included in the report to the owner.

FIGURE 3-4: SAMPLE VACANCY REPORT (RESIDENTIAL)

No. Units	Unit Type	Vacancies	Vacancy Rate
15	Efficiency	1	7%
33	One Bedroom	3	9%
18	One Bedroom, Den	0	0%
27	Two Bedroom, Two Bath	7	26%
7	Three Bedroom	0	0%
100		**11**	**11%**

Delinquency Report

The *delinquency report* is a report that tracks late payment of rent; it is updated monthly and included in the report to the owner. Items included in a delinquency report are: resident name, total amount owed, length of delinquency (0-30 days, 31-60 days, etc.), and what is being done to collect the late payment.

FIGURE 3-5: SAMPLE RENT DELINQUENCY REPORT

Building: Eastwood Period Ending: 09/30/20XX
Prepared by: xxxxxxxxx Date: 10/10/20XX

Suite No.	Tenant	Amount and Length of Delinquency								Remarks
		Rent	30 Days	60 Days	90 Days	120 Days	180 Days	Over 180 Days	Total Amount Delinquent	
101	S. Smith	800	X						800	
102	J. Adams									
103	M. Allan	600		x					1200	
104	H. Wu	500			x				1500	
105	(vacant)		--	--	--	--	--	--	---	
	Totals:								3,500	

Cash Flow Statement

The *cash flow statement* is usually updated monthly and can be included in the report to the owner. Cash flow budgets often include brief descriptions of variances, and for that reason, they are a brief general recap of financial activity.

Variance Report

Variances can be shown in the monthly cash flow budget; however, a *variance report* is a narrative report that describes assumptions, amounts, and plans for managing variances. It communicates to the owner that the real estate manager is aware of the variances and will take action as needed.

Variance analysis is important in analyzing financial statements and reports. Variance analysis asks several questions that focus on financial performance and have an impact on decision making:

- Do the budget and the actual figures differ?
- How significant is that difference?
- What is the reason for the variance?
- Were the forecasting techniques reliable?
- Is action necessary to correct the situation?
- What actions can be taken?

Year-End Reports

A formal year-end report to owners and investors normally is prepared in addition to monthly reports. In large organizations, the annual report can be quite elaborate and often includes a narrative describing the year's business activity, finances, and future plans in addition to financial statements.

The following reports are prepared at the end of the fiscal year for distribution to owners, investors, and other interested parties. Accountants and auditors are usually involved in preparing and assessing these reports.

Cash Flow Statement

As just discussed, the *cash flow statement* is a year-end report that recaps the actual inflow and outflow of cash and its related sources and uses. Only items that involve a cash transaction appear on a cash flow statement. For example, depreciation, which is not a cash outlay, does not appear on a cash flow statement. This document can be prepared using the monthly cash budgets.

Year-End Income Statement

The *year-end income statement* encapsulates the financial transactions for the fiscal period.

An *income statement* (sometimes called a profit and loss statement) gives a summary of the organization's economic activity over a period of time, typically a year. It lists income, expenses, and net income (or loss). The income statement is prepared after all journal entries have been posted to the general ledger.

The following figure shows an example of an income statement for a sole proprietor.

FIGURE 3-6: SAMPLE INCOME STATEMENT: BRIDGEHAMPTON APARTMENTS

Bridgehampton Apartments Income Statement For Year Ending December 31, 20XX		
Income		
Rental	$129,600	
Misc. Income (laundry)	4,000	
Less Vacancy/Collection Loss	1,000	
Total Income		132,600
Expenses		
Operating Expenses:		
Utilities	4,020	
Repairs and maintenance	3,500	
Payroll	25,200	
Payroll taxes	3,780	
Real estate taxes	5,150	
Insurance	4,235	
Depreciation	18,300	
Mortgage Interest	29,000	
Total Expenses		93,185
Net income (or loss)		39,415

Note the following:

- Real estate taxes are included with operating expenses.

- Physical assets used for business, such as buildings and equipment, age and consequently lose value over time. **Depreciation** is the expense of using up an asset.

- **Interest** is included in the income statement for external use. The figure for interest expense represents the amount that the property paid in interest on its loans.

Balance Sheet

The *balance sheet* is a statement of the financial position of a person or business at a particular time, indicating assets, liabilities, and owner's equity (net worth). It balances assets against liabilities to determine what a company is worth at a certain time. Balance sheets are normally prepared at the end of the fiscal year.

Unlike the income statement, which divides the world into income and expenses, the balance sheet focuses on assets and liabilities. This is the heart of double-entry bookkeeping. The same transaction that is classified as income, for example, is also entered another time in the balance sheet as an asset. The double entry is a check to ensure that all financial information is captured and analyzed.

FIGURE 3-7: SAMPLE BALANCE SHEET

Genoa Arms Building: Balance Sheet
December 30, Year 1

ASSETS		
Current Assets		
Cash	1,052	
Accounts Receivable	63,417	
Tenant Deposits	101,600	
Tax Escrow	120,000	
Capital Reserves	15,000	
Total Current Assets		301,069
Long-Term Assets		
Land	500,000	
Buildings	2,000,000	
Total Long-Term Assets		2,500,000
Total Assets		**2,801,069**
LIABILITIES		
Current Liabilities		
Tenant Deposit Payable	101,600	
Accounts Payable	12,500	
Tax Payable	120,000	
Total Current Liabilities		234,100
Long-Term Liabilities		
Mortgage Payable	2,294,202	
Total Long-Term Liabilities		2,294,202
Total Liabilities		**2,528,302**
OWNER'S EQUITY		**272,767**
Total Liabilities and Equity		**2,801,069**

Check Register

A check register is a report of checks dispersed by the property over a set time period, typically organized by date or check number. Items usually included are: check number, date of check, payee, and amount paid.

Payables List

A payables list is a list of all invoices that still have to be paid. Items usually included are the date of the invoice, the payee, and the amount to be paid. A payables list also shows when an invoice was due and how many days past due it is.

CHAPTER 4:
CAPITALIZATION

Understanding how value is determined and how daily decisions impact the NOI, and therefore the value of the property, enables site managers to meet the owner's goals and objectives. A property manager must be able to apply capitalization techniques to project the market value of a property.

What is covered in this chapter:

• **Capitalization**

CAPITALIZATION

As stated earlier, NOI is used to estimate the value of a property and help measure its performance. Income capitalization is the market valuation of a property based upon a one-year projection of income. In other words, it relies on a single year's stabilized NOI to estimate the value of a property. The income capitalization approach estimates the value of a property by applying a proper investment rate of return to the annual net operating income (NOI) expected to be produced by the property, using the IRV formula:

Income (I) ÷ Rate (R) = Value (V)

It may help to think of the IRV formula in the form of a house, as shown below.

Note that in the "house" image the I is "over" R to derive V. That is:

NOI (I) ÷ Capitalization Rate (R) = Value (V)

The income capitalization method real estate managers use is the same one appraisers use. Two key elements in this formula are the stabilized NOI (I) and the capitalization rate (R).

Stabilized NOI

Stabilized NOI (I) is the true earning potential of the property in the absence of undue or extraordinary circumstances. According to the cash flow statement, it is income adjusted for operating expenses, before considering debt service. An accurately projected NOI is a critical component in determining value.

Capitalization Rate

If a property yields $115,000 in NOI each year, and the owner expects 10% in return annually, how much is the property worth? The 10% return becomes the capitalization rate.

The *capitalization rate* (R) is the rate of return used to estimate the property's value based on that property's net operating income. Often called a cap rate, it is the method for determining the attractiveness of the investment for the owner.

Put simply, the capitalization rate is the NOI divided by the sales price and value of a property expressed as a percentage.

The lower the capitalization rate, the higher the value of the property, and vice versa.

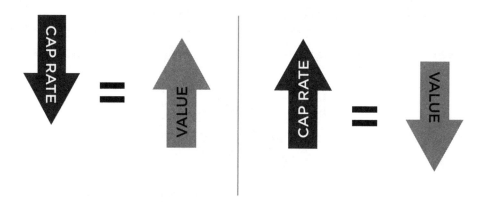

Sources of Capitalization Rates

As you would expect, the capitalization rate varies between properties. Demand for a particular type of property, quality of the property, and future potential benefits are key variables that influence the capitalization rate. For example, a prime residential property with a strong operating history and an excellent future potential may sell at a 7% capitalization rate, while a small multifamily building may sell at a 9.5% capitalization rate. In addition, average capitalization rates for each property type are sometimes listed in newspapers.

Location of the country can also determine cap rates. In urban areas, such as Washington D.C., New York, Boston, and San Francisco, cap rates for Class A properties can be as low as 4-5%.

Many valuable sources are available for finding accurate cap rates, as shown in Figure 4-1.

FIGURE 4-1: SOURCES FOR CAP RATES	
Source	**Features**
RealtyRates.com	• National source for research data on markets • Provides a survey of current and historical average cap rates
NCREIF National Council of Real Estate Investment Fiduciaries	• National Council of Real Estate Fiduciaries • Offers Property Index report that shows capitalization rates or computed from the NPI properties sold • Reports are detailed across each major property type and major U.S. region
CoStar GROUP	• International real estate and financial data firm • Frequently produces reports on market activity and cap rates
Colliers INTERNATIONAL	• Real estate data firm • Provides market-specific research on costs, sales prices, and cap rates for commercial real estate
CBRE CB RICHARD ELLIS	• International real estate firm. • Provides data for markets throughout the United States (and globally)
Appraisal Institute® Professionals Providing Real Estate Solutions	• Association of appraisers who calculate cap rates, adjust NOI, and estimate the market value of a property

Other sources of cap rates can be derived from comparable properties that have recently been sold. Enough comparable properties must be included to have a representative sample.

Major buyers of real estate, such as pension funds, real estate investment companies, and life insurance companies, can be contacted for information on cap rates. These companies are good sources for cap rates for large properties.

TIPS:
Cap rates indicate value as a snapshot in time. Cap rates will fluctuate, in some markets widely, over time.

Using the IRV Formula

The IRV formula (Income ÷ Rate = Value) can be rearranged to calculate any of its elements: Income (NOI), Rate, or Value.

Example 4.1: Finding Income (NOI)

Consider an initial value of a property in Year 1 at $120,000 with a capitalization rate of 8%.

Calculate income:

$$\text{Income (I)} = \text{Value (V)} \times \text{Rate (R)}$$

Income = $120,000 (Value) x 0.08 (Rate) = $9,600

Example 4.2: Finding the Capitalization Rate

A property was bought for $3.25 million and its NOI is $295,000.

Calculate the cap rate.

In this case, the variables are reordered to give the rate as the answer:

$$\text{Rate (R)} = \text{Income (I)} \div \text{Value (V)}$$

R = $295,000 ÷ $3,250,000 = 0.09076, or 9.08%

The cap rate is 9.08%.

Example 4.3: Finding Value and the Importance of Cap Rates

The NOI at a property is $115,000. Comparable properties currently sell at a capitalization rate of 10%.

Calculate the value of the property.

$$\text{Value (V)} = \text{Income (I)} \div \text{Rate (R)}$$

V = $115,000 ÷ 0.10 = $1,150,000

Because the capitalization rate is used to estimate value, extreme care must be used to select the appropriate rate. Minor differences in the rate used can create large variations in the resulting value. For example, what if this same property's NOI were to be capitalized at a 9.5% rate?

Recalculate the value of the property.

V = $115,000 ÷ 0.095 = $1,210,526

This is a difference of over $60,000.

Example 4.4: Finding Value and the Importance of NOI

The NOI at a property is $80,000. Cap rates for similar properties in the market are 10%.

Calculate the value of the property.

$$V = \$80{,}000 \div 0.10 = \$800{,}000$$

What if the property manager were to reduce expenses by implementing energy-efficient systems throughout the property? Now assume the NOI is $100,000.

Recalculate the value of the property.

$$V = \$100{,}000 \div 0.10 = \$1{,}000{,}000$$

The value of the property has increased by $200,000.

Now assume that the property manager has further increased yearly NOI to $110,000 by installing coin-operated washers and dryers and a pay-per-use community room thereby increasing miscellaneous income at the property.

Recalculate the value of the property again.

$$V = \$110{,}000 \div 0.10 = \$1{,}100{,}000$$

The value of the property has increased by another $100,000.

TIPS:
On a more day-to-day basis, site managers impact value tremendously. Consider the following: What is the value of an average rental rate increase of $10 per unit on a 300 unit property if the cap rate is 10%? 5%?

Where can you find $10 on your property?

FIGURE 4-2: WHERE CAN YOU FIND $10?

A $10 increase in rent on 300 units can impact value tremendously. Assuming a $1,000 and $1,010 rent, income is calculated as follows:

$1,000 rent x 300 units x 12 months = $3,600,000
$1,010 rent x 300 units x 12 months = $3,636,000

The first chart shows the value using a 10% cap rate:
$3,600,000 / .10 = $36,000,000
$3,636,000 / .10 = $36,360,000

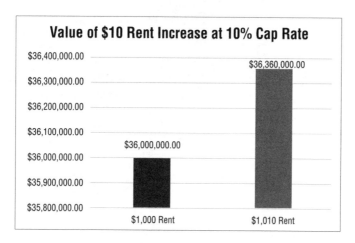

The second chart shows the value using a 5% cap rate:
$3,600,000 / .05 = $72,000,000
$3,636,000 / .05 = $72,720,000

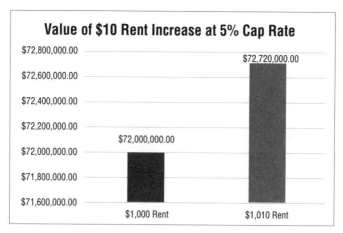

In this scenario, an increase of $10 equates to between $360,000 and $720,000 in value.

CHAPTER 5:
WORKING WITH CAPITAL

Budgeting capital for major expenditures ensures the future of the property. A property manager must budget capital for major expenditures so that the owner's objectives for the property are met.

What is covered in this chapter:

- **Capital**
- **Budgeting for Capital Expenses**

CAPITAL

Capital is money or property that can be used to create more wealth by investing. It consists of the total assets of a business. Capital is also any form of wealth used, or ready for use, in creating more wealth.

Making major improvements to a property involves the use of capital. To ensure the future of a property, real estate managers budget capital for major expenditures, such as renovations, restorations, and additions. Earlier chapters discussed net operating income (NOI) and before-tax cash flow (BTCF) as important indicators of financial viability. NOI is used to determine whether the property produces enough income to pay debt service and to create a capital budget for major expenses.

Capital is often available for investment because investing money is usually the best way of increasing one's wealth. Investors count on the value of their investment to grow over time. Similarly, property owners buy apartment complexes, office buildings, and shopping centers with the expectation that the value of the property will appreciate over the time that the owners hold the properties.

Terminology

Starting with the basic definition of capital as money or property available for investment, we can consider several concepts that describe how capital is used. These basic ideas are helpful for understanding capital and for contemplating capital budgeting:

- **Capital Asset:** a long-term asset, tangible or intangible, needed to generate income. In real estate, capital assets are often defined as land, buildings, and their improvements.
- **Equity:** the value of real property in excess of debt. It is the interest or value that an owner has in real estate over and above the mortgage and other financial liens against it. Sometimes the term equity investment is used.

- **Liquidity:** the ability to convert assets into cash. A savings account is liquid. Generally, real estate is not liquid because it can rarely immediately be sold for cash.

- **Working Capital:** the amount of money a company has on hand to conduct business over the short term (30 to 90 days).

- **Capital Expenditure:** spending on capital assets, such as future major renovations, improvements, or purchases. The purpose of capital expenditures is to add value to the property or to prolong its life appreciably.

- **Capital Reserves:** money that has been set aside for a future major renovation, improvement, or purchase. They are not considered income.

BUDGETING FOR CAPITAL EXPENSES

The process of budgeting for capital expenses estimates the costs of major improvements or replacements:

- **Capital Improvements:** a structural addition or betterment to real property that increases its useful life or productivity or extends the life of a building or its equipment. The improvement must have a life in excess of one year in order for the cost to be recovered for income tax purposes.

- **Reserves For Replacement:** money set aside for the replacement of a property's short-life items and/or for capital improvements. (Note that this step can be included in a cash flow statement; however, this depends upon the owner's requirements and the property's tax situation).

Capital expense budgeting generally results in a long-range plan for improvements to a property. The expenses of capital improvements are not included among operating expenses. The large amount of these expenses is one reason for separating them from run-of-the-mill operating expenses. Various organizations have different requirements for capital expense budgeting. Sometimes these expenses are included "below the line" and sometimes they are entirely separate.

NOI measures the ability to cover day-to-day operating expenses. Capital expenses are concerned with the property's future. Besides the buildings themselves, many features in real estate involve substantial outlays of capital:

- Major renovation programs
- Swimming pools and recreational facilities
- Parking structures
- Restorations of historic facades and interiors
- Complete replacement of major structural components such as roofs, windows, loading docks, lobbies, and atriums

- Replacement of large equipment such as furnaces, elevators, and air-conditioning systems

As with any large financial undertaking, planning for capital improvements and expenses is crucial. The owners and managers of properties often begin by working with architectural and engineering firms to draw up detailed plans for major restorations, additions, and improvements. Cost estimates from architects and engineers are one source for a capital budget.

However, a full *capital needs assessment* is the most thorough approach. The management firm can conduct the assessment, or the real estate manager may ask a large vendor to assess the state of the entire property and recommend priority actions. The capital needs assessment can be the basis of long-term planning for the property. When setting aside cash reserves, a long-term view of at least five years is best.

A short-term mentality may not be appropriate in real estate, where buildings are constructed to last and investors keep their money in properties for decades. Further, planned replacements and improvements are more economical than sudden changes and emergency work, which may entail rush charges and little choice of prices and materials.

TIPS:
Site managers must work closely with other site staff, especially maintenance and cleaning staff, to identify and monitor items to determine what needs to be replaced and when so that they can be included in the reserve plan and not become an unexpected expense.

When budgeting for capital expenses, it is important to show the sources of funds and reflect the owner's and the manager's plans for renovation and replacement. The decision about the source of the funds often rests with the owner. Any reserves for capital improvements that have been set aside should also be included.

In general, the estimated future capital needs divided by the number of years until the capital is needed determines the amount of reserves to be set aside each year. A best practice is to develop a 5- to 10-year reserve plan. Figure 5-1 shows a sample capital expenditure budget/actual report.

Affordable Housing Impact: HUD requires at a minimum a five-year reserve plan. Every HUD property must have a reserve replacement account, and HUD mandates how much money each month you must put into this account. These requirements are based on factors such as the size of the property. The minimum amount that must go into the reserve account is $1,000 per unit. The plan should be reviewed and updated on an annual basis.

FIGURE 5-1: SAMPLE CAPITAL EXPENDITURE BUDGET/ACTUAL REPORT

Building: Silver Creek Property No. 01999   Month/Year: 09/20XX
As of: 9/30/20XX Prepared by: xxxxxxx Date: 10/04/20XX
Reviewed by: xxxxxxx   Date: 10/08/20XX

| Acct. | Account Description | Current Month | | | | Year-to-Date | | Explanation of Variances |
No.		Budget	Actual	Var. %	Budget	Actual	Var. %	
111-xxx	Parking lot renovation	$3,000	$3,150	-5.00	$15,120	$15,500	-2.5	
112-xxx	Walkway repair	2,500	2,150	14.00	13,960	13,100	6.2	
113-xxx	Lobby renovation	2,250	2,560	-13.78	10,870	11,000	-1.2	
114-xxx	HVAC upgrade	1,300	1,600	-23.08	5,670	7,100	-25.2	
	Totals:	$9,050	$9,460	-4.53	$45,620	$46,700	-2.4	

Budgeting and Accumulating Capital Reserves

Some owners request that cash reserves be deducted from the property's cash flow and set aside for future capital expenses. The real estate manager and owner must agree on how much money (and how often) to take from cash flow to set aside as a reserve.

In some instances, the owner may not want to set up cash reserves. If the owner does not wish to set aside reserves, the property is still likely to need capital expenditures at some point. In that case, the budget for the project may have to come directly out of cash flow. A second possibility is using income to the owner to pay for the needed capital expenditures. A third is debt or borrowed funds. If the owner chooses these options, the owner is financing capital improvements out of working capital rather than using capital budgeting and cash reserves as the source of the funds.

A capital budget can be set up and a certain amount added to it each year to reach the needed sum as shown in the following example.

Example 5.1: Divide and Accumulate

Silver Creek has brick walkways and a small, landscaped, brick courtyard. In four years, the walkways will need extensive repair, including replacement of worn and damaged bricks. The courtyard walls will require tuck-pointing. Ornamental tiles will need to be replaced as well. Working from contractors' estimates and expected price increases, the manager estimates that the renovation of the walkways and courtyard will cost $200,000.

The simplest way to accumulate the $200,000 that will be needed four years from now is to divide the forecasted amount by the number of years. Each year, the manager should set aside the amount required to meet the goal.

Estimate of Overall Budget ÷ Number of Years
= Yearly Amount to Place in Reserves

$200,000 ÷ 4 = $50,000

TIPS:
The capital budget can have its own savings and investment goals. For example, the cash can be taken from the property's operating surplus, invested, and kept in reserve until the year that it is needed according to the building's renovation plan.

Tax Considerations

Taxes are another reason to keep capital expenses separate from operating expenses. The tax laws treat normal daily business expenses differently from capital expenses. The tax laws recognize that capital in the form of a building, an addition, an expensive furnace, or even a fleet of company cars should receive special treatment, largely because capital assets last for a long time. Sometimes capital expenses are deducted in the year that they are finished, although they are usually divided up over several years.

Capital budgeting may also involve dealing with debt. Capital assets are often acquired with debt, and capital improvements may involve debt as well. Because of the way money is used, as well as the tax deductions involved in borrowing, taking on debt can be advantageous at times. The details, though, are beyond the scope of this book.

DIG DEEPER WITH IREM RESOURCES

Publications

Glossary of Real Estate Management Terms, Chicago: Institute of Real Estate Management, 2003.

> This book provides definitions for over 2,000 terms encountered in real estate management.

Prassas, Frederick W., *Investment Real Estate: Finance & Asset Management*, Chicago: Institute of Real Estate Management, 2013.

> This book provides insight into the real estate management company and manager's role in the financial analysis and asset management of a property.

Websites

www.irem.org
The IREM website is your first-stop for information on real estate management. With resources organized by topic and property type, you will find the forms, tools, publications, webinars, and tutorials you need to help you manage your business and keep up with the industry.

IREM On-Demand Learning (www.irem.org)
- IREM® Financial Analysis Spreadsheet (Tool)
- IREM® Financial Analysis Spreadsheet Demonstration (Webinar, Recorded Webinar)
- HPIIB Calculator Webinar (Recorded Webinar)

IREM Books (www.irem.org)
- Investment Real Estate: Financial Tools (FIN402)
- Investment Real Estate Financing and Valuation – Part One (ASM603)
- Investment Real Estate Financing and Valuation – Part Two (ASM604)
- Investment Real Estate Financing and Valuation – Part Three (ASM605)

Articles
Published bi-monthly by IREM, the *Journal of Property Management* offers comprehensive coverage of the real estate management industry, including frequent features and columns on financial management topics.

Income/Expense Analysis® Reports
The IREM *Income/Expense Analysis® Reports* are the industry standard in relaying precise property data to owners, investors and tenants. Valuable operating data is collected for Conventional Apartments; Office Buildings; Federally Assisted Apartments; Condos, Co-ops, and Planned Unit Developments; and Shopping Centers. But we can't do it without your help.

Submit your data by April 1 of each year at http://IE.IREM.ORG to receive a FREE Income/Expense Analysis® book (a $450 value) and a FREE Individual Building Report. (Available once published by September.)

The Income/Expense Analysis® Reports are available for purchase in softcover books, downloadable .pdf or Excel, and Interactive online Labs.

PART III:
MAINTENANCE AND RISK MANAGEMENT

The following topics are covered:

- Creating a maintenance and risk management plan
- Types of maintenance
- Property inspections
- Risk management
- Emergency and disaster planning
- Insurance
- Inventory and suppliers
- Working with contractors
- Maintenance systems
- Conservation and recycling
- Environmental issues

CHAPTER 1:
CREATING A MAINTENANCE AND RISK MANAGEMENT PLAN

A well-managed maintenance and risk management plan increases maintenance efficiency, controls costs, extends the life of equipment, ensures the safety of residents and staff, and increases resident and staff satisfaction levels. A property manager must be able to understand the importance of developing a sound maintenance and risk management plan, as well as the factors to consider when developing the plan.

In this chapter:

- • **Maintenance and Risk Management Introduction**
- • **Types of Maintenance**
- • **Maintenance and Risk Management Plan Components**
- • **Benefits of a Maintenance and Risk Management Plan**
- • **Service Request System**

MAINTENANCE AND RISK MANAGEMENT INTRODUCTION

Buildings have life cycles similar to neighborhood life cycles. Life cycles are evolutionary stages that include development, maturity, decline, and rehabilitation. The natural physical deterioration of a building's component materials determines its life cycle.

Maintenance is the process by which a property is maintained in its existing state and preserved from physical deterioration. An important distinction exists between maintenance and repairs:

- • **Maintenance:** keeping something in an existing state
- • **Repairs:** fixing something that is broken

Maintaining a property in good condition is the first step towards managing risk associated with real estate management:

- • **Risk Management:** process of controlling or reducing risk to acceptable levels. It is protecting the owner's asset, the property's residents and guests, and the management company.

TIPS:
Maintenance and risk management go hand-in-hand and are key factors affecting the health, viability, and successful operation of the property.

Site managers play a critical role in managing risk at the property. In fact, the decisions site managers make on a daily basis affect risk management tremendously. For example, a maintenance issue such as carpet that is buckling in the clubhouse could result in a major lawsuit if a prospect trips on it, falls, and breaks an arm.

As problem solvers, site managers are expected to evaluate situations and anticipate consequences. The best way to solve problems is to know and understand risks, and then manage them appropriately.

TYPES OF MAINTENANCE

In order to help extend the useful life of building components, the practice of proactive maintenance is important.

- **Proactive maintenance** is properly planned and scheduled in advance to maximize labor at optimal times of the year, using quality materials purchased at the best price available.

- **Reactive or resident-driven maintenance** is not planned or controlled. It consists of reacting to a problem or emergency and often results in wasted time, energy, people, and materials.

Among the types of maintenance listed in the table below, preventive is the most important and requires the most planning. Emergency maintenance is the least desirable, but the most pressing.

Type	Description
Preventive	• Proactive maintenance approach that requires planning and prioritizing maintenance activities
	• Can add years to the life of equipment and sustain a property in good to excellent condition
	• Minimizes breakdowns and prevents the need for corrective and emergency maintenance work; ultimately saves money • Examples: Replacing belts on mechanical equipment, cleaning drain traps, vents, rain gutters, downspouts, fertilizing lawns and shrubs, etc. Includes the following sub-categories: o **Routine/Custodial:** Day-to-day upkeep of the property which is essential to preserving the appearance and value (e.g. cleaning, waxing floors, removing trash, washing windows, etc.) o **Cosmetic:** Enhances the appearance but does not contribute materially to the operation or preservation of an item (e.g. painting new color)
Corrective	• Reactive, after-the-fact maintenance in which a problem needs to be repaired or corrected (e.g. dripping faucet, frayed fan belt, overheating motor), often notified of problem by resident or tenant
	• May result in inefficient use of staff time; costly in terms of interrupting other projects and purchasing of supplies at less-than-optimum times and prices
	• Includes **emergency** maintenance, which is unscheduled maintenance that must be performed immediately to prevent further property damage or to protect the health and safety of tenants (e.g. broken water pipe, furnace breakdown, broken lighting, broken window, flooding)

Type	Description
Deferred	• Repairs or replacements that should have been completed but were purposely delayed for any reason, and may or may not be corrected depending on the owner's wishes (e.g. filling asphalt cracks instead of resurfacing, delaying exterior painting or carpeting, and waiting to install new appliances or bathroom fixtures.)
	• Sometimes part of the overall planning for the property, seasonal conditions, or scheduling until a full replacement is warranted
	• Sometimes a sign of neglect or poor management if the delay allows damage to expand; can be caused by lack of money and/or proper labor or materials
	• Before deciding to defer maintenance, carefully consider the impact to the property's operations and residents' safety
	• May impact marketability of a property

TIPS:
As the eyes and ears of the property, site managers are uniquely positioned to proactively monitor and respond to maintenance and risk management situations on a daily basis.

MAINTENANCE AND RISK MANAGEMENT PLAN COMPONENTS

An important aspect of proactive maintenance is the creation of a maintenance and risk management plan. A *maintenance and risk management plan* is a structured plan created to preserve, protect, and enhance the property. The plan consists primarily of detailed descriptions of the specific tasks to be performed at the property according to a reasonable schedule. Specific requirements for each property vary depending on its age, condition, size, location, and complexity as well as the number and mix of occupants and the frequency of turnover.

Identify Goals and Objectives

The first step in developing an effective and cost-efficient maintenance and risk management plan is to know and understand the owner's goals and desires for the property. It is then possible to set meaningful objectives that support those goals.

A comprehensive maintenance and risk management plan should set *clear, reasonable, and measurable* goals. For example:

- Obtain maximum rents and occupancy
- Maintain an established functional standard for systems and equipment in the building through a preventive maintenance program
- Prepare a vacant apartment for occupancy within a certain time
- Maintain established standards of cleanliness throughout the common areas of the building
- Respond to residents' service requests within a prescribed period after receipt

- Reduce the number of return calls for the same maintenance problem
- Reduce the number of emergency repair calls
- Maintain established standards for occupant health and safety
- Identify specific maintenance projects
- Reduce liability and insurance risks

TIPS:
A solid maintenance and risk management plan contains specific maintenance goals, guided by owner directives.

Follow Maintenance and Risk Management Cycle

Once the objectives have been determined, the next step is to develop the detailed plan that explains how to attain those objectives. Figure 1-1 shows a comprehensive maintenance and risk management cycle that should be considered when developing the plan.

FIGURE 1-1: MAINTENANCE AND RISK MANAGMENT CYCLE

Assess

In order to create an effective maintenance and risk management plan, the site manager must assess the status of the property with the owner's goals in mind. This involves conducting a visual inspection, inventorying mechanical equipment and appliances, and reviewing previous maintenance records, financial reports, and current vendor contracts. Additionally, reviewing the skills and experiences of the on-site maintenance staff is recommended. Knowing this information will help the site manager determine if the specified goals are realistic.

Plan

Once the assessment component is complete, the site manager plans specifically how to maintain the property and manage risk:

- Address all types of maintenance, with a specific focus on the preventive, routine, and corrective areas in order to control expenses and provide residents with the level of service they expect

- Address emergency and disaster recovery plans, including training and practice for personnel

- Define the scope of each task or project included in the plan, including milestones and completion dates

- Schedule and supervise maintenance work, relying on information such as property inspections, ongoing services, and budget constraints to determine the priorities and schedule

- Manage time well by scheduling in advance, scheduling periodic maintenance on a regular basis, allowing flexibility, and seeking input from staff who perform the work

- Ensure that the right people are available and trained to complete the tasks and projects; plan ways to lead, support, and train personnel

- Create and manage the maintenance and risk management budget; monitor expenses and analyze reports

- Develop control procedures to be sure work is accomplished effectively and on time (referencing the property's maintenance policy and procedure manual). Define acceptable response times.

TIPS:
A maintenance and risk management policy and procedure manual is a collection of all the forms and procedures related to maintenance activities. It describes every maintenance activity that could, would, or should happen at a property. It should be accessible to all staff, and customized for each property. Refer to Figure 1-2 for key components of the policy and procedure manual.

FIGURE 1-2: POLICY AND PROCEDURE MANUAL COMPONENTS

- Routine maintenance
- Resident requests
- Make-ready/turnover
- Property inspections
- Preventive maintenance
- Equipment inventory
- Eviction procedures
- Major systems
- Energy performance records
- Emergency procedures
- Life safety
- Job descriptions
- Contractors
- Handling hazardous materials

LEGAL ISSUE:
Ensure that maintenance and risk management plans comply with applicable laws and regulations (e.g., Americans with Disabilities Act (ADA), Occupational Safety and Health Administration (OSHA)) or are working toward compliance. When creating a renovation program, check with local authorities as some counties and cities require an upgrade to code when renovations are undertaken, adding substantial cost. Some require that a percentage of the total cost be spent on code compliance issues.

Execute

Once the plans are in place, it is time to execute the maintenance and risk management plan:

- Conduct property inspections and monitor projects
- Keep a maintenance record for major systems and equipment
- As necessary, develop bid specifications for certain work
- Meet to discuss the plan with staff and/or the owner on a regular basis

Evaluate

Planning ways to evaluate and monitor the maintenance and risk management plan is another important consideration. This involves evaluating the effectiveness of the plan and the quality of the service provided. Conducting resident surveys is one technique to gather relevant data. Be sure to document and report results, including suggested adjustments or alternate strategies to enhance the plan.

BENEFITS OF A MAINTENANCE AND RISK MANAGEMENT PLAN

Item	Description
Resident Satisfaction	• Yields more lease renewals and higher rents • Fosters a more solid relationship between residents and management
Quality Maintenance Staff	• Provides proper training and the needed supplies and personnel to complete tasks • Helps increase job satisfaction • Works smoothly with office staff • Ensures that maintenance priorities are in line with the overall goals of the property
Property Reputation	• Reduces turnover costs and rent loss from vacancies • Increases the net operating income (NOI) through more efficient and effective use of materials, labor, and time—reduces maintenance costs in general • Increases ability to sell or refinance

Cost and Risk Control	• Reduces the cost of emergency repairs/ replacements:
	  o Anticipating parts that may be needed
	  o Averting a crisis and resident dissatisfaction
	  o Avoiding high-cost orders, delivery, and overtime
	  o Reducing liability and insurance costs

Sound Maintenance and Service (Figure 1-3)	• Yields more attractive property in good condition • Increases units rented (greater operating funds) • More responsive to resident's needs • More satisfied residents and higher renewal rates • Lowers turnover, fewer vacancies, and lower operating costs

FIGURE 1-3: BENEFITS OF SOUND MAINTENANCE AND SERVICE

Q. What are the most frequent resident complaints?

A. Residents are most likely to complain about maintenance issues. Specifically,
- Lack of good housekeeping and maintenance
- Lack of adequate heat, air-conditioning, or hot water
- Delay of repair or decorating
- Attitude of management when notified about a need repair or a complaint
- Attitude of the maintenance worker performing a task

Single Family House Impact: Because they are in multiple locations, single family houses require more time, resources, and logistical considerations. Details of a maintenance and risk management plan for a single family house will be dependent upon terms of the lease, age, location, and amenities of the house, and HOA requirements. Be sure to consider these impacts and include the necessary details when preparing and implementing a maintenance and risk management plan for a single family house. Because different houses require different plans, coordination, record keeping, follow up, and inspections are crucial.

Student Housing Impact: In student housing, it is important to consider "the Turn" (restoring units to move-in condition in the short amount of time available) as part of the overall maintenance and risk management plan. Basically, this involves painting, re-carpeting or cleaning carpets, performing inspections, addressing curb appeal, determining availability, etc. for a massive number of units all at the same time. It is critical to have a detailed maintenance implementation plan in place to ensure The Turn is successful.

Sustainability Impact: For a property with sustainability goals, integrate sustainable maintenance policies and procedures such as waste reduction and purchasing of environmentally preferable materials into a standard maintenance and risk management plan. For more information on sustainable operations and maintenance, see IREM® course "Sustainable Real Estate Management" (SRM001).

SERVICE REQUEST SYSTEM

A critical component of a sound maintenance and risk management plan is an established system for fielding and responding to resident service requests. The following checklist provides a list of components to consider in a service request policy.

CHECKLIST: SERVICE REQUEST POLICY COMPONENTS

□ Office hours for accepting requests
□ Availability of service at night, during weekends, and on holidays
□ Emergency telephone numbers to call when the site office is closed
  o Indicate what constitutes an emergency request versus a standard maintenance request
  o Define circumstances in which residents should call the emergency number
□ Documentation procedures
  o Instruct residents to make requests using the standard service request form available online or in the management office.
  o Residents should not report situations to maintenance technicians, and all requests should be thorough to assist maintenance staff in addressing the situation effectively
  o All requests should be documented immediately
□ Guidelines for billing residents for damage
□ Communications process
  o Define standard response times
  o Ensure compliance with permission to enter (PTE) laws
□ Resident retention considerations
  o Provide instructions for common service requests
  o Follow-up to determine satisfaction and inquire about additional needs
  o Personalizing the maintenance team with cards identifying the name of the team member who completed the work

FIGURE 1-4: SAMPLE RESIDENT HANDBOOK

Procedures for Service Requests

All service requests should be directed to the management office, preferably during office hours. A service request form can be completed in person or by a staff member (over the phone or online, using a service request form). To help us provide better service to you, requests should be stated as clearly and completely as possible. Our goal is to respond to your request within 24 hours, if possible. When work cannot be scheduled that quickly, we will explain why the delay is necessary and when you can expect the work to be completed. Every effort will be made to perform the requested service as soon as possible.

To help us monitor the quality of the service we are providing, a service request "report card" will be left with you after the work has been done. Please complete the questionnaire, grading the quality and timeliness of the service and commenting as appropriate.

In case of an emergency, please call the management office immediately. If the office is closed, call the emergency service number listed in this handbook. Examples of emergencies follow:

• Fire or smoke (call fire department first)
• Security problem (e.g., door that will not shut, broken window or lock)
• No electricity, heat, or air-conditioning
• Leaky plumbing (a broken pipe or overflowing toilet)
• Blocked drain or backed up sewer
• Gas odor
• Failure of an appliance
• Nonworking elevator

This procedure is intended to ensure fast, courteous, and efficient service. If you have any questions regarding this policy, please call the site manager.

NOTE: Power outages and telephone service disruptions should be reported directly to the respective utilities, although the management will appreciate receiving such information. Gas leaks should be reported to the utility company immediately; the management company should be notified afterward.

Maintaining Files

Service Request Form

Proper response to a service request should be documented. Every resident request should result in the preparation of a service request form, whether the form is print or electronic. The completed service request form indicates what is to be done, when it should be completed, and who will do the work. It becomes the maintenance record of the response to the request for maintenance services.

Typically, companies have automated service request systems, including online systems (Refer to Figure 1-5) which can help them identify areas of the property that might need improvement (e.g. timeliness of responding to resident requests for maintenance services).

For companies that use hard-copy service request forms (Refer to Figure 1-6), three copies of the form should be made—one for the management office, one for the unit maintenance file, and one for the resident.

FIGURE 1-5: SAMPLE ONLINE SERVICE REQUEST

Source: **www.buildinglink.com/Public/buildinglink/Screenshots.aspx**

TIPS:
Regardless of the service request system in place, all staff should be trained to collect and document relevant information.

FIGURE 1-6: SAMPLE SERVICE REQUEST FORM

PROPERTY MANAGEMENT COMPANY

CONTACT	PHONE	DATE

ADDRESS	APT.

DEAD BOLT o   ANIMAL o   PERMISSION TO ENTER o

SERVICE REQUEST

DATE	MECHANIC	WORK PERFORMED	HOURS

QUAN.	UNIT	DESCRIPTION OF MATERIAL	AMOUNT

TOTAL HOURS	COMPLETE	INCOMPLETE	TOTAL AMOUNT

RESIDENT SIGNATURE: _____ DATE:_____

MAINTENANCE SIGNATURE: _____ DATE:_____

FOR OFFICE USE ONLY:

RESIDENT BILLED? _____ DESCRIPTION: _____

DATE: _____ AMOUNT: _____

RECORDED IN
ACCTS RECEIVABLE: _____DATE: _____ BY: _____

Unit File

Each unit should have a file, either in electronic or hard-copy format, that documents relevant information and provides a record of specific maintenance performed. These files are typically kept online or scanned to minimize paper. The file for each unit should contain standard information that will expedite responses to residents' service requests and facilitate implementation of inventory controls. Refer to the following checklist for items to include in the unit file.

CHECKLIST: UNIT FILE

- Unit measurements
- Appliance serial numbers, model numbers, colors; purchase dates, source, warranty information
- Plumbing fixture manufacturer, style, color; purchase dates, repair source
- Cabinet and hardware design
- Whether drapes or blinds were provided
- Whether unit was leased furnished or unfurnished
- When the apartment was last cleaned
- When carpet was last shampooed
- Color scheme if more than one is used on the property
- Dates when last painted or wallpapered
- Installation dates of carpet or tile
- Unique characteristics of the unit (e.g., a fireplace)
- Dates and types of maintenance or service performed, especially repetitions
- Resident billing for damage (copies of letters or invoices); these charges should also be recorded in the resident's ledger
- History of pets that have lived in the unit
- Reasonable modifications made to the unit
- Inspections (e.g. according to company policy or to meet HUD requirements)

Maintenance Log or Ledger

All maintenance assignments should be entered in a maintenance log or ledger that serves as a cumulative record. This log can be written by hand or entered into a computer program. The log is used to record specific tasks, their locations, and the time required to complete them, along with the name of the worker and the date. A maintenance log becomes a record of all maintenance work done for the property as a whole, which is important when preparing budgets and analyzing budget variances. A maintenance log also facilitates evaluating the performance of maintenance technicians. Refer to Figure 1-7 for a sample maintenance log.

LEGAL ISSUE:
Note that the maintenance log can also have legal implications. Some tasks are related to compliance with building code requirements or environmental regulations. Therefore, the log should document work sufficiently enough to overcome claims of constructive eviction.

Maintaining Records

Maintaining records is an integral part of the site manager's job. Property management agreements, leases, work orders, invoices and receipts, tax returns, just to name a few. All of these materials must be maintained in a manner that ensures their safekeeping and ease of retrieval. Legal requirements vary from state to state, but many require that property owners keep all documents relative to the management of property for at least three years.

With the increased use of property management software, many records are created and maintained in computer-based systems. Real estate companies that have online records should implement a regular procedure for backing up files and storing them in an off-site location. Many services now offer online, "cloud based" systems which backup user files over the Internet.

TIPS:
Record keeping is an important part of risk management. Having a written record of interactions with residents, contractors and staff provides protection in the event of legal action. Be sure to immediately document any situation that has the potential for misunderstanding – you will never have a clearer recollection of the event.

FIGURE 1-7: SAMPLE MAINTENANCE LOG

	Service Request No.	Unit	Resident Name	Work to Be Completed	Time Written	Date Written	Taken By	Finished On	Cost
1.									
2.									
3.									
4.									
5.									
6.									
7.									
8.									
9.									
10.									

CHAPTER 2:
PROPERTY INSPECTIONS AND MINIMIZING RISK

Regular inspection ensures a well-kept building and eliminates reactive maintenance. Also, identifying, controlling, and reducing risk protects the owner's asset, the property's residents and guests, and the management company. A property manager must inspect all parts of the property on a regular basis to ensure proactive maintenance, reduce risk, and identify risks to be managed.

In this chapter:

- **Property Inspections**
- **Risk Management**
- **Insurance**
- **Incident Management**
- **Emergency and Disaster Planning**

PROPERTY INSPECTIONS

Purpose of the Inspection

The primary purpose of a property inspection is to determine the need for maintenance. Through regular inspections, site managers can anticipate problems, address them promptly, and thus reduce the extent of maintenance work and related expenditures. Additionally, inspections are the single best way to identify risks at a property. In order to know what to inspect, what to look for, and how to evaluate the findings, managers must determine the basic purpose for making the inspection.

Property inspections are often conducted in the following situations:

- When considering taking over a new account (property)
- When working with a new owner (or owner's asset manager) of an established account
- To analyze the property's condition and operations thoroughly in order to develop and implement a management plan
- To determine if the property is being operated and maintained at peak efficiency and in accordance with the operations manual and standard operating procedures as well as to ensure that the manual and procedures are current and realistic
- To monitor the possible development of problems such as leaking windows, deteriorating brick walls, backed up drains, failing paint on surfaces, hazards, etc.
- To develop various budgets
- To comply with local, state, and federal laws
- To evaluate the property's liability risk

Types and Frequency of Property Inspections

Because so many different reasons exist to conduct inspections, categorizing inspections into the following types is often helpful:

- Unit Interior
- Unit Exterior
- Spring and Fall Exterior
- Move-in/Move-out
- Marketing (signage, etc.)
- Life Safety and Risk
- Risk Evaluation
- Lighting
- Pest/Termite
- ADA Compliance
- Big Ticket Items (for budget purposes)
- Capital Improvements
- Maintenance Shop and Inventory Areas

Note that inspection types vary based on the property, the size of the staff, budget, specific goals, and so forth.

Affordable Housing Impact: With affordable housing properties, regulatory inspections are often required, and may include the following:
- Local Building inspections
- HUD Section 8
- Investor inspections
- State agency inspections
- Lender inspections
- Real Estate Assessment Center (REAC) inspections – required for any property with a HUD insured mortgage.
  - o REAC inspections assign the property a specific score that can significantly impact the financial stability and viability of the property. Issues that go uncorrected within a specified timeframe could result in a decrease or withdrawal of federal or state affordable housing funds. (Refer to Figure 2-1 for a list of the most frequently cited deficiencies in REAC inspections)
- NOTE: Each inspection may have a different focus (e.g. fiscal, physical) and any life safety issues identified must be corrected within 72 hours.

Rank	UPCS Area Name	UPCS Item Name	UPCS Deficiency Name	Number of Times Cited **
1	DU	Doors	Damaged Hardware/Locks**	109,517
2	DU	Kitchen	Refrigerator - Missing/Damaged/Inoperable	76,086
3	DU	Bathroom	Lavatory Sink - Damaged/Missing**	46,267
4	DU	Kitchen	Range/Stove - Missing/Damaged/Inoperable**	41,916
5	DU	Doors	Damaged Surface - Holes/Paint/Rusting/Glass**	41,469
6	DU	Walls	Damaged**	37,700
7	BldgExt	Walls	Stained/Peeling/Needs Paint	35,956
8	DU	Walls	Peeling/Needs Paint**	35,628
9	BldgExt	Walls	Missing Pieces/Holes/Spalling**	33,749
10	BldgExt	Roofs	Missing/Damaged Components from Downspout/Gutter**	32,284
11	DU	Windows	Missing/Deteriorated Caulking/Seals/Glazing Compound**	31,469
12	DU	Smoke Detector	Missing/Inoperable**	30,911
13	DU	Windows	Inoperable/Not Lockable**	30,883
14	DU	Outlets/Switches	Missing/Broken Cover Plates	30,642
15	HS	Hazards	Tripping	29,405
16	DU	Bathroom	Plumbing - Leaking Faucet/Pipes	24,962
17	DU	Electrical System	GFI - Inoperable	24,473
18	DU	Call-for-Aid	Inoperable	23,936
19	DU	Ceiling	Peeling/Needs Paint**	22,149
20	HS	Emergency/Fire Exits	Emergency/Fire Exits Blocked/Unusable	21,208
21	DU	Bathroom	Shower/Tub - Damaged/Missing**	20,563
22	DU	Doors	Damaged/Missing Screen/Storm/Security Door**	20,186
23	DU	Doors	Missing Door	19,517
24	HS	Infestation	Insects	19,355
25	BldgExt	Windows	Damaged/Missing Screens**	19,167

DU = Dwelling Unit

BldgExt = Building Exterior

* FHEO defects were excluded for consistency with existing business rules.

** Since the beginning of 2.3 to September 20, 2006

Source: **www.hud.gov/offices/reac/**

There are different types of inspections for different circumstances:

Type	Description
Routine Inspections	• Performed on a predetermined schedule to evaluate the property's condition and the performance of staff and contractors • Regular inspections let the site staff know that the manager is interested in what they are doing and is aware of ongoing operations. Staff know that the manager will follow up on assigned projects, which encourages them to maintain the property on a continuing basis. Refer to Figure 2-2 for a sample. • Normally conducted during the day, when staffing is at its peak and the manager is visible to the staff and residents • Occasional night visits offer the opportunity to see the staff on that shift, check the lighting, and identify any possible security challenges

Type	Description
Special Inspections	• Conducted after a fire or other disaster, when residents move in or out, and when purchasing or selling a property • Special inspections may also be conducted prior to preparing an annual budget
Surprise Inspection	• An opportunity to gather a random and instantaneous look at what goes on during normal business hours and at night • Managers should inform staff in advance that they may occasionally conduct unannounced inspections to prevent staff feeling that they are not trusted

FIGURE 2-2: SAMPLE INSPECTION SCHEDULE

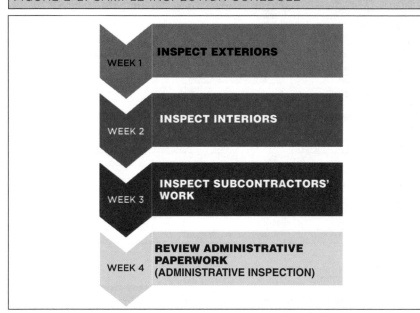

WEEK 1 — INSPECT EXTERIORS

WEEK 2 — INSPECT INTERIORS

WEEK 3 — INSPECT SUBCONTRACTORS' WORK

WEEK 4 — REVIEW ADMINISTRATIVE PAPERWORK (ADMINISTRATIVE INSPECTION)

TIPS:

Note that subcontractors' work should be inspected weekly, but it is especially important to check their work during the third week of the month as they approach their billing cycles.

The site manager should gather data to determine whether to approve payments or to demand further work to fulfill the contract.

Student Housing Impact: With student housing properties, conducting inspections about four times per year is recommended.

Inspection Checklist

Always use an inspection checklist to ensure that everything is inspected properly and nothing gets overlooked. Use of a standard inspection report form (on paper or using an app) facilitates the inspection process and allows the manager to communicate findings to the maintenance staff and the owner. The completed form documents the particular inspection and facilitates scheduling of needed work and estimating costs for the purpose of budgeting or cost benefit analysis.

Risk Evaluation Checklists

When inspections are used to identify risks at a property, the inspection checklists are often called risk evaluation checklists. Such checklists can be obtained from an insurance company or an independent risk consultant, or they can be created in-house. Regardless, they should be customized for the property to yield more specific information. Refer to Figure 2-3 for a sample risk evaluation checklist.

Student Housing Impact: The following items should be included on a student housing risk evaluation checklist:
• Are blood-borne pathogen kits available?
• Are bodily fluid kits available?
• Are restrictive windows used?

Q&A

Q. What is a risk audit?

A. A formal risk audit is performed by professional risk consultants, insurance company representatives, or management personnel. It incorporates an analysis of both site factors (e.g. advice on hidden hazards, review of insurance coverage, adjunct information from claims adjustors and local authorities, etc.) and people factors (e.g. employee reviews, vendors' and workers' compensation, environmental issues, etc.) that serves as an in-depth inspection or an analysis method for determining insurance coverage.

RESOURCES:

Downloadable forms such as inspection checklists and risk evaluation checklists can be found under Resources>Forms & Checklists at **www.irem.org** and are free for members. These sample forms and agreements are not endorsed by the Institute of Real Estate Management. They are presented for informational purposes only.

FIGURE 2-3: SAMPLE RISK EVALUATION CHECKLIST

Property_____
Inspected by_____ Date_____

The following questions should be answered YES, NO, or not applicable (N/A):

1. Are parking areas free of potholes and tripping hazards?
2. Are handicapped parking spaces clearly marked?
3. Are all parking bumpers and speed bumps secured and painted a bright contrasting color?
4. Are porches, steps, sidewalks, and other exterior walkways in good condition?
5. Are lawn sprinklers positioned to minimize tripping hazards?
6. If natural gas meters are located outside the building, are they adequately protected from vehicular traffic?
7. Are all fire hydrants capped and free of obstructions?
8. Are fire lanes clearly marked?
9. Are electrical fuse panels cool to the touch?
10. Is the pool fenced and enclosed on all sides, and does the gate lock securely?
11. Is the required life-safety equipment readily accessible near the pool and in working order?
12. Is all poolside furniture clean and free of defects?
13. Is the "Pool Rules" sign clearly visible, and does it provide emergency telephone numbers? (Depending on the resident profile, these signs may have to be printed in more than one language.)
14. Is a "No Diving" sign posted at the pool?
15. Is the playground area free of debris?
16. Is the playground equipment free of worn parts and other defects?
17. Is all interior and exterior lighting adequate, day and night?
18. Does the emergency lighting system function properly?
19. Are all interior hallways, stairs, and walkways free of tripping hazards?
20. Are all fire exits shut and fully operational?
21. Are all fire extinguishers fully charged and tagged, indicating recent service?
22. Are exit signs clearly visible?
23. Are fire hoses properly stored, without obstructions?
24. Are all fire sprinkler heads unobstructed?
25. Are all sprinkler valves in the open position?
26. Have all fire alarms been tested recently?
27. Is the number of electrical outlets sufficient, eliminating the need for extension cords?
28. Is sufficient clear space present around furnaces, water heaters, radiators, and electrical panels?
29. Are all the electrical applications properly grounded?
30. Are employee annual reviews been compliant with employment laws (as discussed in HR section)
31. Are all vendors covered by workmen's compensation insurance?
32. Have policies and procedures of the property been reviewed for risks to the asset?
33. Are property staff compliant with changes in the law for fair housing? Landlord-Tenant law? Mold and asbestos regulations?

Other hazards or comments:

For negative responses, please indicate below what action will be taken to correct the situation and when. Use a separate sheet if necessary.

Repair Item Number_____ Action Required_____ Scheduled Date of Repair_____

Paper Forms

Paper inspection forms are usually set up as grids in which the checklist items are on the left and blank columns are to the right. The grid generally has at least one column in which to record the condition, plus one in which to indicate the action to be taken and/or completed. The inspection form should be modified and organized to reflect the property's specific features and equipment, and should contain space for the date and a signature. Separate forms for different types of areas is recommended.

Inspection reports should be filed conveniently and should be easy for personnel to review. Employees should be part of the inspection team so they understand the observations and are aware of critical areas. It is important to periodically submit written inspection forms to the owner, indicating actions that are planned to correct any problems found and necessary expenditures. Refer to Figure 2-4 for a sample inspection form.

Inspection Apps

More and more inspections are being done with mobile apps on smart phones or tablets instead of paper forms. Mobile apps make reporting easier by saving documents in an electronic format that can be easily emailed to the owner and the business office. They allow photos or even video to be quickly associated with a problem-area and incorporated directly into the report. Most have simple, easy-to-use interfaces with customizable fields and the ability to save frequently used comments. Some are standalone apps and others are sections of property management software and will import data into a central database.

Carrying a cell phone, tablet and/or 2-way radio during an inspection also allows you to quickly call for help if someone is injured or unsafe conditions are encountered.

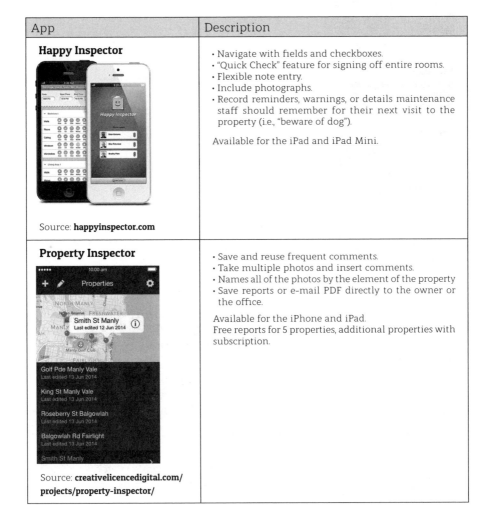

App	Description
Happy Inspector Source: **happyinspector.com**	• Navigate with fields and checkboxes. • "Quick Check" feature for signing off entire rooms. • Flexible note entry. • Include photographs. • Record reminders, warnings, or details maintenance staff should remember for their next visit to the property (i.e., "beware of dog"). Available for the iPad and iPad Mini.
Property Inspector Source: **creativelicencedigital.com/ projects/property-inspector/**	• Save and reuse frequent comments. • Take multiple photos and insert comments. • Names all of the photos by the element of the property • Save reports or e-mail PDF directly to the owner or the office. Available for the iPhone and iPad. Free reports for 5 properties, additional properties with subscription.

App	Description
Snap Inspect  Source: **www.snapinspect.com**	• Inspection checklists or create custom. • Automatically schedule inspection dates/times. • Video inspection and include in reports. • Support collaboration and teams. • AutoText comments and voice dictation. • Produce reports in Microsoft Word and PDF. Available for iPhone, Android Mobiles, iPad, Android Tablets, iPad Mini & iPod Touch.
Tap Inspect  Source: **www.tapinspect.com/**	Supports and organizes multiple types of inspection templates. • Create custom templates. • Search comment library. • Import photos directly into reports. • Share reports between inspectors or devices. • Publish PDF reports to the web. Available for the iPhone, iPod Touch and iPad.
Yardi Inspection Mobile  Source: **www.yardi.com**	• Custom inspection templates. • Track inspector, inspection type status, due date, completion time. • Automatically create work orders and notification letters. • View detailed reports on inspection history. • Communicate with residents and tenants with printed or emailed notifications. • Operate in areas without a cellular or wireless connection, and synchronize data later. • Inspection data stored in centralized Yardi VoyagerTM database. Available for BlackBerry, iPhone, Android, Android Tablet, or iPad – without using the full Voyager browser client.

NOTE: IREM does not endorse any vendor as part of IREM Education

Using the Inspection Results

Depending on the property and the purpose of the inspection, results can be used for the following purposes:

- Create or update the maintenance and risk management plan
- Plan and prioritize maintenance
- Determine annual plans and budgets
- Monitor and report the condition of the property to the owner
- Identify current and future maintenance liability
- Evaluate staff and contractor performance
- Identify and track specific goals

FIGURE 2-4: SAMPLE APARTMENT INTERIOR INSPECTION REPORT

Property_____Address_____

Apt. No._____ No. of Rooms_____

Report Submitted By_____ Date_____

Item	Character and Condition	Needs	Estimated Expense Involved
Vestibule			
1. Door			
2. Hinges			
3. Lock			
4. Safety Chain			
5. Doorplates			
6. Transom			
7. Floor (Carpeting)			
8. Walls			
9. Ceiling			
10. Light Fixtures & Switches			
11. Draperies/Blinds			
Coat Closet			
12. Door			
13. Floor			
14. Interior Walls			
15. Ceiling			
16. Shelves, Rods, Hooks			
Living Room			
17. Floor (Carpeting)			
18. Baseboards			
19. Walls			
20. Ceiling			
21. Windows			
22. Doors			
23. Light Fixtures & Switches			
24. Electric Outlets			
25. Draperies/Blinds			
Dining Room			
26. Floor (Carpeting)			
27. Baseboards			
28. Walls			

FIGURE 2-4: SAMPLE APARTMENT INTERIOR INSPECTION
REPORT (CONTINUED)

Item	Character and Condition	Needs	Estimated Expense Involved
29. Ceiling			
30. Windows			
31. Doors			
32. Light Fixtures & Switches			
33. Electric Outlets			
34. Draperies/Blinds			
35. Buffets			
36. Wainscot or Chair Rail			
Kitchen			
37. Doors			
38. Transoms			
39. Locks			
40. Floor			
41. Baseboards			
42. Walls			
43. Ceiling			
44. Light Fixtures & Switches			
45. Electric Outlets			
46. Dishwasher			
47. Range			
48. Sink			
49. Cabinets			
50. Refrigerator			
51.. Pantry			
52. Doorbell			
53. Ventilating Hood			
54. Disposal			
First Bedroom			
55. Floor (Carpeting)			
56. Baseboards			
57. Walls			
58. Ceiling			
59. Windows			
60. Doors			
61. Light Fixtures & Switches			
62. Electric Outlets			
63. Draperies/Blinds			
64. Closets			
Second Bedroom			
65. Floor (Carpeting)			
66. Baseboards			

FIGURE 2-4: SAMPLE APARTMENT INTERIOR INSPECTION
REPORT (CONTINUED)

Item	Character and Condition	Needs	Estimated Expense Involved
67. Walls			
68. Ceiling			
69. Windows			
70. Doors			
71. Light Fixtures & Switches			
72. Electric Outlets			
73. Draperies/Blinds			
74. Closets			
Third Bedroom			
75. Floor (Carpeting)			
76. Baseboards			
77. Walls			
78. Ceiling			
79. Windows			
80. Doors			
81. Light Fixtures & Switches			
82. Electric Outlets			
83. Draperies/Blinds			
84. Closets			
Housekeeping Room			
85. Floor (Carpeting)			
86. Baseboards			
87. Walls			
88. Ceiling			
89. Windows			
90. Doors			
91. Light Fixtures & Switches			
92. Electric Outlets			
93. Draperies/Blinds			
94. Closets			
First Bathroom			
95. Doors			
96. Floor			
97. Walls			
98. Ceiling			
99. Window			
100. Tub (Glass Door)			
101. Shower			
102. Shower Curtain or Door			
103. Lavatory			
104. Toilet Bowl			

FIGURE 2-4: SAMPLE APARTMENT INTERIOR INSPECTION
REPORT (CONTINUED)

Item	Character and Condition	Needs	Estimated Expense Involved
105. Flush Tank			
106. Faucets			
107. Light Fixtures & Switches			
108. Electric Outlets			
109. Exhaust Fan			
110. Towel Racks, etc.			
111. Cabinets			
Second Bathroom			
112. Doors			
113. Floor			
114. Walls			
115. Ceiling			
116. Window			
117. Tub (Glass Door)			
118. Shower			
119. Shower Curtain or Door			
120. Lavatory			
121. Toilet Bowl			
122. Flush Tank			
123. Faucets			
124. Light Fixtures & Switches			
125. Electric Outlets			
126. Exhaust Fan			
127. Towel Racks, etc.			
128. Cabinets			
Windows & Shades			
129. Frames			
130. Sashes			
131. Sills			
132. Stops			
133. Weights			
134. Locks			
135. Glass			
136. Weather Stripping			
137. Shades			
138. Blinds			
139. Drapery Fixtures			
Linen Closet			
140. Door			
141. Floor			
142. Ceiling			

FIGURE 2-4: SAMPLE APARTMENT INTERIOR INSPECTION
REPORT (CONTINUED)

Item	Character and Condition	Needs	Estimated Expense Involved
143. Walls			
144. Shelves			
145. Drawers			
146. Electrical Lights			
Environmental Controls			
147. Heating Equipment			
148. Air Conditioning Unit(s)			

NOTES

NOTES:
Additional inspection forms such as the following:
• Sample Apartment Exterior & Common Area Inspection Report
• Sample Residential Unit Make Ready Inspection Checklist
• Sample Preventive Maintenance Checklist
• Sample Residential Property Inspection Report

Can be found under Resources > Forms & Checklists at **www.irem.org** and are free for members.

RISK MANAGEMENT

Managing Specific Risks

Once risks have been identified through inspection, the site manager must evaluate the risks and decide how to manage them. Risk management can use several approaches. Each has advantages and disadvantages. In order to select the best approach to a particular risk, the site manager can compare the costs and benefits of retaining a risk versus the costs and benefits of changing the condition. Refer to Figure 2-5 for the four methods of managing specific risk.

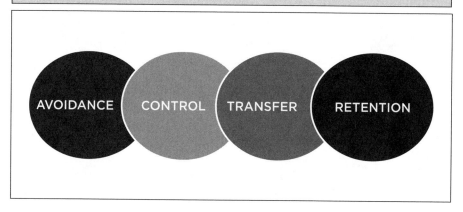

FIGURE 2-5: MANAGING SPECIFIC RISKS

AVOIDANCE   CONTROL   TRANSFER   RETENTION

Avoidance

Characteristics	Example
• Elimination of a known risk • Not always desirable because the benefits that accompany the risk can also be lost	• Filling in swimming pool and converting to landscaped area

Control

Characteristics	Example
• Taking action to reduce loss exposure by correcting conditions that pose risk or by controlling the particular risk • Involves reducing the risk while retaining the benefits associated with the condition that creates the risk • Reduces exposure to injury and lessens owner's and the management company's exposure to liability • Control measures are commonly mandated by local ordinances	• Using example of the swimming pool: removing a diving board, installing safety equipment (e.g., a ladder with handrails), hiring a lifeguard, installing an anti-vortex cover, enclosing the pool area with a fence and lockable gates, and posting and enforcing rules • Scheduling regular fire drills, conducting frequent property and equipment inspections, complying with OSHA standards, and so forth.

Transfer

Characteristics	Example
• Transfer of risk to a professional risk bearer through various types of insurance policies	• Using example of the swimming pool: purchasing property insurance and liability insurance to help cover the risk of having a swimming pool • Securing certificates of insurance for contract workers

Retention

Characteristics	Example
• Risk is accepted "as is" because it is unlikely to occur, or the potential for financial loss is minimal • Often neither pure retention nor pure avoidance is a realistic solution	• Using example of the swimming pool: the decision might be to keep the pool because the benefits of resident enjoyment outweigh the risks of injury or accidental drowning

Types of Risk

Risk takes several basic forms: safety, liability risk, and emergency risk. The types of risks often overlap, but the specific category of risk is not as important as the action taken to reduce liability.

Safety Risk

As a site manager, it is extremely important to minimize safety risks on the premises. The liability associated with injuries that occur on a property can be great if physical safety hazards are not minimized by proper planning, maintenance, and repair.

TIPS:
The safety program's goals should include injury prevention, damage control, compliance with applicable laws and regulations, and liability reduction. Site managers should educate employees and residents on specific steps they can take to minimize their own exposure.

Security

Residents' desire for security is universal, but security must be a cooperative effort that involves building management, residents, local police, and other authorities within a jurisdiction. While site managers cannot eliminate security risks, they can take steps to deter them through proper planning and precautionary measures. The following checklist provides site-level security precautions.

CHECKLIST: SECURITY PRECAUTIONS

- ☐ Check vacant units, storage areas, recreation rooms, and site office
- ☐ Keep existing security devices or systems functioning
- ☐ Repair or replace damaged devices immediately
- ☐ Respond quickly to resident reported problems
- ☐ Perform regular inspections to uncover problems
- ☐ Note that being out of step with local security provision practices can be costly from both a marketing and liability perspective
- ☐ Retain established measures unless a better alternative is found (may be legally responsible for continuing existing measures or providing suitable substitutes)
- ☐ Remember duty to the owner to make security measures as efficient and effective as possible while managing resident perception

---

LEGAL ISSUE:
Recent court cases have ruled that like properties in like areas must maintain like safety procedures—including security. As this is a huge change for property owners, competitive surveys should be updated quarterly at a minimum, and the absence of security should be noted as a red flag to a property owner.

In determining whether to add security measures, consider these issues:

- **Effectiveness:** Does the security measure work fairly easily? Is it superior to what is currently used?

- **Cost:** Is the initial expense justified? Will it translate into lower insurance premiums? What is the cost to maintain it?

- **Quality:** How long has the system been in the marketplace? What kind of service or support can you expect once it is installed?

- **Ease-Of-Use For Residents:** Is the measure something for which residents can assume responsibility?

- **Possible Liabilities That May Be Created:** How will it affect residents' perceptions and expectations? Will security really be increased, or will it be reduced?

• **Possible Impact On Marketing And Resident Retention:** Will this security measure add to the appeal for new residents and help retain current ones? Does it yield a marketing advantage over the competition?

LEGAL ISSUE:
Note that in rent control areas, a landlord may not discontinue any service without a reduction in rent. In addition, a management company that takes over a property in a rent control area should be mindful of any extra programs initiated during the start-up of the property because they may have to remain in-place depending on the wording in the rent control initiative.

Building Access

Probably the most effective component of building safety is limiting access to the inside of the building. The likelihood of danger is dramatically reduced when people who do not belong in the building are kept out. The following checklist provides considerations for limiting building access.

CHECKLIST: LIMITING BUILDING ACCESS
☐ Ensure doors are sturdily constructed and securely installed
☐ Use heavy-duty locks on exterior doors
o Two-inch deadbolts are most secure
o Metal guard plates can be added to strengthen doors and protect against kick-ins.
o Hinges should be mounted on the insides of doors to prevent intruders from gaining entry by merely taking door off hinges
☐ Install emergency alarms
☐ Put mirrors in elevators
☐ Add parking gates to the property
☐ Include peepholes for personal protection
o Should give a wide-angle view (180 degrees)
o Install low on doors to maximize access for children or disabled individuals (or install two peepholes)
☐ Educate residents and guests about not letting strangers into the building. Emphasize this in new resident orientation, resident handbook, and via newsletters and other notices.

Access Control

Keys and key fobs present their own issues. Potential for liability is present if former residents retain keys and/or if management does not change locks between residents.

At the same time, management must have access to rented apartments in emergencies, which raises the risk from multiple copies of individual keys or so-called master keys. To avert such problems, access control is essential. The following checklist provides some suggestions for access control:

- Consider a computerized key control system. Benefits include controlled access to the key box, the ability to monitor key use, rotating codes for key storage, and online reporting data.
- Consider a card access system. Cards have a magnetic strip that is uniquely coded to the lock. When inserted into a reading device, it opens the door.
- Change locks at re-lease
- Keep records of keys issued to residents and staff
- Consider arranging to have extra keys made yourself, rather than permitting residents to duplicate theirs
- Store duplicate keys in a locked cabinet, out of sight of visitors
- Limit who has access to the key box (e.g., only the manager and the maintenance supervisor)
- Always have employees or contractors sign keys out when they start work and sign them in before they leave
    - o Do not provide contractors with keys to occupied units; on-site personnel should admit them
    - o As an additional precaution, make and retain photocopies of contractors' drivers' licenses
- Never label keys with unit numbers or names; use blind codes that are recorded in a secure place separate from the keys
- Require residents to sign a key receipt when they move in and to return all keys related to their occupancy when they move out
- Charge a deposit, such as $100, for keys or key fobs at move-in. If they are not returned at move-out, residents forfeit their deposit.

LEGAL ISSUE:
Check on local laws, because changing locks between residents may be required. Even if changing locks is not required by law, it is a good practice that should be a requirement of the property.

Lighting

Good lighting is essential both inside and outside the building to minimize safety risk. The following checklist provides lighting best practices.

CHECKLIST: LIGHTING

- □ Install lighting wherever people typically walk at night (walkways, parking lots, building entrances)
- □ Place lights so they make it difficult for intruders to hide in the shadows
- □ Check to make sure new hiding places have not been created when lights are on
- □ Install mirrors, windows and additional lighting to eliminate blind spots and increase visibility
- □ Change bulbs and clean fixtures regularly as lighting levels will change over time and light intensity diminishes as bulbs age and dirt accumulates on fixtures
- □ Keep trees and shrubbery properly trimmed to minimize shadows
- □ Use photo cells, timers, and motion detectors to turn lights on and off
  - o Reset timers at the change of seasons or after power failure
- □ Perform regular inspections to ensure that all lights work properly

TIPS:
Crime Prevention Through Environmental Design (CPTED) principles are meant to create safer environments and improve the quality of life through the study of how people tend to act in a given architectural environment. CPTED focuses on how the elements of the spaces in the multifamily property may contribute to or aid in the liability of risk. Refer to Figure 2-6 for sample CPTED principles.

FIGURE 2-6: SAMPLE CPTED PRINCIPLES

Natural Access Control

Balcony railings should never be a solid opaque material or more than 42 inches high, entrances into parking lots should be defined by landscaping, architectural design, or monitored by a guard, dead end spaces should be blocked by a fence or gate, access to the building should be limited to no more than two points, etc.

Natural Surveillance

Exterior doors should be visible from the street or by neighbors, doors that open to the outside should be well lit, visitor parking should be designated, recreation areas should be visible from a multitude of windows and doors, shrubbery should be no more than three feet high for clear visibility, etc.

Territorial Reinforcement

Property lines should be defined by landscaping or post and pillar fencing, building entrances should be accentuated by architectural elements, lighting and /or landscaping, etc.

Courtesy Patrols

Although using courtesy patrols (formerly referred to as *security guards*) to enhance safety is an option, some controversy exists over their use on residential properties.

One option is to subcontract to a courtesy patrol agency because an agency has the means to provide trained, licensed, and supervised personnel and backups.

Another option to consider is using off-duty police officers. One advantage is that they can make arrests. Discounted rent arrangements are often made with police officers who live on-site and serve as a security presence.

TIPS:
Once the property uses courtesy patrols, there is an implication to residents that courtesy patrols are part of what they receive in return for their rent. Canceling such a service raises issues of liability between landlord and resident.

When working with courtesy patrols, site managers should consider the following guidelines.

CHECKLIST: COURTESY PATROL GUIDELINES

- Fully screen and train courtesy patrols (extremely important)
- Provide close guidance and monitoring (present but not oppressive)
- Establish schedule to ensure that the entire property is patrolled and that predetermined locations are checked periodically
- Vary the routes and times of courtesy patrol movements
- Train courtesy patrols to know the layout of the property and the locations of system controls (e.g. shutoff valves, electrical junction boxes). Point out areas of concern and suggest things to look for.
- Ensure the courtesy patrols understand their role and responsibilities
- Provide courtesy patrols with a means of communicating with each other, as well as contact information for management staff, maintenance and repair personnel, and other emergency contacts
- Provide current list of residents and their apartment numbers to help courtesy patrols verify visitors to the property

Q. What is community policing?

A. Community policing, also known as community action policing or CAPS, is a growing trend in urban and suburban residential communities. It involves partnering with the police force to create foot patrols and increase communication between law enforcement and residents.

If the city/municipal government does not have a police/ community program established, residents may still take the initiative to establish a routine of scouts and inspections on activities in the community and share this information at weekly or monthly meetings.

Such programs give residents a sense of ownership in the community and may also strengthen the communication between residents and the management company.

Resident Education

Resident education and cooperation are important elements of safety and loss prevention. Site managers can have tremendous impact in this area due to their frequent interactions with residents:

- Offer programs that involve professional speakers (police officers or representatives of community groups). They can provide residents with timely information about personal safety and loss prevention.

- Provide safety information and tips in the resident newsletter

- Get involved with community watch programs and coordinate with local authorities on property and neighborhood safety initiatives

- Gather brochures and educational materials from agencies and authorities within a community (e.g. local fire departments usually have booklets designed for apartment residents)

- Review safety information during new resident orientation

- Include comprehensive information in the resident handbook.

CHECKLIST: RESIDENT HANDBOOK SAFETY ITEMS

- ☐ Maintain safe housekeeping practices (e.g. keep walkways clear, close cabinets when not in use, never block fire exits or fire equipment, clean-up spills and hazards immediately, etc.)
- ☐ Store cleaning supplies safely (e.g. away from furnace or other mechanicals, tightly closed and labeled, out of reach, etc.)
- ☐ Know the locations of fire extinguishers and emergency utility shutoffs
- ☐ Become familiar with emergency procedures and the property diagram of emergency exits (should be included)
- ☐ Post regular and emergency contact information for police, fire, poison control, utilities, and maintenance (should be included)
- ☐ Always close doors all the way and use deadbolts
- ☐ Always look through the peephole before answering your door
- ☐ Never let a stranger into the building
- ☐ Cancel all deliveries when you are going to be away
- ☐ Use timers to turn lights on and off when you are not at home
- ☐ Leave the radio on when you are gone for an extended period
- ☐ Follow and communicate appropriate guest behavior guidelines
- ☐ Don't use candles and incense
- ☐ Don't distribute alcohol to minors

Student Housing Impact: It may be effective to conduct a town hall meeting with your students in order to review resident education issues effectively. Consider inviting an attorney and a police officer to such a meeting in order to discuss the risk and severity of distributing alcohol to minors.

Staff Safety

Prevention is the most effective way to reduce safety risks for site staff. Following directions, using safety equipment, not taking shortcuts, and reporting problems as soon as they become evident are virtually cost-free ways of reducing risk. The following checklist provides additional methods to minimize staff safety risk.

CHECKLIST: STAFF SAFETY

☐ Train staff to prevent accidents
☐ Implement safety training programs. Occupational Safety and Health Administration (OSHA) at the federal level and some state laws require training, periodic safety inspections, and safety plans.
☐ Teach staff the differences between safe and unsafe work practices
☐ Train staff in the proper use of tools and equipment
☐ Insist on the use of safety equipment (e.g. goggles, gloves, etc.)
☐ Teach staff the proper handling and storage of cleaners, solvents, and other chemicals used on-site
☐ Bring in professionals from your workers' compensation insurance carrier (or state administrator's office) for injury prevention seminars
☐ Conduct regular safety inspections in work areas
☐ Have first aid supplies handy and know how to use them
☐ Make sure all contracts include safety and OSHA standards
☐ Ensure all contractors are properly attired while working on site

Site Office Safety

One of the site manager's major responsibilities is to safeguard the owner's funds and personal property. Fiscal problems can be averted by establishing policies and procedures for handling rent payments and other receipts. Many site offices now offer online payment options to facilitate rent payments, which brings additional safety and security considerations such as data security and technology issues. The following checklist provides strategies to help ensure safety in the site office.

CHECKLIST: SITE OFFICE SAFETY

☐ **Consider A No Cash Policy To Help Reduce Liability.** It's recommended to have a no cash policy (easier to get crime insurance). Encourage residents to pay rent via e-banking websites, direct withdrawal programs, money orders, or credit cards. Payment options can be required in the lease. Check local landlord eviction laws.
☐ **Endorse Checks Immediately And Deposit Them Daily.** Limit the number of people assigned responsibility for handling funds. Require written documentation of transactions (signed by the responsible employee, noting the date and time). This helps determine who is responsible if money is missing.
☐ **Always Give Numbered Receipts For All Money Collected.** Keep copies of receipts in the office to provide additional safeguards. The amounts indicated on the receipts should match the payments required on the respective leases and the amounts recorded in residents' ledgers, all of which should agree with the amount of money collected.

☐ **Records Are Another Issue At The Management Office.** The information contained in office records is personal and confidential, and the agency relationship specifies that the real estate manager is responsible for safeguarding it. If an intruder gains access to information about residents, serious liability issues can be raised, especially if an intruder harms a resident. Keep records in locked cabinets, and make copies of records and backups of software. Consider an alarm system monitored by a security company that will notify the police of a break-in at the management office.

Condominium Impact: Having consistent forms for administration, accounting, maintenance, and association information will guarantee the accuracy of information collection and retention. The records program should be ensure that state legal requirements are met when a unit is sold or refinanced, including file retention guidelines.

Each unit should have a unit file, either in electronic or hard-copy format, that documents relevant information and provides a record of ownership and correspondence between the owner and the Condominium. This will aid the administrative demands upon unit sale or refinancing.

Liability Risk

Residents, their guests, visitors to the property, vendors, and the general public may hold the property owner, the managing agent, and the staff liable for damage to personal property, injuries, or death related to the property and its operation. Such liability is inherent in the other types of risk discussed here.

Liability for injuries suffered at the property is one of the greatest concerns today. The property's liability insurance would financially shield the owner and any other named insured party if a lawsuit were filed. The liability of the managing agent (including the site manager) arises out of his or her involvement in the day-to-day operation of the property.

The following checklist provides tips to help reduce the risk of liability.

- □ Provide reasonable security
- □ Take safety precautions and plan ahead for emergencies to reduce the risk of responding inappropriately
- □ Create a sense of shared responsibility with residents.
- □ Work with an authorized representative to report all incidents to the insurance company as quickly and completely as possible
- □ Make written notes and take photographs at the time of the incident
- □ Records of prior inspections, maintenance, and repairs help prove reasonable care and lower liability risk and insurance premiums.
- □ Ensure use of premise clause in the lease to hold the resident, guests, or visitors to the property liable for property damage due to improper use of the premises, such as illegal substance use.

TIPS:
The risk of liability always exists. Reduce risk exposure by taking proper precautions.

Emergency Risk

Emergency situations may be encountered at any time. Examples of emergencies include fire, natural disasters (e.g., earthquake, hurricane, tornado), and human-caused situations such as criminal incidents, bomb threats, and civil disorders. Other emergencies that pose less serious risks include equipment breakdowns (e.g., lack of heat in the winter or air-conditioning in the summer) and elevator problems in a high-rise building.

TIPS:
In emergency situations, the site manager's primary duties are to protect the lives of residents, guests, and employees and to protect the owner's investment from further damage.

Factors that affect risk exposure and contribute to potential emergencies should be identified so they can be addressed appropriately. Some of these factors may include location, geography, climate, building code requirements, construction materials, availability of emergency support from within the community, and the resident profile of a particular building.

Fire Risks

Fire risks demand systematic preparation. Local ordinances dictate the nature and extent of directional signage and the display of the building address (for fire department access). Fire safety codes dictate the number and placement (location, height) of pull alarms, fire extinguishers, and fire hoses as well as requirements for smoke detectors and fire drills. Most jurisdictions mandate sprinkler systems in buildings over a certain size or height.

Construction materials determine the nature and extent of fire risk at a property. For example, masonry is much less susceptible to fire than frame construction. Some roofing materials may be petroleum-based, which makes them highly flammable and potentially more dangerous than other materials.

 Student Housing Impact: Students have many resources available to them when dealing with various risks. Managers should ensure their students are aware of the following resources:
- Counselor's Office
- Dean's Office
- Campus President
- Campus Safety Organization
- Campus Health Center

 RESOURCES:
Downloadable forms such as sample safety checklists can be found under Resources>Forms & Checklists at **www.irem.org** and are free for members. These sample forms and agreements are not endorsed by the Institute of Real Estate Management. They are presented for informational purposes only.

INSURANCE

Another strategy to minimize risk is the transfer of risk through insurance. *Insurance* is a system under which individuals and companies concerned about potential hazards pay premiums to an insurance company. In return, the insurance company reimburses policyholders (in whole or in part) in the event of a loss. In economic terms, insurance is a means of transferring risk from individuals to a larger group whose pooled funds (premiums) make the group better able to pay for losses experienced by individual members. While insurance does not prevent losses, it does offer financial protection against their consequences.

While site managers are not typically responsible for writing insurance specifications or purchasing insurance policies, the decisions they make on a daily basis affect insurance premiums and availability tremendously. Not only do site managers' decisions affect their own properties, they can also impact the cost and availability of premiums on all other properties insured under the policy as well. In order to meet the owner's goals and objectives and maximize income to the property, the site manager should understand basic insurance concepts and key touch points.

Example: Site Manager Impact

Consider a maintenance technician who cuts his finger stocking the supply room. It wasn't a big deal so the site manager doesn't document the incident. Six months later the same maintenance technician loses a finger conducting an inspection and it's a whole different ballgame now. With the first incident, the insurance company may have required the maintenance technician to see a doctor or sign off on the situation. These little decisions have the possibility to affect insurance and the bottom line in a big way.

Condominium Impact: For condominiums, the generic bare wall concept indicates that there is no responsibility to insure the unit inside the unfinished surfaces of the perimeter walls, floors, and ceilings. Responsibility for the interior of the unit is on the part of the individual unit owner. Note that state laws and the CC&Rs of the CID may stipulate the limits of liability for insurance policies.

TOP 10 INSURANCE CONCEPTS FOR SITE MANAGERS

1. **Liability Insurance** (also known as Casualty Insurance): Coverage that offers protection against claims that allege that a property owner's negligence or inappropriate action resulted in a bodily injury (e.g., resident slips and falls on wet surface and is injured) or property damage to another party (e.g., sprinkler system in hallway turned on suddenly and ruined a resident's couch).

2. **Property Insurance:** Includes coverage for accidental, direct physical loss to the property of the insured from any event that is not specifically excluded or limited (e.g., fire).

3. **Co-Insurance:** Requires the insured to maintain insurance at least equal to a stipulated percentage of the replacement cost of the property in order to collect partial losses in full. If insurance is less than required, the claim is reduced. A lower percentage equals higher risk.

4. **Replacement Cost Coverage:** Loss limit for which the owner sets the value and the insurance company agrees that the value is correct. Note that market value may not equal the replacement cost of the property.

5. **Actual Cash Value:** The value for which a property could be sold, which is always less than the replacement cost. Often used by insurance companies to determine the amount to be paid in the event of a loss.

6. **Use of Premise Clause:** Ensures use is for residential purposes only, and not, for example, a non-licensed childcare situation.

7. **Renters' Insurance:** The contents of residents' apartments are not covered under the owner's policies for the building, so residents are responsible for insuring their personal possessions. The lease should include a recommendation to obtain renters' insurance, and residents should initial that clause. Refer to tip below.

8. **Contractors and insurance:** Refer to checklist below.

9. **Cost and Coverage Comparison:** Particularly important for single-family home coverage.

10. **Typical Conventional and Tax Credit Insurance Policy Coverage should have fidelity bond crime and theft policies.**

TIPS:
Provide residents with information about sources for obtaining renters' insurance such as brochures or contact information for local agents.

Some management companies work with insurance agencies to create insurance packages that can be offered to renters at the time they sign their lease.

At some properties, renters can purchase insurance by signing a lease addendum and the premium can be paid along with the rent.

LEGAL ISSUE:
Check state laws for specific regulations related to renters' insurance, specifically the arrangement of paying renters' insurance premiums along with the rent. A license to sell insurance is often required.

CHECKLIST: CONTRACTORS AND INSURANCE

☐ Include an indemnification (hold harmless) clause is in the contract when independent contractors are hired to work at the property
☐ Ensure that the contractor is bonded as a guarantee of performance (surety) and provides a certificate of insurance
☐ Confirm that the certificate of insurance (Refer to Figure 2-7 below):
  o Lists the coverage carried and shows the property owner and the management company as additional named insured parties. An additional insured is a person, other than the named insured, who is protected by the terms of the policy. Real estate managers and building owners often ask to be named as additional insured parties; they are also asked to include others as insured parties for liability purposes.
  o Includes the limits of liability with sufficient amounts
  o Is provided directly by the insurance company to ensure they are up-to-date. Photocopied certificates or certificates that appear to have been altered are not acceptable.
  o Has at least one limit of liability for each type of insurance
☐ Check the expiration date of the rider and verify that the company is at least an AA rated insurer

FIGURE 2-7: SAMPLE VENDOR CERTIFICATE OF INSURANCE

ACORD

CHEMC-1 OP ID: AP

CERTIFICATE OF LIABILITY INSURANCE

DATE (MM/DD/YYYY) 11/05/2012

THIS CERTIFICATE IS ISSUED AS A MATTER OF INFORMATION ONLY AND CONFERS NO RIGHTS UPON THE CERTIFICATE HOLDER. THIS CERTIFICATE DOES NOT AFFIRMATIVELY OR NEGATIVELY AMEND, EXTEND OR ALTER THE COVERAGE AFFORDED BY THE POLICIES BELOW. THIS CERTIFICATE OF INSURANCE DOES NOT CONSTITUTE A CONTRACT BETWEEN THE ISSUING INSURER(S), AUTHORIZED REPRESENTATIVE OR PRODUCER, AND THE CERTIFICATE HOLDER.

IMPORTANT: If the certificate holder is an ADDITIONAL INSURED, the policy(ies) must be endorsed. If SUBROGATION IS WAIVED, subject to the terms and conditions of the policy, certain policies may require an endorsement. A statement on this certificate does not confer rights to the certificate holder in lieu of such endorsement(s).

PRODUCER Phone: 248-360-4100 Fax: 248-305-5154 360 Risk Management, Inc. 21500 Haggerty Rd Suite 140 Northville, MI 48167 Rebecca Virden	CONTACT NAME: PHONE (A/C, No, Ext): FAX (A/C, No): E-MAIL ADDRESS:
	INSURER(S) AFFORDING COVERAGE — NAIC # INSURER A : Citizens Insurance Co
INSURED One Way of Michigan Carpet Services Inc. 23730 Research Dr. Farmington Hills, MI 48334	INSURER B : INSURER C : INSURER D : INSURER E : INSURER F :

COVERAGES **CERTIFICATE NUMBER:** **REVISION NUMBER:**

THIS IS TO CERTIFY THAT THE POLICIES OF INSURANCE LISTED BELOW HAVE BEEN ISSUED TO THE INSURED NAMED ABOVE FOR THE POLICY PERIOD INDICATED. NOTWITHSTANDING ANY REQUIREMENT, TERM OR CONDITION OF ANY CONTRACT OR OTHER DOCUMENT WITH RESPECT TO WHICH THIS CERTIFICATE MAY BE ISSUED OR MAY PERTAIN, THE INSURANCE AFFORDED BY THE POLICIES DESCRIBED HEREIN IS SUBJECT TO ALL THE TERMS, EXCLUSIONS AND CONDITIONS OF SUCH POLICIES. LIMITS SHOWN MAY HAVE BEEN REDUCED BY PAID CLAIMS.

INSR LTR	TYPE OF INSURANCE	ADDL INSR	SUBR WVD	POLICY NUMBER	POLICY EFF (MM/DD/YYYY)	POLICY EXP (MM/DD/YYYY)	LIMITS	
A	GENERAL LIABILITY X COMMERCIAL GENERAL LIABILITY CLAIMS-MADE X OCCUR GEN'L AGGREGATE LIMIT APPLIES PER: POLICY PRO-JECT LOC	X		07B9345168	11/18/2012	11/15/2013	EACH OCCURRENCE DAMAGE TO RENTED PREMISES (Ea occurrence) MED EXP (Any one person) PERSONAL & ADV INJURY GENERAL AGGREGATE PRODUCTS - COMP/OP AGG	$ 1,000,000 $ 300,000 $ 5,000 $ 1,000,000 $ 2,000,000 $ 2,000,000 $
A	AUTOMOBILE LIABILITY X ANY AUTO ALL OWNED AUTOS SCHEDULED AUTOS X HIRED AUTOS X NON-OWNED AUTOS			ADB9339320	11/15/2012	11/15/2013	COMBINED SINGLE LIMIT (Ea accident) BODILY INJURY (Per person) BODILY INJURY (Per accident) PROPERTY DAMAGE (Per accident)	$ 1,000,000 $ $ $ $
A	X UMBRELLA LIAB X OCCUR EXCESS LIAB CLAIMS-MADE DED X RETENTION $			07B8345168	11/15/2012	11/15/2013	EACH OCCURRENCE AGGREGATE	$ 2,000,000 $ 2,000,000 $
A	WORKERS COMPENSATION AND EMPLOYERS' LIABILITY Y/N ANY PROPRIETOR/PARTNER/EXECUTIVE OFFICER/MEMBER EXCLUDED? (Mandatory in NH) If yes, describe under DESCRIPTION OF OPERATIONS below	N/A		WDB9344884	11/15/2012	11/15/2013	X WC STATU-TORY LIMITS OTH-ER E.L. EACH ACCIDENT E.L. DISEASE - EA EMPLOYEE E.L. DISEASE - POLICY LIMIT	 $ 500,000 $ 500,000 $ 500,000

DESCRIPTION OF OPERATIONS / LOCATIONS / VEHICLES (Attach ACORD 101, Additional Remarks Schedule, if more space is required)

Towers of Southfield and Wedgewood Properties are listed as Additional Insureds.

CERTIFICATE HOLDER	CANCELLATION
Towers of Southfield 20875 Lahser Southfield, MI 48033	SHOULD ANY OF THE ABOVE DESCRIBED POLICIES BE CANCELLED BEFORE THE EXPIRATION DATE THEREOF, NOTICE WILL BE DELIVERED IN ACCORDANCE WITH THE POLICY PROVISIONS. AUTHORIZED REPRESENTATIVE

Source: Sheila Austin, CPM®

Q. What causes insurance policies to be cancelled or not renewed?

A. All insurance policies contain a description of the circumstances under which the insurer may cancel the policy. Examples include failure to pay the premiums, failure to remedy an identified hazard, new risk factors, environmental risks (e.g. hurricanes), filing many small claims or one large claim, and the presence of deferred maintenance. Check state laws for additional cancellation reasons. Site managers play a primary role in managing risk at the property. Typical on-site activities have the potential to affect insurance policy coverage as well as the bottom line.

RESOURCES:
Tutorials can be found under Education>On-Demand Learning>Tutorials at *www.irem.org* and are free.

INCIDENT MANAGEMENT

Even with all the precautionary measures a site manager may take, incidents will occur. It is important for site management staff to report all incidents to their authorized representative, taking care to be as thorough as possible by identifying who, what, when, and where.

An authorized representative should take the following steps in reporting an incident to an insurer.

- **Complete an Incident Report:** An internal report should be kept on file at the property, and should be completed as thoroughly as possible. Refer to Figure 2-8 for a sample incident report form.

- **Report to the Insurance Company:** A report should be sent to the insurance company as FYI in case of a future lawsuit, especially when dealing with a Workers' Compensation Claim because very tight deadlines apply. Even if the employee is late in reporting the incident, the manager should report it immediately.

- **File a Claim:** A claim may be submitted to the insurance company reporting a loss and filing a claim for money. Sometimes a filed claim results in an insurance company inspection of the property.

Affordable Housing Impact: Keep track of invoices and/or repair costs associated with a claim, as requirements vary depending on the specific Affordable Housing program. Track them separately and keep copies on file in the site office.

TIPS:
Failure to report incidents may shift liability to the owner or the management company. An injured party may claim injury or seek monetary damages long after the actual event. If it is revealed that the manager had knowledge of the incident but failed to report it to the insurance company at the time, the duties and obligations of the policyholder may have been breached.

Reporting a Loss

Proper handling of incidents will make filing a claim with the insurance company easier and more successful. The following checklist covers steps to follow in the event of injury or property damage.

CHECKLIST: REPORTING A LOSS

In the event of injury or property damage:
- ☐ Ensure immediate aid is given to any injured person or people
- ☐ Call emergency personnel for assistance
- ☐ Report a crime to the police, and let them take any necessary statements for the police report
- ☐ Obtain the names and addresses of people involved and any witnesses. Write down the name of everyone you see at the site of the loss in case you need to contact them later. Capture who, what, where, how, why.
- ☐ Make any temporary repairs to protect the property from further damage or people from additional injuries. Several restoration companies exist that can handle any form of safeguards 24 hours a day, 7 days a week, and 365 days a year.
- ☐ Have authorized representative as specifically designated by Management Company call the insurance company. Check policy for requirements about reporting a loss. Some policies have time limits to file claims.
- ☐ Do not discuss the incident with anyone other than your insurance representative or attorney
- ☐ Arrange for a claims adjuster to inspect the property
- ☐ Prepare a list of lost or damaged articles. Include diagrams and/or photographs if possible
- ☐ File a signed and sworn Proof of Loss form

FIGURE 2-8: SAMPLE INCIDENT REPORT FORM

Date of Report:_____   Date of Incident:_____   Time:_____am / pm

Property:_____   Weather Condition:_____
  (do not abbreviate)

Property Address _____
  Street / City / State / Zip Code

Type of Incident: Criminal   Potential/Injury   Water Damage   Other Damage
  (circle one or more & mark out the rest)

(In the event of an injury, notify the Risk Admin. immediately via tele. and the Pres. & EVP via e-mail)
Crime Alert *(Circle one)*   has been   will be   will not be   sent.

If you circled "will not be" explain why: _____

Name of Injured Party: _____

(Circle one)   Resident   Homeowner Occupant   Guest   Unknown

Injured Party Address: _____
  Street / City / State / Zip Code

Occupant/Resident Name(s) _____

Occupant/Resident Address _____
  Street / City / State / Zip Code

Occupant/Resident Phone Number: (h) _____ (w) _____

Location where incident occurred _____

List the unit numbers, occupants/owners of other units damaged; *if water damage, note size of area affected*
_____

Name of Any Witness _____

Witness Address   _____
  Street / City / State / Zip Code

Witness Phone Numbers :(h) _____ (w) _____

Police Report # *(attach copy also)*: _____

Claimant/Witness statement attached? *(Circle one)*   YES   NO

Name of person taking report: _____ Phone Number: _____

Original pictures: *(Circle one)*   attached   will follow

Manager's signature *(if available)*: _____

==

Corporate Use Only

Date received: Copy/Fax _____ Original _____

Insurance Agent: Notified On:

_____Record Only_____Insurance Claim_____R. Adm_____Pres_____EVP._____RM

Incident Report for Resident Injury or Property Damage

Description of what happened (Detail who, what, when, how.)
_____
_____

Police Report (Get officer's name and badge #.)
_____

Do any other witnesses have additional information regarding the incident? If so, list the witness
names and additional information. _____
_____

Action taken in response to the condition. _____
_____

Comments _____

EMERGENCY AND DISASTER PLANNING

Planning for emergencies and disasters is little different from planning for safety. However, the key is to plan and prepare responses to emergencies before they happen.

RESOURCES:
IREM® publishes publishes a comprehensive book entitled, *Before Disaster Strikes: Developing an Emergency Procedures Manual,* Fourth Edition. This book provides information and guidelines to assist real estate managers in developing emergency plans and emergency procedures manuals for their properties

The following excerpts are from the IREM® publication, *Before Disaster Strikes: Developing an Emergency Procedures Manual,* Fourth Edition (IREM® Copyright 2012).

Emergency Response Team
It is good practice to form an emergency response team to carry out the emergency plan and take immediate action to assist occupants, lead them to safety, and help secure the property. The size of the team will depend on the size and staffing of the property.

The Resident Profile
Emergency procedures for a residential property must take into account the resident profile. Refer to Figure 2-9 for questions to ask about residents for emergency planning purposes.

Emergency Procedures
Refer to Figure 2-10 for the general components of an emergency procedures manual.

Emergency Support Team
The emergency plan should also identify a support team that comprises certain specialists who may be called on for backup assistance. Refer to the following checklist for a list of potential team members.

Emergency Kit
Having the proper tools and equipment ready and available in an emergency can save property and lives. Equipment should be specifically designed for emergencies and should be capable of handling the size of the building and the number of residents. Include industrial flashlights and batteries, first aid supplies and instructions, blankets and fresh water, communication devices, rope, shovels, and a ladder. Other items should be added as the need is determined. Refer to Figure 2-11 for sample contents of an emergency first aid kit.

FIGURE 2-9: THE RESIDENT PROFILE

- What are their ages? What is the overall age range? How many are elderly?

- Are there small children—infants and toddlers? Teenagers? How many in each age group? Which units do they occupy? Are the children alone during the day or evening? Can their parents be reached in an emergency?

- Are any residents disabled? What is the type/extent of the disability? Do they have assistive animals?

- Do any residents have skills that may be helpful in an emergency situation? Are any residents trained firefighters, police officers, military, or National Guard members?

FIGURE 2-10: EMERGENCY PROCEDURES

1. Reference information

- An extensive, updated list of phone numbers (e.g., team members, management, owner, emergency assistance, restoration, etc.)

- An up-to-date list of phone numbers of all occupants and any needs

- Designated spokesperson to provide information to the media and examples of news release formats

- A general one-page description of the building's statistics (e.g., ownership, occupancy, age, construction materials, plans and specifications, mechanical systems, and equipment that is available)

- A list of the building's current safety features and equipment, their locations and operating instructions (e.g., fire extinguishers, alarms) along with other supplies available onsite (e.g., first aid kit, medical supplies) including quantities and where they are stored

- Floor plans and as-built drawings that show all equipment, systems, and exits to which access may be needed during an emergency

- Insurance information, including the insurance agent's name, business and after-hours phone numbers. Document the type of insurance coverage, policy number, and name of carrier for each policy. Create a current inventory of property possessions.

- The material data safety sheet (MSDS) that lists any hazardous materials or chemicals on the property and where they are stored

FIGURE 2-10: EMERGENCY PROCEDURES (CONTINUED)

2. Directions for the management staff to follow for each possible emergency

- Detailed descriptions of the duties of the emergency management team during the emergency
- A flow chart depicting the chain of command during the emergency
- The person(s) responsible for communicating with the media and with emergency responders
- A copy of the emergency public announcement for the particular emergency
- Procedures to account for all management personnel and residents
- Procedures for notifying families of management employees about the status of personnel on the premises
- Evacuation and re-entry procedures as they apply to each emergency
- Reporting, documentation, and regulatory procedures as they apply to each emergency
- Restoration procedures

3. Directions for building occupants

- Communicate how residents will be notified of an emergency, how they can identify members of the emergency management team, and directions for evacuating residential units
- Post emergency directions prominently throughout the property
- Promote safety guidelines from police, fire officials, and others in a newsletter directed to occupants (e.g., holiday safety tips, reminders to drive and walk carefully on icy surfaces in winter, keeping doorways, corridors, and hallways clear of obstacles)
- Create emergency guide for occupants that includes information such as evacuation directions and procedures, recommended assembly areas, consideration for pets, proper use of appliances, list of safety precautions to take in various emergencies, and so forth.

The emergency support team may include some or all of the following:

- Contractors and suppliers, including electricians, plumbers, elevator and HVAC contractors, board-up services, and glass companies
- Disaster recovery contractors specifically trained and equipped to minimize loss and fast-track restoration of the building and contents
- Building's architect; structural, mechanical, and electrical engineers
- Utility company representatives
- Police and fire department representatives, possibly including hazardous materials and bomb/arson specialists
- Representatives from the local building department
- Contract security services
- Representatives from the property's insurance company
- Attorneys for the property owner and manager
- Resident representatives
- Government and charitable agencies
- A consultant or representative from a disaster restoration firm
- A professional public relations representative
- A representative of the firm whose communication systems and equipment are used in the building
- The on-site staff of adjacent properties

FIGURE 2-11: CONTENTS OF AN EMERGENCY FIRST AID KIT

Taken from *Before Disaster Strikes, Developing an Emergency Procedures Manual*, Fourth Edition

- Sterile adhesive bandages in various sizes
- Sterile gauze pads (2" and 4")
- Sterile roll bandages (2" and 3")
- Latex gloves
- Triangular (cloth) bandages for slings
- Splints
- Scissors
- Tweezers
- Adhesive tape
- Safety pins (assorted sizes)
- Soap or other cleansing agent
- Betadine microbicide (liquid or packaged swabs or wipes)
- Antiseptic solution
- Rubbing alcohol
- Moist towelettes
- Antiseptic wipes
- Cotton balls and cotton swabs
- Thermometer
- Tongue depressors

FIGURE 2-11: CONTENTS OF AN EMERGENCY FIRST AID KIT
(CONTINUED)

- Petroleum jelly or other lubricant
- Aspirin or nonaspirin pain relievers
- Antidiarrheal medication
- Syrup of ipecac or other recommended emetic
- Phone number for poison control
- Activated charcoal
- Chemical cold packs
- Chemical hot packs
- Thermal blankets
- Bloodborne pathogens kit

Eye drops or eye wash and treatment for burns may be appropriate additions; consult a pharmacist or physician for recommendations. Also, preparation for specific emergencies may reveal other items to add to a first aid kit. Prepackaged first aid kits can be purchased, but they often need to be supplemented with specific components and to ensure adequate quantities of bandages and other items. A physician or pharmacist may be able to advise about specific quantities of materials to stockpile. To protect first aid items from dust and contamination, storage in a portable, sealable box or container is advisable.

Guidelines for creating a first aid kit can be found on the American Red Cross Web site at **www.redcross.org** or the FEMA Website **www.fema. gov**. The guidelines may only be part of preparations to address specific types of emergencies.

Several companies have developed bloodborne pathogen kits that include absorbent materials, personal protective equipment, waste disposal bags and labels, and other items to facilitate proper cleanup and disposal of spilled blood or body fluids.

While a comprehensive emergency and disaster plan reduces the threat of emergencies, there's only so much that can be done ahead of time. Once a disaster strikes, it is critical to reduce further risk through control and mitigation of recovery operations.

The following excerpts are also from the IREM® publication, *Before Disaster Strikes: Developing an Emergency Procedures Manual*, Fourth Edition (IREM® Copyright 2012).

To keep things running smoothly throughout the recovery process:

- Focus on the safety and health of employees and residents
- Contact disaster contractor and additional resources as needed
- Make any temporary repairs to protect the property from further damage or people from additional injuries
- Implement business continuity strategies for recovery and resumption of normal business operations (e.g., backup operations site, data recovery, and so forth)
- Communicate with employees and residents. Note that Twitter is an effective tool for real time communication because of its SMS/text abilities in the event of disrupted internet and phone service.
- Depending on the emergency or disaster, provide resources and tips to residents (e.g., tips for food safety guidelines during a power outage, resources on preparing for tornados or hurricanes, etc.)
- When dealing with the media, direct inquiries to a designated spokesperson
- Offer supplies of flashlights, batteries, bottled water, and so forth
- Keep battery-powered radio available to listen to emergency updates and news reports
- Work with authorized representative to contact insurance company. Check your policy for requirements about reporting a loss. Some policies have time limits to file claims. Work with your representative on next steps (e.g., claims adjuster inspection, signed Proof of Loss form, and so forth).
- Complete initial incident report that captures the period immediately before and after the loss. Take photographs or video.
- Create a log to track expenses including cash, purchase orders, credit card charges, and contracts
- Log the contractors and identify the scope of their work
- Continue written and photographic record from inception through the completion of the emergency or mitigation services
- Review and update emergency plan

Q&A

Q. What is the site manager's role in an emergency?

A. The IREM® publication, *Before Disaster Strikes: Developing an Emergency Procedures Manual,* Fourth Edition (IREM® Copyright 2012) states the following:

It may be advantageous to alter the normal chain of command and appoint the site manager, rather than the real estate manager as the "team leader." The site manager is more familiar with the residents, vendors, contractors, and other people involved in the daily operation of the property.

The real estate manager's role should be one of oversight, allowing the site manager to direct the emergency response. If the site manager is to have primary responsibility for overseeing emergency procedures, they should be involved in developing those procedures and trained to implement them.

TIPS:
All media inquiries should be directed to the designated spokesperson, and statements such as "no comments," should be avoided.

RESOURCES:
Additional resources for information on developing an emergency and disaster plan include:
· Federal Emergency Management Agency (FEMA):
 www.fema.gov, www.ready.gov
· American Red Cross: **www.redcross.org**
· Occupational Safety and Health Administration (OSHA):
 www.osha.gov

RESOURCES:
Tutorials such *Developing an Emergency Plan* can be found under Education>On-Demand Learning>Tutorials at **www.irem. org** and are free.

CHAPTER 3:
INVENTORY AND SUPPLIERS

Real estate managers provide the best value for the property by controlling the ordering, purchasing and inventorying of supplies and equipment. A manager must be able to implement a process for purchasing supplies and equipment, and an effective system of receiving and inventorying items to control costs.

In this chapter:

- **Purchasing Decisions**
- **Inventory Control and Storage**

PURCHASING DECISIONS

Most companies have a par stock (inventory levels that are restored Maintenance workers accomplish their work more efficiently if the property purchases and maintains an inventory of commonly used supplies and frequently needed parts.

Most companies have a *par stock* (inventory levels that are restored each time an order is placed), and they use approved vendors. Those two strategies significantly streamline the purchasing and inventory process.

TIPS:
It is important to understand the ordering and inventory process, even if it is not a part of your job. The amount of materials used can have a significant impact on a property's NOI.

Purchasing Assessment

Managers typically assess purchasing decisions during the annual budgeting process:

- Assess history and age of equipment and supplies
- Consider repair vs. replacement
- Identify average use and needs
- Assess the availability of parts in the local market
- Keep a supply of parts that are time-consuming to procure
- Buy in quantity when possible—use standardized colors, floor coverings, and light fixtures
- Research knowledgeable vendors
- Assess quality and quantity
- When purchasing chemicals, follow all health and safety guidelines,

ensure that Material Safety Data Sheets are available, and consider employee training on proper handling and storage procedures

Suppliers

Different types of suppliers present varying advantages and disadvantages:

- **Discount/Warehouse Supply Stores:** These large stores (Home Depot, Lowes, etc.) carry a wide variety of goods at competitive prices. A manager can often purchase supplies in bulk and avoid time-consuming extra purchasing trips and delays.
- **Internet:** Ordering online is an increasingly easy and effective way to compare prices from a variety of vendors and to purchase supplies.
- **Specialty Supply Companies:** Plumbing, electrical, and other specialty suppliers provide a wider selection and inventory of specialty items. They often carry hard-to-find discontinued products from other suppliers. Buying in bulk or setting up an account can help the real estate manager secure the best price.

Sustainability Impact: *Environmentally Preferable Purchasing (EPP)* refers to purchasing materials and supplies that contribute to a property's sustainability goals. The materials and supplies should have less impact on human health and the environment than standard alternatives. Items should be assessed for their environmental and financial benefits. For more information, see **www.epa.gov/epp** and IREM® course "Sustainable Real Estate Management" (SRM001).

INVENTORY CONTROL AND STORAGE

Establish Inventory System

An additional means of controlling costs is using a system to verify inventory levels and track the frequency with which items are restocked. Many types of software and Web sites are available for inventory control. These systems issue maintenance work orders (both for scheduled preventive maintenance and for requested repairs) and keep a variety of data regarding the costs associated with property maintenance. The use of barcodes or QR codes can help reduce inventory loss.

Just implementing a regular system of inventory control can be enough to discourage petty theft on a property. When staff see that materials are being accounted for they are less likely to remove items for personal use.

Whether it uses a simple checklist or a computer database program, an inventory system is a cost-control measure that a real estate manager should implement as part of the purchasing program.

Establish Storage System

Another element of a well-managed maintenance plan is an effective system for inventory storage. The following are guidelines for effective inventory storage:

- **Locate storage room(s) conveniently.** Avoid using a vacant unit for storage. Renting the unit and purchasing storage sheds is more cost-efficient.

- **Provide adequate shelving and storage space** to accommodate all supplies so they are easily found, organized, and maintained damage free

- **Mark boxes or storage containers clearly.** This will help prevent waste and increase safety. Use of a painted silhouette of each piece of equipment behind its proper storage position can help facilitate storage and organization.

- **Distribute chemicals only in proper containers** that are correctly marked as prescribed by OSHA and that are labeled as follows: product name, chemical content, product use, instructions for use, dilution instructions, and hazard warnings. Never rebottle chemicals.

- **Keep the storage room locked and limit access** to discourage theft. Develop a sign-out system or log to monitor usage. Or consider an alarm system for which each employee has an access code number, especially for areas used to store high-dollar volumes of equipment, supplies, and tools. Entry after business hours can be monitored by the alarm security system.

- **Shelve new items behind old.** Use date codes for items with limited shelf life

- **Record new purchases** along with the purchase order number and vendor for reference

- **Note the service request numbers** as items are removed to fulfill service requests in order to trace faulty parts

Manage the Maintenance Shop

If your property has a maintenance shop on-site, it is important to manage it as effectively as you do the rest of the property. The maintenance shop is often the real estate manager's weakest area of administration. Many managers who have limited knowledge of maintenance issues tend to defer all decisions to the maintenance supervisor. If the maintenance supervisor is not well organized, the result will be a poorly organized shop. Many managers may accept this situation as a necessary trade-off. Unfortunately, that is usually detrimental to the property's operations. The manager should take an active role in making sure the maintenance shop is organized, clean, and safe.

To help ensure an effective maintenance shop, visit other buildings in the area. Study the organization of their maintenance shops and the systems they use to track tools and supplies.

Single Family Home Impact: Since single family homes are on scattered sites and don't have onsite maintenance shops, contractors are used extensively. See Chapter 4 for more information on working with contractors.

Inventory the Shop

Before any meaningful change can take place, the shop's contents must be reviewed to determine which items should be discarded and which should be recorded in inventory. One inexpensive and effective method for quickly inventorying supplies and equipment is the "tag and tear" system. In this method, inventory items are counted and the information is recorded on two sections of a perforated card. Then the card is attached to the specific inventory item or container (tag) and the perforated copy is removed (tear). This system works best when you have one person to tag the items and another to collect the copies. The information from the cards is tabulated at the site office and entered into the system or maintained by hand.

Maintain a Clean Shop

Cleanliness is important for safety as well as for cosmetic reasons. A clean maintenance shop projects a positive image, which helps improve employee morale.

CHECKLIST: MAINTAINING A CLEAN SHOP

☐ Sweep and mop floors once a week
☐ Wipe down shelves periodically
☐ Make sure containers are properly closed. (Open containers of oil-based paint and other combustible liquids can be fire hazards, which threatens the health and safety of all employees and pose a liability risk for management and the property owner.)
☐ Store chemicals and flammables in a locked cabinet with signage posted to promote safety and avoid liability
☐ Display posters that give safety tips around the maintenance shop

---

Use Material Safety Data Sheets

Managers, as well as the maintenance staff, need to know how to read Material Safety Data Sheets so they are aware of potential hazards. A *Material Safety Data Sheet* (MSDS) is an informational document that outlines the specific characteristics of a substance and includes specific information about such potential hazards as flammability, explosion potential, toxicity, and other health hazards.

The real estate manager or the maintenance supervisor must post MSDS information to make employees aware of spill and leak procedures, recommended protective devices, and special precautions. The manufacturer is responsible for preparing the MSDS and making it available to those who use the product. Each time a new product is purchased, a new MSDS document must be posted. Personnel who will handle or work directly with the product should read all product hazard information and safety recommendations before using the product. Maintaining MSDS forms is a federally mandated OSHA requirement and is subject to unannounced OSHA inspections.

NOTES:

Refer to **Appendix C** for a sample Material Safety Data Sheet (MSDS)

CHAPTER 4:
WORKING WITH CONTRACTORS

Selecting and overseeing the work of contractors helps to control costs and ensures the work is performed to specifications. A manager must understand when to use contract labor, and how to develop an effective bidding process, including well-written contract specifications.

In this chapter:

- **Site Employees vs. Contract Workers**
- **Contract Specifications**
- **The Bidding Process**
- **The Maintenance Contract**
- **Monitoring a Contractor's Work**

SITE EMPLOYEES VS. CONTRACT WORKERS

Labor constitutes 80 percent of total maintenance costs. Therefore, the real estate manager must ensure proper employee selection as well as supervision, scheduling, and training of maintenance employees. The size of the maintenance staff and the skills needed to perform specific tasks will determine the most appropriate approach to maintenance.

Hiring contractors to perform certain work or to provide certain services and/ or products is often necessary. The choice between using site employees and contracting for maintenance services will depend on many factors. Conducting a work assessment can help clarify specific job requirements in order to determine the best use of resources. A work assessment considers the following:

- Length of job
- Timing of each task
- Skill requirements (specialized training, licensing, or certification)
- Equipment requirements (specialized tools or parts)

Once the specific job requirements are defined, the real estate manager should support a decision to hire a contractor with a cost benefit analysis. A *cost benefit analysis* is a technique designed to determine the feasibility of a project or plan by quantifying its costs and benefits. In this case, a cost benefit analysis will weigh the cost associated with hiring a contractor against the benefit of having the contractor perform the work.

□ A staff shortage exists due to vacation, illness, or unfilled positions

□ Staff does not have the necessary skills, such as HVAC or elevator maintenance

□ The work requires special equipment or materials

□ The work requires licensed technicians, such as plumbing or electrical work

□ The total in-house cost of a project, including licensing fees, special insurance, and payroll administration, is not cost-effective, and a contractor can handle it more efficiently

□ Training staff members and purchasing equipment would be more expensive than hiring a contractor

□ Some materials and supplies may not be available locally

Types of Maintenance That May Require Contractors

Management companies frequently have policies regarding specific types of jobs that are always, sometimes, or never awarded to contractors. Whenever possible, contracts should stipulate "caps"—limits for time and material that are not to be exceeded. Outside maintenance services are commonly used due to the complexity of equipment, the specialization and expense of the repair and maintenance tools, and/or the special licenses required. The real estate manager may hire some contractors on a retainer basis and others only as needed. Additionally, situations may arise when hiring a technical expert in the field may be appropriate. The manager may hire engineers or architects due to structural requirements or the need for highly specialized and licensed skills.

Situations when hiring contractors or other specialized experts might be appropriate include:

- Heating, ventilation, and air conditioning (HVAC) repair or replacement
- Swimming pool cleaning or repair
- Plumbing
- Security
- Waste disposal (trash removal/recycling pickup)
- Snow removal
- Extermination (pest control)
- Parking lot patching and striping
- Major landscaping
- Laundry facilities
- Janitorial
- Carpet shampooing
- Unit reconditioning (vacant)

- Complete rehab or renovation
- Large capital improvements
- Electrical rewiring
- Lead paint removal
- Mold removal
- High-rise exterior window washing
- Exterior work, including painting, tuck pointing, balcony maintenance, etc.
- Elevator repairs, renovations or updates

<table>
<tr><td></td><td>Single Family House Impact: Note that contractors are used extensively in single family house management.</td></tr>
</table>

<table>
<tr><td></td><td>Sustainability Impact: Properties with ambitious sustainability goals related to the reduction of energy, water, and material use, as well as improvement of indoor air quality, will require the use of contractors and consultants with experience, and preferably certification, in their fields of expertise. For instance, retrofitting lighting with compact fluorescent lamps (CFLs) may be accomplished cheaply and with regular maintenance staff, but a more advanced project such as solar water heating should be assessed for its financial viability and installed by qualified technicians. Even with these additional contractors, many sustainable systems can provide financial benefits through lower operating expenses—the system just has to be right for the specific property.</td></tr>
</table>

Advantages of Using Contract Workers

- **Workload:** Site staff already have full workloads
- **Re-allocate staff:** Hiring contractors may allow the real estate manager to make better use of staff skills
- **Specialization:** A contractor has more specialized workers
- **Insurance:** A contractor has insurance that is more specific
- **Licensing:** The job requires specific licensing from local, state, and/or federal agencies
- **Technical Expertise:** A contractor's greater technical expertise may translate into greater efficiency and lower costs
- **Warranties:** Equipment service not performed by a certified contractor may void warranties or insurance coverage
- **Payroll:** The contractor deals with the details of payroll, union negotiations, and training
- **Monitoring Work:** The contractor handles scheduling and monitoring of work

- **Parts:** The contractor often can purchase parts or supplies more efficiently and more economically

Disadvantages of Using Contract Workers

- **Cost:** Contractors frequently charge high hourly rates; they may also mark up the cost of parts and supplies that could be purchased directly for less

- **Quality of Work:** Monitoring and ensuring that the contracted job is done right the first time can be difficult

- **Corrections or Changes:** If follow-up work is required, getting a contractor to correct problems can be difficult

- **Scheduling:** A contractor's schedule may not be optimal for your property. In addition, if the job was awarded at an agreed price that is low, the contractor may not be motivated to stay on schedule

- **Flexibility:** Contractors may not be as flexible in meeting changing conditions at the property

- **Personnel:** Selection and direction of personnel are not under the manager's control

The decision to use outside contractors requires careful consideration. The manager must review the advantages and disadvantages when determining what is best for the property.

CONTRACT SPECIFICATIONS

When the real estate manager has made the decision to contract a service, he or she must complete a contract specification that details the work required. These specifications are then incorporated into a *Request for Proposal (RFP)* or *Invitation to Bid.*

The Request for Proposal is a document that is provided to qualified contractors requesting that they bid on a job according to the specifications outlined. Contractors are asked to include an estimate of time and costs for materials and labor or to quote a fee for a period or for each time a service is provided.

The more information about the project that is provided, the better the resulting bids will be. With more information, contractors can prepare more accurate bids for the required work. A well-written specification often becomes part of the actual contract.

In addition to specific contract specifications, the Request for Proposal or Invitation to Bid should require that contractors complete a cost breakdown analysis that lists labor and materials separately. This helps compare bids from different contractors using the same service and line items. Also, stating that alternative proposals are acceptable only if they are additional to a bid that follows your specifications and if they are priced separately will help ensure that all bids can be compared appropriately.

Items to include in contract specifications:

- Detailed description of the work expected, its duration, and the timing of its performance and completion (include start and end time each day)
- Description of the preparation work (e.g., demolition and removal of old materials)
- Requirement for contractor to clean up the site when all work is completed
- Details about the ownership, removal, and disposal of old material
- Description of the specific materials to use (and who supplies them), acceptable material substitutions, temporary storage of materials, and final approval of substitutions (i.e., brand of paint, its color, flat or gloss, where painters are to use rollers, airless or other spray application, and brushes)
- Type of equipment to be used (and who provides it)
- Building standard specifications (e.g., same ceiling grid, lock set, door type)
- Applicable OSHA requirements
- Explanation of how repairs and/or replacements will be made should additional problems occur during contracted work
- Required licenses, permits, and insurance as well as the person responsible for obtaining them
- Terms of payment, including submission, lien releases, permits, retention, etc.
- Maximum amount the work can cost (i.e., a "cap")
- Behavior of contract workers and the safety equipment required
- Hours work is permitted on-site, including the days of the week
- Requirements for listing an additional insured

THE BIDDING PROCESS

While the site manager may not write the RFP, it is important to understand the bidding process as it is often the site manager who meets with contractors, answers questions, and collects the bids.

Establishing Procedures

Procedures for a bidding process should be part of the property's policies and/ or management plan. Having a written procedure and following it precisely is a good management practice, especially if any legal action is needed or taken. Refer to Figure 4-1 for a sample.

FIGURE 4-1: SAMPLE BIDDING PROCESS POLICIES AND PROCEDURES

- Decide a minimum dollar threshold before requesting bids
- Give all bidders equal consideration
- Neither management nor staff will accept personal gifts or gratuities from current or potential bidders
- All bids will be kept confidential
- Bids must meet bid requirements
- Bids must respond to and meet all specifications
- Bids must be submitted during the specified time limit
- Bids must be complete and signed
- The company will issue a contract or purchase order before a contractor may begin work or provide a service or product
- A performance bond, provided by the contractor, may be required for all contracts in excess of a fixed amount. The performance security required may depend on the type of bid and dollar amount of the contract. Types of bid securities include surety bonds, irrevocable letters of credit, and cashier's checks or officer's certified checks.
- Contractors are required to have Certificates of Insurance for general liability, automobile coverage, and workers' compensation
- Contractors will be notified by telephone or letter about bid acceptance

Evaluating Bids

All bids received should be based on the specifications provided so they are truly comparable. A 20 percent or greater difference in price range is typical. A bid outside that range suggests that the contractor has made a mistake, has purposely bid out of the job, or has come up with a creative alternative.

Remember the lowest bid may not always be the best. A low bid may be the result of a contractor's lack of experience in estimating job costs. The contractor may not be able to carry out promises made on the level of income requested. Be certain the contractors will not water down paint, shorten the life of the equipment, or impair its effective performance by not attending to it with sufficient frequency.

It is important to decide on evaluation criteria and priorities such as quality, time frame, price, or reliability. One suggestion for evaluating bids is to conduct a preliminary screening of potential contractors and choose at least three who seem most qualified. Having at least three contractors submit written bids allows a choice based on the predefined priorities and helps provide the best quality service at the lowest possible cost. Note the following considerations when evaluating bids:

CHECKLIST: EVALUATING BIDS

- ☐ Check industry statistics to determine if the prices given in the bid are within the range normally charged for this type of work or service
- ☐ Request references and investigate business history
- ☐ Check the principal's creditworthiness through references and credit bureaus
- ☐ Check whether the company pays subcontractors and suppliers in a timely fashion
- ☐ Speak with a recent or current client of the contractor
- ☐ Inspect jobs in progress or finished jobs at other sites
- ☐ Investigate the knowledge, training, and ability of the people who will work on your property. Refer to Figure 4-2 for sample questions.
- ☐ Verify that the contractor employs people legally eligible to work in the country
- ☐ Determine employee turnover
- ☐ Ensure that the contractor has the staff available to complete the work, even if you have worked with the company before
- ☐ Consult other property managers and people with related experience with such contractors
- ☐ Compare details such as insurance coverage and warranties
- ☐ Compare the contractor's ability to estimate costs through its cost breakdowns. Consider what credits are allowed for work not required or visits not needed (such as fewer snow removal days because of a mild winter). Did the contractor have add-ons or change orders due to inadequate scope of the job?
- ☐ Learn whether the contractor starts and finishes jobs on a timely basis
- ☐ Develop a spreadsheet to ensure an "apples-to-apples" comparison of costs and scopes of work. The information documented will identify areas of a bid that are lacking, thereby, prompting the property manager to obtain additional information for comparison purposes.

When requesting information from a contractor's reference, use the following questions to solicit comments that will provide you with an idea of the contractor's business ethics and attitude toward customers.

- Do they follow through on promises or do they overpromise and under-deliver?
- How quickly do they respond to problems or changes? Do they deliver on time?
- What is the attitude of the contractor's employees toward problems? Toward the property? Toward residents?
- If problems occurred, did the contractor resolve them to your satisfaction?
- If warranty work needed to be performed, did the contractor respond in a timely fashion and to your satisfaction?
- Would you hire this contractor again? Why or why not?
- How much of the work was performed by the contractor's employees and how much by subcontractors?
- Do they pay their subcontractors and supply houses in a timely manner?
- Do they have adequate support staff for supervisors to monitor the work?

THE MAINTENANCE CONTRACT

After the real estate manager has carefully decided on a contractor to perform a job, creation of a documented contract is imperative. The maintenance contract should provide the manager with a known price, detailed specifications, cancellation rights, and insurance protection to ensure the maintenance work is performed correctly, in a timely fashion, and at little risk to the owner. A contract may take several forms, including the following:

- Signed copy of the bid
- Signed and initialed set of specifications
- Purchase order
- Service agreement
- American Institute of Architects (AIA) short form

All nontechnical maintenance, such as custodial service, snow removal, or parking lot sweeping, can be negotiated on a standard maintenance contract. The manager should have an attorney review all contract forms before use. However, technical maintenance, such as elevator or HVAC, requires a maintenance agreement designed specifically for that service.

Contract Standards

Below are some points to consider regarding contract standards:

1. Contracts must be in writing to ensure specific performance and to be enforceable. Even emergency projects should be written up prior to work commencing.

2. The contract should be written in the owners' names and signed by them as the party ultimately responsible. If the other party sues, they sue the signatory of the contract. Many management companies do not allow site management personnel to sign any contracts.

3. Terms that will govern renewal or cancellation penalties of the contract should be included

4. Specific insurance coverage requirements should be stated. Either require a certificate of insurance as proof of the type and quality of the contractor's coverage, or obtain copies of insurance policies covering the contractor's work on the property and proof of liability and workers' compensation insurance. Make certain the policy includes a hold-harmless clause and indemnifies the owner and the property management firm against any third-party claims. Indicate that the insurance provider must submit notice of cancellation if the policy is canceled.

5. All agreed specifications from the bid letter must be spelled out in the contract along with any appropriate diagrams

6. The contract should spell out what the contractor will provide and what the real estate manager will provide

7. The contract must include warranties—what and how long the work or equipment is warranted

8. The contract should specify the fees for the services named and stipulate fees for extra services. It should also address payment procedures. A retention fee (usually 10 percent) to be paid upon successful completion of the work is advisable. Discuss late fees and discount fees if applicable.

9. A specific completion schedule should be documented. Provide a weather contingency plan if the specification is for construction or rehabilitation work. Provide an illness contingency plan. Indicate holidays allowed and work coverage.

10. Some major contractors want the owner or real estate manager to sign their standard contract rather than the property's contract. Make certain their contract includes all the information required on the property's contract. Have an attorney review the document.

TIPS:
Avoid contracts longer than 12 months in duration to keep options available and to avoid being stuck with a service that is no longer needed or that can be found for a better rate.

Discounts

If the manager has multiple properties or an extensive portfolio, a national discount, usually 10 percent, can be negotiated with many contractors.

Elevators

When negotiating an elevator maintenance contract, consider the contractor's supply of parts and the availability of after-hours service and after-hours prices. Negotiate a *light load credit* in the elevator maintenance contract. This credit is a discount for vacancies. For instance, a discount of 20 percent in the contract fee may be allowed for a 50 percent or greater vacancy rate.

Landscaping Contracts

Climate and soil conditions weigh heavily in the choice of trees, shrubs, flowering plants, and grass or ground cover, as does the cost of their installation and maintenance. The contract should address types of plants, placement and replacement, lawn care (mowing, seeding, fertilizing, pest control), and other specific services as may be appropriate. It should state how often repetitive services such as lawn mowing will be performed. Selection of plants and seasonal color changes should be a consideration as well as the cost of changing plantings in flower beds. Since perennial bulbs are usually taken out of the ground over the winter, timing of their removal, storage, and replanting must be addressed. The contract should be specific about when shrubs will be trimmed and the plant height that will be maintained.

The contract should spell out the costs and payment requirements. Charges may be stated as a flat rate for a particular service, which may or may not include plant materials, or as an hourly rate for labor, with itemized costs for plant materials and special equipment. Multiple bids are in order here, and the manager should draw up specifications or a Request for Proposal (RFP) stating how the bids should be submitted so comparing them will be easy.

Supplies

The contract should provide the property with control over supplies and sources of equipment. Make sure that contractors do not provide equipment without replacement parts. If the contractor buys supplies but charges them back in billing, require actual supply invoices with the billing statement. You should have the right to buy supplies directly if the markup is unreasonable.

MONITORING A CONTRACTOR'S WORK

Real estate managers are responsible for ensuring that contracts are fulfilled properly and for monitoring progress. In order to get started on the right foot, the manager should meet the contractor at the site on the first day work is to begin. It is important to be visible early on and to get to know who is working on the property.

Ensuring Work Quality

Below are specific suggestions for checking the quality of a contractor's work:

- **Walk the property** and discuss problem areas with contractors who will provide services on a consistent basis, such as security, landscaping, etc., at least two weeks before they start. This will familiarize them with the situation and prevent future problems.

- **Ask that the contractor's workers not talk** to residents about their work or about the facility

- **Conduct inspections as often as necessary** to ensure that the contractor is performing work to bid specifications. Ask the contractor for a specific schedule of work progress to facilitate planning these inspections.

- **Time inspections for the best observation of conditions.** For example, conduct a roof inspection when old roofing material has been removed and inspect a landscaper weekly. If a contractor is building a fence, monitor the work daily to make sure specifications for the job are followed.

- **Require lien releases** (refer to Figure 4-3) from all contractors and suppliers and have them provide all sign-offs from the city. Both partial and full waivers should be used. At each draw or payment, a partial waiver of lien must be obtained from the contractor to be sure that all material/ suppliers are paid to date. A full unconditional waiver is obtained at the final payment (usually the retention payment) in which the contractor verifies that all parties are paid in full.

- **Before making interim and final payments** make sure that no violations of local codes exist and that no liens will be placed on the property

- **Ensure agreed health and safety procedures are observed**, including the following:
    - o Following MSDS Sheets
    - o Using personal protective equipment
    - o Working at safe heights
    - o Using warning signs
    - o Controlling noise, dust, fumes, and chemical vapors
    - o Using fire safety precautions
    - o Preventing the unauthorized use of equipment
    - o Taping off or restricting access in construction areas
    - o Posting signage to notify the public of service as necessary
    - o Notifying residents if there is a potential to remove more than two square feet of drywall containing lead-based paint

Any contractor who performs excavation—plumbers, telephone, or electrical workers—should be given clear, written instructions about the type of barricades and warning signals required on the property, as well as the absolute need for an underground utility mark out. These types of notices can be important, especially if legal action is taken later because of a contractor's negligence.

LEGAL ISSUE:
Make sure contractors are aware of and abide by applicable federal, state, and local employment laws—i.e., Illness, Injury, Prevention (IIP), Occupational Health and Safety Administration (OSHA).

Paying Contractors

Below are some points to consider regarding contractor payment:

- Specify payment procedures in the contract. Periodic progress payments may be tied to phases of construction work.

- Consider *retainage*, or holding money back from payments, usually a percentage of the total cost of the project, until any outstanding work, (e.g., punch list items) is completed satisfactorily.

- Include a monetary damage or forfeit clause in the agreement that states that if the contractor does not finish work in a timely fashion, or by a certain date, a penalty will be assessed.

- Pay annual contracts, such as those for extermination or elevator maintenance, on a monthly basis with annual adjustments for work not required.

- Obtain details of all associated warranties, plans, diagrams, schematics, sources of supplies, code numbers for paint, and information on who did the work.

- Obtain a complete invoice for your records and for the owner.

- Require that all bills show labor, supplies, fees, and taxes to avoid any disputes with government agencies.

- Inspect the work thoroughly before paying for services provided or work performed (both interim and final payments). Tie approval of each section to the building inspector's signature.

FIGURE 4-3: RELEASE OF LIEN

Waiver and Release of Lein
Upon Final Payment

The undersigned lienor, in consideration of the final payment in the amount of $_____, hereby waives and releases its lien and right to claim a lien for labor, services, or materials furnished to _____

_____

(Insert name of customer)

on the job_____

 (insert name of owner)

to the following described property:

_____

_____

_____

(Insert description of property)

 DATED on _____, _____.

 _____

 BY:_____
 (Lienor)

Prepared by:

_____

CHAPTER 5:
BIG TICKET MAINTENANCE

Understanding the maintenance of major components allows the real estate manager to effectively maintain them, supervise staff, and oversee contracted work. A manager must be able to identify key maintenance considerations for the major building mechanicals and systems.

In this chapter:

- **General Guidelines**

- **Big Ticket Maintenance**

GENERAL GUIDELINES

To establish good property maintenance procedures, the site manager must keep many factors in mind. Some general guidelines follow:

- Blueprints of the facility should be inventoried and readily accessible.

- The manager and maintenance personnel should know the location of all water and gas shutoff valves.

- The manager and maintenance personnel should know the location of all electrical circuit breakers and main breakers. The breakers should be labeled.

- The manager should have an elevator override key in order to call an elevator car to an emergency site.

- Safety should always be a priority.

    o Conduct regularly scheduled inspections.

    o Use personal protective equipment (PPE).

    o Refer to and follow recommendations of MSDS sheets.

- Using qualified, licensed, and insured contractors and consultants is a sound practice.

NOTES:
Refer to **Appendix D** for information about other major building mechanicals and systems including:
- Electrical Systems
- Swimming Pools
- Elevators
- Life Safety Systems

RESOURCES:
IREM publishes *The Real Estate Manager's Technical Glossary*. This useful book explains terms managers encounter in dealing with service providers, including construction architecture, HVAC operations and maintenance, electrical systems, environmental management, etc.

BIG TICKET MAINTENANCE

Roofing

The ultimate condition of a roof depends on three factors—design, construction, and maintenance. Roofs with certain features tend to cause fewer problems and generally last longer than average. These features include prompt drainage of water from the roof; good sealing procedures for the many edges, walls, and pipes; materials used; and good access to the roof and around equipment on the roof, so that regular maintenance can be carried out easily.

Catching roof problems before they become serious is important. Roofs should be inspected twice a year and after any significant weather event. The surface of the roof should also be inspected shortly after a rain to gather information about the roof's condition. Additional inspections or more frequent minor maintenance may be scheduled for roof areas that are particularly vulnerable.

Visual inspection is the traditional method used and is adequate in many instances. However, more comprehensive inspection using infrared technology may be warranted every few years. If patches are constantly required but do not seem to resolve the leak, a comprehensive inspection may be needed to find the real source of the problem.

Roofing Terminology

While managers may not always have an influence on how a building's roof is constructed, they should be aware of some of the factors that may affect how well the roof will resist deterioration. In this way, the manager can anticipate potential problems with the roof and budget accordingly. Knowledge of basic roofing terminology can assist the real estate manager in effectively maintaining the property's roof. The following is an overview of terminology related to common roof styles, general roofing terms, and roofing materials. Refer to Figures 5-1, 5-2, 5-3, and 5-4.

TIPS:
Poor design or installation of items like roofs, parking areas, and landscaping, may have ramifications for future maintenance and repair. Understanding these drawbacks can be useful in determining appropriate solutions.

FIGURE 5-1: ROOFING STYLES

Gable or Pitched:
A roof that has two equal sloping sides and forms a triangle at each end.

Flat:
A horizontal roof that frequently has a slight inclination to allow it to shed water

Gambrel:
A gable roof that has two slopes on each side with a steeper lower slope; as seen on many barns.

Cross Hipped:
A roof that has sloping ends at the same pitch as the sloping sides. Variations include pyramid hip or pavilion *(see below)*

Mansard:
A French-style gable roof that has two slopes on each of four sloping sides with the lower slope being steeper than the upper slope; in some versions, the top has a flat area instead of coming to a peak

Pyramid Hip:
A roof having sloping ends as well as sloping sides.

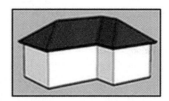

Saltbox:
Similar to a gable roof except that it is asymmetrical—one side is longer.

Pavilion:
A shallow, polygonal hip roof typically found topping gazebos and other pavilion structures

Image Source: Maier Roofing Co. Inc. **www.maierroofingcompany.com**

FIGURE 5-2 ROOFING TERMS

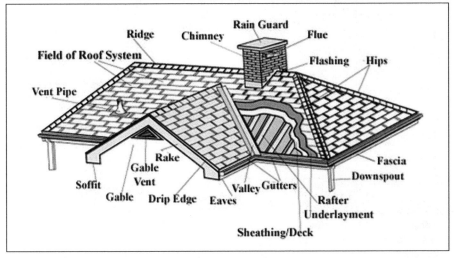

Source: Mad City Roofing. **www.madcityroofing.com**

FIGURE 5-3: ROOFING TERMS

Cornice	• Uppermost section of moldings along the top of a wall or just below the roof
Eaves	• Beam ends of a sloped roof that overhang the wall and allow water to drip away from the building
Soffit	• Exposed underside of the eaves or other structures of a building
Dormer	• Window set vertically into a small structure that projects from a sloping roof; also the structure itself, which has its own roof
Flashing	• Thin impervious material (metal, rubber, etc.) or connecting device that seals membrane joints at expansion joints, roof drains, and other places where a membrane ends (e.g., where a roofing membrane meets a wall) • Purpose is to prevent water penetration and/or provide water drainage, but is often a common source of leaks • Base Flashing: essentially an extension of the membrane that forms the upturned edges of a water-tight membrane • Counter Flashing: thin strip of material, typically sheet metal, attached to or built into the building structure and turned down over the exposed edges and joints of base flashing; prevents water from entering the joints and exposed upturned edges of base flashing
Parapet	• Low wall or barrier positioned to denote the edge of a platform or other sudden drop (e.g., the edge of a roof, where the parapet wall is usually an upward extension of the exterior curtain wall of the building)

Joint	• Gap between structural elements of a roof to allow expansion and contraction of roof materials
Roof Drain	• Drain designed to receive rainwater collecting on a roof and discharge it to a drain pipe or downspout
Gutter	• Trough that runs along the eaves and slopes toward a downspout • Helps drain water from a roof
Downspout	• A vertical pipe that carries water from gutters down the side of the building and expels it away from the building

FIGURE 5-4: ROOFING MATERIALS AND MAINTENANCE RECOMMENDATIONS

Asphalt/ Composition Shingles	**Description:** • Shingles manufactured from roofing felts saturated with asphalt and coated with aggregate particles on the side exposed to the weather • Most common materials used; made in a variety of weights, colors, and designs • The weight of the shingles, slope of the roof, exposure to the sun, color, and climate conditions all influence the aging process. In warm, sunny climates, these shingles may last 12 to 14 years. In northern climates, they may last 25 years. **Check For:** • Condition of shingles (flexibility and granule cover) • Flashing at walls, chimneys, roof intrusions • Gaps at gable overhang
Built-up, Pitch and Gravel, Hot Tar	**Description:** • Continuous roof covering comprised of layers (plies) of felt paper alternated with thin layers of adhesive tars or asphalts and surfaced with a layer of gravel in a heavy coat of asphalt or coal-tar pitch • Also referred to as a tar-and-gravel roof • Older installations may have been held down by ballast (weight) of slag or gravel. Modern installations do not have slag or ballast and are called bald installations. **Check For:** • Exposed felt at parapets damaged by UV rays • Bald spots • Flashing at walls, chimneys, roof intrusions • Condition of protective coating • Degraded roofing material at perimeter flashing laps • Degraded pitch at roof penetrations

Ballast	Description:
	• Coarse stone or gravel used to hold down the roofing material (membrane, felt layers, insulation, etc.) on a building • Advantages include economical installation, superior tolerance of building movement, protection of the membrane from sunlight degradation and other weather conditions, and protection from debris • Rock-ballasted roofs consist of tar paper or a rubber membrane held in place by the weight of rocks • Paver-ballasted membranes are smooth coated roofs **Check For:** • Exposed membrane at parapets damaged by UV rays • Flashing at walls, chimneys, roof intrusions • Flashing of above-roofline equipment • Bald and thin spots

FIGURE 5-4: ROOFING MATERIALS AND MAINTENANCE RECOMMENDATIONS	
Tile 	**Description:** • Made from clay, ceramic, slate, or manufactured • Heavier and costlier than other materials **Check For:** • Cracked tiles • Flashing at walls, chimneys, roof intrusions • Hip and ridge mortaring
Bitumen (used in built-up, pitch and tar, hot tar, roofs) 	**Description:** • Mixture of complex hydrocarbons obtained from petroleum or coal by distillation, usually in semi-solid form • Usually asphalt and coal-tar pitch. The bitumen is usually heated to a liquid state, dissolved in a solvent, or emulsified before being applied. • Modified bitumen combines the waterproofing qualities of asphalt with the advanced polymer technology and flexibility of single-ply sheets. Single-ply or multi-ply applications. **Check For:** • Generally, same inspection as built-up roofs • Primary problems for APP (Atactic polypropylene) membranes are crazing or cracking, blisters, open or loose laps, loose bare flashings • For SBS (styrene butadiene styrene) membranes, problems include open or loose laps, blisters, cracking, granule loss

Membrane	Description:
	• Thin, flexible, weather-resistant component of a roofing system, as elastomeric (EPDM) sheets or alternate layers of felt and bitumen (a tar-like substance)
	Check For: • Exposed membrane at parapets damaged by UV rays • Flashing at walls, chimneys, roof intrusions • Flashing of above-roofline equipment • Degraded roofing material at pipes/vents

Image Sources: (Composition, Tile): Maier Roofing Co. Inc. **www.maierroofingcompany.com**, (Ballast): Deer Park Roofing **www.deerparkroofing.com**, (Built-up, Bitumen): Professional Roofing Service **www.proroofingservices.com**, (Membrane): Warburton's Inc. **www.warburtonsinc.com**

 Sustainability Impact: Cool Roofs, those constructed from light, reflective materials, contribute to energy efficiency goals. Green or Vegetative Roofs can provide storm water management benefits and a relaxing, enjoyable environment for residents. More information about Green and Cool Roofs will be provided in Chapter 6.

Checking for Adequate Drainage

Look for roofs with sufficient slope to remove water promptly. Standing or ponding water has a detrimental effect on the structure and may cause interior damage if a membrane fails. Too steep a slope, however, may cause water to rush into the drains too quickly, creating backups and causing water to overflow the base flashing.

Make sure no obstruction, such as a skylight, a satellite dish, or an HVAC unit, interferes with the flow of water to the drains. If the flow is blocked, install *saddles* or *crickets*, which are devices used to divert the water away from obstructions. Schedule cleaning of gutters and downspouts on a regular basis as well.

Drains located in the middle of a *load span*, where the sag of the roof is greatest, are more effective in eliminating standing water than drains located at the columns. Drains should be located no more than 50 feet apart to prevent pooling. If the roof is sectioned, each section should have at least two major drains. If each section has only one pump, a drain sump should be installed in each section's drain to prevent accumulated debris from blocking the drains.

Evaluating Equipment Installation and Roof Access

The manager should evaluate the installation of the HVAC and other equipment on the roof. Whenever possible, equipment should be mounted on flashed curbs or pipe pedestals. If pitch pockets are used to seal around penetrations, they should be inspected every six months and refilled as needed.

When the roofing membrane is attached to metal, the different thermal expansion-contraction coefficients are likely to cause damage to the roof membrane. All metal penetrations should have a simple flashed curb installed around them to prevent seepage. All HVAC ducts and coping covers should have sloping top surfaces to shed water.

The roof and its components must be easily accessible for inspection. At the same time, the manager must control unauthorized access. The roof is not a playground, a sundeck, a storage site, or a solar experiment station. Limit access to the roof to inspections and repairs of the roof or related equipment.

RESOURCES:
The following organizations provide more information on selecting a roofing contractor or consultant
• National Roofing Contractors Association (NRCA): **www.nrca.net**
• Roofing Consultants Institute: **www.rci-online.org**

Residential high-rise buildings and garden apartments require different approaches for equipment installation and roof access. Consider the following:

	High-Rise Apartment Buildings	Garden Apartment Buildings
Equipment Installation	• Install HVAC equipment in penthouse instead of roof to avoid damage from repairs. • Enforce a NO resident installation policy.	• Establish careful procedures to control resident installations of HVAC equipment, antennas, and other equipment on the roof to prevent structural overloads and water entry.
Roof Access	• Have multiple access points so repair workers do not have to walk or carry tools over the entire roof surface. • Install ladders between areas if there are multiple levels; attach the ladders to the wall; do not tie them to the roof, which might create seepage at that point. • Protect the roof from foot traffic with installation of raised metal or fiberglass grating mounted on flashed curbs across the most frequently accessed areas.	• Access the roof from the third floor attic crawl space or an exterior portable ladder.

Handling Roof Leaks

Another major consideration is how easily leaks can be located. If an inspection locates leaks, do not ignore them. Establish a definite system by which maintenance or custodial personnel keep a simple log of when and where leaks were observed and what happened after they were repaired.

When repairs are made, they must do more than just stop the water entry. Have all wet and damaged materials removed and replaced. If necessary, have a new membrane installed in the localized area and add flashings to protect the roof. One new layer of membrane may be added over the existing one (a less expensive process than tearing off the entire covering). However, the existing membrane must first be thoroughly dried out to prevent mold.

The manager should also define the quality control measures expected during repair. Full-time inspections are more important to a useful roofing system than all the bonds and warranties available. It is far better to detect and correct workmanship problems while the roof is being installed than to find and argue about them once the installation has been completed. If you obtain a warranty, however, make certain that it clearly defines the procedure to follow if problems occur.

CHECKLIST: ROOFING PRECAUTIONS

If working around an occupied building, take the following precautions:
□ Define what areas the contractor can use for work
□ Ensure that the contractor uses proper signage and barricades as necessary to protect residents and keep them away from work areas
□ Define what areas the contractor can use for storage. Have storage trailers or temporary sheds in place for the storage of roofing materials
□ The contractor should take only enough supplies for each day's work to the roof.
□ Define what machinery is acceptable for use in construction
□ Determine how to dispose of removed materials
□ Ensure that the contractor protects the building from damage by bitumen or sprayed foam

---

Heating, Ventilation, and Air-Conditioning (HVAC) Systems

If a building cannot be cooled adequately in the summer and heated comfortably in the winter, it won't be as marketable.

Before the manager can properly operate and maintain a heating, ventilation, and air-conditioning (HVAC) system, he or she must develop a basic understanding of the types of systems, terms, concepts, and theories associated with HVAC.

Most systems have two cycles: the refrigeration cycle and the air-distribution cycle.

The Refrigeration Cycle

The ASHRAE (American Society of Heating, Refrigeration, and Air-Conditioning Engineers) Guide defines air-conditioning as "The process of treating air so as to control simultaneously its temperature, humidity, cleanliness, and distribution to meet the requirements of the conditioned space." The strategies for controlling air to address each factor of air-conditioning include:

- **Temperature:** adding heat or removing heat
- **Humidity:** adding moisture or removing moisture
- **Cleanliness:** removing all or a portion of the impurities from the air, such as dust, smoke, bacteria, and non-atmospheric gases
- **Distribution:** circulating room air using unit air conditioners, or distributing air through ductwork using central handlers

Refrigeration is a process that removes heat, rather than adding cold. The process of refrigeration transfers heat from one place to another. Heat flows from an object or substance of higher temperature to one of a lower temperature. In refrigeration, optimizing the rate of heat transfer is important.

To better understand refrigeration, it is helpful to understand how the measurements are derived. Heat energy has two components:

- **Intensity:** measured by temperature
- **Quantity:** measured by BTUs (British Thermal Units)

A *BTU* is the amount of heat that must be added to one pound of water to raise the temperature one degree Fahrenheit. In refrigeration, a BTU is the amount of heat that must be removed from a pound of water to lower the temperature one degree Fahrenheit.

To designate the rate of flow, the BTUs per hour are measured, and that indicates the amount of heat that flows from one substance to another in one hour. In air-conditioning, the term "a ton of refrigeration" is used. *One ton of refrigeration* provides the same amount of cooling as melting one ton of ice over a 24-hour period. One hundred forty-four BTUs are absorbed when one pound of ice melts at 32°F. One ton of refrigeration absorbs 288,000 BTUs over a 24-hour period or 12,000 BTUs per hour (288,000 divided by 24 hours).

A mechanical refrigeration system consists of four main components (See Figure 5-5):

1. The **compressor** compresses the refrigerant gas and sends the compressed gas to the condenser.
2. The **condenser** is a heat exchanger that removes heat from the hot compressed gas and allows it to condense into a liquid. The liquid refrigerant is then routed to a metering device.
3. The **metering device** restricts the refrigerant's flow by forcing it to go through a small hole that causes the pressure drop in the liquid and allows it to begin to evaporate into a gas.

4. The **evaporator** is where the refrigerant evaporates. It is then routed back to the compressor, completing the cycle. The refrigerant is used repeatedly, absorbing heat from one area and relocating it to another, generally through a cooling tower in a large central system or a condenser in a small apartment unit.

FIGURE 5-5: REFRIGERATION CYCLE DIAGRAM

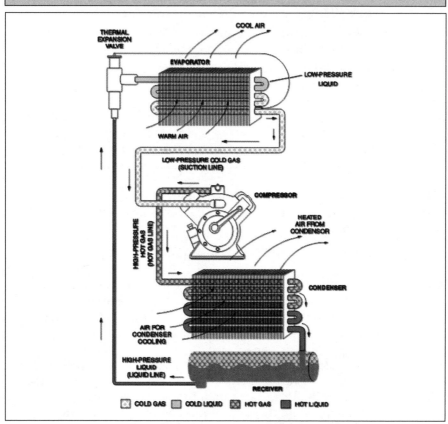

Thomas J. Griffin, CPM®. *The Real Estate Manager's Technical Glossary.* IREM® Copyright 1999. Reprinted with permission.

The Air Distribution Cycle

While the refrigeration cycle works to remove heat, the air-distribution cycle works to move air evenly throughout a building or space. The process of air-conditioning involves bringing outside air in to provide a positive, higher-than-outside pressure in the building. The building becomes a pressurized box, which prevents infiltration of unfiltered, unconditioned outside air through any openings such as doors or cracks.

The air-distribution cycle typically involves some type of air handling unit that includes fans, ductwork, filters, dampers, and heating and cooling coils (see Figure 5-6). Figure 5-7 shows how the refrigeration and air-distribution cycles work together in a complete air and refrigeration cycle for a typical building

FIGURE 5-6: AIR DISTRIBUTION CYCLE

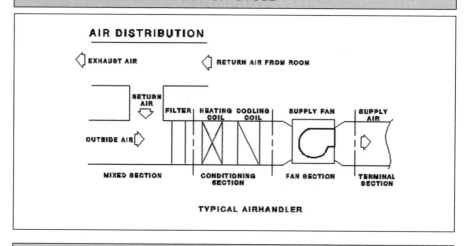

AIR DISTRIBUTION

TYPICAL AIRHANDLER

FIGURE 5-7: TYPICAL ALL AIR SYSTEM

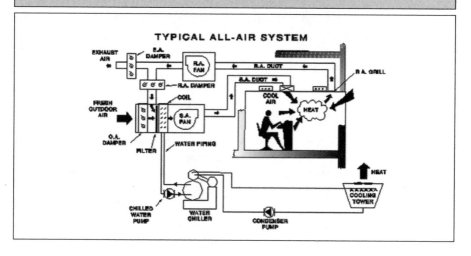

TYPICAL ALL-AIR SYSTEM

Energy Management Systems

Energy management systems are available that regulate HVAC systems to conserve energy. These systems can be programmed to maintain an optimum temperature level by taking readings throughout the day. The system raises and lowers temperatures at certain times of the day (when energy costs are lower) and turns systems off and on. The use of energy management systems can help prevent people from tampering with thermostats, which can waste a tremendous amount of energy.

Maintaining HVAC Equipment

Generally, only large national companies with facilities in several locations can afford the staff, training, and equipment required to carry out all of their own HVAC maintenance activities. Even those firms use maintenance contractors to supplement their efforts, especially on complicated maintenance procedures such as overhauling a centrifugal chiller.

In deciding what kind of HVAC service the property needs, consider two questions: What *can* we do in-house? What do we *want* to do in-house?

It is helpful to start by examining HVAC maintenance manuals, which are usually available from the equipment manufacturer or a qualified service contractor. These manuals specify the inspection and preventive maintenance (PM) routines required to ensure that the equipment operates as designed. From these maintenance specifications, often in checklist form, you can determine how much (if any) maintenance work can be performed by on-site staff and how much should be performed by a service contractor.

Types of HVAC Service Contracts
Depending on the property's equipment and maintenance objectives, a variety of HVAC service contracts are available.

- Consider an *inspection-only plan* if the objective is to evaluate and document equipment operations periodically and to perform minor adjustments.
- Consider an *inspection-plus plan* if systematizing PM is a priority.
- Consider a *maintenance-and-labor plan* if the goal is to use staff more effectively by reassigning HVAC operating personnel to other critical building functions.
- Consider a *total service contract* if the property has a combination of these objectives and wants to establish stricter control of HVAC maintenance costs.
- This type of agreement places full responsibility—including that for all labor and materials—on the contractor.
  - o All HVAC maintenance costs become a budgeted monthly payment, based on a negotiated price.
  - o The contractor has a strong incentive to keep the HVAC system in top condition because that company bears the cost and headaches of any equipment failures.

Most total service contracts, as well as many inspection-type agreements, also provide for consulting services from the contractor. They may recommend energy-saving measures and equipment retrofits to keep the HVAC system efficient and technologically up-to-date. This is a function on-site maintenance personnel often are not qualified to perform. The HVAC system manufacturer can often send a representative to review the system and make recommendations for improvement.

Keys to Running Successful HVAC Operations
1. Understand the operating parameters, hours of operation, and levels of resident comfort for the property.
2. Identify maintenance objectives as specifically as possible.
3. Match the objectives with the appropriate mix of on-site staff responsibilities and an appropriate maintenance contract type.

4. Support these efforts with a realistic budget, including the purchase of software upgrades for monitoring equipment.

5. Consider special insurance, such as Boiler and Equipment Coverage, for sophisticated HVAC systems. These policies cover major breakdowns and replacements.

6. Test and balance, using an HVAC contractor, to maintain peak HVAC efficiency. This helps measure air flow through dampers to ensure even air distribution.

Unit Air Conditioners

Many properties use smaller wall unit or window unit air conditioners, which are typically serviced by on-site maintenance personnel. Unit air conditioners work in much the same way as a refrigerator. An evaporator coil cools the interior (in this case the room), and the condenser coil releases the hot air outdoors. Refrigerant is moved by a pump through tubes between the two coils to transfer the heat. A fan blows the cool air into the room.

Some simple maintenance tips can help keep wall and window units working properly. Keep the filter and coils clean and replace the filter as recommended by the manufacturer. To clean, remove the inside grill, carefully take out the foam filter, and wash it in warm soapy water. If the filter is extremely dirty, more than one washing may be needed. Be sure to rinse and allow the filter to dry before replacing. Filters that are no longer effective can be inexpensively replaced. Filter maintenance alone will increase the air conditioner's efficiency, but to get the most from a unit, a thorough cleaning is required.

RESOURCES:
The following organizations provide more information on regulating HVAC temperatures:
• Occupational Safety Health and Safety Administration (OSHA): **www.osha.gov**
• The American Society of Heating, Refrigerating and Air-Conditioning Engineers (ASHRAE): **www.ashrae.org**

Plumbing Systems

Domestic Water Systems

Domestic water systems are composed of a supply system and a waste system.

Supply System

The supply system includes the following:
• Pressure regulator to maintain a constant water pressure
• Meter to measure water usage
• Heater or boiler to provide hot water (Tankless hot water heaters use gas to heat hot water only when it is needed. That can lead to energy efficiencies. Although tankless hot water heaters are often the best choice, some debate exists about the advantages of using them due to the high initial cost, their reliability in colder climates, and temperature fluctuations of the heated water.)

- Filters to remove minerals and purify drinking water
- Copper piping of various sizes to maintain pressure throughout the building
- Various fittings to control the flow of water: valves, elbows, reducers, tees, and caps
- Risers to act as shock absorbers (*Risers* are vertical pipes that should contain air; they are placed near water outlets to reduce *water hammer*–the sound that occurs when air is trapped in the system.)

Waste System
- The waste system includes the following:
- Traps to keep gases from entering the building
- Vents to allow gases to leave the building
- Clean-outs to allow cleaning of lines
- Removable caps to allow access to lines
- PVC or cast iron piping of various sizes to allow for uniform flow of wastes
- Backflow valves to keep sewage from backing up into the building (Some municipalities require backflow valves and annual inspection)

Some of the biggest maintenance headaches a manager may experience are those associated with plumbing. When building occupants experience a shortage of water, they get upset. When a pipe bursts, insulation and other building materials can be damaged, which may result in structural problems. Carpeting, wallpaper, furnishings, and valuable records can also be damaged.

Given the complexity and cost of such problems, managers should include specific inspections and actions relative to the plumbing system in their maintenance plans. Residents usually call management for repairs only after the plumbing has broken down or become a nuisance. Encourage residents to report all maintenance issues by calling the management office as soon as they discover a problem.

Sanitary Sewer System
A sanitary sewer system consists of three basic elements:

Element	Description
1. Waste Lines and Drainpipe	• Carry sewage from each of the fixtures in the building down through the walls and under the floor then outside the building to either a public sewer system or a septic tank below ground on the property • A clog in any of these pipes stops waste from reaching its destination
2. Vent Pipes	• Travel from each plumbing fixture (or group of plumbing fixtures) upward (inside walls) and out through the roof • The vents allow air into the sewer lines so that they drain freely • A clogged vent pipe can be a serious problem and can prevent good drainage of the waste

3. P-Traps (Refer to Figure 5-8)	• P-traps are curved plumbing fittings resembling a broken letter "p" • Traps are in every fixture: sinks, toilets, washing machines, floor drains. If the fixture drains into the sewer system, the water or waste first travels through a p-trap. • The trap allows water and waste to enter the sewer system while at the same time preventing sewer gases from backing up into the building • A clogged p-trap can inhibit the flow of waste and allow malodorous gases to back up into the building

The most common causes of sewer service line backups are improper disposal of household items, such as paper towels, sanitary napkins, disposable diapers, and cooking grease; garbage disposal misuse; and food debris, such as fruit and vegetable peelings, in kitchen sinks. Grease, roots, and rags that are inappropriately discharged into the sewer system can also cause problems in sewer lines that are connected to main or city sewer lines.

FIGURE 5-8: P-TRAP DIAGRAM

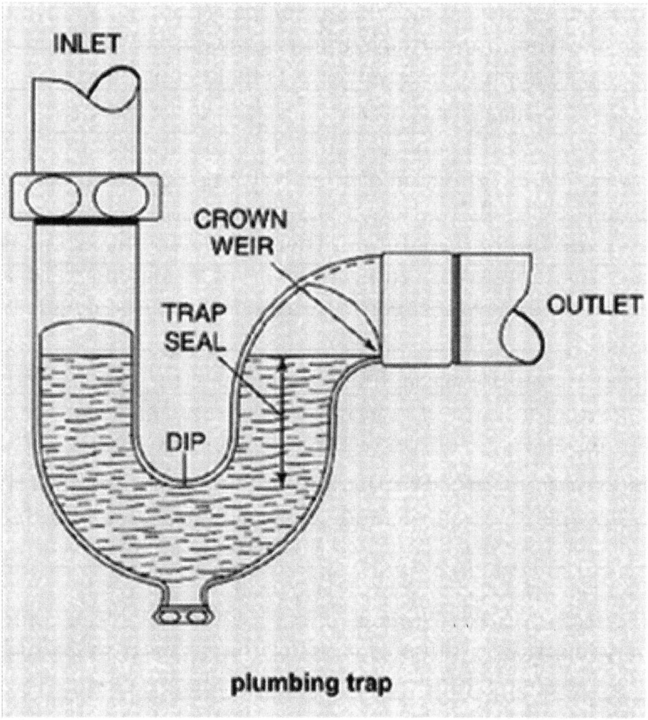

Source: Reprinted with permission. Thomas J. Griffin, CPM®. *The Real Estate Manager's Technical Glossary.* IREM® Copyright 1999.

Preventive Procedures

A typical preventive maintenance inspection should be performed at least annually and should include the following activities:

- **Examine all faucets.** This requires a unit-to-unit or space-to-space inspection to ensure that no leaks are present. The cost of repairing a simple leak is small compared to the cost of repairing a neglected leak.

- **Examine all fixtures.** When checking faucets, also examine fixtures and drains. If a sink or bathtub has a greenish stain, for example, minerals in the water are corroding the copper pipes. An immediate water analysis should be done and remedial measures should be taken. The age of a building can play a large role in maintaining the plumbing system. A manager may change a faucet and realize the pipes in the wall need replacing.

- **Look under sinks.** Are any signs of leakage visible inside vanities, on items in vanities, on the floor, at joints, or at connections of piping? Small drips can cause rotting, permitting water to get under tiles, into the subfloor, into the ceiling below, and so forth.

- **Examine laundry equipment.** If the building has a laundry room, check all hoses closely. On-site personnel often overlook them when the equipment is vendor-owned. Vendors often make repairs on a breakdown basis. Look for signs of leaks (which can bring in pests or lead to structural damage) and examine hoses for signs of cracking. The same applies to laundry units inside apartments.

- **Inspect accessible piping.** Wherever piping is accessible, it should be examined visually and then be tapped with the grip end of a screwdriver. In the case of metal piping, corrosion occurs from the inside, due to the friction created by the moving water and, in some cases, the mineral content of that water. The sound or "feel" derived from the tapping can indicate if the pipe is about to break. In some cases a pipe may be paper-thin, and the tapping itself can cause it to break.

- **Inspect inaccessible piping.** Inaccessible piping can be "observed" by checking for stains or rot. The most obvious place for them to appear is in pipe insulation, on baseboards, or on floors.

- **Check standpipes and sprinkler systems.** Depending on the size of the building, its occupancy, location, and other factors, other plumbing systems may need review. Check the sprinkler system extremely closely to see that it is working properly.

- **Check the lead content of the water.** Be sure to check the lead content because many existing buildings have plumbing that uses lead-based solder. This also applies to any water from drinking fountains. If unacceptably high traces of lead are found, the problem must be remedied. If no such problems are found, the fact should be documented in case someone files a claim.

- **Check for appropriate water use and potential leaks.** Look at past water consumption data closely. If consumption is checked annually, how does this year's consumption compare with the water consumption from last year and the year before? About the same? Significantly more? If significantly more, why? If no reasonable explanation is apparent, such as a higher occupancy rate, or building expansion, then the problem is likely to be an underground leak of some type. If that is the case, it is necessary to use a leak detection system.

- **Ensure water lines are clear.** One major problem in older properties is that roots from trees may interfere with water lines. Use a quarterly preventive maintenance program to clean out the system and avoid this problem.

In addition to the considerations above, the manager and maintenance supervisor should document the location of all water shutoff valves and know how to turn them off. This includes knowing how to turn off fire sprinklers that have accidentally activated.

Special Plumbing Problems

For sewer problems, the use of cameras to capture a real-time visual analysis of conditions can help solve problems quickly and cost-effectively. For water line leaks, computer-based hydroacoustics can determine where lines are, whether they are leaking, and, if so, where.

The equipment required to perform sewer inspections and water line leak detection and location is expensive and is not usually used on a regular basis. As such, it is not cost-effective for even a major property management company to invest in the equipment, except through a separate operating subsidiary that services other companies, too.

When working with owners during the acquisition of a property, advise them that they can avoid the possibility of receiving a major water and/or sewer line repair bill by having lines thoroughly surveyed before making the purchase.

Review billing records for each meter to monitor water consumption. Establish typical usage patterns for each meter to reflect different sizes of the resident units on the meter and varying types and sizes of commercial occupancies. When consumption exceeds levels established for each meter, determine the cause. If the source cannot be located (leaking faucets, nonfunctioning diverters, running toilets), then an underground leak exists. Call for a leak detection immediately.

Preventive maintenance of sewer lines calls for regular cleaning. Conduct preventive maintenance of water lines by surveying for leaks on an annual basis, typically in mid-spring. The initial survey should include line location and preparation of as-built drawings (measured drawings of the existing conditions) of the water lines. Thereafter, leak detection alone is needed. Regular monitoring of meters should make annual line surveys unnecessary.

Paved Surfaces

All paved surfaces are subject to wear and tear, and no paved surface is permanent. During the first 75 percent of a pavement's life cycle, it performs well and maintains a good appearance. After that, deterioration occurs rapidly.

Preventive maintenance of asphalt pavement requires completion of routine maintenance tasks as well as early detection and repair of minor defects. These actions will limit situations that bring on deterioration and that could lead to a major corrective program. Caring for an asphalt surface requires a basic understanding of the components and structure of asphalt.

There are two types of paving materials:

Type	Description
Asphalt Paving/ Blacktop	• An extremely durable paving material. • Typically, a dark brown to black cement-like material of solid, semisolid, or liquid consistency. • May also be red, green, orange, or white. • Primarily made up of bitumen (obtained as residue in refining petroleum) which works as an adhesive to bind other materials.
Asphalt Concrete	• A tough, flexible traffic-bearing surface. • A mixture of angular stone, slag, or gravel aggregate and sand with asphalt, combined with quantity of mineral filler to fill the voids between the larger aggregates.

Pavement Design

Pavement design is based on several factors: maximum load to be carried, frequency of each category of loading, and supporting capacity of the foundation soil. These factors determine the required thickness of the asphalt pavement and its component layers. The layers that make up the pavement are materials of successively higher bearing value from subgraded soil to pavement surface.

The quality of the foundation soil determines the thicknesses required for the various pavement layers. A good, solid foundation soil that has been graded and power rolled to provide proper drainage and strength will not have the thickness requirements of soft clay soils.

The first book, the *subbase* layer, should be built of crusher-run stone or slag, back-run gravel, or other inexpensive materials. This may not be needed, however, if the foundation surface provides a satisfactory subbase.

The *asphalt base* is the layer immediately beneath the asphalt surface and may be composed of crushed stones, crushed slag, crushed or uncrushed gravel with sand, or combinations of these materials. It may also be bound with asphalt.

The asphalt surface should be 2 to 5 inches thick and should be well compacted (rolled) and pitched for proper drainage. For driveways, the slope should be at least 2 inches per 10 feet or roughly 1.5 to 2 percent. Proper drainage is very important, since standing water is destructive to asphalt pavement.

Pavement Damage

All pavement requires timely maintenance because stresses that produce minor defects are constantly at work. No matter what climate you live in, weather—sun, rain, snow and heat—is a major factor in the life cycle of paved surfaces. The following stresses may be caused by traffic loads, temperature fluctuations, ground settlement, and changes in moisture content:

- **Raveling.** This is a progressive separation of aggregate particles in pavement, beginning on the surface and moving downward. Usually, the fine aggregate comes off first and leaves pock marks in the pavement surface. Raveling can result from lack of compaction during construction, construction during wet or cold weather, dirty or disintegrating aggregate, or poor mix design.

- **Shrinkage.** Shrinkage creases are interconnected cracks forming a series of large blocks, usually with sharp corners or angles. They are caused by changes in the asphalt mix, in the base, or in the subgrade.

- **Potholes.** The most common and easiest problem to recognize is a pothole. The holes in the pavement are bowl-shaped and of various sizes. The holes result from localized disintegration of the pavement (base) under stress. Contributory factors include improper asphalt mix design, insufficient pavement thickness, and poor drainage. Potholes may simply be the result of neglecting other types of pavement distress.

- **Alligator Cracks.** These interconnected cracks form a series of small cracks resembling alligator skin or chicken wire. Alligator cracking generally is caused by excessive deflection of the surface over unstable subgrade or lower books of the pavement.

- **Upheaval.** This is the localized upward displacement of a pavement due to swelling of the subgrade or some portion of the pavement structure. In colder climates, the expansion of ice in the lower books of the pavement or subgrade commonly causes upheaval. It may also be caused by the swelling effect of moisture or expansive soils.

- **Grade Depression.** Depressions are localized low areas of limited size that may or may not be accompanied by cracking. They may be caused by traffic heavier than the pavement design can accommodate.

- **Moisture Damage.** Excess moisture is probably the most destructive of all the types of pavement damage. Excess moisture reaching the soil under the pavement decreases the soil's ability to resist stresses. Pavement should provide a good seal over the soil.

Surface repair of a pavement defect caused by poor drainage will merely be a temporary solution. It treats only the symptom. The repair must stop water from getting beneath the pavement surface. This can prevent larger maintenance expenditures in the future.

Prevent excess moisture buildup by using proper drainage. Properly designed inlets and culverts efficiently conduct storm water from the parking lot surface to a convenient outlet.

When necessary, use subsurface drains to collect and dispose of ground water before it can reach the foundation soil of the parking lot.

Check sprinkler systems. Where possible, move them away from curbs and parking lots. If the parking lots have little islands, convert them to desert landscaping or concrete slabs that do not require watering.

Repair Alternatives

Once the specific pavement problems are identified, take corrective action to prolong and preserve the asphalt investment.

The following is a summary of the proper methods of correcting deficiencies for three general conditions of pavement. While some parking lots will develop problems other than the more common pavement defects, these examples serve as a guide to the repairs generally required to maintain a parking lot appropriately:

Condition	Characteristics	Action Required
Good	• Might show fine cracking, some raveling of the fine aggregate, or other minor effects of wear and tear.	• Apply a light sealcoat to the pavement to help it remain in good condition.
Fair	• May have cracks up to half an inch in width and raveled aggregate.	• Fill random cracks with hot rubberized crack filler. • Prepare the cracks for filling by removing vegetation, cleaning with a broom or a stream of compressed air, and applying a soil sterilant if weed growth is anticipated. • Use a hand torch or weed killer to destroy existing vegetation. • Then fill the cracks using a pour pot and a hand squeegee. • Fine cracks up to 1/8 inch wide are too small to effectively fill and can usually be ignored, especially when an overlay or slurry seal is to follow. • A fine sand and asphalt hot mix can also be used for filling very large cracks. After the cracks have been filled, cover the parking lot with the appropriate asphalt overlay or a sealcoat.
Poor	• May display random cracks, raveled aggregate, depressions, locally alligatored areas, potholes, and perhaps upheaval.	• Repair pavement in this condition first by constructing a full-depth asphalt patch to repair the alligatored areas, potholes, and upheavals. • Restore depressed areas to the proper cross section. Apply a leveling or wedge book. This is an asphalt layer of variable thickness intended to eliminate irregularities in the contour of an existing surface prior to an overlay. Then apply an asphalt overlay or an asphalt sealcoat.

Infrared Patching

Another repair alternative is *infrared patching*. Using infrared rays to repair asphalt does not alter the inherent characteristics of the asphalt. The infrared rays penetrate the asphalt, repair, and reclaim it without burning or scaling the aggregate. With infrared, the repair area and surrounding areas are worked at the same temperatures. This means that any cold joints or seams are eliminated to create an area that is thermally bonded to the existing pavement. Without cold joints or seams, water and debris are less likely to enter and cause a failure in the patch.

Asphalt Coatings

A *sealcoat* (or sealer) is a thin asphalt surface treatment used to waterproof and improve the texture of an asphalt surface. There are two basic types:

- **Emulsified asphalt sealer** is derived from crude oil. This product will last three to five years, depending on the application rate. It is vulnerable to breakdown by gasoline and other chemicals and is susceptible to oxidation and fading.

- **Coal tar sealer** is derived from a coal extraction method and does not oxidize or fade. Further, it is a true sealer in that it is not vulnerable to breakdown by gasoline and other chemicals. However, it is a harder substance (less flexible) than emulsified asphalt and has a tendency to crack in areas that experience temperature extremes.

Using these two types of sealers as bases, four types of sealers are commonly used today. Depending on the purpose, sealers may or may not contain sand or aggregate.

- **Fog sealer** is an emulsified asphalt or coal tar base sealer diluted one to five parts with water. Usually applied under pressure to give a light protective coating to an asphalt surface, this type is best suited to a surface in good condition or to new construction. Due to its diluted state, it is necessary to apply this sealer about every two years.

- **Sand sealer** is an emulsified asphalt or coal tar base diluted with 25 percent water and 2 to 10 pounds of 60-mesh-silica sand per gallon. This is used for additional traction in a light traffic resident parking lot or driveway.

- **Aggregate sealer** is an emulsified asphalt or coal tar base sealer using more sand for additional traction and to accommodate heavier or commercial traffic. Application of this sealer is made where trucks are common, such as in business centers.

- **Slurry sealer** is an emulsified asphalt or coal tar base using sand that is not as diluted with water as are the other sealers. The purpose of this sealer is not only to protect the existing asphalt surface but also to fill cracks.

CHAPTER 6:
CONSERVATION AND RECYCLING

Implementing energy and water conservation measures can have a positive impact on natural resources and the owner's profit. Conservation and recycling can also be a marketing feature for residents who are concerned about sustainability. A manager must be able to identify ways to implement conservation techniques to improve sustainability and efficiency while reducing operating expenses

In this chapter:

- **Sustainability**

- **Energy Conservation**

- **Water Conservation**

- **Resident Education**

- **Green Building**

- **Recycling**

SUSTAINABILITY

Sustainability means the responsible use of resources to prevent depletion or damage. It is becoming more and more important for owners and property managers to manage all property resources (e.g., electricity, natural gas, water, waste, building materials, land use) to reduce consumption, ensure efficient and cost-effective use, and contribute to long-term sustainability. Market demand, the bottom line, government regulations, and personal voluntary awareness is driving the demand for sustainability in property management.

Sustainability: Initial Steps

Professionals in sustainable real estate management often refer to the "low-hanging fruit" of sustainability measures. These are low-cost/no-cost, easy-to-implement actions that result in greener real estate. The first step to identifying what you can change, is to determine where you stand now. There are many self-assessment tools available to help you begin to identify those areas where you can begin "greening" your building. Energy and water efficiency measures, and changes in operational strategies like product purchases are often easy "quick wins."

RESOURCES:
IREM Sustainability provides three comprehensive tools to help you operate more energy-efficient and sustainable properties, including a web-based platform to enter data about your property and discover savings; a challenge to improve sustainability and earn prizes; and a certification to distinguish your property as a high-performance building.
iremsustainability.com

ENERGY CONSERVATION

The Environmental Protection Agency (EPA) and the U.S. Department of Energy (DOE) have created an extremely helpful program, ENERGY STAR, to help businesses and individuals work to conserve energy and use energy efficiently. ENERGY STAR also has a benchmarking and performance measurement tool called ENERGY STAR Portfolio Manager. This tool became available for multifamily use in 2009. Refer to Figure 6-1 for an image of ENERGY STAR Portfolio Manager.

Much of the following information is based on information from the ENERGY STAR website.

RESOURCES:
The ENERGY STAR website provides resources, guidelines, and useful examples of what companies across the nation have done to increase efficiency and reduce costs: **www.energystar.gov**

FIGURE 6-1: ENERGY STAR PORTFOLIO MANAGER

Analyzing Energy Consumption

An *energy audit* is a systemized approach to measuring, recording, and evaluating the operational performance of a building or building system with the intention of improving performance and conserving energy. Energy audits help identify how much energy is used in a building, where the energy is used, and what opportunities exist for conservation. Refer to Figure 6-2 for one look at how energy is typically used in homes.

Tracking Energy Consumption

One technique to help analyze energy consumption is to track consumption compared to monthly and yearly temperature variations. This can be accomplished by analyzing kilowatt consumption per cooling or heating degree day, as appropriate. A *heating degree day* is each degree that the average temperature drops below 65°F on a given day. A *cooling degree day* is each degree above 65°F. Often the heating degree days are given on the monthly utility bill.

RESOURCES:
Visit the National Climatic Data Center, which is part of the U.S. Department of Commerce, for additional information on heating degree days: **www.ncdc.noaa.gov**

FIGURE 6-2: HOME ENERGY USE

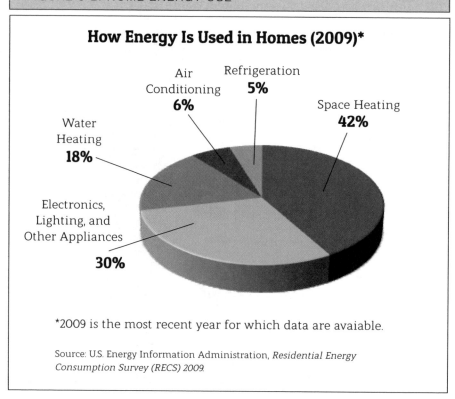

How Energy Is Used in Homes (2009)*

Air Conditioning **6%**

Refrigeration **5%**

Space Heating **42%**

Water Heating **18%**

Electronics, Lighting, and Other Appliances **30%**

*2009 is the most recent year for which data are avaiable.

Source: U.S. Energy Information Administration, *Residential Energy Consumption Survey (RECS) 2009.*

Understanding Electric Bills

Electric bills can consist of customer charges, energy use charges, demand charges, a power factor penalty, and taxes. The manager must clearly understand and agree with each element of the charges paid each month on the electric bill.

- **Customer charges** help the utility recover the cost of meter equipment and billing.
- **Energy use charges** include fees for the direct use of electrical energy in kWh and applicable fuel adjustment charges.
- **Demand charges** are designed to help the utility recover part of the investment necessary to meet peak customer demand. They are based on the highest demand interval in a billing period, usually a 15- or 30-minute period. Some electric utilities offer rate structures with a separate demand charge and without a demand charge.
- **The power factor penalty** is based on a utility's provision of both real (kWh) and reserve or reactive power (KVA). Reactive power doesn't show up on the kWh meter, but the utility has to invest in generating, transmitting, and distributing the equipment to provide it. Customers are penalized if their monthly power factor falls below a specified value.
- **Taxes** may be reduced if a company has several sites with meters and it can add the meters together and tax the total at a lower rate. The manager should talk with the utility company about this possibility.

The utility company can analyze alternatives such as billing with or without a separate demand charge if the company qualifies for the demand-based rate. The manager can compare billing for all rate schedules that apply. A solid base of information about what the electric bill means and how much each component of the bill costs the company or how much it saves will help with an energy audit.

Conservation Measures
The following is a list of common conservation measures and their benefits. Payback from the investment will depend on climate and energy costs.

CHECKLIST: ENERGY CONSERVATION STRATEGIES - LIGHTING

Operations & Maintenance
☐ Employ daylight harvesting (taking advantage of free natural lighting) and combine with automatic photosensing controls that shut lights off when daylight is at pre-set levels

Equipment and Technology
☐ Replace T12 fluorescent bulbs with T8 or T5 (use an electronic, more efficient ballast instead of a magnetic ballast)
☐ Replace incandescent light bulbs with compact fluorescent lights (CFLs), which use 75% less energy, produce 75% less heat, and last 10 x longer
☐ Install occupancy sensors and timers to turn lights off in spaces that are unoccupied such as conference rooms, offices, and restrooms
☐ Install light-emitting diode (LED) exit signs instead of fluorescent or incandescent light bulbs
☐ De-lamp, or remove unnecessary lamps; disconnect unused ballasts; install lower-wattage lamps or use partial lighting
☐ Add skylights to provide natural lighting.

Operations & Maintenance

☐ Inspect and seal air ducts

☐ Clean up the system to remove dirt, dust, and grime from chillers, air conditioners, and heat pumps. Regularly clean and change air filters.

☐ Adjust thermostats up a few degrees during cooling season and down a few degrees during heating season.

☐ Use an Energy Management System (EMS) and take advantage of its capabilities such as automatic notifications to engineering staff when systems vary outside of set parameters

Equipment and Technology

☐ Use programmable thermostats for more precise control

☐ Install individual heat controls for every heating zone.

☐ Install electronic or mechanical ignitions in gas furnaces, boilers, ovens, and ranges in place of pilot lights.

☐ Install air-conditioning units away from the sunny side of a building, where they can operate more efficiently

☐ Upgrade central HVAC units when it comes time to replace them

☐ Install ceiling fans in units to circulate air.

☐ Use water-cooled systems as air-cooled HVAC systems use a lot of energy

☐ Look into porous and/or high-albedo (reflective) surfaces that reject solar heat and can significantly lower cooling costs if exterior hardscape surfaces need to be replaced

☐ Use light-colored, reflective roof coatings or materials for any upgrades

☐ Consider green roofs (specially designed layers of soil and grass)

☐ Consider passive solar energy systems for charging batteries and supplementing a building's electrical service.

Operations & Maintenance

☐ Unplug all office equipment (computers, printers, fax machines, copiers, LCD projectors) and domestic appliances (coffee machines, washing machines, dryers, dishwashers, refrigerators and more) to avoid constant energy draw when they're plugged into the wall (considered "phantom plug loads")

Equipment and Technology

☐ Purchase ENERGY STAR qualified equipment

☐ Consider more efficient appliances such as ventless clothes dryers that use natural gas instead of electricity or dryers with a moisture sensor to automatically stop the machine when clothes are dry

CHECKLIST: ENERGY CONSERVATION STRATEGIES – WATER HEATING

Operations & Maintenance

☐ Lower the temperature

☐ Insulate older water heaters to keep heat from escaping

☐ Insulate electric water heaters' hot water pipes using pipe sleeves

☐ Eliminate water heating in warmer climates

Equipment and Technology

☐ Install times on water heaters that shut them off at night

☐ Use solar water heating (investigate rebates and incentives available)

CHECKLIST: ENERGY CONSERVATION STRATEGIES – BUILDING ENVELOPE

Operations & Maintenance

☐ Weatherize by regularly check all seams, cracks, and openings between conditioned and unconditioned spaces, and update caulking, air sealing, and weatherstripping as necessary

Equipment and Technology

☐ Consider upgrading windows, doors, and skylights to more efficient models as 1/3 of heat loss occurs through the windows and doors

☐ Insulate attic space, if applicable. Consider insulating roofs (insulate during reroofing); walls (drill and blow in insulation); ducts and pipes (wrap with insulation); and slab floors (insulate by putting a vapor barrier under the structure, between it and the earth).

☐ Consider radiant floor heating and cooling systems that allow even heating and cooling throughout the whole floor.

TIPS:

Don't forget vacant units! They offer opportunities to reduce energy usage:

· Keep heating and cooling to a minimum

· Unplug appliances

· Turn off water heaters

· Close windows and blinds

RESOURCES:

Additional resources for information on energy conservation include:

· U.S. Environmental Protection Agency and U.S. Department of Energy ENERGY STAR website: **www.energystar.gov**

· U.S. Department of Energy's Efficiency and Renewable Energy website: **www.eere.energy.gov**

· The IREM® publication: *A Practical Guide to Energy Management*

Computer-Based Energy Accounting

The use of computer software energy accounting programs provides speed, convenience, and high-quality reports and summaries that are produced automatically. Some offer complete records of utility costs and use, automated monthly billing, a search for billing errors, printed graphs and reports, consumption trends, and energy cost calculations based on building size or guest occupancy.

Typical energy accounting software should allow for the following considerations:

- **Incorporation of building data**, including types of fuel used as well as total heated and cooled square footage
- **Site data entry** from multiple meters at each site
- **Comparison of climate records** with consumption records for at least the past 24 months
- **Tracking liquid fuel, water, electricity and natural gas**, and providing flexibility in units of measure—for example, the program might convert all entries into BTUs
- **Adjustments for temperature variations** by calculating the need for space heating or cooling caused by outside temperature differences (measured in heating degree days or cooling degree days)
- **Report production** on a monthly, quarterly, or yearly basis, from each site, along with executive summary reports
- **Side-by-side comparison of energy use**, monthly, with base period data from each metered site
- **Adjustments for irregular billing periods** such as 28-day or 31-day months
- **Calculation of percentage of changes** in fuel use, cost per square foot, total BTUs per square foot, actual fuel use per square foot, and other indices management chooses
- **Explanations of all data entry screens** that document information in terms the reader can understand
- **Blank data organization screens** to assist in inputting data directly from utility bills
- **The ENERGY STAR Portfolio Manager** is a good tool for multifamily benchmarking and performance monitoring

WATER CONSERVATION

The amount of water and quality of water fit for human consumption is a serious issue across the entire United States, even in areas where fresh water seems plentiful. Demand for fresh water supplies continue to increase while supplies ebb and flow with weather and climate changes. Like energy, water conservation measures do not have to be capital-intensive, but can make a noticeable difference in the NOI of a property. Refer to the Figures 6-3 and 6-4 for statistics on water usage.

FIGURE 6-3: RESIDENTIAL WATER USAGE

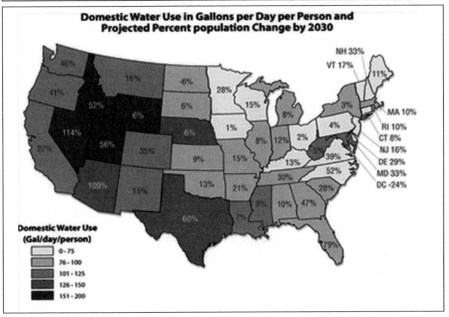

Domestic Water Use in Gallons per Day per Person and Projected Percent population Change by 2030

Source: **http://www.epa.gov/watersense/our_water/tomorrow_beyond.html**

FIGURE 6-4: RESIDENTIAL WATER USAGE

How Much Water Do We Use?

Faucet 16%
Other 5%
Shower 17%
Clothes Washer 22%
Toilet 27%
Leaks 13%

Source: **http://www.epa.gov/watersense/our_water/tomorrow_beyond.html**

Conservation Strategies

Water-efficient Fixtures and Appliances

Changing to water-efficient fixtures and appliances is one option that can reduce water usage without sacrificing performance. The EPA sponsors the WaterSense partnership program to label quality water-efficient products such as showerheads, faucets, and toilets. These products often exceed efficiency standards.

RESOURCES:
Visit the WaterSense website to learn more about
WaterSense-labeled products for your properties:
www.epa.gov/watersense/

Laundry Machines

A recent study of water and energy consumption in multifamily housing found that residents who had in-apartment laundry machines used more water, and consequently more energy, than those who used common area laundry facilities. Water usage was 3.3 times higher among residents who had in-apartment laundry machines and energy usage was approximately five times higher.

Residents with in-unit washers and dryers do many more, smaller and less-efficient loads. An apartment with an in-unit washer wastes approximately 8,500 gallons per year on laundry. For a 150-unit building, that would be 1.275 million gallons more per year.

Most of the energy use associated with laundry comes from heating the water. Apartments with in-unit washing machines tend to have electric water heaters; while most common area facilities have gas water heaters. Residents with in-unit machines that used electric water heaters to heat water used 580.71 kWh per unit per year compared to 117.71 kWh per unit per year for those residents who used common area facilities.

Dryers are a comparable drain on energy. Approximately 96% of domestic dryers used in in-apartment-unit applications are electric, but only 36% of the dryers in typical community area laundry rooms are electric. The cost of electricity needed to dry a typical load of laundry is twice the cost of gas needed to do the same, according to the California Energy Commission.

CHECKLIST: WATER CONSERVATION STRATEGIES – BATHROOMS, KITCHENS & LAUNDRY ROOMS

Operations & Maintenance
☐ Identify and fix leaks

Equipment and Technology
☐ Use aerators in restroom faucets to limit flow of water by mixing air with fine water droplets
☐ Use automatic shut offs on faucet water flows or install pedal-operated faucets
☐ Use low-flush toilets and urinals
☐ Use low-flow showerheads
☐ Use ENERGY STAR dishwashers and washing machines
☐ Find out if the State or municipality offers rebates on water-efficient washing machines

RESOURCES:
Additional information on laundry rooms can be found on the
Multi-housing Laundry Association website:
www.mla-online.com

CHECKLIST: WATER CONSERVATION STRATEGIES – HVAC

Operations & Maintenance

- ☐ Control thermostats and make sure they aren't set too low during cooling season or turned on when they don't have to be
- ☐ Consider acid treatment in recirculated water to control buildup
- ☐ Conduct preventive maintenance on HVAC system

Equipment and Technology

- ☐ Use or convert to closed-loop systems where water is re-circulated through the cooling system or used in other systems
- ☐ Fit cooling system with controls that shut the systems off at night or during weekends

Occupant Behavior

- ☐ Educate tenants on smart thermostat control

Irrigation Systems

Adapting your irrigation methods can be an effective way to conserve water usage. You will need to consider the type of plants, plant size and weather conditions and adjust irrigation amounts as appropriate.

Other considerations for adjusting irrigation amounts follow:

- **Evaporation:** A typical sprinkler operated at noon on a hot, windy, dry day in summer can lose 30 percent or more of the water to evaporation.

- **Runoff:** Water is wasted because it is applied too quickly and the soil cannot absorb it. Sandy soils accept water more quickly than clay soils and dry soil accepts water more quickly than moist soil.

- **Frequency:** Irrigating once deeply is better than irrigating twice or three times shallowly.

- **Municipal Water Systems:** To save money, install an irrigation water meter. Sewer usage usually involves no fees since the water is not returned to the municipal sewer system.

- **Sprinkler Heads:** Place each head so that its stream of water actually touches the next sprinkler (or is within one to two feet of touching). The overlap ensures good, uniform coverage.

- **Timers:** Operate a sprinkler automatically, reducing the possibilities of overwatering and the number of staff hours devoted to the task.

Xeriscaping

Xeriscaping is a practice that uses slow-growing, drought-tolerant plants to conserve water and reduce yard trimmings. Xeriscaping generally requires less fertilizer and fewer pest control measures, which results in reduced impact on air and water quality. Xeriscaping varies from region to region. Plants that are appropriate in one climate may not work well in another. Landscapes need to be planned to be compatible with locally available resources, including water, soil types, and sunlight.

Xeriscaping has been adopted in areas in the desert Southwest and the states of California and Florida as well as other areas. In Albuquerque, New Mexico, residents and businesses can receive a rebate on their water bill for xeriscaping.

RESOURCES:
Tutorials such as *Water-Efficient Landscaping* can be found under Education>On-Demand Learning>Tutorials at **www.irem.org** and are free.

CHECKLIST: WATER CONSERVATION STRATEGIES – LANDSCAPING

Operations & Maintenance
- ☐ Reduce watering times by at least 25%
- ☐ Water during cooler times of the day to prevent less evaporation, and don't water on windy days
- ☐ Position sprinklers correctly so they aren't watering pavement
- ☐ Check for leaks
- ☐ Create irrigation zones (not all plans require same amount of water)
- ☐ Sweep instead of using water to clean sidewalks, driveways, and parking lots
- ☐ Use mulch around shrubs and garden plants to reduce evaporation.
- ☐ Raise the lawn mower height as longer grass blades help shade each other, cut down on evaporation, and inhibit weed growth.
- ☐ Minimize fertilizing that requires additional watering.
- ☐ Only use water ornamental features that operate on recycled water.
- ☐ Investigate rebates for business that use water conservation measures
- ☐ For swimming pools consider installing a water-saving pool filter, use pool filter backwash for landscape irrigation, and use a pool cover to reduce evaporation.

Equipment and Technology
- ☐ Use rain shut-off mechanisms and timers
- ☐ Use water efficient nozzles
- ☐ Use smart irrigation controls (sophisticated alternatives to irrigation systems that monitor variables such as land gradation, plant types, plants' evaporation and transpiration rates, soil moisture, and local real-time weather to determine when/how long to water)
- ☐ Replace sprinkler systems with a drip irrigation system which deposits water directly to plant roots
- ☐ Use drought-resistant landscaping

Water submetering can control costs and lead to lower rents. Simply put, just as billing residents individually for the electricity they use significantly reduces energy usage, submetering reduces water usage.

TIPS:

In properties that are **submetered** residents consume **18-39% less** water than in properties that include a shared water meter.

Another option is *Ratio Utility Billing System (RUBS)*, which bases its billing on the size of a unit or the number of residents occupying it and does not require additional equipment or metering services. RUBS can be used for most utilities including water, wastewater, electric, gas and trash.

Automatic meter reading (AMR) automatically collects consumption data from water meter or energy metering devices (gas, electric) using wireless technology, and transfers that data to a central database for billing. This allows billing to be based on actual consumption rather than estimates and saves utility providers the expense of staff travel to a physical location to read a meter. AMR also allows companies to give time-of-day-based conservation incentive plans for their customers.

A *network meter reading (NMR)* system requires a communications device that is typically retrofitted to a utility's existing meters. This device sends signals through the system's local area network to a pole-top device, which begins to process the information from the meter. For example, this device will route alarm signals back to the system's head end with a higher priority than it sends back standard meter reads.

RESIDENT EDUCATION

One of the least expensive and most effective ways to conserve energy and water is to educate residents on the role they play in conservation. The following are some strategies you can use for educating residents, including conservation tips that can be included in the resident handbook or discussed in meetings:

□ Educate residents on water conservation (offer pamphlets with conservation tips, hold a workshop, etc.)
- o Always notify the manager or leasing office regarding plumbing leaks or needed repairs to appliances or fixtures
- o Don't use the dishwasher or washing machine for small loads unless the appliance has a load setting
- o Use showers instead of tubs for bathing
- o Don't use the toilet as a trash receptacle

□ Educate residents about energy efficiency and the property's goals
- o Always use cold water when operating garbage disposals
- o Use cold water and warm water cycles more often when washing clothes
- o Leave thermostats at a specified temperature, rather than constantly adjusting the controls
- o Maintain thermostat settings at no less than 75°F during the cooling season and no more than 68°F degrees during the heating season
- o Do not block registers and outlets; allow air-conditioning and/or heat to flow through the unit
- o Close fireplace dampers tightly when fireplace is not in use so the chimney doesn't draw heated or cooled air from the unit
- o Adjust drapes, blinds, and shades to act as insulation

□ Turn off TVs, radios, and lights when not in use

□ Unplug appliances when not in use

□ Market your water-efficient landscaping as part of education plan

GREEN BUILDING

Green or *sustainable building* is the practice of creating healthier and more resource-efficient models of construction, renovation, operation, maintenance, and demolition. Research and experience increasingly demonstrate that when buildings are designed and operated with their lifecycle impacts in mind, they can provide great environmental, economic, and social benefits. Elements of green building include:

- Energy Efficiency and Renewable Energy
- Water Stewardship
- Environmentally Preferable Building Materials and Specifications
- Waste Reduction
- Indoor Environment
- Smart Growth and Sustainable Development

Why Build Green?

In the United States, buildings account for the following:

- 39 percent of the total energy use
- 12 percent of the total water consumption
- 68 percent of the total electricity consumption
- 38 percent of the carbon dioxide emissions

Adopting green building strategies can maximize both economic and environmental performance. Green construction methods can be integrated into buildings at any stage (e.g., design, construction, renovation, deconstruction). However, the most significant benefits can be obtained if the design and construction team takes an integrated approach from the earliest stages of a building project.

Green Roofs

Green roofs have become popular in recent years as a method of reducing energy costs. A roof that has a full or partial covering of vegetation is defined as "green," although roofs with container gardens with plants in pots, are not generally considered to be true green roofs. There are two types of green roofs:

- **Extensive (Low Profile):** Simpler, lighter weight, better suited to roofs with slopes. Easier to implement, needs no permanent irrigation system, and requires little maintenance once established. Tends to include alpine-like groundcover plants adapted to extreme climates.

- **Intensive (High Profile):** A complex system like a conventional garden, or park, including large trees and shrubs, which can provide a garden environment for residents. Intensive green roofs are heavier, require more structural support, more maintenance and a greater initial investment.

GREEN ROOFS: FACTORS TO CONSIDER

Benefits

- **Lower Energy Costs:** Green roofs absorb heat and act as insulators for buildings, reducing energy needed to provide cooling and heating.
- **Extend Roof Life:** Green roofs have a longer expected life than most roofing products, perhaps as much as double the length.
- **Roof Drainage:** Green roofs may absorb as much as 70% of a one-inch rainfall, slowing storm water runoff and filtering pollutants from rainfall.
- **Cleaner Air:** Green roofs can decrease the production of associated air pollution and greenhouse gas emissions by lowering air conditioning demand.
- **Lower Heat Stress:** Reducing heat transfer through the building roof can improve indoor comfort and lower heat stress associated with heat waves.
- **Attractive Amenity:** Green roofs improve roof aesthetics. Intensive green roofs can provide an urban garden space for residents.

Considerations

- **Installation:** Estimated costs of installing a green roof start at $10 per square foot for simpler extensive roofing, and $25 per square foot for intensive roofs. Reduced energy, storm water management and longer life expectancy may offset the initial higher costs of implementation.
- **Structure:** Green roofs tend to be easier to design into new rather than existing buildings. Retrofitting older buildings depends on the current structure. Concrete systems require the least intervention; steel decks may require the most. A flat or low-sloped roof generally will be easier than an installation on a steep-sloped roof.
- **Design:** Consultants are necessary to evaluate, design, install and maintain green roof systems.
- **Maintenance:** Inspections and maintenance of drainage layer flow paths and roof membrane should be performed regularly. Annual maintenance costs for either type of roof may range from $0.75–$1.50 per square foot.

TIPS:
Another option for reducing energy costs but with fewer maintenance issues than a green roof is to install a cool roof.

Cool roofing products are made of highly reflective and emissive materials that can remain approximately 50 to 60°f (28-33°C) cooler than traditional materials during Peak Summer Weather.

Traditional roofs in the united states can reach summer peak temperatures Of 150 To 185°F (66-85°C).

RESOURCES:
- National Association of Home Builders (NAHB) and International Code Council (ICC) National Green Building Standard: **www.nahbgreen.org**
- U.S Environmental Protection Agency: **www.epa.gov/greenbuilding**
- U.S. Green Building Council: **www.usgbc.org**
- Other resources include the IREM® publication: *A Practical Guide to Green Real Estate Management,* the IREM® course "Sustainable Real Estate Management" (SRM001), and JPM® magazine includes a recurring column titled "Green Scene."

RECYCLING

In many areas of the United States, *recycling*–the collection and reuse of waste materials–is mandatory. This means residents must be taught how to dispose of their garbage and what to do with recyclable materials. However, even if it is voluntary, the majority of residents will gladly participate in a recycling program. The resident handbook should include the trash pickup schedule, bagging requirements, and instructions for separating recyclable materials. Managers may need to reinforce these instructions by holding a meeting or including a reminder in the resident newsletter. Scheduling meetings with residents to discuss the recycling program will not only increase their awareness, but it will also provide opportunities to answer their questions.

Place trash receptacles in convenient locations to minimize spillage and prevent indiscriminate dumping. Any spillage should be picked up on a regular basis to eliminate the unsightly and unsanitary spread of items by the wind. All receptacles should be cleaned and deodorized regularly to eliminate unpleasant odors, prevent infestation by vermin, and reduce health risks. Large Dumpsters provided by the disposal service should be reasonably clean and odor free when the vendor leaves them.

Instructions for Separating Recyclables

Depending on local facilities and practices, a waste disposal contractor may collect recyclable materials. Usually such arrangements require separation of specific categories of materials. Typical guidelines follow:

- **Glass:** Separate by color (green, brown, clear)
- **Aluminum:** Soda cans may have to be crushed. Foil, pie plates, and other aluminum materials may or may not be accepted.
- **Plastics:** Sort by type. Soda bottles made of polyethylene terephthalate (PET) have a number 1 inside the recycling logo. Milk jugs and detergent bottles made of high density polyethylene (HDPE) have a number 2. Some recyclers accept only one of these types of plastic, and they may not accept other types.
- **Newspapers:** Recyclers usually accept newsprint only (no inserts, magazines, or "slick" advertisements). The agency you select may sort this separately for you
- **High-Grade Paper:** Computer paper, stationery, office papers
- **Packaging Materials:** These are primary collection targets. While paper labels usually can remain in place, metal and plastic caps must be removed. All containers must be free of foodstuffs, which attract vermin.
- **Manufacturing Recyclables:** Exploring separate arrangements for collection of recyclables that are reused in manufacturing processes may be worthwhile because they may have a market value.

Benefits of Recycling

Establishing a recycling program has several benefits. Recycling reduces the trash deposited at landfills and thus has a positive effect on the environment. In some areas, waste disposal costs may be reduced because of the lower volume of trash. However, in some areas, removal of recyclables by a waste handler may increase waste disposal costs because of the need for extra containers and additional trips.

Despite their benefits, establishing recycling programs in rental communities requires extra effort. Separating recyclables is a learned habit, and the process can be inconvenient for participants. The more convenient the program is, the greater the participation from residents will be. The keys to success are ease of collection, timeliness of removal, and reminders to participants that reinforce positive behaviors.

CHAPTER 7:
ENVIRONMENTAL ISSUES

Real estate managers are responsible for protecting residents, preserving the property, reducing operating costs, and improving resident satisfaction. A manager must understand the environmental issues that damage properties and threaten the welfare of residents.

In this chapter:

> • **Environmental Issues**

ENVIRONMENTAL ISSUES

Mold	
What is mold?	• Mold is the common term for a variety of types of fungus that are found in the environment.
Where can mold be found?	• Mold spores circulate in indoor and outdoor air almost constantly. When they land, they only need a little humidity to grow. • Mold grows on wood, paper, carpet, and food, so there is no practical way to eliminate all mold and mold spores in an indoor environment
How can you control mold?	• The only way to control mold is to reduce and control moisture (refer to "Mold: Prevention Measures" checklist)
What are the dangers of mold exposure?	• Mold exposure can cause nasal stuffiness, eye irritation, wheezing, or skin irritation. People with serious allergies to molds may have fever and shortness of breath, and people with chronic lung illnesses may develop mold infections in their lungs.
Why should the site manager be concerned?	• In some cases, insurance claim payouts and jury awards have gone as high as $195 million. Like many claims, once a claim is filed, coverage may be dropped or premiums increase dramatically.

TIPS:
It is important to contact a professional when mold is detected to determine the extent of contamination and recommend next steps.

RESOURCES:
For current and complete information pertaining to identification, prevention and remediation of mold, **visit www.epa.gov/mold**.

Tools such as *Mold - Detection, Prevention and Remediation* can be found under Education>On-Demand Learning>Checklists, Tools and More at **www.irem.org** and are free.

MOLD: PREVENTION MEASURES

☐ Maintain appropriate humidity levels
  o Mold grows at humidity levels from 65% to 99% at the surface on which it grows
  o Maintaining relative humidity below 50% inhibits mold and mildew growth, dust mite infestations, and bacteria
  o In colder climates, wintertime humidity levels must be even lower at generally 25% to 40%
  o To keep peoples' respiratory systems healthy, humidity should be above 25%
☐ Check the ground slope from exterior walls:
  o The ground should slope at least six inches within the first 10 feet from the wall
  o Rain and water should not be allowed to stand and possibly saturate walls or floors that contact the earth
☐ Use the proper size air-conditioner for the space and/or room
☐ Use dehumidifiers
☐ Install exhaust fans in places such as kitchens, bathrooms, and laundry rooms
☐ Use a heat recovery ventilator or energy recovery ventilator to remove excess humidity from kitchens, baths, and laundry areas
☐ Do not store anything in basement in contact with the basement walls
☐ Pay special attention to carpet on concrete floors
☐ Do not shut down ventilation systems during unoccupied hours

LEGAL ISSUE:
There are no federal laws, and few state or local laws related to exposure limits for mold in residential properties. Nevertheless, mold-related lawsuits continue to grow in number, and so do the damage awards associated with them.

If you fail to take care of leaks and mold grows as a result, you may be liable for not "maintaining a fit and habitable property," particularly if it can be proved that the mold has caused a health problem.

Lead	
What is the risk of lead?	• Excessive amounts of lead can cause lead poisoning and serious disabilities. • In children, lead poisoning can cause learning disabilities, hearing and/or visual impairment, permanent hearing and/or visual loss, and brain and nervous system damage. Lead poisoning can also affect adults, causing anemia, headaches, hallucinations, hypertension, and kidney damage • Lead is most dangerous in flake or dust form.
Where can mold be found?	• Paint (note that in 1978, the federal government drastically limited the lead content in paint) • Lead pipes and lead-based solder used on copper pipes (note that few lead pipes were used in buildings built after 1930. In 1988, lead-based solder was banned in home plumbing.) • Soil that can be released into drinking water when acidic or soft water corrodes pipes or solders or when leached from brass fixtures and lead-lined tanks in water coolers • Leaded gasoline also contributed to lead in the soil prior to its ban • Common renovation activities like sanding, cutting, and demolition can create hazardous lead dust and chips by disturbing lead-based paint
Why should a site manager be concerned?	• Since a manager acts as an agent for a property owner, the manager may be liable to a buyer or resident if he or she knowingly violates lead-based paint regulations. Penalties include fines, liability for damages, court costs, and attorney fees.

LEAD: LEGAL ISSUES

Residential Lead-Based Paint Hazard Reduction Act

- This act, often referred to as Title X, calls for the evaluation of lead-poisoning risk in each residence and action in reducing that hazard.
- Since 1996, it also requires landlord and seller disclosure in connection with the rental or sale of pre-1978 dwellings.
- Copies of the regulation and the information pamphlet that must be given to renters of pre-1978 buildings can be obtained from the National Lead Information Center: **www2.epa.gov/lead**
- All leases, rental, and real estate sales agreements must also include certain language to ensure that disclosure and notification actually take place.
- Both OSHA and the EPA have written regulations explaining this rule.

Toxic Substances and Control Act (T.S.C.A.), Section 406(b)

- Applies to residential properties built before 1978
- Requires that tenants be given notification every time a painted surface of more than two square feet is disturbed
- Specifies that information about the work in an occupied unit as well as common areas must be provided to tenants

2008 EPA Rule Requiring Use of Lead-Safe Practices

- Beginning in 2010, contractors and firms performing renovation, repair and painting projects that disturb lead-based paint in residential properties and child-care facilities built before 1978 must be certified and must follow specific work practices to prevent lead contamination
- Additionally, firms must use certified renovators who are trained by EPA-approved training providers to follow lead-safe work practices. Individuals can become certified renovators by taking an eight-hour training book from an EPA-approved training provider.

LEGAL ISSUE:
Landlords may open themselves to litigation if they fail to maintain premises containing lead-based paint. Lead toxicity may take years to manifest and lawsuits may be filed as long as a decade after a resident inhabited a unit. Landlords should maintain detailed records, including records of repairs and any past lead testing or abatement. A company which no longer manages the property may still be sued, even if they no longer operate the property.

LEAD: ACTION ITEMS

New Residents
- ☐ Provide residents with the EPA booklet (September, 2013), "Protect Your Family from Lead in Your Home."
- ☐ Disclose information about lead risks on the property to prospective and/or renewing tenants before they sign a lease. This includes records and reports concerning common areas and other units when such information was obtained as a result of a building-wide evaluation
- ☐ Add a lead disclosure attachment to the lease or insert language that includes a "Lead Warning Statement" and confirms that you have complied with all notification requirements.

Existing Residents
- ☐ Monitor the condition of any surfaces that contain lead-based paint, and keep a log to on the condition of the paint and date of inspection.
- ☐ Determine the frequency of inspections by considering the age of the building, condition of the paint, and whether children are present.
- ☐ Develop a maintenance program to keep paint in place, such as wet-scraping any loose paint, priming it, and painting over it at least once a year with lead-free paint
- ☐ Inform residents when repairs or renovations will take place. Give the tenants another copy of the EPA booklet before beginning work.
- ☐ Test for lead hazards in paints or pipes. If lead is present, take appropriate action.
- ☐ Consult an expert before removing lead-fixtures
- ☐ Clean up lead-contaminated dust with a specifically designed vacuum and detergent
- ☐ Ensure contractors use lead-safe work practices and follow these three simple procedures:
  - o Contain the work area
  - o Minimize dust
  - o Clean up thoroughly

RESOURCES:
For current and complete information pertaining to identification, prevention and remediation of mold, visit **www.epa.gov/mold**.

Bed Bugs

What are bed bugs?	• Bed bugs are one of several species of insects visible to the naked eye. They are reddish brown and about the size of lentils or apple seeds. • Younger bed bugs are white or translucent yellow and are small enough to be almost invisible
Where are they found?	• Bed bugs thrive in sofas, mattresses, and other furniture and are mainly active at night
Why are they a problem?	• Bed bugs are blood-sucking insects. They tend to bite the exposed skin of the face, neck and arms of a sleeping individual. Their bites often go unnoticed until they develop into low itchy welts that may take weeks to go away. • Infestation can lead to problems beyond medical treatment and extermination; some people develop anxiety and insomnia • Residents may not be forthcoming about a bed bug infestation due to stigma

Bed Bugs: Myths

Myth	Reality
You can't see a bed bug	• You should be able to see adult bed bugs, nymphs and eggs with your naked eye
Bed bugs won't come out if the room is brightly lit	• While bed bugs prefer darkness, keeping the light on at night won't deter them
Bed bugs live in dirty places	• Bed bugs are not attracted to dirt and grime; they are attracted to warmth, blood and carbon dioxide. However, clutter offers more hiding spots.
Bed bugs transmit diseases	• There have been no cases or studies that indicate bed bugs pass diseases from one host to another
Pesticide applications alone will easily eliminate bed bug infestations	• Proper use of pesticides will not by itself eliminate bed bugs • Bed bug populations in different areas of the country have developed resistance to many pesticides • With a resistant population, some products and application methods may only make the problem worse • Bed bug control requires a treatment strategy that includes a variety of techniques plus continued monitoring • A qualified pest management professional (PMP) should be consulted to address any bed bug infestation

Source: **www.epa.gov/bedbugs/**

BED BUGS: ACTION ITEMS

Prevention
- Train staff and contractors and educate residents about bed bugs
- Encourage residents to avoid secondhand furniture or to check it before bringing it onto the property

Identification
- Look for bed bugs near seams and tags of mattress and box spring; cracks in frame and head board. Also, curtain rods, baseboard heaters, and behind chipped paint or loose wallpaper.
- Look for physical signs of bed bugs: Dark spots, smears or reddish stains on bedding or mattresses; tiny white eggs or eggshells; molted skins; live bugs
- Bed bug sniffing dogs can be used to find bugs in various stages of development

Treatment
- When bed bugs are detected, it is important to take immediate action. You don't want them spreading to other units or areas on the property. Also, it is much more cost effective to treat a small infestation than a large one.
- Hire knowledgeable pest control specialists who understand effective extermination of bed bugs, ideally without use of pesticides
- Heat infested articles and/or areas to at least 113 °F (45 °C) for 1 hour. The higher the temperature, the shorter the time needed to kill bed bugs at all life stages.
- Cold treatments (below 0 °F (-19 °C) for at least 4 days) can eliminate some infestations. The cooler the temperature, the less time needed to kill bed bugs. Home freezers usually are not cold enough to reliably kill bed bugs.

Communication
- Inform residents about treatment efforts, including sending a preparation letter before treatment and any follow-up measures
- In condo buildings, the cost of pest control services should be charged to the unit owner of the original infestation, if possible
- Have an attorney review rules and riders related to pest management

LEGAL ISSUE:
In a recent case in Maryland, a jury awarded $800,000 to a woman whose landlord failed to clean up a known bed bug infestation prior to her taking residence. Some landlords add specific bed bug addenda to leases to require residents to pay the expenses for bed bug treatment, if it is determined that the resident was responsible of the infestation.

RESOURCES:
JPM® magazine article "Don't Let the Bed Bugs Bites into Your NOI" by Greg L. Martin and John L. Berg, July/August 2011.

Environmental Issues

CHECKLIST: DEALING WITH ENVIRONMENTAL ISSUES

☐ Whatever the issue, act on it. If you ignore it, it will only get worse and cost more to remedy.

☐ Keep your supervisor informed of any issues, communication with residents, and actions taken

☐ Document the issue and any remedies

☐ Make sure there are company guidelines and policies pertaining to environmental issues

☐ Ensure that staff are trained on company policies and that there are ongoing conversations about environmental issues

☐ Make sure that staff and contractors are aware of any local or state ordinances on environmental issues

☐ Use licensed/qualified contractors

TIPS:
Both the property manager and the owner have legal exposure and the potential for legal liability if environmental hazards are found on the property.

NOTES:
Refer to **Appendix E** for information about other environmental issues:
• Asbestos
• Carbon Dioxide
• Carbon Monoxide
• Fiberglass
• Freon/Chlorofluorocarbons
• Hazardous Waste
• Indoor Air Quality (IAQ)
• Leaking Underground Storage Tanks (USTs)
• PCBs
• Radon

DIG DEEPER WITH IREM RESOURCES

Publications

Ashley, Brad J., Gallagher, John N., Howard, Mary Jayne, Muhlebach, Richard F., Whitman, Lee A. *Managing Your Maintenance Programs: A Guide to Implementing Cost-Effective Plans for Properties.* Chicago: Institute of Real Estate Management, 2010.

> This publication provides a guide to implementing cost-effective maintenance programs.

The Real Estate Manager's Technical Glossary. Chicago: Institute of Real Estate Management, 1999.

> This book provides nearly 2,000 terms and definitions that describe commonly encountered technical items.

Klein, John, Levin, Sharon, Cloutier, Deborah. *A Practical Guide to Energy Management.* Chicago: Institute of Real Estate Management, 2005.

> This publication addresses creating an energy management plan, achieving energy reduction goals and the resulting financial benefits, purchasing energy, working with tenants, and more.

Klein, John, Drucker, Alison, Vizzier, Kirk. *A Practical Guide to Green Real Estate Management.* Chicago: Institute of Real Estate Management, 2009.

> This publication provides a guide to implementing green real estate management programs.

Websites

www.irem.org
The IREM website is your first-stop for information on real estate management. With resources organized by topic and property type, you will find the forms, tools, publications, webinars, and tutorials you need to help you manage your business and keep up with the industry.

Note that the IREM® Code of Professional Ethics can be found on the IREM® website at **www.irem.org/ethics**

iremsustainability.com
The IREM Sustainability website features three comprehensive tools to help you operate more energy-efficient and sustainable properties.

IREM On-Demand Learning (www.irem.org)

• Top 10 Building Systems To Inspect Now (Tutorial)
• Maintenance Mobile (Recorded Webinar)
• Energy and Water Conservation (Tutorial)
• Developing an Emergency Plan (Tutorial)
• Understanding Insurance Coverage (Tutorial)
• Mold: Detection, Prevention, Remediation (Interactive Tool)

IREM Courses (www.irem.org)
· Sustainable Real Estate Management (SRM001)

Articles
Published bi-monthly by IREM, the *Journal of Property Management* offers comprehensive coverage of the real estate management industry, including frequent features and columns on maintenance topics.

Income/Expense Analysis® Reports
The IREM Income/Expense Analysis® Reports are the industry standard in relaying precise property data to owners, investors and tenants. Valuable operating data is collected for Conventional Apartments; Office Buildings; Federally Assisted Apartments; Condos, Co-ops, and Planned Unit Developments; and Shopping Centers. But we can't do it without your help.

Submit your data by April 1 of each year at http://IE.IREM.ORG to receive a FREE Income/Expense Analysis® book (a $485 value) and a FREE Individual Building Report. (Available once published by September.)

The Income/Expense Analysis® Reports are available for purchase in softcover books, downloadable .pdf or Excel, and Interactive online Labs.

PART IV:
MARKETING AND LEASING

The following topics are covered:

- Demographics
- Target markets
- Comparison grid analysis
- Marketing strategies and social media
- Leasing tactics
- Affordable housing wait list procedures
- Fair Housing and Americans with Disabilities Act (ADA) compliance
- Landlord-tenant laws
- Lease-term provisions
- Resident retention strategies

CHAPTER 1:
ANALYZING THE MARKET

In order to set appropriate rental rates and conduct effective and profitable marketing and leasing activities, the site manager and property team must first understand the property's position in the market and have solid knowledge of the subject property. A manager must be able to conduct market, property, and comparison analyses, which are critical to setting optimal rents for the property and meeting the owner's goals and objectives.

In this chapter:

- **Market Analysis**
- **Property Analysis**
- **Establishing Rents**

MARKET ANALYSIS

Q&A
Q. What is marketing?
A. Real estate marketing is the methods used to rent space and retain current residents. In order to conduct effective and profitable marketing and leasing activities, the site manager must first understand the property's region, neighborhood, and demographic profile by conducting a market analysis.

Conducting a market analysis should be the first step performed in any marketing and leasing activities. Based on facts rather than opinions or assumptions, a market analysis helps answer the following key questions:

- What are the property's region and neighborhood boundaries?
- What is the economic climate in the market?
- What is the demographic profile of the area?

Within a market analysis, a site manager studies the economic climate of the area and identifies the property's region, neighborhood, and demographic profile. The goal is to describe the market area as it relates physically and economically to the property. Refer to Figure 1-1 for the components of a market analysis.

FIGURE 1-1: MARKET ANALYSIS

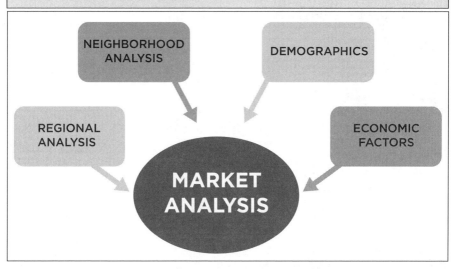

Regional Analysis

A *region* is the market area in which changes in economic conditions are likely to affect the fiscal performance of a particular property and thereby determine its value. A region is often defined as the metropolitan statistical area (MSA) in which a property is located. Refer to Figure 1-2 for additional details on MSAs.

A regional analysis determines economic information, such as employment and per capita income, and demographic information, such as age, race, and gender. Population data are also factors—a careful study of the region may determine that the area does not have enough large households to support any additional three-bedroom units.

FIGURE 1-2: A CLOSER LOOK:
METROPOLITAN STATISTICAL AREAS (MSAS)

- Metropolitan and micropolitan statistical areas (metro and micro areas) are geographic entities delineated by the Office of Management and Budget (OMB) for use by Federal statistical agencies in collecting, tabulating, and publishing Federal statistics
- The term "Core Based Statistical Area" (CBSA) is a collective term for both metro and micro areas
- A metro area contains a core urban area of 50,000 or more population, and a micro area contains an urban core of at least 10,000 (but less than 50,000) population
- Each metro or micro area consists of one or more counties and includes the counties containing the core urban area, as well as any adjacent counties that have a high degree of social and economic integration (as measured by commuting to work) with the urban core

RESOURCES:
For the most recent MSA information, visit the U.S. Census
Bureau website: **www.census.gov/population/metro**

Neighborhood Analysis

While regional analysis generally describes a given area, *neighborhood analysis* indicates the potential for a specific site to be successful. *Neighborhood* refers to the section of the larger region within which buildings generally compete with one another for residents. The area generally has common characteristics of population and land use. The neighborhood analysis should identify the selling points of the surrounding area as well as the undesirable features and the types of residents that will be attracted to the area. The neighborhood analysis is similar to the regional analysis, but more narrowly focused.

Mapping the Neighborhood

Determining the boundaries of the neighborhood is important in order to begin investigating demographic information and trends for the area. Boundaries can be natural, such as rivers and lakes, or manmade, such as highways and streets. Representations of the neighborhood on a map provide an excellent resource when prospecting for residents. Boundaries can be established, and competing properties will be revealed. Marketing efforts can be focused in the designated area.

TIPS:
An effective way to map the neighborhood of a residential property is to determine the place of employment of each of its residents. Plot these points, along with the location of the property, on a map drawn to scale. Also keep track of the number of retired or nonworking residents. Refer to Figure 1-3 for a sample neighborhood map.

FIGURE 1-3: MAPPING THE NEIGHBORHOOD

Single Family Home Impact: For the management of single family home rentals, neighborhood analysis may include data on the quality of the school systems.
- Fee-based websites offer searches of available statistical rankings based on academics
- Free websites, such as **www.greatschools.org** are growing in popularity as a means of providing "user-generated" content on the quality of local public and private schools

Affordable Housing Impact: There is a fundamental difference between the market for affordable housing and the market for conventional housing. Whereas conventional housing is often an amenity-driven market, affordable housing is a price-driven market. As a result, it is important to clearly identify the competition, considering that apartments compete less on the basis of proximity than on affordability.

Campus Analysis

Student Housing Impact: Another level of analysis required when managing student housing is the completion of a campus analysis. A campus analysis looks at the following items:
- University and field of study
- Types of students (traditional, day/night, etc.)
- Age (average)
- Percentage of out-of-state residents and in-state residents
- Ratio of school beds to enrolled students (a lower ratio is better for student housing income)
- Campus political environment
- Administration
- Health of university
- Supporting funds
- Housing requirements (e.g. co-ed not allowed, etc.)
- A great source of information to assist with the campus analysis is the National Center for Education Statistics: **www.nces.ed.gov**

Demographics

After the region and neighborhood have been established and plotted, the site manager must gather additional information to complete the picture. The following data comprises the demographic profile of an area that is needed to forecast residential property demands accurately:

- Population size
- Density
- Age
- Race
- Household
- Family composition
- Education
- Occupation
- Income
- Spending habits

In addition to examining current population data, site managers should analyze population growth to determine the area's future needs. Population growth projections are based on the assumption that established patterns will continue from year to year. However, many factors besides normal increases in growth must be considered. New industries or new schools and colleges may stimulate growth, but a factory shutdown or economic setback may lead to a decline.

Site managers use demographic information about the local market to target advertising efforts to appropriate market niches. For example, the senior demographic has vastly different needs and interests than people under the age of 30. Identifying the occupant profile and desired property amenities will determine the property's target market and its position in the market.

RESOURCES:
The American Fact Finder website (**factfinder2.census.gov**) is the U.S. Government's most comprehensive census research tool for the general public and can be used to find specific demographic data.

Vendor Demographic and Market Research

Apart from the U.S. Census Bureau, private companies conduct market/demographic research to provide a snapshot of the "segmentation" of the area. These reports analyze multiple factors including the psychographics, or customer buying trends, of an area. Where the U.S. Census Bureau will track the relative proportional spending habits of a demographic segment, the vendor-produced reports may include the spending choices of a demographic segment. This type of report is increasingly seen as valuable, as it saves the time required to compile exhaustive demographic data.

Economic Factors in Market Analysis

In addition to demographics, examining the economic characteristics of the area and their effect on the rental market is important. Supply, demand, occupancy rates, and vacancy rates provide insight into the economic environment of the area.

Supply and Demand

Supply refers to the quantity (units) or amount (square feet) of space available in the market at a given time to meet demand. *Demand* is the need or request for that available space. Supply and demand for residential property can be affected by demographic characteristics such as household income, age, and family composition.

Landlord's Market

When supply is less than demand, it is a landlord's market. There is less competition for residents, therefore the value and rent of the space increase.

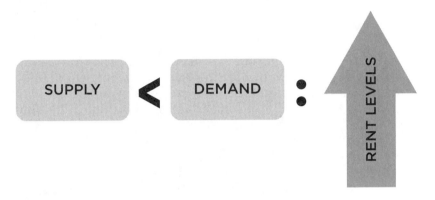

Renter's Market

On the other hand, when supply is greater than demand, it is a renter's market. Increased competition for residents leads to a decline in rents and difficulty leasing.

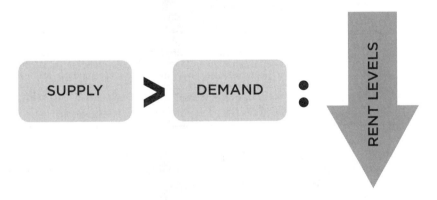

Occupancy and Vacancy Rates

The *occupancy rate* is the number of occupied residential units expressed as a percentage of the total number of units. When subtracted from the total, the difference is the *vacancy rate* (the ratio of vacant space to total rentable space).

Occupancy Rate = Amount of Occupied Space ÷
Total Amount of Available Space

Vacancy Rate = Amount of Vacant Space ÷ Amount of Available Space

For rental housing, the vacancy rate includes vacant units in existing buildings plus vacancies in new construction (the unleased inventory of newly built apartments) but excludes vacancies that are, for any reason, not available for occupancy. Reasons may include awaiting demolition, rehabilitation, conversion, or seasonal occupancy.

Additional sources for obtaining vacancy data for the market area include:
- Research published by larger real estate corporations
- Tracking the fluctuations of local print and online newspaper advertisements for available units
- Real estate online listing services such as **Rentals.com**
- Anecdotal evidence produced through research
- In some areas, utility companies provide a snapshot of vacancy rates in local cities estimated from the number of units that are not current with a resident user account

Single Family Home Impact: Vacancy rates in the market area affect supply and demand for single family homes as well, as these rental properties are competing for the same market. With the single family home itself, vacancy is always 100%. Vacancy of the single family home is therefore the most costly to the owner of any property type.

Collecting Data

There are a myriad of resources one can use to analyze the region, neighborhood, and demographic profile for a specific property.

Source	Description
American Fact Finder **factfinder2.census.gov**	• Population size, density, distribution • Population forecasts • Age, education, and family size • Per capita income, disposable income • Consumer spending and savings

Source	Description
American Housing Survey **www.census.gov/housing/ahs**	• Vacant housing units • Household characteristics • Housing and neighborhood quality • Housing costs, equipment, fuels • Size of housing unit • Recent movers
U.S. Bureau of Economic Analysis **www.bea.gov**	• Reports on regional business activity and personal income • Employment data on available labor force, types of jobs, area employers • Forecasts of expanding job markets
State Agencies and Local **Governments** **www.statelocalgov.net**	• State and local taxing authorities • Zoning laws and use restrictions • Construction permits issued for housing
Local Chambers of Commerce	• Local tax regulations • Variety of companies and industries • Strength and vitality of businesses
Review and Recommend Websites	• Examples: **www.RentAdvisor.com** and **www.Yelp.com**

RESOURCES:
Numerous publications such as the *Income/Expense Analysis®* reports published by the Institute of Real Estate Management (**www.irem.org**) and Dollars & Cents® published by the Urban Land Institute (**www.uli.org**) provide a wealth of data and information. The National Apartment Association (**www.naahq.org**) compiles economic data that details housing and vacancy statistics on a national and regional level.

PROPERTY ANALYSIS

So far, our analysis has centered on gathering and studying a variety of data regarding the region and neighborhood of the property. The next component of the analysis is to examine the subject property as well as comparable properties in the market area. Comparable properties are used to identify differences from the subject property for the purposes of estimating market rents. As a site manager, your daily presence on the property enables you to become deeply familiar with various site attributes. It is important to consider the strengths and weaknesses of the property as they relate to the following:

Factor	Description
Location	• Location is one of the most important factors when assessing the property • A well-located property can command higher rents despite a lack of amenities or the presence of other negative features, but a well-maintained but poorly located site may not generate the income necessary to operate efficiently • Of concern for any site is where it is located in relation to residential areas, schools and college campuses, offices, and neighboring industries • The immediate surroundings of the property are also an issue; what is across the street and adjacent to the site affects the property's image
Space and Amenities	• The square footage, layout, numbers of rooms, and amenities are other important site attributes • Amenities include items such as parking, washers/dryers, fireplaces, hardwood floors, fitness facilities, high-speed Internet access, or anything else the resident finds valuable • Whether the resident must pay for certain utilities is also an important consideration
Property Appearance and Condition	• Examine the average age and character of the property, including the building condition, grounds, landscaping, and signage • Curb appeal goes beyond the appearance of the exterior to include common areas and interiors • Prospects make judgments regarding the quality of the building based on their first impression of its appearance, which either motivates them to consider signing a lease in the building or convinces them to look elsewhere for the qualities they are seeking. Prospects also consider the interior condition of the building when making a rental decision
Property Management and Staff	• Prospective residents will be concerned about how well the property is maintained and what security features it offers, such as entry systems, intrusion alarms, and/or 24-hour security staff • Strong first impressions are created in prospects' minds when public areas are clean and well lighted, the lawn is trimmed and edged, the parking lot pavement is smooth, and trash is removed at regular intervals • In addition, on-site staff must be friendly and helpful, and they must look professional

Single Family Home Impact: Single Family Houses are increasingly common providers of residential rental space. Increasingly, real estate management companies are recognizing that multifamily properties are competing with single family housing in some areas.

Student Housing Impact: Additional staffing considerations include a Resident Assistant (RA) and/or a Community Assistant (CA). These positions may be responsible for enforcing rules and regulations, serving as a resource to students, and fostering a sense of community. Due to the nature of these responsibilities and the student environment, hours of operation are not typical and often include evenings, nights, and weekends.

Sustainability Impact: Depending on the demographics of your target market, there may be a marketing value for residential properties that have taken steps toward sustainability. Some prospects will seek out sustainable space. If their choice comes down to an apartment in a sustainable building and an apartment in a non-sustainable one, they will likely choose the sustainable building, especially if they are committed to social responsibility. Some may even be willing to pay a little more in rent.

Even the inexpensive sustainable upgrades can have an impact. Advertise your activities and achievements along with the property's amenities, and maximize the marketing impact of your sustainability efforts. If your occupancy rates go up, or you are able to raise rents, this demonstration of success may interest the owner in more substantial upgrades.

Studying the Competition

After assessing the subject property's features, it is time to see how it relates to the competition. Visiting the property's competitors will show exactly what it is up against in terms of competing properties and how to play up its strengths compared to others. The site manager can observe and implement others' effective ideas and solutions and build a collection of information on properties that compete for residents. This information will also be important in applying one of the methods of establishing rental rates, such as comparison grid analysis, that the next section discusses.

By regularly visiting each competitor and compiling a list of its features, real estate managers can gather relevant facts about the property. In addition, they can determine the economics of the residents' leases, such as rental rates, concessions, vacancy rates, and any additional charges.

Q&A

Q. How do you identify comparable properties?

A. Many site managers struggle with how to do this, especially when dealing with an existing property. It is important to look for commonalities in age, building type, price point, amenities and floor plans. However, the most effective way to identify comps is to ask your prospects and your former residents (at the time they give notice). For example:
- "Where else have you looked for apartments today?"
- "I'm sorry to hear you're moving, what community will you be calling home next year?"
- "Since you didn't rent from us, do you mind telling me where you did rent?"

By asking these questions of every prospect and former resident, it will be possible to identify communities you're hearing about often and to determine who you're truly competing against. Depending on product type and price point, those options that are your "true comps" may not be in the neighborhood or immediate area.

ESTABLISHING RENTAL RATES

Once you are familiar with the demographic and economic outlook for the local market, as well as the features of the subject property and its competitors, you can begin to determine rental rates for the property.

Income Considerations

When considering a pricing strategy, it is important to understand any income guidelines or restrictions for the community. Some communities are market rate, while others may have a government mandated affordable income component that sets limits on pricing. When dealing with affordable income communities, the following factors may affect the site manager's ability to set competitive pricing:

- Income restriction (e.g., low-income or ultra low-income housing)
- Section 8
- Communities with 80% market rate and 20% affordable rate
- Tax credit properties
- Zoning restrictions

Affordable Housing Impact: In general, communities with an affordable income component have limited income potentials.

Rent-Setting Methods

Site managers often assist in establishing rental rates for the property. Rent setting is more common for market rate communities than for those with an affordable income component due to the rent restrictions inherent in affordable income communities.

TIPS:
Site managers are on the front lines of their communities every day. They will have intimate knowledge of their market and communities that other people within their company may not have. A great site manager will make recommendations and drive the pricing process for their community.

Cost vs. What the Market Will Bear

The most common initial pricing method focuses almost entirely on what is possible in the marketplace. It combines knowledge of what is needed to pay the bills with awareness of which rent levels will result in an unacceptable number of vacancies. A great manager will constantly be pushing to find the balance between highest possible rents while still maintaining a high occupancy percentage. Regularly evaluating your company's pricing within your market and making small adjustments to your rental rates as market conditions change (e.g., traffic, closing ratio, competitor prices, market demand for apartments) will enable you to successfully find that balance.

Best-of-Type Pricing

Best-of-type pricing involves categorizing the units into similar groups. Once the site manager has a thorough knowledge of the rents set by competitors, he or she can establish rent levels for similar units. For example, all of the one-bedroom units with a den would be one group, and one-bedroom units without a den would make up another.

The site manager should visit each and every unit and identify the best unit for each group. The most desirable unit may have extra subtle features, such as a better view, an extra window, or more closet space. A rent should first be set for that unit. Based on that rent, the rents for the less desirable units in the same group can be altered accordingly. Appropriate deductions should be made in descending order of unit desirability. This process is repeated for each apartment type.

The main disadvantage of this pricing method is the time that must be initially spent to make your determinations; however, after it has been completed, this method results in the highest total rent for your community.

In an ideal situation, a manager would be utilizing best-of-type pricing in conjunction with what the market will bear pricing. It is not either/or, many times they are used together.

Example: Best-of-Type Pricing

Consider an example of a building 25 stories tall, with 24 floors of 12 apartments each—a total of 288 units. The residential floors are numbered 1 through 24, and the four corner units on each floor are one-bedroom-plus-den apartments. The remaining units are efficiencies and two-bedroom units.

For convenience, we will discuss only the one-bedroom-plus-den units on the front corners of the building. The front of the building faces a row of similar buildings across a wide boulevard. Twenty-five feet away from one side of the building is an aging nine-story apartment residence. On the other side is a large, picturesque park. The process for determining rents is as follows:

1. First, the site manager changes the floor numbering system. Apartments on higher floors have greater status appeal, and that means more rent dollars. Because the lobby level is about one and a half stories high, the numbering sequence can logically begin with the third floor. The manager can omit the thirteenth floor because superstitious people avoid it. The resulting top floor number is 27 rather than 24.

2. After a thorough study of the competition, the manager identifies the best one-bedroom-plus-den apartments in the building—the top apartments overlooking the park. Based on the manager's complete knowledge of the market, the rent for those apartments is estimated at the highest rate the market will bear. Before the

---

rent is set, however, improvements are made to the top two floors to create special penthouse-type units. When the improvements are complete, the manager assesses their market value.

3. After comparing both floors and finding virtually no difference in view, the manager establishes identical rents for all of the one-bedroom-plus-den penthouse-type units.

4. Moving downward, the manager finds the corner units on the next three floors share the same view as the top floors, so their rent is reduced by the market value of the penthouse upgrades only.

5. Continuing the inspection, the manager discovers that the view suffers slightly on the next three floors and lowers the rent accordingly. Toward the middle of the building, further rent reductions are applied to blocks of units to adjust for loss of view and the reduced status appeal of lower floors (Refer to Figure 1-4).

During the inspection, the site manager discovered that the older building does not impede views or have a negative influence above the fifteenth floor, so rent realignment to account for the different views from the two sides of the building was not a factor. On the fifteenth floor and below, the presence of the older building was obvious, and the rent adjustments began to reflect that.

FIGURE 1-4: BEST OF TYPE PRICING EXAMPLE

Floor	Tier Facing Park	Tier Facing Building
27	$920	$920
26	920	920
25	890	890
24	890	890
23	890	890
22	878	878
21	878	878
20	878	878
19	865	865
18	865	865
17	865	865
16	865	865
15	852	855
14	852	845
12	852	835
11	852	825
10	842	815
9	842	805
8	835	795
7	830	785
6	825	775
5	820	765
4	810	755
3	800	745

Monthy Total: $20,616 $20,204
Average Monthly Rent: $850.42

Best-of-type pricing can also be used for a variety of property types and features. The principle works the same way, as the best-of-type unit sets the top rent level. Features that may impact rent include:

☐ Corner units
☐ Units with cathedral ceilings
☐ Dumpster view
☐ Pool view
☐ Private yards/green space
☐ Preferred community location (e.g., near laundry, front of community)
☐ Newer appliances
☐ New carpet

Comparison Grid Analysis

A comparison grid analysis involves comparing the rents and features of local competitors to the subject property. For purposes of comparison, it is important to choose properties that are similar to the subject in type.

While contemporary methods of comparison analysis rely upon automated software and other technology, it is important to understand the conceptual methodology of comparison analysis as a foundation in order to maximize the value of such tools. Site managers must rely upon their own knowledge and instincts to complete an effective comparison analysis, regardless of tool.

To begin, the features you observed in the property analysis are evaluated in comparison to the subject property and given a rating. For each feature,

> • If the comparable is rated superior to the subject property, a **NEGATIVE** number is assigned to adjust the comparable downward.

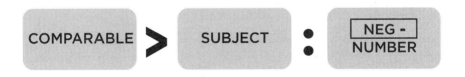

> • If the comparable is rated inferior to the subject property, a **POSITIVE** number is assigned to adjust the comparable upward.

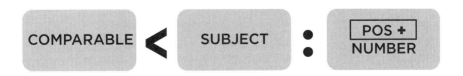

The adjustments for each property are totaled, and added or subtracted to the property's rent to determine the adjusted market minimum rent for that property. Finally, the average of these adjusted market minimum rents is found to determine an approximate market rent for the subject property.

For most properties, the value of the variables in the comparison grid will be determined by management company policy and computed by the spreadsheet or software. The value of any variable (for example, a reserved parking space) may also be set in the software.

In addition to helping establish rental rates, the use of a comparison grid should highlight the strengths and weaknesses of the subject property relative to the competition. In multifamily properties, a comparison grid should be completed for each unit type (e.g. one bedroom apartments are compared to one bedroom apartments.)

Although intended to be data-driven, comparison grid analysis is subjective by nature because the choice of features compared and the values assigned to them are usually arbitrary. For this reason, only one person should conduct the analysis. Keep this limitation in mind, especially in regard to setting rents.

TIPS:
The IREM Financial Analysis Spreadsheet contains a Comparison Grid tab that automatically calculates the values for you. The Financial Analysis Spreadsheet is free for IREM Members at **www.irem.org**.

App	Description
	Smart Phone Application: The IREM comps app is a tool that allows you to establish competitive rents for your residential property. You can enter data for three comparable properties, and the app will calculate the adjusted effective rent for your subject property. You will also have the ability to e-mail the results in spreadsheet format to anyone.

	Student Housing Impact: Consider the following additional criteria when completing a comparison grid analysis for student housing: computer center, wifi, cable TV, tanning beds, social programming, transportation, bike storage, furnished vs. unfurnished, and so forth.

RESOURCES:
Downloadable forms such as residential comparison grids can be found under Resources>Forms & Checklists at **www.irem.org** and are free for members. These sample forms and agreements are not endorsed by the Institute of Real Estate Management. They are presented for informational purposes only.

FIGURE 1-5: SAMPLE IREM COMPARISON GRID

Residential Comparison Grid

	Subject	Comparable 1	Comparable 2	Comparable 3
Property Name	Silver Creek	Casablanca Apartments	Sky Harbor	
Base rental rate		$920.00	$935.00	$925.00
- Concessions				
+ Other income				
= Effective rent/unit		$920.00	$935.00	$925.00
÷ Square feet/unit	600	715	760	625
Effective rent/sq ft		$1.29	$1.23	$1.48

Categories	Description	Description	+/- Adj	Description	+/- Adj	Description	+/- Adj
Location	Very Good	Very Good	$0.00	Good	$5.00		
Age	3	4.5	$0.00	5	$0.00		
Building condition:							
Exterior	Good	Good	$0.00	Very Good	-$5.00		
Grounds	Fair	Fair	$0.00	Poor	$5.00		
Common areas	Good	Good	$0.00	Fair	$5.00		
Public lighting	Good	Good	$0.00	Good	$0.00		
Other							
Unit interior:							
Recent kitchen upgrades	No	Yes	-$10.00	Yes	$10.00		
Stainless appliances	Yes	No	$5.00	Yes	-$5.00		
Washer/dryer	No	No	$0.00	No	$0.00		
Closets/storage	Good	Very good	-$5.00	Very good	-$5.00		
Flooring	Poor	Good	-$5.00	Good	-$5.00		
Central air	Yes	Yes	$0.00	Yes	$0.00		
Other							
Type of parking	Reserved	Covered	$10.00	Open	$15.00		
Fitness center included	No	Yes	-$10.00	Yes	-$10.00		
Access to Interstate	Yes	No	$5.00	Yes	$0.00		
Conference rooms/work stations	Yes	No	-$5.00	No	-$5.00		
Owner paid utilities	water/sewer	water/electric/sewer	-$10.00	water/sewer	$0.00		
Total rent adjustments		-$25.00		$5.00		-$25.00	
Adjusted effective rent/unit		$895.00		$940.00		$0.00	
Average adjusted effective rent/unit	$917.00						
Average adjusted effective rent/sq ft	$1.53						

Revenue Management Software

Regardless of the pricing strategy used, the goal is always the same: to maximize income to the owner. Revenue management software relies upon real-time modeling and the forecasting of demand behavior in the market to calculate the best pricing policy for optimizing profits. The software recommends the best possible price for each unit on a daily basis in order to maximize revenue. Each management company sets up their software based on unique criteria, but the general concept is similar across property management companies.

TIPS:
There are many revenue management systems available, including YieldStar™, Yardi RENTmaximizer™, RentPush.com, Rainmaker LRO™, and more.

Site managers must be vigilant about pricing guidelines and revenue management software can assist. For example, it may be difficult for a site manager to adjust rents quickly enough to match supply with demand, so potential income is not realized because prices should have been raised. Or, apartments are not leased because prices were not lowered.

TIPS:
While there are many advantages to the use of revenue management software, nothing takes the place of a site manager's critical thinking skills, deep property knowledge, and common sense. Revenue management software should not be considered a replacement for the value a site manager brings to the transaction.

Revenue management systems are a great tool, but the site manager should not be bound by the system if an alternate pricing approach makes more sense towards meeting the owner's goals and objectives and enhancing the overall value.

Example: Revenue Management Software Limits

Revenue management software doesn't always take the condition of the unit into account or the value of excellent customer service. The system may recommend a rate of $840, but you know your property leads the market for that floor plan and you think you can get $860. The incremental difference of $20 per month translates into real value.

CHAPTER 2:
CREATING A MARKETING PLAN

Selecting appropriate marketing plans and techniques attracts residents to the building, increases signed leases, and maximizes income for the owner. A manager must be able to determine appropriate marketing plans and strategies for the property.

In this chapter:

- Marketing Plan vs. Leasing Plan
- Marketing Plan Components
- Marketing Techniques
- Measuring Effectiveness

MARKETING PLAN VS. LEASING PLAN

After assessing the market in which the property is located, it is time to develop a plan for attracting residents. Two types of plans are commonly used in the leasing of property:

- The **marketing plan** is used to advertise and relay information about the property for the purposes of attracting residents. This plan provides the marketing goals for the property.

- The **leasing plan**, or more detailed plan, typically includes a site plan, unit numbers, square footage dimensions, and unit rental rates.

This chapter describes the components and functions of the marketing plan; the leasing plan will be discussed further in the next chapter.

Single Family Home Impact: Having a single marketing plan for multiple single family home contracts is highly unlikely. This form of real estate management is sometimes referred to as "scattered site" management. As marketing plans are highly location driven, it is typical to have separate marketing plans for each single family house. This is one of the more challenging aspects of managing single family homes, as it requires research for each unique location, subdivision, and neighborhood.

Affordable Housing Impact: Note that the discussion of marketing plans in this chapter is different from the affirmative fair housing marketing plans often required with affordable housing (depending on the financing vehicle and state requirements).

Student Housing Impact: With student housing, the timing of marketing is extremely important, and a solid plan should be in place. As students all move in at the same time, there is only a small window of opportunity available to market to these potential students.

MARKETING PLAN COMPONENTS

The site manager is exposed to feedback from the leasing team and working with the results of the marketing efforts every day. To be an exceptional manager, site managers should be able to develop, implement, and analyze their own marketing plans. Refer to the table below for elements of a typical marketing plan.

Component	Description
Purpose	• Shapes all marketing and leasing efforts • Reflects owner's goals and objectives • Reflects life cycle of the asset (lease-up, stabilization, rehabilitation) Repositioning requires a specific strategy/plan • Should be spelled out clearly and apply to all levels of the leasing team • Should use SMART goals (Refer to Figure 2-1)
Target Market	• Identifies the segment of the overall market for which the property is likely to have appeal • May be composed of a particular age group or income bracket that matches the current resident profile • Determined as part of the market analysis (Refer to the Tip below)
Image/ Messaging	• Should be what is communicated to the target market to distinguish the property from others • Emphasizes the most important features as perceived by the target market • Should position the property for competitive advantage, gained by promoting the features that set it apart from competitors as determined in the property analysis and comparative analysis (e.g., lower rent, location, reputation)
Timetable	• Establishes a schedule for the planning, production, and release of marketing materials, public relations events, and so forth • Provides a means for plotting the goals for the property on a calendar, determining how long it takes to achieve them, and assigning the staff member responsible for each marketing item (Refer to Figure 2-2)
Budget	• Specifies the money allocated for each activity related to marketing the property • Must be allocated in order to fulfill the owner's goals and objectives effectively

---

FIGURE 2-1: SMART GOALS

SMART is an acronym for the following characteristics of goals:

• **Specific:** the goal should be precise and explicit, not general or broad. For example, a general goal for the property would be "To acquire more residents." A specific goal might be "To decrease the vacancy rate by 4 percent within the next six months." Writing out these goals helps visualize them more clearly.

• **Measurable:** the more specific a goal is, the easier quantifying results will be. Measuring the effectiveness of the marketing plan is discussed later in this chapter.

• **Agreed Upon:** using the owner's objectives as a foundation, the site manager must gain commitment from all leasing professionals on the marketing and leasing goals for the property.

• **Realistic:** increasing occupancy by 20 percent in two months may not be an attainable goal for the property. To be realistic, the goal must be one that management is both willing and able to achieve.

• **Time-Based:** a specific deadline is set for completion of the goal. To use the examples above, "To decrease the vacancy rate by 4 percent within six months" would be an effective, time-based goal.

Q&A

Q. What's the difference between marketing and messaging?

A. In real estate, **marketing** consists of the methods and strategies used to rent space and retain current residents. **Messaging** on the other hand conveys what the property is all about and is what you wish to communicate to your target market in order to distinguish the property from others. Messaging is a strategic approach that goes beyond a color scheme and logo to relay information such as key property strengths, credibility, professionalism, and so forth. Regardless of the marketing method used, it is important to ensure that the messaging is on target.

FIGURE 2-2: SAMPLE MARKETING TIMETABLE

Event	Timing	Comments
Direct mailing of brochures	February 2	
Property Health Fair	Fair March 11	Distribute promo flyers March. 1-10
Classified ad: *Apartment Locator*	April issue	
Vacancy listing on www.rent.net	Runs April 2-30	Add link to www.rent.net on property website

MARKETING TECHNIQUES

In order to attract prospective residents to a new or existing space, the space and the property as a whole must be promoted. Always keep in mind the owner's goals for the property and the desired return on investment (ROI).

Developing a Theme

The property's theme is a concept for the property on which all marketing efforts are based. It uses design, symbols, fonts, and color scheme to convey the message, and is reflected in all signage, websites, and marketing pieces to create a consistent property image in the mind of the prospect.

□ Internet Listing Service(s) (ILS)
□ Company/property website
□ Google/Bing adwords and search engine optimization (SEO)
□ Grand opening costs
□ Apartment locator services
□ Signage
□ Print advertisements
□ Production of brochures, letterhead, forms, business cards
□ Promotional items printed with the property name or logo
□ Postage for direct mailings
□ Public relations events
□ Leasing team/leasing bonuses
□ Social activities
□ Resident retention and appreciation events
□ Resident newsletters

Student Housing Impact: It is often effective to use the university color scheme for a student housing property's theme.

Advertising

The following table provides various advertising outlets, or paid forms of presentation and promotion of the property. Specific outlets will be chosen based on the target market and positioning for competitive advantage. Consider two key elements when selecting advertising outlets:

- **Reach** is the specific audience exposed to the medium. The reach of the selected medium should be the largest possible number of prospects who mirror the target market.

- **Frequency** is the number of times the ad appears in the medium

Type	Description
Property Website	• Includes photographs, floor plans, features and amenities, directions and maps, social media feeds, as well as leasing contact information for interested prospects • May include capability to check availability of units, submit online application, or talk to live help desk • May include embedded YouTube full-motion video, flash-animated video, or extended galleries of unit types • May have a mobile version of the website
Real Estate Management Company Website	• Can index all the available units at properties under management, searchable by location or unit type • Commonly include embedded Web video (or Flash animation of still images) for the properties, live help desks to set appointments, online reservations for apartments, and online lease application • May have a mobile version of the website.

Type	Description
Apartment Search Website/ILS	• Includes Apartmentfinder.com, Apartments.com, RentAdvisor.com, etc. • Serve as "proxy" property websites; include features such as embedded video (YouTube), live contact info, or additional features
Apartment Locator Services	• Provide service to residents and management companies including showing apartments, referring prospects to the property, shopping the competition, conducting marketing studies, training leasing personnel, or even carrying out entre marketing and leasing programs tailored to specific properties on behalf of the management company • Charge a fee (usually a percentage of the first month's rent) that is paid by the owner of the property or the resident
Adwords (Google)	• Places a link and a short description of the link target on a Google search results page • Also known as "sponsored links," which are separate from the search results, these links can advertise your property with one or two sentences and a link to the property website. • Includes "pay-per-click" and display advertising • May be adjusted to only run in searches that are initiated by prospects in your zip code
Search Engine Optimization (SEO)	• Considers how prospects search for space and seeks to improve the ranking of the property website in the search engine results page the prospect sees • Seeking higher search engine results means more visibility for the property • May be contracted to a vendor that specializes in SEO techniques as part of a coordinated search marketing campaign • Should have analytics set up for the website owner to track improvements in ranking and source of hits • May include both search engine buys (see "adwords" below) and "display network" buys (see "display advertising" below)
Display Advertising	• Ranges from large or small ads for your property placed on another Web or mobile page—ad sizes and position on page will vary • Entails finding the websites likely to be viewed by your target market to advertise • May include still images or rich media (e.g., video, Flash animation) embedded in a display ad that will not "activate" unless a website user selects the image area.
Classified Advertising	• Includes classified ads for local print newspapers, online versions of local news organizations, and websites that look similar to "traditional" print-based classified advertising such as Craigslist.org • May provide opportunity to capture wide range of prospects with no placement cost, as in the case with Craigslist
Print Display	• Includes apartment guides and rental magazines published monthly or quarterly; contains full-page listings of available apartments • In larger markets, competing apartment guides may cater to different renter profiles • Offers a range of opportunity in display ad size and color; larger image and graphic space afford the opportunity to convey property brand, theme, or competitive advantage message
Collateral Materials	• Includes brochures and flyers that are passed out to potential residents, available for download on websites, or included in a direct marketing campaign • Should be more general and timeless and maintain consistency with the property's messaging and theme
Other Forms of Advertisings	• Billboards, broadcast media (television and radio), "bootleg" or temporary sidewalk signs, mall kiosk, onsite property kiosk

TIPS:
Be sure to offer exclusive content to prospects who have reached out via email, text, QR code, and so forth. They've responded to a "call to action" so the content must be meaningful and worth the extra effort. For example, effective pricing, floor plans in greater detail, virtual tours of amenities, and so forth.

To ensure prospects and residents come back to your website, it must be updated with fresh and new content on a regular basis, at least every week.

CHECKLIST: WRITING AN AD

Regardless of advertising outlet, the following items should be included:
- ☐ Photographs that focus on high value areas (e.g. interiors of the apartments, kitchens).
- ☐ Consider using a watermark with your logo, company name, and phone number on the image to prevent unauthorized use and fraud.
- ☐ Maps and directions
- ☐ Sizes and types of units
- ☐ Rental rates and any promotions
- ☐ Features and amenities
- ☐ Floor plans
- ☐ Pet policy
- ☐ Contact information (address, phone number, website)

Also, consider the following tips:
- ☐ Grab the prospect's attention with a sharp graphic or headline; appeal to emotions
- ☐ Maintain consistency with the property's image and theme
- ☐ Clearly communicate appealing features of the property, especially its competitive advantages
- ☐ Focus graphics on the interior of the apartment rather than the building exterior
- ☐ Base the message on your assessment of the target market and their desires
- ☐ End with a "call to action" that prompts the reader to respond by calling or visiting the property
- ☐ Brochures should use a timeless design with blank space for rental rates, include colorful maps and photographs, use a typeface that is easy to read, and use an active voice instead of a passive voice (e.g., "The property features an exercise room" is more desirable than "There is an exercise room."

Single Family Home Impact: Typically, the company is the focus of general marketing for Single Family Homes. An example: "2-3-4 BR Homes available all across the Southside; Check our website for current listings of homes available for immediate occupancy!"

Affordable Housing Impact: All advertisements for affordable housing properties should include a statement indicating that "income limits may apply." Additionally, all advertisements should have the Fair Housing logo and a wheelchair logo to demonstrate ADA compliance.

Student Housing Impact: Advertising via the Internet is extremely important when trying to attract a tech-savvy student population.

Direct Marketing

Direct marketing is the use of leasing professional-to-prospect channels without using marketing middlemen. These channels include direct mailings and email broadcasts.

Mailings can also be customized, in the form of a personal letter that focuses on the features of the property that the particular prospect is likely to perceive as most valuable. Developing personal letters can be comparatively expensive and time-consuming; however, the personalization itself can greatly influence the prospective resident. Disadvantages of direct mailings include the high and rising cost of postage and typical low response rates.

As a lower-cost option, broadcast email can be sent to a group of prospects at once, including the same content that would appear in a direct mailing. The email should be nicely formatted, and it should be tested on a variety of email software to ensure that it appears correctly when the recipient opens it.

TIPS:
Referrals are an excellent source of prospects. Satisfied residents, persons in influential positions, business associates, and friends can generate valuable referrals. Some properties establish referral programs that compensate the resident whose referral results in a signed lease. Incentives may consist of cash payments, rental discounts, or improvements to the leased apartment. Note that in some states, brokers or anyone holding a real estate license cannot pay cash except to another licensed person.

LEGAL ISSUE:
In accordance with the CAN-SPAM Act of 2003, all commercial emails should:
• Include a legitimate return email and physical postal address
• Include a clear and conspicuous opt-out mechanism that offers the recipient of the email the option to not receive similar messages from the sender
• Include a clear and conspicuous notice that the message is an advertisement

TIPS:
It is essential to track direct marketing piece effectiveness due to the high cost. Use tracking numbers and mailing-specific URLs added to your property website to monitor success rates.

Social Media

A social media presence is an integral part of the overall marketing strategy. Various channels such as Facebook, Twitter and LinkedIn offer opportunities to expand the property's visibility and market to both potential and existing residents. Social media is a participatory back-and-forth social connection between you and your customers and requires an intentional approach.

Site managers should work with management to determine the overall goal of social media efforts. The specific platforms used, how to best engage the target audience, and how to dedicate staff resources appropriately will stem from answers to the following questions.

- What are your goals?
- Who is your audience?

RESOURCES:
Best practices on using social media, as well as specific "how-to" information, can be found in the Institute's eBook publication *Social Media for Real Estate Managers.* Visit **www.irem.org** for additional information.

This concept is explored further in the following excerpts from the IREM eBook publication, *Social Media for Real Estate Managers* (2012):

To learn how to use social media most effectively, you must start with a strategy and determine your marketing and communications goals. If you plan to use social media accounts for individual properties, your goals might be to:

- Improve communication with tenants or residents
- Increase awareness of property among potential tenants or residents
- Improve reputation of property
- Effectively market properties to potential tenants or residents
- Improve tenant/resident retention

Always keep in mind the reasons for incorporating social media tools into your business. Don't feel pressured to use social media because it seems like everyone else is doing it. While social media is an effective tool for real estate managers and is becoming increasingly important for today's businesses, it's important to be able to execute it well. Most importantly, do not jump into the social space half-heartedly, uninterestedly, or without a solid strategy.

As you begin to think about your audience, consider their motivations. What problems do they have? How can you help them with those problems? Which platforms allow you to offer the service, information or personal interaction they need?

For example, residents of an apartment community are very likely to be on Facebook, and are already comfortable interacting with brands and businesses with a social media presence. So, a Facebook business page may be the best way for you to communicate with your residents.

The following table provides some common social media platforms and how they are used for marketing.

Platform	Description
Facebook facebook	• Most popular social networking site • Often considered a purely personal network for friends and family • Users increasingly comfortable interacting with their favorite brands or companies • If target audience includes residents or the general public, you are likely to find them on Facebook • Great for building a sense of community, belonging, and loyalty • Ability to establish business pages to encourage interaction and engagement between your company and your fans • Offers tools for administrators of business pages to post content and track success • Provides ability to create events and post photos, videos and polls
Twitter twitter	• Fastest-growing social network • Post 140-character (or about 30 word) updates. Other users can "follow" you to receive your updates and you can follow other accounts that are of interest. • Professionals use for breaking news updates, industry information, and networking • Consumers use for communicating with friends and family, receiving breaking news, hearing about deals, and so forth • Users have developed norms of use and lingo that help them form communities and improve communication.
LinkedIn Linked in.	• Social networking site focused on professionals in the workforce or those looking for work • User profiles set up like resumes • Users can indicate if they want to connect for career opportunities, expertise requests, recommendations, and so forth • Because of its business focus, many companies find LinkedIn to be a logical place to start with social media • Ideal for reaching out to working professionals and expanding network • Offers the ability to create company pages, as well as groups for gathering and interacting with other users
YouTube You Tube	• Video sharing website to upload, share, and view videos • Users create channels that others subscribe to for real time updates • Channels can be customized to compliment branding and highlight key content • Can link YouTube videos to website, Facebook, or Twitter for easy sharing • Ability to provide in-depth look at the property and amenities
Instagram Instagram	• Photo-sharing, video-sharing, and social networking service that allows users to take pictures and videos, apply digital filters to them, and share them on a variety of social networking services like Facebook, Twitter, Tumblr, and Flickr • Can follow users, like or comment on uploads, and use hashtags to search for or categorize uploads • Ability to showcase interesting or unique property images and convey a sense of the living experience
Foursquare foursquare	• Location-based social networking site for mobile devices where users "check-in" at venues to let others know where they are and figure out where others are as well • Users collect points and badges and receive recommendations on things to do or discounts/coupons for frequent visits • Ability to claim your property and set up a foursquare page to monitor activity and comments about your property, offer tips on things to do nearby, and promote your services and amenities

Platform	Description
Tumblr tumblr.	• Microblogging platform and social networking site • Users can post multimedia and other content to a short form blog; text is limited • Users typically follow other users' blogs based on shared interest • Opportunity to share visually engaging property images
Pinterest Pinterest	• Pinboard-style photo sharing website for saving and organizing images • Often used to get inspiration for interests or hobbies • Can collect tips and resources for residents such as neighborhood and city information, local restaurants and attractions, design inspirations, packing and moving tips, tips to go green, organizational ideas, recipes, and so forth

CHECKLIST: USING SOCIAL MEDIA

☐ The type, source, and frequency of posts should support the established goals

☐ Promotional or sales content should be avoided

☐ Content can include blog updates, events at the property, press releases, market analyses, links to other content, neighborhood news, local deals and discounts, and so forth

☐ Establish a regular posting schedule. Generally, Facebook and LinkedIn users expect one post per day to one post per week. Twitter users expect from one to five or more posts per day.

☐ Stagger the timing of posts so as not to overwhelm your followers

☐ Focus on interaction to keep users coming back. Ask questions and solicit feedback.

☐ Acknowledge and respond to complaints publically, even if you resolve them via phone or email

☐ Include icons and links to social media pages in as many places as possible (e.g., website, email signatures, brochures, etc.)

☐ Establish ways to measure and monitor success (e.g., number of referrals to website from Facebook or Twitter, number of retweets, number of comments, ☐ Facebook Insights once you have 30 fans, etc.)

Source: *Social Media for Real Estate Managers*, IREM® 2012

Corporate Outreach/Business Development

Corporate outreach or business development efforts involve contacting institutions, such as human resources departments or military housing offices, to determine if they have new hires or other personnel who may need a place to live.

Successful outreach involves becoming a partner in the community. This goes beyond just knocking on doors and leaving a basket of goodies. Successful business relationships and strategic alliances are established over time with intentional effort. Keep the following principles in mind:

• Ensure you're talking to the right person, such as the HR contact or relocation director (i.e., move beyond the front desk staff)

• Be prepared with an intentional agenda and key talking points

- Bring something to the table and incentive them to partner with you. Specific tactics vary by market and business, but one example is to let a company present an offer to their employees for a waived application fee. This can help them look good to their employees.
- Select potential partners strategically. Target elite partnerships by focusing on companies that hire your target market.

Signage

Property signage is the one of the first things a prospect sees at the property. It establishes the visual theme for the site, and if well-designed, can enhance the prestige of the property. Signage is durable and requires minimal maintenance, while providing a continual, cost-effective form of advertisement. Consider the following best practices:

- Ensure signage is easy to read, upright, and perpendicular to traffic flow if possible
- Keep the amount of information on the sign to a minimum
- Maintain upkeep of signage to enhance the prestige of the property

In general, there are five types of signage:

Type	Description
Identification Signs	• Establish character and display the name of the property • Typically located at the entrance to the property
Directional Signs	• Direct prospects to the property, visitor parking, and the leasing office • Usually include arrows and other directional symbols
Informational Signs	• Provide general information about the property, such as hours of operation and speed limit
"For Lease" Signs	• Indicate available space and provide leasing contact information • Usually placed at key entrances to the property
Project Signs	• Introduce a site prior to and during construction and may include a rendering of the property, availability date, names of the developers, and leasing contact information

LEGAL ISSUE:
Size and placement of signs, including temporary sidewalk signage (known in some markets as "bootleg" signs), may be regulated by local laws and ordinances.

MEASURING EFFECTIVENESS

Many tools are available to monitor and record the success of marketing efforts. Reports also assist in monitoring against the owner's goals and sharing the status of leasing activities with the owner.

TIPS:
Measuring the effectiveness of various marketing tactics is critical to meeting the owner's goals and objectives. Constant evaluation ensures that necessary modifications can be made, and that the set budget amount is used effectively.

Reporting to the Owner

As the eyes and ears of the property, the site manager is uniquely positioned to track the status of marketing activity and prepare reports for management and the owner. Note that the level of detail and number of reports requested varies by owner. The key to success here is the input and gathering of information. Remember the old adage, "garbage in = garbage out."

Report	Description
Traffic Report	• Can be daily, weekly, or monthly • Logs telephone calls and visits to the property, source of the traffic, result of each contact, competitors visited, and why the visit did not result in a lease (if applicable) • Call tracking through 1-800 numbers is an additional source of tracking data • Refer to Figure 2-3
Internal Marketing Report	• Records the frequency of advertising, public relations events, and outreach initiatives • Identifies effectiveness of techniques and areas in need of modification
Website Traffic Report	• Provides statistics such as how many users visited the site and when, the approximate location of the user, and the amount of time spent on each page • This information can help determine what pages are most popular and the demographics of your market.
Leasing Activity Report	• Keeps owner informed of leasing activity such as active prospects and signed leases • May include progress charts comparing actual leasing progress to projected activity • Refer to Figure 2-4

RESOURCES:
Downloadable forms such as traffic reports can be found under Resources>Forms & Checklists at **www.irem.org** and are free for members. These sample forms and agreements are not endorsed by the Institute of Real Estate Management. They are presented for informational purposes only.

FIGURE 2-3: SAMPLE TRAFFIC REPORT (EXCERPT)

Product Name	Home Phone	Desired Requirement	Date Needed	Source	Agent	Event Type	Event Date	Result/Reason
Napp, Christen	512-502-5231	Rent: 0.00	10/1/13	Craigslist	Joelle Smith	E-mail	8/1/2013	
		Bedrooms: 1			Joelle Smith	E-mail	8/1/2013	
		Amenities: None			Joelle Smith	E-mail	8/21/2013	
					Joelle Smith	Canceled Guest	8/23/2013	
McIntyre, Allysa	650-740-5883	Rent: 0.00	10/7/2013	Craigslist	Joelle Smith	Call	8/21/2013	
		Bedrooms: 1			Joelle Smith	Appointment	8/21/2013	
		Amenities: None			Emily Wade	Show	8/21/2013	
Dunn, Igor	512-944-2233	Rent: 0.00	10/7/2013	Drive-by/Walkin-in	Joelle Smith	Call	8/5/2013	Set appointment
		Bedrooms: 1			Joelle Smith	Appointment	8/8/2013	
		Amenities: None			Joelle Smith	Canceled Guest	8/21/2013	
Jones, Ethan	214-667-7226	Rent: 0.00	8/21/2013	Drive-by/Walk-in	Joelle Smith	Walk-In	8/5/2013	Submitting application
		Bedrooms: 1			Joelle Smith	E-mail	8/21/2013	
		Amenities: None			Joelle Smith	Canceled Guest	8/23/2013	
Pei, Sara	505-404-3217	Rent: 0.00	10/7/2013	Locator	Joelle Smith	E-mail	8/21/2013	Leased elsewhere
		Bedrooms: 1			Joelle Smith	Canceled Guest	8/21/2013	
		Amenities: None						

Source: Reprinted with permission from Steven Rea, CPM®.

FIGURE 2-4: SAMPLE ACTIVITY REPORT

NO OF UNITS: _____ (D+E) **PROPERTY NAME:** _____

LEASING AGENT: _____ **PROPERTY NO:** _____

A + B - C = D G + H - I - J = K

WEEK ENDING	A BEG	B MOVE IN	C MOVE OUT	D END	E VACANT	F NOTICES TO VACATE	G BEG	H DEP	I CANC	J MOVE IN	K END	L AVAIL. LEASE	TRA CALLS
12/31	0			0	0		0				0	0	
1/7	0			0	0		0				0	0	
1/14	0			0	0		0				0	0	
1/21	0			0	0		0				0	0	
1/28	0			0	0		0				0	0	
2/4	0			0	0		0				0	0	
2/11	0			0	0		0				0	0	
2/18	0			0	0		0				0	0	
2/25	0			0	0		0				0	0	
3/4	0			0	0		0				0	0	
3/11	0			0	0		0				0	0	
3/18/	0			0	0		0				0	0	
3/25	0			0	0		0				0	0	
4/1	0			0	0		0				0	0	
4/8	0			0	0		0				0	0	
4/15	0			0	0		0				0	0	
4/22	0			0	0		0				0	0	
4/29	0			0	0		0				0	0	
5/6	0			0	0		0				0	0	
5/13	0			0	0		0				0	0	
5/20	0			0	0		0				0	0	
5/27	0			0	0		0				0	0	
6/3													
6/10													
6/17													
6/24													
7/1													
7/8													
7/15													
7/22													

D+E= Total number of units on the property
A=D (From previous week)

G+H-I-J=K
E-K=L
G=K (From previous week)

Source: Reprinted with permission from Sheila Austin, CPM®.

Evaluating Results

Analyzing these reports reveals the effectiveness of different marketing tactics used in the marketing plan. Consider the following questions:

- Which techniques produced the most interest in the property?
- Which led to a signed lease?
- Which media does the target market read most frequently?
- How will I modify the plan to be more effective in the future?

One of the most important measures of success is cost-effectiveness. If a marketing campaign costs $4,000, it needs to draw in enough leads and eventual residents to cover that cost. If a campaign nets three new residents whose rent payments total multiple times that expense, the campaign has been a success. By estimating marketing campaign costs, it is possible to determine in advance the needed break-even response rate. Cost-effectiveness is often calculated using ratios such as cost per prospect, and cost per signed lease.

Cost per Prospect

Cost per prospect is the ratio of marketing costs to the number of prospects attracted to the property:

Cost of Marketing ÷ Number of Prospects = Cost per Prospect

Example

If an online ad costs $500, and 10 prospects respond to the advertisement, the cost per prospect would be $50 ($500 ÷ 10).

Conversion Rate

A conversion rate compares the number of prospects to the number who actually sign a lease:

Number of Leases Signed ÷ Number of Prospects = Conversion Rate

> **Example**
>
> If 2 out of 10 prospects sign leases, the conversion rate is 20% (2 ÷ 10).

The conversion rate can help identify ineffective leasing professionals, but it should be used with caution. A new property may have a much higher conversion rate. If the conversion rate is very high at an established property, the manager may want to examine the rental rates and determine if they are too low. If the conversion rate is very low, the property may have flaws, or the marketing plan may need adjustment. Compare the numbers to those of competitors for realistic market conversion rates.

Cost per Signed Lease

Cost per signed lease is the ratio of marketing costs to the number of leases signed:

Cost of Marketing ÷ Number of Leases Signed = Cost per Signed Lease

> **Example**
>
> If an online ad costs $500, and 2 out of the 10 prospects end up signing leases, the cost per signed lease is $250 ($500 ÷ 2).

These assessments assist in determining effective and ineffective marketing techniques used in a campaign. The site manager should apply what is learned through measuring effectiveness to make modifications to the marketing plan going forward.

FIGURE 2-5: EVALUATING RESULTS

Consider the simplified comparison example. Which ad do you think has the most return? What would be different in your market?

	Apt. Guide	Website	Billboard
Ad Cost	$1,200	$210	$500
Traffic generated	10	3	2
Cost per prospect	$120	$70	$250
Amount of leased conversion	6 (60%)	0	1 (50%)
Cost per signed lease	$200	0	$500

CHAPTER 3:
LEASING THE APARTMENT

Knowledge of effective leasing tactics leads to more signed leases and directly impacts the success of the apartment building. Managers need to establish effective leasing practices in order to successfully lease apartments to potential residents.

In this chapter:

- **Leasing Plan Components**
- **Leasing Team**
- **Leasing Tactics**

LEASING PLAN COMPONENTS

After the marketing plan is implemented and begins attracting prospects to the property, it is necessary to develop an outline for leasing to and placing the residents in the property. This in-house leasing plan typically includes items listed in the following checklist.

CHECKLIST: LEASING PLAN COMPONENTS

- ☐ Site plan, preferably drawn to scale
- ☐ Unit numbers
- ☐ Square footage
- ☐ Rent schedule
- ☐ Expiration dates
- ☐ Concessions

TIPS:
The leasing plan should always reflect the goals and objectives of the owner.

LEASING TEAM

Leasing success depends on staff members having a shared commitment to the goals determined by property ownership and management. A variety of staff members may perform leasing activities, including the site manager and on-site leasing professionals. But, everyone on staff can impact the prospect's decision to lease or renew at the property. As such, the entire staff must work as a team to achieve the leasing objectives.

Consider the following best practices for on-site leasing professionals:

- Establish a professional dress code that aligns with the property's image or theme
- Provide clear job descriptions with detailed tasks and responsibilities
- Familiarize staff with leasing goals
- Provide initial and ongoing training. For example:
    o Legal compliance
    o Problem-solving skills
    o Communication skills
    o Online leasing system procedures and troubleshooting
    o Sales techniques
- Learn what motivates staff
    o **Ego**: awards, contests, letters of recognition, public acknowledgements
    o **Power:** tough challenges, increased authority
    o **Money:** potential for increased compensation such as bonuses and incentive plans
- Recognize and reward success

TIPS:
Be sure to set the priority that retaining residents in addition to converting prospects is a key leasing team goal.

LEASING TACTICS

Leasing professionals are critical to a property's financial health, especially in uncertain economic climates. Interacting with the prospects is a tremendous opportunity to customize your message and sell the benefits of the property on a more personal level. The leasing process can be broken down into three steps:

1. Getting acquainted with the prospect
2. Showing the apartment for lease
3. Confirming the close

TIPS:
A two-bedroom apartment is always a two-bedroom apartment; the difference is in the leasing professional and the service he or she provides as the face of the community.

RESOURCES:
Best practices on residential marketing techniques and leasing tactics can be found in the Institute's publication *Marketing Residential Properties The Science and the Magic* by Laurence C. Harmon CPM®, CRE and Kathleen M. Harmon, CPM®, ARM®. Visit **www.irem.org** for additional information.

Getting Acquainted with the Prospect

The initial contact with prospects, whether by phone, in person, or via email or online submission, provides the opportunity to make a good first impression. It will leave prospects with a perception of the level of service at the community and the professionalism of staff. Regardless of initial contact method, the goal is to secure a face-to-face appointment.

TOP 10 TIPS FOR INITIAL CONTACT

1. Recognize that voice and tone are important sales tools.
2. Provide a sincere, warm, welcoming greeting.
3. Recognize that the first two to three questions identify the prospect's hot button issues.
4. Engage in the prospect's situation to deepen the exchange of information and uncover unique wants and needs. This also helps in qualifying the prospect. Refer to the examples below.
5. Probe on the "why" behind the prospect's questions and preferences in order to focus on applicable features and benefits that make the property a good fit.
6. Ask the prospect to set up an appointment to visit and learn more about the property.
7. Ensure all leasing team members can answer basic questions about the property and application process.
8. Ensure proper coverage during business hours to accommodate phone and walk-in inquiries.
9. Provide email templates to address common property inquiries and facilitate response time, including a signature with contact information and proper grammar/punctuation.
10. Reply to phone and email inquiries immediately or at least within the same business day regardless of property size/staff. The prospect likely sent multiple emails and the first to respond well is the most likely to get the lease.

Example

Questions that can help uncover unique needs and wants:
- How many people will be living in the apartment? That's yourself and who else?
- What is important to you about your new home? Why?
- Where have you looked? What did you like? Dislike?

"Let us begin by discovering their goals. Then work our goals into theirs. We should place our agenda inside of theirs. People don't care how much you know until they know how much you care. Each important bit of information you share can be shared as a result of a request rather than unsolicited advice."

Toni Blake
Greeley, Colorado

The leasing professional's goal is to uncover the prospect's unique wants and needs in order to determine how the property fits those needs. It is then possible for the leasing professional to sell those features that are important to the prospect. This concept is explored in the following excerpts from the IREM publication, *Marketing Residential Properties: The Science and the Magic* (2008):

As buyers became more sophisticated and more self-reliant consumers, high-pressure sales tactics became less successful. With the increasing use of the Internet to provide comparative data, buyers now come to the marketplace more knowledgeable, more inquisitive, more critical, and more intent on finding a "perfect fit" for every purchase they make.

In the residential environment, when prospects come to the marketplace, it's because their current housing situation doesn't "fit" anymore and they need a better one. As the seller, you may have a perfect place but how do prospective buyers figure out whether that place will be a good fit for them? Fact: your job is to figure out what the customer came to buy or lease. Unfortunately, that's not what our industry has taught you to do.

Historically, the residential real estate industry has trained its salespeople to be tour guides armed with canned closing statements. We've been taught to recite a script that's loaded with facts about the neighborhood, the building, the common areas, and the unit features. The problem is that the traditional sales presentation fails to find the fit between the real estate product and prospects' needs and wants.

Bottom line: Renters and buyers have an image, a vision hidden in their minds, of what they want their living space to be. As the salesperson, you need a way to unlock that image and understand it before you can find a product in your inventory that mirrors it.

Guest Cards

Guest cards (also called prospect cards) serve as a tracking tool to gauge the prospect's needs. They document key information about a prospect, and can be either physical cards or electronic software solutions. Often, electronic guest cards can be scaled to match mobile applications enabling real time completion. Recording prospect information during and after initial contact helps the leasing professional prepare for the site visit. Refer to Figure 3-1 for a sample guest card.

TIPS:
The leasing professional, not the potential resident, should complete the guest card.

CHECKLIST: GUEST CARD INFORMATION

□ Prospect's name
□ Current home address
□ Home and work telephone numbers
□ Email address
□ Occupation
□ How the prospect learned about the property
□ Reason for moving
□ Rental requirements
□ Special needs
□ Section to document apartments shown to the prospect
□ Section to log follow-up contact (Refer to Figure 3-2) below
□ Section to record any questions the prospect poses:
  o Remember the first two questions are the prospect's "hot buttons"—the factors this prospect considers vital in leasing the apartment.
  o Questions typically involve price or availability and other vital factors for the prospect. Unless these factors are satisfied, the prospect will look elsewhere.

Effective guest cards:

- Collect information that tells when to follow up with prospects and how to concentrate on the strongest sources of guest traffic

- Identify peak periods for showings and become an excellent resource and reference on where prospective residents live and work and why particular prospective residents did not choose the property

- Provide valuable marketing information regarding the effectiveness of specific advertising, particularly whether it is reaching the target market:
  o By asking the prospective resident how they found out about the property and listing the item
  o By tracking this information on the card—listing sites, outdoor

signs, drive-by, referral–the agent can determine the source of the traffic

- o Prospective residents' home addresses tell what geographic areas the advertising has reached
- o If management is planning an open house or a large-scale promotion of a property, this information, along with a zip code breakdown of qualified prospective residents, will help generate a targeted mailing list

TIPS:
It is imperative that guest card information be limited to information necessary to help serve the prospect's interests in the community. Doodles, pictures, or opinion and speculation regarding a prospect's application, before it has been duly processed (e.g., "Prospect may have bad credit") should never be allowed. Guest cards and software records of leasing professional contact with the prospect may be subpoenaed in court as evidence of the will of the management company regarding the prospect.

FIGURE 3-1: SAMPLE GUEST CARDS

GUEST CARD

Leasing Professional: _____ Date: _____

Contact Information
Prospect Name: _____ Home Phone: _____
Email Address: _____ Work Phone: _____
Present Address: _____
_____

Company Name: _____ Job Title: _____

Requirements
No. Occupants: _____ Date Needed: _____ Desired Rent: _____
No. Bedrooms: _____ No. Bathrooms: _____ Parking: _____

Reason for Moving:_____

Additional Needs:_____
_____

Source of Traffic
_____ Online Ad   _____ Apartment Guide   _____ Website
_____ Resident Referral _____ Newspaper Ad   _____ Drive By
_____ Other: _____

Student Housing Impact: A guest card for student housing prospects would also include the following:
- Class standing
- College
- Major
- Smoking preference, Music preference
- Study habits
- Cell phone number

This type of information is important when assigning roommates.

Online Leasing and Mobile Leasing Applications

Many companies offer integrated web-based leasing services to improve response times, professionalism, and tracking of prospects. Key features of online leasing systems include:

- May include screening fee and screening process before completion of application
- Online prospects fill out leasing application online with 24-hour access (i.e., paperless)
- Application reviewed by vendor in accordance with the qualifying criteria set by the owner's objectives
- Approved prospects sent lease and addendums in PDF form for signing
- Prospects pay additional fees and deposit through online payment system
- Prospect portal is replaced by a resident portal (where applicable)
- Information and fees posted into property management software

Showing the Apartment for Lease

The desirability of a property as a place to live is embodied in the condition of the apartment that prospects are shown and the emphasis placed on its features.

First Impressions

The condition and appearance of the property is a critical component of the site visit. Just like the old saying goes, "you never get a second chance to make a first impression." Consider the following excerpt from leasing expert Toni Blake's *Five Sensory Selling. Reprinted with permission.*

Visual stimulation in selling is used effectively in many areas. Retailers work very hard to increase revenue with colorful product displays, signage, photographs and merchandizing, especially in the main path of the customer. Retailers identify the highest revenue path in each store. This is called the "Golden Path." The world's largest manufacturers spend millions of dollars on research designed to discover the right color, style, words and image to influence the customer's decision process.

It is time for multifamily to find their Golden Path and implement better practices for high visual impact. Once this "high profit" – "high impact" path through your property is established, it should be separated out for special maintenance, landscaping, and marketing enhancements. For example - weekly touch up painting of the front curbs to keep a "new," "clean" image to the front area. A planter with a dead flower and a welcome mat that is missing letters is a very expensive mistake in the visual marketing. I might not be able to afford to remodel my whole property - but I will be clean, neat and freshly painted with manicured landscape on my golden path.

At every step, your leasing team should be supported by visual displays, added merchandizing, and success tools that will help them weave their magic into Gold. I have created totally new leasing tools & procedures designed to influence the customer's decision: The telephone, office display area, guest card, the apartment demonstration, and the follow up/closing cards.

Residential Models

Because a model apartment conveys the desired image of the property, the apartment's location and appearance are very important. Most prospects assume that models represent the best the property has to offer and that any apparent defects in the model will be magnified in the rental apartments.

The following are some guidelines for using model apartments:

- Use an apartment(s) with a less-desirable location or layout since the most-desirable apartments are the easiest ones to lease
- Be sure the model(s) is easily accessible from the leasing office
- Clean and inspect the model regularly
- Use decorations that accentuate the best features of a unit/its layout
- Be sure the furnishings used reflect the income level of the target market and are appropriate for the size of the unit

TIPS:
Mini-models are another means to showcase apartments at a lower cost. They are full-sized models, but they do not contain any furniture. The mini-model can be supplied with small housewares, such as utensils, dish towels, and garbage cans. Leasing professionals can use cutouts of full-size furniture to lay out the apartment so that the prospect may envision how the apartment might look. Setting up a "theme" such as a non-denominational holiday scene can attract more attention to the model and create a charming impression.

Single Family Home Impact: Each property is unique in single family housing and no models are available for showing. Therefore, the single family home for rental should be rent-ready before it is shown by converting the paint and carpet to neutral colors. The owner may be surprised that this is necessary, but the owner should be informed that he or she is converting the family home to a family business, and that neutral color schemes are most successful. Encourage the owner to visit local apartment communities to see how they present their product for comparison. Also, as single family homes are location driven, direct the potential resident in the most positive direction to the house.

Affordable Housing Impact: Mini-models are often used in affordable housing properties due to their lower cost. An example of a leasing incentive may include supplying a mini-model with items such as a shower liner, dish towels, and a wooden basket with kitchen utensils, and including them with a signed lease.

Vacant Apartments

For residential properties, the condition of vacant apartments is as important as the condition of a model. At all times an assortment of vacant apartments should be in market-ready condition—thoroughly clean with all improvements made. A daily walk-through first thing in the morning by a leasing professional will assure that the apartment is in presentable condition.

CHECKLIST: KEY INSPECTION ITEMS

- ☐ All walls and ceilings should be freshly painted, including closets or shelving
- ☐ Carpeting should be freshly shampooed; burns or stains should be removed or the carpeting should be replaced
- ☐ All windows should be washed inside and out
- ☐ Windowsills, ledges, and shelves should be wiped clean
- ☐ Light fixtures and switches should be in working order
- ☐ The temperature should be set at an appropriate level for the season
- ☐ The kitchen should be immaculate with all appliances clean and in working condition
- ☐ Bathrooms should be spotless; watch for dripping faucets, stains, and tub and tile grout that should be replaced

Preparation

In order to prepare for a showing, leasing professionals must have a thorough background of the property and the neighborhood. They should learn the shopping areas, schools and their bus routes, businesses, churches, local governments, and public transportation. Knowing the key competitive advantages of the property is essential; visits to competitors should have helped determine the relative strengths and weaknesses of the property.

Part of preparing for the site visit is to review the prospect card and information collected at the last point of contact with the potential resident. This will help determine which space to show based on layout, price, amenities, and availability. Before the prospect arrives, the leasing representative should plan a few route options that arrive at the space quickly and easily. Staff should make a habit of walking the grounds and following the various routes that leasing professionals use during presentation tours. Apartments should be ready for viewing and keys should be obtained in advance. If models are available, show them first. All of this preparation should help minimize surprises during a tour and help develop an effective sales presentation.

TIPS:
Security should be of utmost importance when showing a space for lease. If the property is master keyed, safeguard all keys in a separate facility. Keep key codes locked at all times, and restrict access only to employees who have had a background check. If other key access systems are used, follow manufacturer protocols concerning controlling access.

Benefit Selling

To understand the benefits the unit holds for the prospect, the leasing professional should learn the prospect's unique needs and wants, and note specific features that will appeal to the prospect. Selling features requires matching the benefits of the apartment to the prospect's needs.

> **Example**
>
> Simply saying "here is the kitchen" is obvious; however, adding that the kitchen has an "an extra set of cabinets and an unusually large pantry that make it perfect for entertaining" gives a good indication of how the feature improves lifestyle and meets a particular need.

Benefit selling should be delivered with enthusiasm since buying is partly an emotional process. Any promotional materials, such as brochures, should be prepared and ready to be handed to the prospect.

Personalization

The sales approach the leasing professional uses depends on the prospect and his or her reasons for searching for an apartment. A single person looking for an apartment will not have the same "hot buttons" as a retired couple who just sold their large house. The leasing professional should modify the sales approach to accommodate varying motivating forces behind moving.

> **Example**
>
> If the prospect indicates that he or she hates to waste money, a skilled agent may respond by explaining the benefits of the energy-efficient heating plant and high insulation in the walls and ceiling that reduce energy costs.

It is commonly believed that sales are more likely to close when the prospect has a favorable impression of the leasing team member. However, this may lead to the leasing team member trying to identify too closely with the prospect. "Over-personalizing" the discussion of the apartment can backfire, triggering a negative reaction from the prospect. The examples below demonstrate the negatives and positives of this technique.

> **Example 1**
>
> *Leasing professional:* "Isn't this a great kitchen backsplash? The green and brown pattern just came on the market!"
>
> *Prospect:* "It's very nice."
>
> *What the prospect really thinks:* "My small appliances are red; they would look terrible in here."
>
> **Example 2**
>
> *Leasing professional:* "How do you like the color and pattern of this backsplash? Would it go with your belongings?"
>
> *Prospect:* "My small appliances and artwork are red. Do you have a more neutral color?"
>
> *Agent:* "Sure. I have the same apartment layout down the hall. It has a more neutral backsplash. Shall we look at that one?"
>
> *Prospect thinks:* "This person is interested in my satisfaction. I think this might be the right apartment for me."

Source: *Contemporary Apartment Marketing.* Reprinted with permission.

Problem Solving: Countering Objections

The leasing office should expect common objections to layout or features of a unit and be prepared to counter them. It is important for your team to know that if a prospect begins raising objections that is a sign of the prospect's continuing interest in the apartment. In general, people are hesitant when faced with major purchasing decisions and raise objections to avoid making a decision. The leasing team member must listen carefully to the objections and be receptive, not defensive. Uncovering objections and turning them into positives is the key to success.

Example 1: Objection to Price

Prospect: "Your 1000-square foot two-bedroom, one-bath costs $1,200 a month? I saw a 1275-square foot two-bedroom, two-bath apartment down the street for $975."

Leasing professional: "You're absolutely right. Their apartments are less expensive than ours. I'd like you to give me an opportunity to show you our two-bedroom, two-bath apartment. We'll start out by looking at a model apartment that displays the open floor plan and stainless steel and granite features we talked about. As entertaining is important to you, these features will work well. At [the competing property], they have standard appliances and galley kitchens."

Example 2: Objection to Amenities

Prospect: "This property doesn't have cable included?"

Agent: "We've found that many of our residents are turning to Internet streaming models for TV viewing and weren't interested in that feature. But, we do provide complimentary high-speed Internet access and cable is available in the resident lounge."

Common objections should be anticipated and potential solutions noted. How can the following negatives be turned into positives?

- Small space
- Old building
- Remote location
- Busy street
- Higher rent than competitors

Confirming the Close

The culmination of the leasing efforts is the closing or the invitation to the prospect to sign an application and/or a lease. The following are common closing techniques:

Technique	Description
Summary Close	• Summarizes the benefits the prospect is seeking • For example: "This apartment meets all of your needs; it has a separate dining room, big walk-in closets, and the room layout that you liked. Let's go back to the office and fill out an application."
Silent Close	• Simply handing the prospect a rental application and a pen
Assumptive Close	• Hand the application to the prospect and say, "Let's do the paperwork."
"If I Could..., Would You?"	• Ask the prospect if he or she will agree to sign the lease after you make a particular negotiated concession
Emphasize the "Pros"	• Convince the prospect that the reasons in favor of signing the lease are stronger than those against it • This can be done by comparing the space to the competitors and emphasizing all of the property's competitive advantages as they relate to the prospect
Sense of Urgency	• Explain that this is the only apartment with the desired features, or that you have another appointment shortly to show the apartment

Although leasing professionals may be uncomfortable with the idea of closing the deal, prospective residents expect it. The closing should be a natural result of all marketing and leasing efforts.

CHAPTER 4:
LEGAL ISSUES

Site managers must comply with legal requirements to protect the property and avoid the penalties and liability for noncompliance. A manager must be able to identify the legal issues involved in residential management.

In this chapter:

- **Legal and Fair Housing Guidelines**
- **Qualifying Prospects**
- **Landlord-Tenant Law**
- **The Lease Document**
- **Delinquencies**
- **Eviction**
- **Collections**

LEGAL AND FAIR HOUSING GUIDELINES

LEGAL ISSUE:
Real estate managers must ensure that their leasing practices comply with a number of laws, including fair housing laws and the Americans with Disabilities Act.

The Fair Housing Act

The Fair Housing Act was passed in 1968 as part of Section VIII of the Civil Rights Act. Amendments followed in 1974 and 1988. Fair Housing laws are designed to protect against discrimination on the basis of one or more of the seven federally protected classes.

- Race
- Color
- Religion
- Sex
- National Origin
- Familial Status
- Handicap

FIGURE 4-1: FEDERAL PROTECTED CLASSES

The following acronym is an easy way to remember the federally-protected classes: "Renters Can Really Sue Now For Housing"

RENTERS	(RACE; caucasian, Black, Hispanic, etc.)
CAN	(COLOR; skin color or pigmentation)
REALLY	(RELIGION; Catholic, Muslim, etc.)
SUE	(SEX; gender, sexual harassment)
NOW	(NATIONAL ORIGIN; immigrant origin)
FOR	(FAMILIAL STATUS; children or pregnancy)
HOUSING VIOLATIONS	(HANDICAP; physical or mental disability)

LEGAL ISSUE:
States and some municipalities have separate laws dealing with fair housing. These laws may be stricter than the federal laws—e.g., they may include additional protected classes based on such things as lifestyle or sexual orientation—so it is imperative to become familiar with all the fair housing laws that apply in the local area.

The federal law is just the beginning with fair housing. State and local laws often include additional protected classes, and the stricter of the laws must be followed. Each member of the management company must know the laws at the federal, state, and local levels. Depending on the state and city, the following classes could be protected:

Class	Example
Sexual Orientation	Same-sex couples
Gender Identity	Transgendered individuals
Marital Status	Single mothers, cohabiting couples
Ancestry	Culture/ancestral history
Age	Young adult renters or the elderly
No Income/ Periodic Income	Contractors and freelancers
Source of Income	Recipient of state or federal monetary or rental assistance, self-employed
Students	Having or not having standing as an enrollee of a school

The state and local codes for fair housing protection are dynamic and more subject to change than legislation at the federal level. It is essential to continually monitor state websites and the sources of local code information (city or county) for legislation extending fair housing protections that may impact the businesses' operations. At the state website, go to the equal rights or human rights commission and other enforcing agencies, not to the state real estate commission.

TIPS:
There are only a handful of states that just follow the federal guidelines. All other states, cities, and municipalities have additional protections that must be understood.

TOP 3 KEY CONCEPTS

1. Know your local market.
2. Consistency is key; treat everyone exactly the same.
3. Don't discriminate.

TIPS:
Download HUD's Fair Housing App for iphone and iPad. The app provides the public with a quick and easy way to learn about their housing rights and to file housing discrimination complaints, and informs the housing industry about its responsibilities under the Fair Housing Act. Learn more at **www.hud.gov/fairhousing.**

Single Family Home Impact: Note that fair housing laws, from federal, to state and municipal laws, are relevant to leasing the single family rental.

Types of Discrimination

The most common allegation of fair housing violation is discrimination due to differential treatment, such as in the refusal to rent to a prospect on the basis of a protected class. According to the law, there are two types of discrimination:

Type	Type
Different Treatment	Means treating people from protected classes differently–intentionally or unintentionally
Disparate Impact	Means that a neutral-appearing action or policy that applied equally to everyone still results in a negative impact on some classes

Example: Different Treatment

A leasing professional may believe (mistakenly) it is correct to tell a Jewish prospect that the community has a large Jewish population so the prospect should have a lot in common with other residents.

Example: Disparate Impact

Your company has a policy of charging an additional security deposit of $50 per person for each person in excess of two in a unit. This impacts three working roommates differently than it would a single mother with two young children. This is discrimination on the condition for rental or purchase and terms and conditions.

A good test is to ask, "Would I treat this person differently if he or she were not from a different protected class?" In the different treatment example above, the leasing professional would not make such a comment to a non-Jewish prospect.

CHECKLIST: DISCRIMINATORY ACTIVITIES EXPLICITY PROHIBITED

Discriminatory activities against one or more of the protected classes include:

- Refusal to rent
- Refusal to negotiate rental
- Advertising indicating discriminatory preference or limitation through language or the use of locations, logos, or human models
- Selective use of media (e.g., advertising only in newspapers/online communities whose readership is predominately white)
- Refusal to show available units
- Refusal to supply rental information, such as rental rates
- False representation of non-availability
- Imposition of different rental charges, security deposits, or different rental terms or conditions
- Requesting discriminatory information on rental applications (e.g., asking about number of children or about the presence of handicap)
- Discriminatory qualification criteria, applications, or procedures
- Delay tactics to frustrate a person from pursuing rental
- Steering (channeling minorities to certain parts of a community, building, or floor)
- Restrictions or different provisions in lease contracts
- Provision of different levels of services or facilities
- Eviction on the basis of a protected class
- Discriminatory notices or statements
- Sexual harassment

Fair housing laws impact almost every aspect of the leasing process—from advertising to prospecting to continued enjoyment of the property under the terms of the lease, to move-out. Managers must design policies, procedures, and programs that are not discriminatory and that assist staff in avoiding inadvertent discrimination. It is wise to seek advice of legal counsel regarding specifics to ensure compliance. Most importantly, the policies and procedures should be followed to the letter for every ad design, phone call, or prospect visit to ensure that each prospect is treated identically.

Fair Housing in the News: Tenn. Community Settles Claims of Discrimination Against Hispanic Tenants (May 2013):

The owners and managers of a Nashville, Tenn., community agreed to pay more than $170,000 as part of a settlement resolving allegations that it discriminated against Hispanic tenants based on their national origin. According to HUD's complaint, the community's owners and management company allegedly terminated leases, ignored maintenance requests, and intimidated/harassed Hispanic tenants.

Under the terms of the agreement, the manager and owner agreed to establish a $150,000 victims' compensation fund for former residents administered by an independent agency and to pay $10,000 each to two nonprofit organizations to identify potential claimants. They also agreed to adopt fair housing policies and provide fair housing training.

Source: HUD

Fair Housing in the News: Management Company Settles Claim of Discrimination Against Non-English Speakers (January 2013):

HUD announced that a VA property management company agreed to pay $82,500 to settle allegations that it refused to allow an Hispanic woman to apply for an apartment because she didn't speak fluent English.

According to the complaint, the company refused to give her a rental application because she couldn't speak English well and refused the translation assistance of the bilingual person she brought with her. During its investigation, HUD allegedly found that the company had a written policy expressly requiring all prospective residents to be able to communicate with management staff in English without assistance from others, and to complete rental applications only while they were in the office.

The settlement requires the company to pay $7,500 to the woman and $25,000 each to three fair housing organizations. Among other things, the company also agreed to adopt a plan to more effectively serve Limited English Proficient residents and prospects by providing translation and interpretation services.

Source: HUD

Familial Status and Occupancy Guidelines

Discrimination on the basis of familial status refers to discrimination against people under the age of 18 who live with a parent, legal guardian, or any person designated by law to have custody of a child. This includes pregnant women and anyone who is in the process of securing legal custody of a child under the age of 18. The law applies not only to the sale and rental of housing but also to financing for housing.

Familial status remains one of the most confusing areas of fair housing and is the fastest growing area for complaints. Site managers and leasing professionals must know the most current information on this issue.

Occupancy guidelines for residential apartments relate directly to the familial status protected class. Occupancy guidelines cannot be created that limit the number of children in a unit. For example, four people in a two-bedroom unit could mean two adults and two children or one adult and three children. Real estate management personnel must be careful not to impose occupancy guidelines based on the number of children who will occupy the unit. "People" means people—regardless of age.

What rules could be violations, and what rules are safe to impose? Consider the following:

- If property hazards are present, the parents have the right to decide if the property is safe for their family.
- Real estate managers cannot charge persons with children higher rents or higher deposits than those without children.
- Steering based on familial status is discriminatory. Therefore, families cannot be limited to living only on the first floor or in other undesirable units or be relegated to certain buildings. In 1993, the Department of Justice sued two Spokane, Washington, apartment communities for restricting families to the first floor.

In December 1998, the Department of Housing and Urban Development (HUD), which enforces the Fair Housing Act, released a statement of policy of the factors it will use when evaluating a housing provider's occupancy policies to determine whether discriminatory conduct is occurring against families with children. This is a policy, not a rule or law. HUD believes that an occupancy policy of two persons per bedroom, as a rule, is reasonable under the Fair Housing Act.

However, HUD also states that it will not evaluate compliance solely on the number of people permitted in each bedroom. For more restrictive policies, HUD will take into account such factors as the number and size of the bedrooms or sleeping areas, the overall size of the dwelling unit, capacity of sewer, septic and other building systems, and any city or state occupancy requirements governing the property to determine if discrimination against families with children is occurring. If a rented property is governed by state or local occupancy requirements, and the property owner's occupancy policies reflect those requirements, HUD would consider them as a special circumstance tending to indicate that the owner's occupancy policies are reasonable. HUD also states that an occupancy policy that limits the number of children in a unit is less reasonable than one that limits the number of people in a unit. Keep in mind that rental housing groups must adopt state and local policies if they are stricter than HUD's policy.

Example 1:
Consider two theoretical situations in which a housing provider refused to permit a family of five to rent a two-bedroom dwelling based on a "two-people-per-bedroom" policy. In the first, the complainants are a family of five who applied to rent an apartment with two large bedrooms and spacious living areas. In the second, the complainants are a family of five who applied to rent a mobile home space on which they planned to live in a small two-bedroom mobile home. Issuing a charge of discrimination might be warranted in the first situation, but not in the second.

Example 2:
Another example involves the age of the children. Consider the following hypothetical situations involving two housing providers who refused to permit three people to share a bedroom. In the first, the complainants are two adult parents who applied to rent a one-bedroom apartment with their infant child, and both the bedroom and the apartment were large. In the second, the complainants are a family of two adult parents and one teenager who applied to rent a one-bedroom apartment. Issuing a charge of discrimination might be warranted in the first situation, but not in the second.

Affordable Housing Impact: Note that there may be differences in the familial status category depending on the specific affordable housing program. It is extremely important to understand the program requirement and additional laws.

Single Family Home Impact: The two-person per bedroom guideline can be a questionable policy in a single family home that, generally speaking, has more square footage per occupant than an apartment unit. Tenants may choose to use dens, family rooms, and bonus rooms as bedrooms.

Fair Housing in the News: Community Must Pay $38K for Discriminatory Craigslist Ad (June 2013):

A Massachusetts landlord and property manager have been ordered to pay more than $38,000 in a housing discrimination case alleging discriminatory online advertisements against families with young children, according to a recent announcement by Attorney General Martha Coakley.

In May 2013, a court found the owner and property manager violated state law by posting an advertisement on Craigslist stating that an apartment "is not deleaded, therefore it cannot be rented to families with children under six years old." Under Massachusetts law, it's illegal to refuse to rent or steer families away from rental properties because they have young children whose presence triggers an owner's duty to eliminate lead hazards that pose serious risks.

The court order requires the owner and property manager of the 20-unit community to pay a civil penalty of $10,000 and more than $28,000 in attorneys' fees and costs. They must also delead the next two-bedroom units that haven't yet been deleaded when they become available for rent.

Source: Massachusetts Attorney General's Office

Fair Housing in the News: Occupancy Policy Leads to Discrimination Charge (April 2013)

The owners and managers of 23 rental properties in Mississippi recently agreed to pay $27,000 to settle allegations of housing discrimination against families with children.

The lawsuit, filed by the Justice Department in 2011, alleged that the community violated federal fair housing law by refusing to rent a three-bedroom home to a woman with four children because she had "too many children" under the community's occupancy policy. The suit also alleged that by setting a lower maximum number of children than adults who could reside in each home, the community engaged in a pattern or practice of discrimination or denied rights protected by the Fair Housing Act to a group of persons.

The settlement requires the community to pay $20,000 to the family and a $7,000 civil penalty. In addition, the owners and managers agreed to adopt a nondiscriminatory occupancy policy of two persons per bedroom and receive fair housing training.

Source: U.S. Department of Justice

Provisions for the Disabled

Under provisions of the 1988 FHA Act, a property owner cannot refuse to permit a disabled tenant to modify the leased premises at his or her own expense, as long as the modifications are necessary to allow full enjoyment of the premises. Nor can an owner refuse to implement reasonable rules and policies that will allow a disabled person the same right to use and enjoy the dwelling as tenants who are not disabled. Finally, certain multifamily dwellings designed and constructed after March 13, 1991, must be accessible to people with disabilities.

The definition of *handicapped* is extremely broad. Currently, the preferred terminology is *disabled* instead of *handicapped*. The Fair Housing Amendment defines handicapped or disabled as follows:

- A physical or mental impairment that substantially limits one or more of such person's major life activities
- A record of having such impairment
- Being regarded as having such impairment, but such term does not include current, illegal use of, or addiction to, a controlled substance

A physical impairment may be any physiological disorder, cosmetic disfigurement, or anatomical loss that affects any of the body's systems. This would include AIDS, alcoholism, drug addiction (other than addiction caused by current illegal use of a controlled substance), and environmental illnesses from pesticides and ventilation systems.

Unlike with other protected classes, those renting to the disabled must take affirmative action. The Fair Housing Act states that housing providers are required to make reasonable accommodations in rules, policies, practices, or services and to allow reasonable modifications of existing premises.

Term	Description
Reasonable Accommodations	• Changes to policies and procedures that may be required to allow a disabled person to use and enjoy the property • For example, if the current policy on maintenance requests requires the resident to file a written request, management can change the policy to allow residents to make verbal maintenance requests
Reasonable Modifications	• Physical changes to a property that allow a disabled person full use of the premises • Modifications may be made to the interior of a unit or to any common area not open to the public (e.g., laundry rooms, clubhouses, or storage areas) • A lift on the outside of the building to allow a person with a wheelchair to have access to a second floor apartment is an example of a reasonable modification • Modifications do not need to be made only at the beginning of the tenancy; they may be made at any time

Modifications are made at the disabled person's expense and the property owner is entitled to protection against poorly done or improper modifications. The tenant is required to remove the modifications to the unit at the end of the tenancy if it is reasonable to do so or if the modifications interfere with enjoyment of the unit by a nondisabled tenant. Modifications to private common areas do not (and in most cases, should not) be removed.

> **Example 1:**
> If a wheelchair-bound prospective resident needs to have sinks and countertops lowered within the unit, doorways widened within the unit, and ramps installed to the laundry room, the owner must allow the resident to make those changes to the property. The owner can require the resident to restore the unit if reasonable (e.g., raising the sinks and countertops but not necessarily narrowing the doorways) but cannot require the removal of the ramp.

Examples of common modifications include:

- Installing grab bars in the bathroom
- Lowering or removing kitchen cabinets
- Installing a visual doorbell or fire alarm
- Removing a bathtub to install a roll-in shower
- Widening a doorway to the building laundry room

The property owner may not require the tenant to pay an additional security deposit because of the modifications. The regulations do allow for the establishment of a restoration escrow fund in certain limited situations, such as when extensive modifications are made on a short-term lease. The tenant must pay funds into an escrow account with interest accruing to the tenant. The owner may only use the funds for the restoration of the modifications and not as an additional security deposit.

If a property already has units modified to accommodate disabled residents, that fact should be advertised in a nondiscriminatory manner. Any accommodations that have already been instituted, such as the availability of a TDD (telecommunication device for the deaf), can also be advertised.

Service Animals

Discrimination charges are often levied against rental companies that do not alter a "no pets" rule to allow for service animals. Guide dogs for the blind commonly provide assistance, but they are not the only animals that provide support. Persons with a variety of disabilities may have a variety of animals to assist them in many ways, including providing emotional support.

In 2011, HUD issued a memo clarifying that DOJ amendments to ADA regulations limiting the definition of "service animal" do not apply to enforcement of the FHA. The HUD memo reiterates that under the FHA an individual with a disability may have the right to an animal with or without training if the animal provides equal opportunity for the individual to use and enjoy a dwelling. This means that a community with pet restrictions must make reasonable accommodations allowing a resident to keep an animal in his or her unit if that resident, upon making the request for accommodation, can provide documentation from a health care provider that (1) they have a disability and that (2) the animal allows them equal opportunity to use and enjoy the community. The FHA standard is expansive, including many types of animals providing physical as well as emotional support. And because a service animal is not a pet, the resident with a disability will not pay a pet deposit, pet fee, or pet rent.

RESOURCES:

HUD's "Fair Housing Accessibility Guidelines" provide builders and developers with technical guidance on how to comply with the specific accessibility requirements of the Fair Housing Amendments Act of 1988. The guidelines presented in this document discuss in depth specific barriers to equal access. The "Fair Housing Accessibility Guidelines" can be viewed at **www.hud.gov.**

Fair Housing in the News: N.M. Owner Settles Disability Discrimination Claim for $200K (April 2013):

The owner and manager of rental property in Albuquerque, N.M., recently agreed to pay $200,000 to settle allegations of discrimination and retaliation against a tenant with a disability.

The government's complaint alleged that the tenant became disabled as a result of a medical condition more than two years after he and his family moved into the rental home. Allegedly, the owner unlawfully refused to permit the tenant, who uses a wheelchair, to make reasonable modifications to the home at the tenant's own expense and with the assurance that the tenant would restore the premises to its original condition after moving out. The complaint also accused the owner of unlawfully retaliating against the tenant by evicting him after he requested permission to make reasonable modifications to accommodate his disability.

In addition to the monetary award, the settlement requires the owner to implement standards and procedures for receiving and handling requests made by persons with disabilities for reasonable modifications and accommodations at his rental properties and to submit to the government written reports regarding his efforts for three years.

Source: U.S. Department of Justice

Fair Housing in the News: Housing Authority Settles Complaint Involving Deaf Resident (December 2012):

HUD announced that the Houston Housing Authority agreed to settle allegations of disability discrimination for initially refusing a deaf resident's requests to have a sign language interpreter present at a hearing to determine her eligibility to remain in HUD's Housing Choice Voucher (HCV) program.

The Fair Housing Act prohibits housing providers from discriminating against persons with disabilities. Furthermore, Section 504 of the Rehabilitation Act of 1973 bans discrimination against qualified individuals with disabilities in any program or activity receiving federal funds.

In her complaint, the resident claimed that she twice asked the housing authority to provide a translator for the hearing, but none was provided. She said she was forced to use her daughter, who is a minor and is not fluent in American Sign Language, to interpret for her, and that the complex nature of her HCV eligibility hearing prevented her daughter from effectively interpreting for her. The outcome of the hearing was that the resident's housing assistance was terminated. After the resident filed a complaint with HUD, the housing authority held a second hearing, during which an interpreter was provided. Following the second hearing, the resident's housing assistance was reinstated.

Under the agreement, the housing authority paid $4,251 in rental assistance payments that were owed to the resident's landlord for the period her rental assistance was terminated. The housing authority also notified its employees of its intent to provide sign language interpreters for individuals who are deaf or hard of hearing, agreed to inform new HCV program participants of their right to request reasonable accommodations, including interpreters, and agreed not to retaliate against the resident or her children in any way.

Source: U.S. Department of Justice

Discrimination Post-September 11th

In the wake of the attacks of September 11, 2001, property owners and real estate managers have inquired about procedures for screening tenants on the basis of citizenship status. Real estate professionals must ensure that, while working to keep their buildings safe, they do not infringe on the fair housing rights of current or potential residents.

After September 11, 2001, reports of housing discrimination against persons who are perceived to be Muslim or of Middle Eastern descent have increased. To clarify this issue, the FHA does not prohibit discrimination based solely on a person's citizenship status. However, there is the risk that it might be closely tied to national origin or religious discrimination.

Requesting documentation of citizenship or immigration status from a housing applicant does not violate the FHA, but it may violate state or local statutes. Many federally assisted housing properties require this documentation when screening applicants in order to determine who is qualified to receive the subsidy in each household. In such cases, HUD regulates the guidelines for defining and verifying acceptable documents. Real estate managers and property owners who plan to use similar measures must implement them uniformly for all applicants. Note that such inquiries regarding citizenship or immigration status are illegal in California (although the law does not prohibit required verification for HUD programs.

Example 1:

A man applies for an apartment. Because he looks like he is from the Middle East, the landlord requires him to provide additional information and forms of identification and then refuses to rent the apartment to him. Later, a person from England applies for an apartment at the same community. Because he is from England, the landlord does not have him complete the additional paperwork and rents the apartment to him. This is discrimination by differential treatment on the basis of national origin.

Example 2:

A person who is applying for an apartment mentions in the interview that he left his native country to study in the United States. The landlord, concerned that the applicant's visa may expire during tenancy, asks him for documentation to determine how long he is legally allowed to be in the United States. If the landlord requests this information, regardless of the applicant's race or specific national origin, the landlord has not violated the FHA. Source: www.hud.gov

---

When enforcing rules and privileges of tenancy, a leasing professional, real estate manager, or property owner cannot impose stricter penalties on a person because of his or her nationality. Action should only be taken because of a legitimate property management concern.

Example:

Imagine a property owner receives a complaint from a resident who claims another resident whom he believes to be Muslim is "having a group of about five or six men over to his apartment every Monday night." The resident claims "the men appear unfriendly" and thinks they may be "up to something." The resident's visitors do not disturb the other residents in their peaceful enjoyment of the premises. A property owner could be accused of religious or national origin discrimination if he or she asks the resident to refrain from having these guests over when no evidence of any violation of established property management rules exists. Additionally, everyone in the U.S. has the right of "free association," which is the right of adults to freely choose their associates for whatever purpose they see fit.

Fair Housing Assessment

Representatives from HUD and other organizations can legally visit and "test" your property for violations of fair housing laws. In addition, it is legal for these testers to file a fair housing complaint.

Therefore, it is good practice to test yourself and your staff to ensure there are no discriminatory policies at the property. Be sure to check whether your prospects are shown all available apartments that they are qualified to rent. Ask yourself and your staff the following questions:

CHECKLIST: FAIR HOUSING ASSESSMENT
☐ Am I treating this applicant any differently because he or she is a member of a protected class group?
☐ Am I acting in any way that will potentially exclude as residents a higher number of minorities?
☐ Does what I am doing have a valid, nondiscriminatory business purpose? Could I accomplish this in a way that would have less impact on a protected class?
☐ Are there any written or verbal instructions from an owner or other authority stating or implying that apartments should not be rented to members of a protected class?
☐ Do I or do any of my employees falsely tell prospects that an apartment is unavailable? Could this be based on a prospect's protected class status?
☐ Do I or do any of my employees in any way discourage renting an apartment because of an applicant's protected class status?

Source: *Contemporary Apartment Marketing.* Reprinted with permission.

Affordable Housing Impact: Waiting lists should be maintained for all current units, and should contain the following information:
- Name and contact information
- Date and time application is received. It is important to maintain the waiting list according to chronological order or as required by the specific affordable housing program requirements. Residents on the wait list may have rights of first refusal. If they decline the unit they may remain on the wait list, but would then be moved to the bottom.
- Also, all notices of intent to vacate should be dated and time stamped as well.

RESOURCES:
Tutorials such as the Fair Housing tutorial can be found under Education>On-Demand Learning>Tutorials at **www.irem.org** and are free.

The Americans with Disabilities Act (ADA)

The Americans with Disabilities Act (ADA) of 1990 is the civil rights legislation for the disabled. Both residential and commercial properties are subject to the guidelines outlined in the ADA, which mandates equal access to the following:

- Employment
- Public service
- Public accommodations
- Telecommunications services

Accessibility

Title III of the ADA addresses accessibility of areas open to the public for people with disabilities and therefore affects all types of properties. It requires that all buildings that are open to public commerce be made accessible to disabled people to the maximum extent. This includes the removal of architectural (physical obstructions that inhibit movement) and communication barriers (those that inhibit interaction with others) in existing public accommodations.

The Department of Justice has listed twelve types of public accommodations. These include leasing offices and other parts of residential properties that are open to the public, such as pools and clubhouses. Common areas, such as building entrances and lobbies, must also be accessible to disabled individuals. According to the act, the property owner is responsible for installing access ramps and changing parking areas to accommodate applicants with disabilities. These changes may include reserving certain parking areas for vehicles belonging to disabled people and installing ramps with railings.

Commercial facilities are required, among other things, to make public restrooms, drinking fountains, and pay telephones accessible to disabled people, including those in wheelchairs. With regard to pay telephones, it may be necessary to include a TDD (telecommunication device for the deaf) for use by hearing-impaired individuals. Keep in mind that a "No Pets" policy does not apply to individuals who need assistive animals such as guide dogs.

Barrier Removal

If barrier removal is not readily achievable (easily accomplished without much difficulty or expense), management must find an alternative. For example, if the leasing office is not accessible by wheelchair and the cost of making it accessible is prohibitively expensive, the leasing professional can arrange to meet a prospect at another location, such as at the clubhouse or a nearby restaurant. Alternatives to barrier removal can only be used when barrier removal is not readily achievable. They are not a substitute for removing barriers in the first place.

Q. What is the difference between FHA and ADA?

A. The differences between reasonable modifications under the Fair Housing Act and barrier removal under the Americans with Disabilities Act are what modifications need to be made and who is responsible for making them. Modifications within a unit (provided it is not new construction) and to private common areas under the fair housing laws are made at the discretion and expense of the resident. Barrier removal is mandatory under the ADA, and the property owner bears the expense.

NOTES:
In certain circumstances, the property owner may be able to pass on the cost of barrier removal. Such discussion is beyond the scope of this book. For more information on ADA, contact IREM's Legislation and Research Department, or access the ADA website at **www.ada.gov**

RESOURCES:
More information on avoiding illegal discrimination can be found in the seminar "Fair Housing and Beyond" developed in collaboration between the Institute of Real Estate Management and the National Apartment Association Education Institute. Contact your local IREM® chapter or visit **www.irem.org** for additional information.

Affordable Housing Impact: The determination of who is responsible for payment may vary based on circumstance, affordable housing program regulations, as well as what is considered reasonable. Reasonableness is determined by the regulating authority consistent with the ADA and FHA programs.

QUALIFYING PROSPECTS

Once a prospect has filled out an application, it is time to assess his or her feasibility as a resident at the property. This process is called qualifying. Qualifying a residential prospect involves examining household income, references, and credit history. To qualify as a potential resident, a prospect must show the ability to pay rent and demonstrate acceptable prior performance as a renter.

Establishment of minimum standards in a resident selection process, the resident selection criteria, is determined by owner's goals and crucial to the success of the property. Selection criteria should be in writing and must be applied consistently to all applicants. They should include:

- Minimum rent-to-household income ratio (may be affected by state guidelines)
- Minimum period of employment with current employer
- Satisfactory references from one or more prior landlords
- Satisfactory references regarding credit
- Appropriate ratio of residents to apartment size
- Minimum age requirement
- Screening service for criminal background check (applied to all potential occupants, not just potential leaseholders)

To ensure an applicant's ability to pay rent, most properties use the following guidelines:

- The yearly income should be around three or four times the amount of the annual rent

- A reasonable period of employment is a measure of stability and financial security. Often the requirement is that each applicant must have been employed by the same employer for at least 12 months during the preceding two years. An applicant who has been working with a current employer for less than six months is likely to have worked at least a year for a prior employer. An exception to this might be a prospect whose primary employment is seasonal (e.g., construction) or a young adult who is new to the workforce.

- Satisfactory references from two previous landlords are verified (e.g., on-time payments and responsible behavior)

- Limits on the number of residents in an apartment is usually based on the number of bedrooms. In some states, HUD has said two persons per bedroom is "reasonable" but in California for example the rule is two persons per bedroom plus one. As long as the number used by the landlord is not more restrictive than two persons per bedroom there is less chance that it will be challenged as discriminatory. This criterion is aimed at minimizing wear and tear on the apartment and assuring a quality lifestyle for the residents. Before establishing specific limits, check with local jurisdictions since they may have set maximum occupancy levels.

- Residents must have attained the age of majority—depending on state law, this may be 18, 19, or 21—before they can sign a lease

Checking credit references to determine how much debt the prospect is handling is extremely important. This can be done by following up on online vendor reports, verifying rental history, and confirming employment history through pay stubs.

Refer to Figure 4-2 for information on the Fair and Accurate Credit Transaction Act.

FIGURE 4-2: FAIR AND ACCURATE CREDIT TRANSACTION ACT

In 2003, responding to the dramatic increase in identity theft and fraud, the Fair and Accurate Credit Transaction Act (FACTA) was signed into law. The act substantially changes the FCRA's impact on property owners. In addition to reauthorizing the FCRA, the act addresses consumer concerns about identity theft and inaccuracies in consumer reports and gives consumers the right to limit how businesses can use their nonpublic personal information.

For the leasing professional, consumer reports may now appear with fraud alerts and file blocks when consumers claim identity theft or fraud. Similarly, if the community provides data to consumer reporting agencies such as collection agencies, there are new requirements for responding to notices of alleged identity theft. Leasing professionals should always confirm these reports with the management and respond according to company policy and screening criteria.

Leasing professionals should be aware that the act also impacts:
- The types of records that will be submitted to collection agencies
- New procedures for verifying collection account accuracy and re-investigating if the account is disputed
- Limitations on a corporate entity to "share" information between its sister properties for the purposes of marketing

All of these factors impact applicant screening at the community. The leasing professional should be aware of what his or her role is in applicant screening.

Vendor Resident Screening

Effective resident screening services are provided by vendors for real estate professionals. These screening tools use proprietary data collection and grouping systems that can be as broad or as targeted as policy of the management company determines is necessary in order to meet the objectives of the owner for the property. For example:

- **Financial History:** Credit report, check writing history, credit score, risk score
- **Criminal Background:** Felony, misdemeanor, sex offender, terrorist DMV

- **Landlord/Tenant History:** Evictions, landlord tenant court data, verbal verifications

The advantages to using vendor-collected data for these more robust screening goals include the ability of searches to reach across jurisdictions in the case of criminal background checks, and also the reduction of lost property staff time in investigating "false positives"; with a contracted resident screening service the vendor runs additional matching data against a simple return of a "John Smith" conviction for auto theft (for example). Such leasing software may have a proprietary "scoring engine" built in that assigns a risk level to results from a variety of factors.

TIPS:
Be sure to perform criminal checks on both the lessees (18 and over) and the occupants (child or minor) of an apartment. Also, document both the lessees' names as well as the occupants' names on the lease. Check state laws, as some states may not allow for criminal checks.

LEGAL ISSUE:
To avoid potential fair housing issues, it is important to record the date and time of every prospect's visit if your property has a waitlist for apartments. If one of the apartments becomes available, the first person on the waitlist must be contacted about the availability.

RESOURCES:
Downloadable forms such as prospect cards, rental applications, and prospect qualification forms can be found under Resources>Forms & Checklists at **www.irem.org** and are free for members.

Single Family Home Impact: It is extremely important to obtain credit reports on prospective residents and to make phone calls to verify employment history.

Affordable Housing Impact: The process for qualifying prospects is slightly different for affordable housing properties due to the variety of affordable housing programs available. Each program has specific requirements.

In general, to qualify as a resident, a prospect must meet eligibility criteria established for the particular affordable housing program, the property, and the company policies. The real estate manager's responsibility to the owner is to maximize the income of the property. Failure to ensure that prospective residents qualify can result in very serious financial repercussions to the owner/partner.

An approved tenant selection plan must be available and applied consistently to all applicants (see above for specific items to include). Conducting a criminal background check on anyone 18 or older whether they are a lessee or an occupant can also be one of the criteria as long as it is applied to all potential occupants, not just potential leaseholders.

To ensure an applicant's ability to pay rent, the prospect must be income eligible for the program at the particular property.

Student Housing Impact: The following additional criteria should be considered when qualifying potential students:
- Obtain proof of income or guarantor for the lease
- Verify credit of student or parent
- Verify student loan information with financial aid office
- Conduct criminal background check
- Research 501(c)3 stipulations on bond documents (Often tax-exempt 501(c)3 corporations finance or develop student housing properties and there may be specific qualification requirements related to this business arrangement)

LANDLORD-TENANT LAW

The landlord-tenant law spells out the respective *rights and responsibilities* of landlords and tenants. Note that while site managers are encouraged to refer to residential renters as "residents" to foster a closer relationship with them, the parties to a lease are designated landlord (lessor) and tenant (lessee).

LEGAL ISSUE:
Local ordinances may also address the handling of security deposits and identify specific "tenants' rights" in regard to the relationship with the landlord. These laws also affect the contents of application and lease forms.

Landlord's Duty

The landlord's duty under landlord-tenant law includes the following:

TOP 8 LANDLORD DUTIES
1. Deliver the premises at the beginning of the lease term
2. Maintain the premises in a habitable condition
3. Provide for the tenant's quiet enjoyment of the premises
4. Supply essential services, including heat and hot water (the landlord does not have to pay, just make available)
5. Give proper notice of changes to rules and regulations or a change of ownership
6. Notify the tenant of any changes to the terms of the lease (including rent increases)
7. Notify the tenant before lease expiration
8. Return the security deposit within the prescribed period

In exchange for fulfilling these obligations, the landlord is to receive timely payment in the form of rent. The lease should clearly state what the rent is, when it is due, how often it is to be paid, and where payment is to be made. It should also specify any fees or other charges, such as the late payment of rent. If the rent is not paid or if the tenant is otherwise in violation of the lease, the landlord has the right to terminate the lease agreement and evict the tenant.

Landlord's Rights

Landlord-tenant law also provides the landlord the following right:

- **Right of Reentry** to make repairs and improvements and provide agreed services. Usually, specific notice is required—except in an emergency. The landlord is also allowed to show the apartment to prospective tenants, contractors, purchasers, and lenders. The landlord has the right to set reasonable policies and rules for the property. Such rules generally concern promotion of the convenience and welfare of all the tenants, preservation of the landlord's (owner's) property, and allocation of services and facilities.

Possession

A tenant's right to possess and use the premises is the counterpart of the landlord's responsibility to deliver possession of a leased apartment on a specified date. Delivery of possession by the landlord is an important point. Usually, this is specified in the lease agreement as well as in landlord-tenant law. However, possession involves two issues:

- If the landlord has possession of the leased premises at the beginning of the lease term but is unable to deliver it to an incoming tenant, the landlord may be obligated to abate the rent (refund prior payment) until he or she is able to deliver the apartment to the tenant. Alternatively, the tenant may choose to terminate the lease and have prepaid rent, deposits, and fees returned, or the tenant may sue for possession of the premises and recover damages from the landlord.

- If the landlord does not have possession of the dwelling unit because a previous tenant has not vacated it, the landlord's liability may be partially mitigated by that of the current occupant, if proper notice had been given.

Tenants' Duty

Tenants also have specific responsibilities under landlord-tenant law, including the following:

TOP 7 TENANT DUTIES

1. Comply with the terms of the lease
2. Maintain the dwelling unit in a clean, safe condition and use the fixtures and appliances appropriately
3. Respect the privacy and right to quiet enjoyment of other tenants
4. Abide by the rules and regulations of the premises, provided the purpose is to promote the welfare of all the tenants and preserve the property from abuse. (These rules must be reasonable and apply uniformly to all tenants. They are typically an addendum to the lease.)
5. Grant the landlord reasonable access to the dwelling unit to make repairs or show the unit to prospective renters, purchasers, or lenders
6. Use the dwelling unit only as a residence, unless otherwise agreed
7. Give proper notice before vacating the premises

In return for the tenant's payment, the landlord agrees to provide a habitable apartment—one that is safe and clean. Local building codes usually define specific standards that generally include the following:

- The common areas are maintained in a clean and safe condition

- The apartment is maintained in a safe condition

- The structure (roof, exterior walls) is free from leaks

- Appropriate fixtures and facilities are provided and maintained in safe working order

- Essential services, including heat, running water, gas, electricity, sewerage, and waste disposal, are supplied (again, the landlord does not have to pay for these services, just make them available)

Tenants' Rights

Landlord-tenant law also provides the tenant the following rights:

- **Quiet Enjoyment:** This includes the right to privacy, peace and quiet, and lawful use of the apartment, common areas, and facilities. Tenants are expected to respect each other's rights to privacy and peaceful enjoyment. Quiet enjoyment also means that the tenant can occupy the premises free from interference by the landlord, except for the landlord's right of reentry and obligation to make repairs discussed previously.

- **Warranty of Habitability:** If the landlord does not maintain the leased premises in habitable condition or does not provide essential services, the tenant may have the right to withhold rent, vacate the apartment without penalty, make repairs and deduct their cost from the rent, and/or collect damages in court based on the landlord's breach of contract. In general, tenants are required to provide the landlord with formal notice of the breach (usually in writing) and give the landlord the opportunity to make corrections before exercising any of these remedies. However, the tenants' specific rights and responsibilities under the warranty of habitability are subject to the applicable landlord-tenant law.

- **Constructive Eviction:** If a tenant can document that a landlord was aware of a problem and failed to correct it that may constitute violation of the implied warranty of habitability. In that case, the tenant may be able to vacate the premises on the basis of constructive eviction. That type of eviction may also apply if the tenant's right to quiet enjoyment is disturbed by some action of the landlord that renders the leased premises uninhabitable or deprives the tenant of enjoyment of the premises. The key to constructive eviction is that the tenant must vacate.

LEASE DOCUMENT

A *lease* is an agreement that grants a tenant the rights of exclusive use and occupancy of a specific space for a defined period in return for the payment of rent or other consideration to the landlord. To be enforceable, a lease must be in writing. As a legal contract, it is enforceable if: The space is not used for illegal purposes, both parties enter into the lease by mutual consent, and the document is signed and dated.

Usually the tenant's signature is affixed before the lease is presented to the landlord for acceptance and signature. Both parties receive an original, signed copy of the lease. To maintain their tenancy, tenants must pay their rent on time and abide by all provisions of the lease.

Most qualified residential prospects sign a one-year standard lease for a set rent payment without engaging in any formal negotiations. Discussions of the starting date of the lease term or specific inducements to lease (i.e., decorating to be done before move-in, rent concessions) may be considered "negotiations."

CHECKLIST: LEASE DOCUMENT ELEMENTS

☐ Names and signatures of all parties to the agreement
☐ Description of the leased premises
☐ Duration of the lease term, including the commencement and expiration dates
☐ Rental fee and payment terms
☐ Purpose for which the leased premises will be used
☐ Abandonment of the residence: the rights of the landlord upon the relinquishment of the residence before the end of the term of the lease without consent of the owner
☐ Additional clauses (also called "provisions and attachments")

LEGAL ISSUE:

Note that negotiating rent can potentially violate Fair Housing Laws. Ensure that standard and consistent policies and procedures for rent negotia tions are in place.

Affordable Housing Impact: HUD provides the leases and addendums for most property types they oversee. Separate leases or addendums specific to affordable housing assistance programs must be approved by the local HUD office.

FIGURE 4-3: SAMPLE RENTAL AGREEMENT WITH PROVISIONS AND ATTACHMENTS

RENTAL AGREEMENT

This agreement is made and entered into _____ on between _____ hereinafter "Landlord" and _____ hereinafter "Resident". Subject to the terms and conditions below, Landlord rents to Resident and Resident rents from Landlord, for residential purposes only, the premises located at_____, The lease term shall be for _____ months. The tenancy term shall commence on _____ with a completion date of _____. The rent for the above premises shall be $_____ per month. Security deposit shall be $_____, Other deposits $_____ for_____.

1. *Month-to-Month Tenancy after Fixed Term.* This is a tenancy for a fixed term, but after the expiration of the Minimum Lease Term this will be a month-to-month tenancy. A "month" for purposes of this Agreement means a calendar month, The Resident's obligation to pay rent will continue until terminated in the manner set forth in this Agreement.

2. *Notice of Non-Renewal or Termination.* If Resident intends to vacate at the end of the fixed term, Resident must provide written notice of the non-renewal of this lease at least 30 days prior to the end of the term. Thereafter, either party may terminate this lease upon 30 days written notice to the other.

3. *Rental payment.* Rent is due on the FIRST day of each month. If the rent has not been received by the end of the 3rd day of each month, the Resident agrees to pay a Late Payment Fee in the amount of $25.00 and $5.00 a day thereafter for each day any amount of rent remains unpaid until the end of the month. Returned check fees (NSF) will be $25.00. Resident will be responsible for rent payment for 30 days from the date that the Landlord receives a written 30-day notice to vacate or until Resident returns the keys to the premises, whichever is longer. Resident shall be responsible for rent for the entire term of this Agreement even if the Resident vacates the premises prior to the termination of this Agreement. If a rent discount, move-in special or concession is provided with this Agreement, and if the Resident does not fulfill the terms and conditions of this Agreement, the discount, move-in special or concession must be repaid in full along with all other provisions of the Agreement.

4. *Deposits.* Any deposits received from the Resident will be applied as provided in the PROVISIONS AND ATTACHMENTS. For health and safety purposes, all carpets will be professionally cleaned after each vacating resident and the cost deducted from the deposit unless the resident makes other arrangements with the Landlord in writing. Any remaining balance will be returned to the Resident within thirty (30) days after the Premises have been vacated as evidenced by the return of the keys to the Landlord,

5. *Utilities Provided by Landlord:* _____.

6. *Resident Agrees to Obey Rules.* Resident agrees to abide by such reasonable rules and regulations as Landlord may from time to time establish for all Residents of the same multiple dwelling unit. A copy of the current Community Rules and Regulations is attached hereto. Resident acknowledges that these Rules and Regulations are a legally binding part of the Rental Agreement.

7. *Attorney Fees.* The prevailing party to a suit or other proceeding to enforce the terms of this Rental Agreement will be entitled to all court costs and attorney's fees from the non-prevailing party.

8. *Agreement Binding on Each Party.* It is expressly understood that this rental Agreement is between the Landlord and each Resident jointly and severally, and that in the event of default in payment of rent, or any other provision of this Agreement, each and every Resident can be held individually responsible for complete payment of rent or any other costs,

9. *Forbearance not a Waiver.* Any forbearance by Landlord to strictly enforce all of the terms and conditions of this Agreement will not be construed as a waiver of Landlord's right to strictly enforce all of such terms and conditions in the event of any further, continued, or additional default by Resident.

10. *Other Terms, Conditions or Regulations, if any: (Initials of both parties are required for any changes or additions.)* This instrument, any attachments, and the Rules and Regulations constitute the entire agreement between Landlord and Resident and there are no other promises or agreements whatsoever. It supersedes all prior or existing written or oral agreements and may be modified only by a written instrument, signed by all parties, expressly modifying the terms of this Agreement.

NOTICE: BY EXECUTING THIS AGREEMENT, YOU ACKNOWLEDGE THAT YOU HAVE RECEIVED A COPY OF THIS AGREEMENT, ANY ADDENDUMS OR ATTACHMENTS, INCLUDING ANY CURRENT RULES AND REGULATIONS AND THAT YOU HAVE READ THEM AND UNDERSTAND THEM TO THE BEST OF YOUR ABILITY AND ARE WILLING TO ABIDE BY THE AGREEMENT. YOU AGREE AND UNDERSTAND THAT THIS IS A BINDING LEGAL CONTRACT DESCRIBING YOUR AND YOUR LANDLORD'S RIGHTS AND OBLIGATIONS. In Witnesss Whereof, Landlord and Resident have executed this Agreement as of the day and year first above written.

BY: _____   _____   _____
    Landlord or Agent   Resident   Resident

PROVISIONS AND ATTACHMENTS (SAMPLE)

1. **RENT:** Resident agrees to pay Landlord the amount of Rent agreed to in the Rental Agreement each month in the exact amount due. Any amount tendered that exceeds the amount due will be applied to the following month's rent. All payments tendered will first be applied to any outstanding debts in the order they were incurred, if any, then to the current month's late charges, if any, and only then to the current rent owed. Rent for the first and last month will be prorated on a daily basis if the lease commences or terminates on a day other than the last day of the month.

2. **PLACE OF PAYMENT:** Rent will be paid at the Landlord's Rental Office or at such other address as Landlord may from time to time designate in writing as the place for payment of rent. Mailed envelopes containing rent must be postmarked on or before the due date. Landlord will not be responsible for cash delivered through the mail/mail drop.

3. **DEPOSITS:** The deposit will be used as a security/rent deposit. It will first be applied to damages and cleaning, then to unpaid late charges and administrative fees, and then only to unpaid rent. Any remaining balance will be returned to the Resident within thirty (30) days after the Premises have been vacated. However, if the Resident terminates the tenancy prior to the end of the Minimum Lease Term, the Resident will forfeit all deposits at Landlord's option. Resident cannot apply the Deposit for payment of the last month's rent.

4. **RETURNED CHECKS:** All checks returned for insufficient funds must be redeemed by money order. An administrative fee will be added to the rent due for any such returned check. Late charges and other fees will continue to accrue until the check is redeemed. If the Resident has more than two (2) checks returned for insufficient funds within twelve (12) months of each other, the Resident must pay all rent thereafter by money order. FOR SAFETY REASONS LANDLORD DOES NOT ACCEPT CASH. DO NOT ATTEMPT TO PAY YOUR RENT IN CASH.

5. **RESIDENT'S RESPONSIBILITY FOR UTILITIES:** The Resident will pay in full all utilities not provided by Landlord as they become due. The Resident agrees to place utilities in Resident's name upon occupancy of the Premises and not to remove Resident's name until the termination date. The Resident further agrees to notify the Landlord of any interruptions of utility services to the Premises prior to such interruption. Any damages or loss incurred by the Resident's failure to pay utilities, or to inform the Landlord of any shut off, will be the responsibility of the Resident. The Resident will hold the Landlord harmless for utility charges incurred by the Resident.

6. **MAXIMUM OCCUPANCY:** The Premises will be occupied as living quarters by no more than 2 persons per bedroom, not including children under the age of 2 years. Only those persons who have signed the Rental Agreement and their minor children (including foster and step children) may reside there.

7. **TERMINATION UPON THREE (3) DAY NOTICE:** If the Resident fails to pay the rent when due or any of the other terms and conditions of these Rules or the Rental Agreement are breached, the Landlord may terminate this tenancy and Agreement upon three (3) days written notice. The Resident will have until the end of the third day following delivery of the notice to correct the matter in default or deliver possession to Landlord. During this time, Resident's rights are only forfeited, not terminated and Resident remains liable for rent for the balance of the lease.

8. **LEGAL ACTION BY LANDLORD:** Should the Landlord institute an unlawful detainer or any other legal action to recover possession because of non-payment of rent, and should Resident tender payment after commencement of such action, the Landlord will not be required to accept such payment unless the Resident pays all actual administrative, attorney's and service fees, court costs and moving and storage costs incurred by Landlord and also the entire rent in default. Acceptance by the Landlord of any or all amount will be at Landlord's option and will-not operate to stay said legal proceedings or act as a waiver of Landlord's right to possession of the Premises, unless specifically waived in writing by the Landlord. The Landlord is not required to dismiss an unlawful detainer action, even if the full sum is paid.

9. **VACATING PREMISES:** Resident will leave Premises in the same or better condition (normal wear and tear excepted) than when first occupied. Upon returning keys to Landlord, Resident represents and affirms to Landlord that the Premises are thoroughly cleaned and in good repair. If further cleaning and/or repairs are required, Landlord will not be Obligated to notify Resident other than noting deficiencies along with other charges, if any, on the security/rent deposit refund request form, which will be mailed to Resident's forwarding address, provided one is given by Resident, within thirty (30) days from receiving keys in Landlord's office. If Landlord is required to change locks or do further cleaning and/or repairs after Resident has vacated the Premises Resident agrees to pay for Landlord's loss of rental income during any period which is reasonably required to perform such lock changes, cleaning and/or repairs.

10. **PETS:** No pets or animals are permitted unless there is prior written approval by Landlord. If Pets are permitted, Resident agrees to pay an additional Pet Deposit and sign a separate pet agreement. A violation of the Pet Agreement will be considered a default under this Rental Agreement. Support animals for handicapped individuals are not considered pets and will be allowed on the Premises with no deposits contingent upon a written prescription issued by an appropriate licensed professional. Handicapped individuals will be responsible for any and all damage caused by the support animal and agree to control their support animal so as not to interfere with the safety or quiet enjoyment of the premises by other Residents.

11. **GUESTS:** Guests may stay for a maximum of ten days unless there is prior approval by the Landlord. If such persons cumulatively or consecutively stay on the Premises for more than two (2) weeks within a twelve (12) month period, the Landlord may require them to sign this Rental Agreement.

12. **RESIDENTS:** Any co-Resident vacating the Premises must sign off the Rental Agreement or continue to be liable under these Rules or the Rental Agreement. Such an action will be acceptable at the sole discretion of the Landlord.

13. **NO SUBLETTING:** Resident agrees not to sublet dwelling or any part thereof without the prior written permission of Landlord.

14. **RE-APPLICATION REQUIRED:** In the event that there is a desire to change the number or identity of the Resident(s) who initially entered into this Rental Agreement, Resident(s) will submit an additional Rental Application which will be evaluated using established Resident selection criteria prior to the Landlord accepting new or changed Residents.

15. **INSPECTION:** Landlord or Landlord's assign may enter the Premises at any time with at least 24-hours notice to make repairs. Landlord will give the same notice of intent to inspect or show the Premises to prospective buyers. Landlord may show the Premises to prospective Residents, if the current Resident has submitted a written 30-day notice to vacate the Premises.

16. **NO EXCESSIVE NOISE:** Resident agrees not to play or operate any musical instrument, radio, television, stereo or other machine loud enough to unreasonably disturb other Residents or neighbors; not to have gatherings, parties or to make noise of any kind loud enough to be heard by other Residents or neighbors during the hours before 8 am or after 10:30 p.m.

17. **QUIET ENJOYMENT FOR OTHER RESIDENTS:** Resident agrees not to interfere with the right of other Residents to peace and quiet, not to allow offensive odors, to park properly and to use common areas properly; not to use abusive language, threaten, or physically assault other Residents, the Landlord, Landlord's employees or representatives, or allow any such behavior from Resident's family or guests. Resident, any member of resident's household, or guest, or other person in association with or under the control of the Resident shall not engage in the unlawful discharge of firearms, on or near the Premises. Such action will constitute grounds to terminate occupancy and a notice may be issued to vacate the Premises.

18. **NO ILLEGAL ACTIVITIES:** Resident agrees not to use the Premises for any unlawful purposes; not to violate any regulations of the Board of Health, City or County ordinances or other State or Federal laws of whatever nature. The covenants contained in this paragraph herein, once breached cannot afterward be performed, and in that case unlawful detainer proceedings may be commenced.

19. **CRIMINAL ACTIVITIES AND DRUG ABUSE:** Resident, any member of the Resident's household, or a guest or other person under the resident's control or person in association with the Resident, shall not engage in criminal activity, including drug-related activity, on or near the Premises. "Drug-related criminal activity" means the illegal manufacture, sale, or use of a controlled substance (as defined in Section 102 of the Controlled Substances Act- 21 U.S.C. 802.) A single violation of the above provisions shall be a material violation of the lease and good cause for termination of tenancy. Unless otherwise provided by law, proof of violations shall not require criminal conviction, but shall be by a preponderance of the evidence.

20. **KEYS, LOCKS:** Any changes, alterations or additions to existing locks require prior written approval by Landlord. Should Resident misplace or lose the key to the Premises and become locked out, Landlord may charge Resident to open Premises and/or to provide a key to Resident or the Resident may at his own expense call a Locksmith. Any damages caused by break-in by Resident will be attributed to Resident. Upon vacating the Premises ALL keys will be returned to the Landlord. In the event the keys are not returned the locks will be changed at Resident's expense. Rent may be charged until all keys are received by Landlord.

21. **PLUMBING:** Resident is responsible for unplugging drains, toilets and sinks and for preventing freeze damage to any pipes. Unless it can be ascertained that blockage or damage to the plumbing was not Resident's fault, Resident will pay to have tile pipes repaired or unplugged.

22. **ABANDONMENT:** Abandonment will occur if either (1) without notifying Landlord, Resident is absent from the unit for seven days while rent is due and owing, even though Resident's possessions (all or part) remain on the Premises; or (2) without notifying Landlord, Resident is absent one day while rent is due and owing and the Resident's possessions have been removed from the Premises. If Resident abandons Premises, Landlord may retake possession of the Premises and attempt to rent it at a fair market value.

23. **ABANDONED PROPERTY:** Resident has left personal property in or on the Premises Landlord may remove it to storage and attempt to notify the Resident of this action. Resident may claim said personal property by paying moving and storage charges in addition to any other charges due and owing. If Resident fails to claim said personal property within thirty days of removal from Premises, Landlord may, at Landlord's discretion, dispose of the personal property and apply any proceeds toward any amount the Resident may owe. Personal property left on the Premises, after Resident has relinquished tenancy will be deemed abandoned and may be disposed of as Landlord deems appropriate.

24. **NOTICE:** All notices will be in writing. Notices to Landlord will be deemed given when delivered personally or by certified mail to Landlord at the Landlord's office, at the address herein stated. All notices to Resident may be served by mail, by depositing the same in the United States Mail, postage paid, addressed to Resident at the post office address of the Premises unless otherwise provided by law. Mailed notices will be deemed delivered on the date following the postmarked date on envelope. Landlord will not be required to prove delivery to Resident. If the Premises are occupied by husband and wife or by more than one person not husband and wife or co-Residents, such Resident(s) will appoint the other(s) as his/her Landlord for the purpose of receiving notices hereunder.

25. **ATTORNEY FEES:** The prevailing party to a suit or other proceeding to enforce the terms of these Rules or this Rental Agreement will be entitled to all court costs and attorney's fees from the non-prevailing party. Even if no suit or action is filed, the parties agree, that if due to a default in the payment or performance of any terms in these Rules or the Rental Agreement the non-defaulting party occurs costs or fees in enforcing these Rules or the Rental Agreement, the defaulting party will pay, upon demand, the other party's costs and fees, including, but not limited to attorney fees and costs.

26. **SEVERABILITY:** If any part of these Rules or the Rental Agreement is invalid or unenforceable by law or government regulation, or if any provision herein is deemed waived, the remaining portions of these Rules or the Rental Agreement will remain in force and in effect.

BY SIGNING BELOW YOU ACKNOWLEDGE THAT YOU HAVE RECEIVED A Copy OF THE RENTAL AGREEMENT, ANY ADDENDUMS OR ATTACHMENTS, INCLUDING THESE RULES AND REGULATIONS AND THAT YOU HAVE READ THEM AND UNDERSTANDS THEM TO THE BEST OF YOUR ABILITY AND ARE WILLING TO ABIDE BY THE AGREEMENT.

RESIDENT _____ DATE

RESIDENT _____ DATE

Lease Clauses

The various other clauses in the lease describe the obligations of the parties under the agreement. These clauses are usually specifically identified. They cover everything from security deposits to requirements for notices.

A lease should never contain any clause that could reasonably be considered unconscionable. This refers to any part of a contract that is unenforceable because it is grossly unfair (i.e., a lease clause under which a tenant waived key rights guaranteed under landlord-tenant law). If a tenant contested such a clause in court, a judge could invalidate the entire lease or only the offensive part. An attorney should always review lease forms prior to implementation to identify such problems.

Some common lease clauses follow:

Lease Clause	Description
Rent	• Spells out the amount of rent and the form, time, and place of payment, as well as any penalties that may apply (i.e., late fees)
Renter's Insurance	• States that personal property of the tenant(s) is not covered by the building owner's insurance, and that the tenant(s) must carry renter's insurance for their personal property
Security Deposit	• Explains the purpose of the deposit and the conditions for its return; serves as a guarantee of the tenant's performance of the lease
Delivery of Possession	• Protects the owner in case of inability to deliver possession of the apartment on the agreed date; applies to new or rehabilitated properties when leasing predates completion of construction or when a departing tenant has not vacated the apartment on time
Quiet Enjoyment	• Grants the tenant the right to enjoy the premises without disturbance or disruption
Utilities and Services	• Specifies the tenant's responsibilities for initial utility deposits or service fees and the services provided by the owner
Maintenance and Repairs	• Specifies maintenance responsibilities of each party under the lease
Alteration	• Limits the types of alterations and repairs tenants can make and specifies the extent of the owner's control over them
Assignment and Subleasing	• Gives the owner control over how the space may be occupied if a tenant leaves prematurely
Default	• Explains what constitutes default, the procedures to be followed, and what rights will exist in case of default by either of the parties to the lease
Hold-Harmless/ Indemnification	• Specifies that neither party (landlord nor tenant) will hold the other responsible for certain types of damage or injuries sustained in, on, or about the leased premises
Destruction	• Defines the rights and procedures of the tenant and owner in the event of partial or complete damage to the property
Holdover	• Specifies the tenant's and owner's rights when a tenant occupies the space after the lease has expired
Policies and Procedures	• Allows ownership to change the rules governing the building activities and common area use; usually an addendum because they change from time to time
Separate Addendums or Riders	• Specific rules and regulations may be incorporated in the lease as a separate addendum, or rider, that allows the rules to be modified without altering the lease terms • Examples include mold and lead-based paint disclosures • Note that all addendums or riders should be initialed at the time of the lease signing • Check state and local statutes, as specific requirements may apply

In addition to the general lease clauses, residential leases may include any of the following:

Lease Clause	Description
Condition of Premises	• States that residents have inspected the premises and accepted their condition • A related clause may prohibit alterations to the leased premises without the landlord's consent. Any permanent installation becomes the property of the landlord • Use of a checklist is good business practice. The manager and tenant should initial the checklist both at move-in and at move-out. Note that most states require this initialed checklist to provide for withholding any part of the security deposit for repairs
Right of Reentry	• Gives the landlord the right to reenter the space for specific purposes • Access is usually permitted at any time in case of emergency. Otherwise, proper notice and the tenant's consent must be given to enter during reasonable hours for inspections, repairs, necessary services, or showings to prospective residents • This clause is based on the applicable landlord-tenant law
Surrender of Premises	• States that the tenant will vacate the premises when the lease terminates • If the tenant remains beyond the termination date, he or she becomes a tenant at will and is obligated to fulfill the terms of the original lease on a month-to-month basis
Automatic Renewal	• Provides for automatic renewal of the lease, on the same terms or conditions and for the same period, unless the landlord or tenant gives notice before expiration • The landlord is required to provide notice of lease expiration regardless of the automatic renewal clause
Foreclosure	• Specifies the conditions of foreclosure • In some states, leases may be terminated and all deposits forfeited • In other states, tenants' rights may be better protected

Cancellation Provisions

Tenants may seek to terminate a lease for many reasons, including marriage, divorce, or job transfer. If they are not permitted to terminate a lease legally, some will do so illegally. Management companies can reduce the number of tenants who "skip out" on leases by providing reasonable alternatives within the lease itself.

A lease may be cancelled early in certain situations, including the following:

Lease Clause	Description
Transfer Clause	• May require several months' notice and proof of job transfer; landlord may impose a penalty or "buyout"
Home Purchase Clause	• May require several months' notice and proof of home purchase; landlord may require a "buyout"
Death Clause	• States number of months an estate would be obligated for rent
Soldier/Sailor Act	• May require advance notice, proof of transfer orders, and up-to-date rent payment
Condemnation (also known as eminent domain)	• Acquisition of the property by a government agency for public use. This term may also apply to seizure by governmental agency that determines the building is uninhabitable.
Notice of Authority	• Authorization to act on behalf of resident • Refer to Figure 4-4 for a sample notice of authority form

Student Housing Impact: A graduation clause may require advance notice. Additional fees may apply for early termination of the lease.

FIGURE 4-4: SAMPLE NOTICE OF AUTHORITY FORM

Notice of Authority to Act on Behalf of Resident

Resident Name_____ Address_____

In case of an emergency, or the event of my incapacitation whether due to hospitalization, incarceration or other circumstances beyond my control, or in the event of my demise or death, I hereby grant access to my apartment at the above identified address to the following individual(s).

Name_____Address_____Phone_____

Name_____Address_____Phone_____

Name_____Address_____Phone_____

This access is for the purpose of removing all of my possessions from the property, including vehicles, and administering to all necessary legal responsibilities contracted in my lease, including payment of any and all rent fees that may be owed.

Resident Signature_____Date_____

Manager Signature_____Date_____

If management policy allows tenants a right to terminate their leases prematurely, this should be handled based on a standing policy to reduce the likelihood of inconsistent treatment. Addressing particular situations that are likely to arise and indicating a requirement for extra consideration may also be appropriate. Since job transfers are not always within the individual's control, providing for that occurrence with a transfer or collection rider that can be added to the lease is a good idea.

In addition, if a tenant has personal financial problems that may interfere with his or her ability to honor the lease obligations, finding a replacement tenant before the lease expires may be to the advantage of the management company. Whether the standard lease requires the departing tenant to find a replacement or the landlord assumes the responsibility, the lease should contain a subleasing clause.

A lease may also be cancelled if a landlord breach of contract occurs. This includes the landlord's failure to maintain the leased premises in a habitable condition or unlawful removal of the tenant. Destruction or condemnation of the premises also results in lease cancellation.

LEGAL ISSUE:
Residential managers must occasionally deal with the death of a resident. This unpleasant experience is made more difficult by the legal responsibilities associated with it. The first step is to notify the police. After that, it is important to secure and seal the apartment because the manager or landlord may be liable for the safety of personal belongings until the proper authority takes over. Authorities will most likely secure and seal the apartment while investigating the cause of death. As much as a month may pass before the landlord regains possession of the premises because the estate may be under the supervision of a local public administrator until processing is completed. Administrative details must be handled properly (i.e., notifying the resident's next of kin). Following a careful accounting of any charges to the tenancy and removal of the deceased resident's property, the security deposit can be returned to the resident's estate.

RESOURCES:
Visit **www.irem.org** for sample forms and tools related to the leasing process such as residential lease addendums. The IREM website is your first-stop for information on real estate management. With resources organized by topic and property type, you will find the forms, tools, publications, webinars, and tutorials you need to help you manage your business and keep up with the industry.

DELINQUENCIES

Encouraging timely payment of rent begins with the qualification process and continues with the reiteration of management's collection policies during orientation. However, even the most exacting qualification processes will occasionally miss an irresponsible person and require the site manager to begin the collection process.

The effectiveness of a collection process depends on the diligence of the people who implement it. Personnel who deal with collections should be familiar with company policy and apply it uniformly, without exception. The following figure shows the steps to take as part of an established collection policy.

FIGURE 4-5: COLLECTION PROCESS

Grace Period

- Typically 3–5 days is appropriate

Reminder Notice

- Sent on the first day rent is delinquent
- Strongly worded, but friendly, reminder
- States rent was not received and to contact office
- Manager should also contact tenant by phone or in person

Another Notice (Second Reminder or Notice to Pay or Quit)

- If reminder gets so response, send another notice and visit tenant personally
- Either an eviction notice or a second reminder notice as required by local law
- By law, such a notice to pay or quit is usually the first step in a formal eviction proceeding and may require notarization and proper service
- Must understand implications (may automatically terminate the lease)

LEGAL ISSUE:
State and local laws prescribe the period of time allowed and the form and content of the notice to pay or quit, as well as how it is to be served and witnessed. The notice should also state any late or legal fees, if they are permitted. Generally, the landlord may not be able to accept partial payment without jeopardizing the effectiveness of the notice or the right to bring suit. However, local requirements differ so widely that an attorney should be consulted to determine what applies in each jurisdiction.

Student Housing Impact: Notices should be sent to both the student and the guarantor.

EVICTION

Sometimes legal action may be necessary to remove a tenant from the leased premises. Eviction of tenants is a very serious undertaking. Although it can be unpleasant, it is sometimes necessary.

LEGAL ISSUE:
Because the specific legal requirements of eviction vary from state to state and even between municipalities within states, the site manager must be familiar with the particular requirements in his or her jurisdiction and know when to confer with legal counsel prior to initiating eviction proceedings against a tenant.

Nonpayment

The most common reason for eviction is nonpayment of rent. If the tenant has not complied with the demand for payment within the time allowed, a complaint must be filed in court by an attorney. However, in some jurisdictions, the owner's agent (the manager) may be able to file the complaint without an attorney accompanying him or her. When the complaint is filed, the judge issues a summons to appear in court. Then the summons and the complaint are served on the tenant by a third party (i.e., sheriff or process server).

LEGAL ISSUE:
If the summons and complaint cannot be delivered to the tenant personally, state or local law will specify alternate procedures. Sometimes a notice may be affixed to the front door of the premises or in another conspicuous place.

The prescribed procedures must be followed to the letter, or the entire eviction proceeding may be invalidated. Even a minor procedural inconsistency may permit the tenant to avoid the eviction, and the process will have to be restarted. Harassment or intimidation of the tenant should be avoided at all costs. Denying the tenant access to or use of the apartment or denying or limiting specific services may be considered harassment and could be cause for a countersuit.

In court, the judge may give the tenant an opportunity to pay the rent. State and local laws determine whether the landlord has any legal obligation to accept payment at this point. If the tenant offers to pay, the judge may direct the landlord to accept payment. If the tenant cannot pay, the judge usually awards judgment in favor of the landlord. This award often includes possession of the apartment, rent due, and court costs, depending on the judge. As part of the judgment, the tenant will be given a date by which to vacate the premises.

If the tenant does not vacate the apartment by the specified date, he or she may be guilty of unlawful detainer. *Unlawful detainer* (term for the action being committed by the holdover tenant) means remaining in possession of the premises after proper notice to vacate has been served. In such a case, further action must be taken. Here again, applicable local law dictates specific procedures. In some jurisdictions, removal by the sheriff follows automatically. In other jurisdictions, the landlord's attorneys must obtain a writ of possession and, if that is ignored, they must return to court for a writ of eviction, which orders an officer of the court to physically eject and dispossess the tenant.

Other Reasons for Eviction

Other grounds for eviction for cause are:

- Violation of the lease terms, including nonpayment of monies other than rent (i.e., utilities, deposits, fees)

- Misuse of facilities,

- Destruction of property

- Failure to maintain the premises

- Creating a nuisance (i.e., unlawful activities, persistent noisy behavior).

LEGAL ISSUE:
A *no-cause action* is the landlord simply calling an end to the lease. This is more likely with a month-to-month lease, which either party can terminate with sufficient notice. Eviction procedures and definitions of cause and no cause are prescribed by statute and site managers must be familiar with both law and practice. If a tenant fails to move out at the end of a tenancy, an unlawful detainer action may be required to terminate what has become a holdover tenancy.

Another trigger for eviction may result with foreclosures on small investment properties. If the owner of a property defaults on the loan, the lender that seizes control may order all leases terminated and residents evicted. If the management contract is renegotiated with the bank, the site manager may be responsible for initiating the evictions.

Affordable Housing Impact: Eviction must be for a specific cause (e.g. illegal occupants, excessive traffic in and out) as mandated by the specific assistance program. Note that residents have the right of an administrative hearing in eviction situations. Often, judges are reluctant to evict affordable housing residents as they may have difficulty finding alternate accommodations.

Student Housing Impact: Additional reasons for eviction may include violation of the campus code of conduct or the inability or refusal of the resident to adjust to group living. Furthermore, the lease guarantor must fulfill their obligations as well.

Eviction is a costly and time-consuming remedy. Even in the best of circumstances, completion of the process may take several months, although, in some states, eviction can take place in as few as 10 days. The best way to minimize the need for evictions is to be diligent in screening prospective tenants. This can be done by checking credit references and verifying information provided on the lease application. In the book of a tenancy, the best ways to maintain harmony on the property are by documenting tenants' payment records, being respectful of their privacy, and performing maintenance promptly. If this is done, the majority of the tenants will observe the requirements of the lease.

COLLECTIONS

Collecting rent can be difficult after a tenant has abandoned an apartment or has been evicted. The site manager must ensure that proper abandonment procedures have been followed before proceeding with the collection process. The landlord has several options, including use of a collection agency. The management company may have a standard procedure for determining whether this option is financially viable. Of course, the agent does have a fiduciary responsibility to attempt to collect delinquent rent. Collection agencies typically charge a fee that is a percentage of the amount recovered. Although the fee may reduce the money recovered, collecting some money is better than collecting none or spending valuable time pursuing delinquent tenants. An advantage of using collection agencies is that they assume responsibility for all legal costs. The landlord is not relieved of liability, however, and can be sued if the agency harasses a former tenant.

Small Claims Court

In some states, the site manager may be able to pursue collections in small claims or "housing" court. In small claims courts, the dollar amounts and procedures vary by jurisdiction: Dollar limits may be as low as $500 or as high as $5,000. Depending on the amount owed, the costs of a court appearance (manager's time, attorney fees) may limit the effectiveness of this alternative. For the manager who goes to court, the following checklist details court preparation steps.

CHECKLIST: COURT PREPARATION STEPS

- Document authority by showing a copy of the contract that authorizes him or her to act for the property owner
- Give proper notice to a tenant in a letter or legal document that outlines the complaint. Technicalities can be the basis for dismissal of a case, which must then be refiled.
- Know how the tenant responded to the complaint and be prepared to refute any false claims. Documenting the exact sequence of events is a good idea. Furnishing supporting documents is essential.
- Prepare extra copies in advance of a court appearance. Not only will this save time and legal fees in the preparation of an attorney's formal complaint but it will also help focus the judge's attention on the primary issue. Photographs and the testimony of witnesses may also be important.

Fair Debt Collection Practices Act

The Fair Debt Collection Practices Act may have an important impact on how landlords send notices of rent due and eviction notices for nonpayment. According to the act, a third party, such as a lawyer or collection agency, that attempts to collect a debt must give 30 days' notice to the debtor (in this case, the tenant who owes back rent). However, the act does not apply to persons or businesses that try to collect their own debts or to their employees. The law has not yet determined whether a real estate management company is a third party under the act (and, therefore, subject to the 30-day notice provisions).

Most pay or quit notices give three to five days as a deadline. This difference from the 30-day notice provisions in the act is a potential source of legal conflict, especially if an owner involves a third party in the collection process. To avoid conflict with the act, property owners should not have lawyers or collection agencies send notices to pay or quit on the law firm's or the collection agency's letterhead. All correspondence concerning collections should use the property's letterhead.

RESOURCES:
For additional information on fair debt collection practices, visit the Federal Trade Commission website at:
www.ftc.gov/os/statutes/fdcpa/fdcpact.htm

IREM® publishes two comprehensive books: *Practical Apartment Management, Sixth Edition* and *Principles of Real Estate Management, Sixteenth Edition* that cover the lease document, delinquencies, eviction, and collections in additional detail.

CHAPTER 5:
INCREASING RETENTION

The site manager can reduce turnover, maintain occupancy, improve NOI, and meet the owner's goals by implementing a resident retention program. A manager must explore resident retention strategies to increase lease renewals.

In this chapter:

- **Importance of Retention**
- **Retention Techniques**
- **Lease Renewals**

IMPORTANCE OF RETENTION

Retaining existing residents—renewing their leases year after year—is important because it helps owners and managers avoid the expense and hassle of turnover.

TIPS:
Site managers must realize that an occupied apartment for
The resident is the only asset of the property that appreciates!

Renewing an existing lease is more profitable than finding a new resident for the following reasons:

- Eliminates the loss of rental income while space is vacant
- Significantly reduces marketing and leasing expenses
- Costs less to improve a unit for a current resident than to prepare a vacated unit for a new resident
- Eliminates need to establish relationship all over again with new residents
- Creates loyal residents and promotes positive word-of-mouth advertising and referrals

Refer to Figure 5-1 for an example of how retention impacts value.

FIGURE 5-1: RETENTION IMPACTS VALUE			
Customer Type	**Marketing Effort**	**Value to Marketer**	**Cost**
New	High	Low	High
Current	Moderate	High	Moderate

Source: Kevin J. Clancy and Robert S. Shulman, *The Marketing Revolution*

Example: Cost of Losing a Resident

Consider a resident who occupies a two-bedroom unit, whose lease will expire in two months. Recent maintenance issues and other service problems have created a negative impression, and it is unlikely this resident will renew the lease at the current terms, which are as follows:

Lease Term:	1 year
Rental Rate:	$1,100/month

Assuming it will take two months past move-out in the current soft market to have a new resident in place and paying rent, the property will incur the following costs:

Lost Rent	$1,100 x 2 =$2,200
Ad: www.apartments.com	$125
Ad: Local Newspaper	$550
Cleaning Service	$200
Repainting: Labor & Materials	$250
Maintenance Preparation	$200
Total Cost	$3,525

In this example, it would cost the owner $3,525 in lost rent, marketing fees, and preparation of the apartment for a new resident. The cost to retain a current resident may only include repainting, carpet cleaning, or other minor expenses.

TIPS:

It is critical for the site manager to understand the thread of value with resident retention. Renewals can make a huge difference to the bottom line.

Suppose you're the site manager for a community with 320 units that averages a 50% retention rate, or 160 move outs. If each move out costs you $3,000, how much money is that? If you can cut that down by 5%, or 8 move outs, how much money do you save the owner in NOI? What is the overall value if the owner looking for a 5% return? 10% return?

RETENTION TECHNIQUES

Properties that have sound retention programs show that they care about their residents from the beginning, instead of only when leases are about to expire. Thus, retention should be an ongoing process, beginning with initial contact and continuing throughout the term of the lease. The entire management staff must continue selling the property, long after move-in.

How a property strategizes retention efforts will depend on many factors, including resources, budget, and ownership objectives. However, a sound retention program should include the elements listed below.

TIPS:
Constant communication with residents and great customer service are the best ways to avoid complaints and retain residents.

Customer Service

Customer service is the single most important factor to consider as part of resident retention. The bar has been raised across the board in terms of what customers expect from the service industry. This concept is explored in the following excerpts from the IREM publication, *Marketing Residential Properties The Science and the Magic* (2008):

> We believe that a customer service "revolution" needs to happen in residential marketing. Why? Because great service generates loyalty, which leads to renewed leases and, most important, to positive word of mouth. When customers are so delighted about the service they have received that they repeat the experience in conversations with coworkers, friends, and relatives, that statement—a testimonial, really— provides the most powerful and least expensive advertising available.
>
> Sadly, many in our industry give only lip service to how their customers are handled. They fail to deliver decent service to their clients and soon forget their customers after the paperwork is completed and the commission or bonus is paid. On the other hand, savvy real estate managers and leasing agents recognize that service is just as important as price (and location) in leasing and buying decisions. And service is *the* factor that determines the decision to renew a lease.

Site managers have a unique opportunity to "wow" residents with exceptional customer service as their interactions take place on a daily basis. The bottom line is that site staff must go above and beyond the transaction to create an experience for residents. Refer to the following checklist for some tips.

In general, there are two levels of customer service:

Service Level	Description
Baseline Requirement	• Leased area will be clean, presentable, and in good working condition
Service Expectation	• Management will ensure high-quality and timely repairs in the leased space • Quality is based on whether a problem was fixed or only temporarily repaired • Timeliness is measured in terms of whether the work was done immediately or put off until another time

CHECKLIST: TIPS FOR CREATING A CUSTOMER SERVICE EXPERIENCE

- ☐ Deliver packages to residents doors
- ☐ Offer a trash pick-up service
- ☐ Make your service visible
- ☐ Provide necessary management contact information and encourage residents to get in touch
- ☐ Respond to emails and phone calls immediately
- ☐ Conduct personal visits to answer questions or explain items
- ☐ Set up automated reminders to check in with residents
- ☐ Add a personal touch to standard communication touch points
- ☐ Publish and distribute a monthly newsletter and include scheduled construction, upcoming events, or other news at the property
- ☐ Ask for feedback via surveys or informal conversations
- ☐ Make it as easy as possible for residents to submit service requests. Consider automating the service request process.
- ☐ Respond to service requests or other feedback in a courteous and professional manner
- ☐ Follow-up on service requests to ensure issue resolution and resident satisfaction
- ☐ Make the time to take the time at the resident orientation/move in

Residents also factor in how they are treated each time they come into contact with building management—whether their concerns were received with courtesy or with rudeness or indifference. A moment of truth can be defined as any episode in which the customer comes into contact with any aspect of the organization and gets an impression of the quality of its service during which they decide to do business with you in the first place or consider giving notice to move.

- A **passive moment of truth** is one that is inherent in the business of real estate management
  - o Examples: housekeeping, maintenance service requests, routine tasks that include interactions between residents and staff, deferred maintenance
- An **active moment of truth** is one that is created intentionally
  - o Examples: phone calls to just check in, training staff to be visible and routinely greet residents by name, newsletters, morning coffee/bagels, repaving the parking lot, building repairs

TIPS:
Curb appeal is as significant to retaining residents as it is to attracting prospects. Residents want to feel proud of where they live and complaints about the appearance of the property or the quality of maintenance and repairs should be taken seriously.

Soliciting Feedback

An important component of customer service is soliciting resident feedback. This can be done formally by asking the resident to complete a questionnaire or informally by having a face-to-face conversation with the resident. Figure 5-2 shows an example of a resident questionnaire. Consider posting a questionnaire to a website and allowing residents to complete the survey anonymously. Note, however, that giving residents an opportunity to complain, establishes in their minds an expectation that steps will be taken to resolve each problem.

Example: Soliciting Feedback

In person check points are a great way to solicit feedback. For example, ask, "On a scale of 1 to 10, how would you rate your overall satisfaction with our community?" If the answer is less than 10, use a follow-up question such as, "What would it take for us to rate a 10 in your mind?"

RESOURCES:
Best practices on customer service can be found in the Institute's publication *Marketing Residential Properties The Science and the Magic* by Laurence C. Harmon CPM®, CRE and Kathleen M. Harmon, CPM®, ARM®. Visit **www.irem.org** for additional information.

Responding to Complaints

Residents will find various ways to communicate when they are not satisfied with the service management provides. Complaints and issues should be handled promptly and courteously. Welcoming and responding to resident complaints has an abundance of positive effects:

- Retaining those who might have chosen to move at lease expiration
- Alerting management to areas that need to be changed or improved
- Minimizing any negative word-of-mouth to current and prospective residents
- Enhancing the property's reputation of being committed to its residents
- Nurturing the partnership between management and residents
- Empowering staff, which increases job satisfaction
- Providing a learning experience in the process of complaint handling

FIGURE 5-2: RESIDENT SURVEY

Resident Survey

Date_____ Apt. Building _____ Apt. No. _____

Your opinion is important to us! We want to make sure that living in your apartment is as enjoyable as possible. Please take a few minutes to complete this questionnaire and return it in the enclosed, postage-paid envelope. Thank you

A. The attitude of our staff, and how they treat you, is extremely important. Please CIRCLE the number that best describes how friendly, prompt, and respectful they are.

1	2	3	4	5

Attitude Needs Improvement   Terrific Attitude

B. We hope that you are proud of the condition of your apartment and the apartment community. Are the common areas of the building (entries, hall carpeting, elevators) clean and well maintained? Are the equipment and other facilities in good repair?

1	2	3	4	5

Poor Condition   Excellent Condition

C. Tell us about how comfortable you are with your apartment and your feelings about your building and grounds. Please indicate whether you have had problems with noisy neighbors, difficulties with the entry system, outside lighting, or other concerns about your well-being.

1	2	3	4	5

Serious Concerns About Well-Being   No Concerns About Well-Being

D. How responsive are we to your needs for maintenance and other staff assistance? Let us know if our management and maintenance personnel respond promptly to your requests for work orders, if the work is completed to your satisfaction, and if our staff handles your other requests adequately.

1	2	3	4	5

Major Maintenance Problems   Fast, Excellent Maintenance

E. Based upon your apartment living experience, would you recommend us to a friend, relative, or associate who might be considering living in an apartment?

1	2	3	4	5

Wouldn't Recommend   Would Recommend/No Hesitation

F. There are "extras" we provide that many of our residents enjoy. Have you had an opportunity to participate at resident parties or other apartment community activities? Have you read the newsletter? Please evaluate the "extras" below.

1	2	3	4	5

Inadequate/Poor "Extras"   "Extras" Just Right

Q. What is the best way to deal with comments from online review sites?

A. Reputation management is an important piece of the overall marketing strategy. Considering that many prospective residents turn to online review sites first to get a feel for the property, site managers must be vigilant about acknowledging posted comments. Responding to all posts, preferably within 24 hours, shows readers that management is paying attention.

Avoid being defensive or argumentative in response to negative reviews. Don't hesitate to correct inaccurate information or invite additional discussion offline, but a simple, "Thanks so much for the feedback, we're always trying to improve." response is sufficient. Often, a resident just wants to be heard. Let them know you're taking notes and show empathy. You will usually have an idea as to who posted the comment. Contact them directly to see if you can resolve any "burning issues." Once resolved, don't hesitate to ask for another post from them.

Site managers should encourage positive reviews whenever possible. When residents comment about exceptional service, invite them to post a positive review online: "Thank you so much. We love hearing that. Do you have five minutes? We'd appreciate you sharing that." Then, send a direct link via email for ease of posting. Some resident portals even synch directly to review websites.

Staff Training

A manager may develop the best retention program for a property, but it will not be successful unless a properly selected and trained staff is in place that is dedicated to providing residents with the best service. The most successful programs are those that are developed by the entire staff. People who are involved in the development are most successful in the execution. Management must provide ongoing training, encouragement, and recognition for individual employee's accomplishments and empower employees to solve problems without being constrained by rules and procedures.

TIPS:
Technical competence and people-friendly orientation are different skill sets. You can provide technical training, but you may not be able to train a technically competent candidate to be a "people person."

Move-In

Another important component of a resident retention program is an established move-in policy. This is especially important if a number of moves occur in the same building on the same day. A smooth move-in procedure will create a good impression for new residents and guarantee fewer management problems later. Keep the following tips in mind:

- Require new residents to let you know the date and approximate time of move-in so that you can be on hand to welcome them and coordinate elevator use if applicable
- Be prepared if things don't go according to plan. If the existing residents have not departed when moving day arrives, contact the new residents immediately and tell them to remain where they are. You will have to work out some means of pacifying and compensating these people, even though you may not be at fault.
- Allow early move in (e.g., one or two days early) if the unit is already vacant. Although technically not on the lease for those days, earlier occupancy may allow for easier scheduling and you will gain some goodwill at little or no cost.
- Be present at move-in to give whatever assistance is needed, explain procedures and answer questions, arrange for a tour of the premises, make note of any necessary adjustments or shortcomings, and explain how and when corrections will be made. For markets in which English is commonly a second language, consider hiring a translator to assist you with communications during move-in.
- Use a checklist before the move-in itself to keep track of last-minute items. The apartment should be given a final inspection—the temperature should be set to a comfortable level, all keys should be ready, the resident's name should be on the mailbox, and the storage locker or facility should be clean and secured.

The move-in orientation is your opportunity to share a "Resident Kit" or move-in package to familiarize new residents with the property and the rules and regulations—to inform them of what they can expect from you and what you expect of them. Refer to the following checklist for topics to cover during the move-in orientation.

CHECKLIST: TOPICS FOR MOVE-IN ORIENTATION
□ Keys or access codes
□ Mail delivery
□ Parking
□ Maintenance
□ Utilities
□ Waste disposal
□ Emergency/evacuation procedures
□ Building rules and regulations
□ 24 hour emergency maintenance stipulations
□ Owner's and resident's responsibilities under the lease
□ Rent collection policies

When difficulties arise, it is often because people are uninformed. They cannot evaluate a situation fairly if they lack all the facts. A well-conducted orientation helps avoid problems or eviction for nonpayment of rent and other violations of the lease.

Single Family Home Impact: In the case of single family home rental, one of the most common means of losing a resident is from negative experiences of residents with the owners' upkeep of the ground, landscaping, and other maintenance issues. If the owner of the single family home is not educated of the importance of their responsibility to keep the single family home in tenable "working condition" they may undergo the burden of high turnover with residents.

Student Housing Impact: As all students move in at the same time, coordination of a move-in event is extremely important. Consider serving refreshments, providing entertainment, having a clear process with stations to move students through (ensure appropriate staffing), monitoring traffic, and scheduling parent activities.

Appreciation Events

Resident appreciation events are an integral part of a comprehensive resident retention strategy as they show gratitude and bolster relations. Management can show appreciation for residents in many ways. Refer to the following checklist for some suggestions.

CHECKLIST: RESIDENT APPRECIATION IDEAS
□ Pool parties
□ Holiday events
□ Health fairs
□ Ice cream socials
□ Movie night with snacks
□ Drawing for free iPad
□ Gift certificates
□ Coupons
□ Free cleaning service for a day
□ Golf tournaments
□ Sporting leagues
□ Bingo or game nights
□ Art displays
□ Periodic windshield cleanings, car washes, and wiper fluid refills
□ Anniversary gifts
□ Flowers and cards

LEASE RENEWALS

The lease renewal process begins from the very first contact with the resident. Every interaction with the resident is an opportunity to encourage subsequent lease renewals and foster resident retention. There is a relationship with residents that must be nurtured throughout the term of the lease, not just at the beginning or end of the lease period.

In many cases, revenue management systems automate the lease renewal process. These systems provide reminders for contacting residents about their lease expiration and offer a range of potential price adjustments for the resident renewal. Regardless of the tool, the site manager must:

- Compile and maintain lease expiration dates
- Work with management to develop a strategic renewal strategy that maximizes NOI while providing renewal incentive

TIPS:
Online lease renewals should only relate to the execution of the renewal. You can't automate customer service and the most effective retention policies start with an in person meeting in the resident's apartment – not a letter or an email with renewal rates.

Before a lease expires, it is standard practice for management to offer the resident a renewal lease or a lease extension agreement. Common renewal incentives are listed in the table below.

Incentive	Description
Renewal Rewards	• Establish a policy that offers an apartment improvement at each lease anniversary • For example, for the first anniversary the resident might receive a ceiling fan, new paint, or new light fixtures. With each subsequent anniversary, the improvements have more value (e.g. new carpeting, tiling, an appliance) • Additional rewards may be a "free" unit inspection or other incentives such as an iPad
Security Deposit Reduction	• Common approaches include returning a percentage of the deposit upon lease renewal • Returning the security deposit may partially offset any rent increases • Should all of the security deposit be returned over many lease renewals, the resident may be incentivized to stay for the additional reason that the security deposit cannot be rolled over to the next property

Affordable Housing Impact: Security Deposit Reduction does not apply for affordable housing.

TIPS:

The renewal process goes beyond dropping letters under the residents' doors. It is an opportunity to engage with residents face-to-face and remind them why they rented at your property in the first place. Be sure to follow state requirements about lease expiration notification.

RESOURCES:

Downloadable forms such lease expiration reports, resident surveys, and move-in checklists can be found under Resources>Forms & Checklists at **www.irem.org** and are free for members. These sample forms and agreements are not endorsed by the Institute of Real Estate Management. They are presented for informational purposes only.

Consider joining one of the IREM® Shared Interest Communities on LinkedIn to exchange ideas and share knowledge with peers on industry topics, such as marketing and leasing strategies. The Shared Interest Communities are open to all IREM® members.

DIG DEEPER WITH IREM RESOURCES

Publications

Harmon, Laurence C., Harmon, Kathleen M. *Marketing Residential Properties The Science and the Magic*, Chicago: Institute of Real Estate Management, 2008.

> This book provides practical and relevant "how-to" strategies to revolutionize your marketing strategy and increase your property's bottom line.

Altes, Karen. *Social Media for Real Estate Managers*, Chicago: Institute of Real Estate Management, 2012.

> This eBook provides guidance on developing a social media strategy and using tools such as Facebook, Twitter, and LinkedIn.

Websites

www.irem.org

The IREM website is your first-stop for information on real estate management. With resources organized by topic and property type, you will find the forms, tools, publications, webinars, and tutorials you need to help you manage your business and keep up with the industry.

IREM On-Demand Learning (www.irem.org)
- Comparison Grids Learning Section (Tutorial)
- Tenant Retention Strategies (Tutorial)
- Revenue Management: Lease Renewal (Video)
- Marketing Analytics for the Multifamily Industry (Video)
- Reputation Management (Recorded Webinar)
- Fair Housing (Tutorial)

IREM Courses (www.irem.org)
- Fair Housing and Beyond (FHS201)
- Marketing and Leasing: Multifamily Properties (MKL405)

Articles

Published bi-monthly by IREM, the *Journal of Property Management* offers comprehensive coverage of the real estate management industry, including frequent features and columns on residential marketing and leasing topics.

Income/Expense Analysis® Reports

The IREM *Income/Expense Analysis®* Reports are the industry standard in relaying precise property data to owners, investors and tenants. Valuable operating data is collected for Conventional Apartments; Office Buildings; Federally Assisted Apartments; Condos, Co-ops, and Planned Unit Developments; and Shopping Centers. But we can't do it without your help.

Submit your data by April 1 of each year at http://IE.IREM.ORG to receive a FREE *Income/Expense Analysis®* book (a $450 value) and a FREE Individual Building Report. (Available once published by September.)

The *Income/Expense Analysis®* Reports are available for purchase in softcover books, downloadable .pdf or Excel, and Interactive online Labs.

abandonment A relinquishment of leased premises by the tenant before the lease expires without consent of the owner or the owner's agent. What defines abandonment varies widely and should be determined separately for different locales.

abatement A reduction of rent, interest, or an amount due; also, any reduction in amount or intensity.

absorption rate The amount of space of a particular property type that is leased compared to the amount of that same type of space available for lease within a certain geographic area over a given period of time, accounting for both construction of new space and demolition or removal from the market of existing space. Also, the rate at which a market can absorb space designed for a specific use. Absorption rate for rental apartments can be computed as follows:

> Units vacant at the beginning of the period
> *plus* units constructed new during the period
> *minus* units demolished during the period
> *minus* units vacant at the end of the period
> *equals* units absorbed during the period.

access control systems Security measures designed to limit access to buildings and leased premises and to parking lots and garages. Specifically, electronic locks on doors that are controlled and released with smart card keys or coded card technology.

accessibility The quality or state of being reached, easily approached, or used as an entrance. An important component of the Americans with Disabilities Act is removal of barriers that limit or complicate access to buildings and areas of public

accommodation by people with physical disabilities. More broadly, the law also requires accommodation to make facilities accessible for those who are hearing and vision impaired. See Americans with Disabilities Act (ADA).

ACCREDITED MANAGEMENT ORGANIZATION® (AMO®) An accreditation conferred by the Institute of Real Estate Management on real estate management firms that are under the direction of a CERTIFIED PROPERTY MANAGER® and comply with stipulated requirements as to accounting procedures, performance, and protection of funds entrusted to them.

ACCREDITED RESIDENTIAL MANAGER® **(ARM®)** A professional certification conferred by the Institute of Real Estate Management on individuals who meet specific standards of experience, ethics, and education. See also CERTIFIED PROPERTY MANAGER®.

accrual accounting The method of accounting that involves entering amounts of income when they are earned and amounts of expense when they are incurred–even though the cash may not be received or paid. Compare cash accounting. In real estate management, it is common to account for items that repeat at regular intervals on a cash basis and those requiring accumulation of funds toward a large dollar payout (e.g., real estate taxes) on an accrual basis. This is referred to as modified accrual accounting or modified cash-accrual accounting.

actual cash value (ACV) Insurance that pays a claim based on the purchase price of the item, usually allowing for depreciation because of age and use. Compare replacement cost.

addendum A legal document that adds to or amends the terms of a written agreement, as a lease or management agreement; also called amendment or rider.

additional insured endorsement An endorsement to an insurance policy of an insured party that names another individual or entity as an additional insured party. In real estate management, an endorsement to the building owner's insurance policy or policies that names the manager or managing agent as an additional insured party.

adjuster In insurance, an individual employed by a property and/or casualty insurer to settle loss claims filed by insured parties on behalf of the insurance company; also called insurance adjuster. The adjuster investigates individual claims and makes recommendations to the insurance company regarding their settlement. See also public adjuster.

ad valorem tax A tax levied according to the value of the object taxed; a tax in proportion to the value. Most often refers to taxes levied by municipalities and counties against real property and personal property.

agent A person authorized to transact some business or perform some act for another (the principal) within the limits of the authority bestowed by the latter. A managing agent is one who supervises the operation of a property on behalf of the owner in consideration of a management fee.

aggregate rent The total or gross rent amount for the lease term.

agreed amount insurance A policy under which a coinsurance clause is waived if the insured carries insurance in an agreed amount. The insurer then agrees to pay the face amount on the policy in the event of total loss of property covered or upon occurrence of a stated contingency.

all-risk coverage Insurance that covers losses caused by all perils except those specifically excluded in the policy contract; also called special property coverage.

amenities Features that enhance and add to a property's desirability and perceived value. These might include a gated entry, clubhouse, pool, tennis court, or relaxation garden.

Americans with Disabilities Act (ADA) A federal law that prohibits discrimination in employment on the basis of disability and requires places of public accommodation and commercial facilities to be designed, constructed, and altered in compliance with specified accessibility standards. The accommodation portion of this law may apply to "common areas" of residential properties (e.g., rental offices).

ancillary income See unscheduled income.

annual budget A 12-month estimate of income and expenses for a property. See also operating budget.

arbitration The submitting of a matter in dispute to the judgment of one, two, or more disinterested persons, called arbitrators, whose decision, called an award, is binding on the parties.

asset manager One who is charged with supervising an owner's real estate assets at the investment level. In addition to real estate management responsibilities that include maximizing net operating income and property value, an asset manager may recommend, be responsible for, or participate in property acquisition, development, and divestiture. An asset manager may have only superficial involvement with day-to-day operations at the site (e.g., supervision of personnel, property maintenance, tenant relations). Compare property manager.

assignment The transfer of an interest in a bond, mortgage, lease, or other instrument, in writing.

assisted housing Privately owned rental property that either receives government assistance in the form of mortgage insurance, a reduced mortgage interest rate, or tax incentives, or houses residents who receive some form of rental subsidy.

below-market interest rate (BMIR) A rate offered by a government agency (e.g., HUD) for mortgage insurance on certain types of housing.

betterment Improvements upon real property other than mere repairs.

blanket policy An insurance policy covering all of a specified quantity or class of property, or a variety of risks, or both.

budget An itemized estimate of income and expenses over a specific time period for a particular property, project, or institution. See also annual budget; operating budget.

budget variance The differences between projected and actual amounts of in- come and expenses. Higher income and lower expenditures than expected constitute favorable variances, while lower income and higher expenditures are reported as unfavorable variances. Usually a component of the monthly management report sent to ownership.

cannibalization To strip equipment or housing units of parts for use in other equipment or units to help keep the latter in service.

capital expenditure Spending on capital assets, such as major improvements, large equipment, additions to buildings, buildings themselves, and land.

capital improvement A structural addition or betterment to real property other than a repair or replacement; also, the use of capital for a betterment that did not exist before.

capitalization rate A rate of return used to estimate a property's value based on that property's net operating income (NOI). This rate is based on the rates of return prevalent in the marketplace for similar properties and intended to reflect the investment risk associated with a particular property. It is derived from market data on similar, recent sales (NOI ÷ property value/sales price = capitalization rate) or from calculations based on expected returns to debt and equity. Also called cap rate.

cash accounting The method of accounting that recognizes income and expenses when money is received or paid. Compare accrual accounting.

cash flow The amount of cash available after all payments have been made for operating expenses and mortgage principal and interest.

cash-on-cash return A measure of the productivity of an investor's initial investment that compares the yearly cash flow of a property with its initial investment base: cash flow ÷ initial investment base; sometimes also called return on equity. The result is given as a percentage.

certificate of occupancy A document issued by an appropriate governmental agency certifying that the premises (new construction, rehabilitation, alterations) complies with local building codes and/or zoning ordinances. Some jurisdictions require a certificate of occupancy for apartments based on inspection of units between each tenancy.

Certified Apartment Manager (CAM) A professional designation conferred by the National Apartment Association (NAA) on apartment managers who have demonstrated a level of experience and proficiency.

CERTIFIED PROPERTY MANAGER® (CPM®) A professional designation conferred by the Institute of Real Estate Management on individuals who distinguish themselves in the areas of education, experience, and ethics in property management. See also ACCREDITED RESIDENTIAL MANAGER®.

chart of accounts A classification or arrangement of account items by type of income or expense (e.g., rent, advertising, insurance, maintenance), as well as assets and liabilities, accounts receivable, and accounts payable.

close-in location A phrase used by real estate marketers that refers to a property's convenience and proximity to a central business district. Often this is a downtown area but can also refer to a town center or other area enjoying easy access.

coinsurance An insurance option under which the insured (e.g., the property owner) is obligated to maintain insurance coverage at a stipulated level (e.g., 80 percent of the property's value) in order to receive the full value up to the limits of the policy in case of a loss, in exchange for a lowered premium rate. (Coverage is based on actual cash value of the improvements, which reflects a deduction for depreciation.) Failure to maintain that level of insurance coverage will reduce the amount reimbursed (in proportion to the property value). In the event of a loss, the insured shares in losses in proportion to the amount that the insurance coverage was less than the required percentage. See also actual cash value.

collateral Security given as a pledge for the fulfillment of an obligation.

collateral materials As applied to advertising and promotion, includes printed items such as brochures, leaflets, floorplans, and posters, as well as photographs, lapel pins, book matches, etc.

commingle To mix or combine; combining the money of more than one person or entity into a common fund is commingling of funds. (A prohibited practice in real estate.)

common interest realty association (CIRA) A term commonly used by accountants and real estate managers to describe real estate that is operated for the mutual benefit of the owners. Condominiums, cooperatives, townhouses, zero-lot-line homes, and manor homes are the more popular examples.

comparison grid analysis A method of price analysis in which the features of a subject property are compared to similar features in three or more comparable properties in the same market. The price (or rent) for each comparable property helps to determine an appropriate price (or rent) for the subject. This method involves assigning values for different attributes such as square footage, amenities, parking, floor and window treatments, age, location, and view. In making a rent comparison for rental apartments, features are compared for a specific type or size of unit (e.g., one-bedroom apartments). The process should take market trends into consideration and is obviously subjective. Each comparable property is compared to the subject, feature by feature. When the feature being examined is superior in the comparable property, the comparable rent should be reduced by the amount that a particular feature is worth in the marketplace. When the feature being examined is superior in the subject property, the comparable rent should be appropriately in- creased. Rent for the subject property is determined by adding up the adjustments to the rent of each comparable and then either averaging the adjusted rents or using the final rent of the comparable that has had the fewest adjustments (because this comparable is most like the subject property).

condemnation The taking of private property for public use; also, the official act to terminate the use of real property for nonconformance with governmental regulations or because of hazards to public health and safety.

condemnation clause A provision in a lease stating the agreed rights, privileges, and limitations of the owner and tenant, respectively, in the event of the taking of the subject property for public use.

condominium Outright or fee ownership of an individual unit within a multiple-unit structure along with a prorated share of the undivided ownership of the land and common areas.

condominium association A private, usually not-for-profit corporation comprised of the unit owners of a condominium that is responsible for the operation of the condominium community. The operation of a condominium association is governed by legal documents known as the declaration, bylaws, and articles of incorporation. Also called community association.

constructive eviction A legal term used as a defense pleading when a tenant breaks his/her lease, moves out, and fails to pay rent obligations because the leased premises were uninhabitable, the owner failing to correct the problem.

consumer price index (CPI) A way of measuring consumer purchasing power by comparing the current costs of goods and services to those of a selected base period, which is revised from time to time. Sometimes used as a reference point for rent escalations as a measure of inflation. The CPI is published monthly by the U.S. Department of Labor, Bureau of Labor Statistics.

contract An agreement entered into by two or more persons which creates an obligation to do (or not do) a particular thing. The document that serves as proof of such an obligation. The essentials of a contract are legally competent parties, the obligation created between them, consideration or compensation (e.g., a fee), and mutuality of agreement. Examples in real estate management include management agreements, leases, and maintenance service agreements related to building systems and equipment.

contract rent The rent stipulated in an existing lease, which may differ from the economic or market rent. See also market rent; street rent.

conversion ratio The number of prospect contacts in a defined period compared to the number of leases that result from those contacts. For example, if 20 prospects visit a property, resulting in 4 leases, the conversion ratio would be 5:1. This may also be expressed as a percentage: 1:5 = 20 percent.

cooperative Ownership of a share or shares of stock in a corporation that holds the title to a multiple-unit residential structure; shareholders do not own their units outright but have a proprietary lease granting the right to occupy them.

corporation A legal entity that is chartered by a state and treated by courts as an individual entity with the ability to buy, sell, sue, and be sued separate and distinct from the persons who own its stock.

credit score A numerical value that measures the relative degree of risk of a potential borrower. A credit score takes into account payment history, amounts owed, length of time credit has been established, acquisition of new credit, and types of credit established (credit cards, installment loans, mortgage, etc.).

curb appeal General cleanliness, neatness, and attractiveness of a building as exemplified by the appearance of the exterior and grounds and the general level of housekeeping. The aesthetic image and appearance projected by a property; the first impression it creates.

death clause A special clause in a lease that provides for termination of the lease before its expiration date in the event of the tenant's death.

debt service Regular payments of the principal and interest on a loan.

deed of trust The document used in some states in place of a mortgage. An instrument by which legal title to real property is held by a third party (trustee) as collateral to secure the repayment of a loan. Title is conveyed by the borrower (mortgagor) to the trustee to hold for the benefit of the lender (mortgagee) with the condition that title shall be reconveyed upon payment of the debt.

deferred maintenance Ordinary maintenance of a building that, because it has not been performed, negatively affects the use, occupancy, and value of the property. Also, an amount needed for repairs, restoration, or rehabilitation of an asset (e.g., real property) but not yet expended.

degree-day A unit that represents one degree difference in the mean outdoor temperature for one day. Temperatures above 65° F represent cooling degree-days; those below 65° F represent heating degree-days.

demographics The statistical analysis of populations, using information derived primarily from census records, including overall population size, density, and distribution, birth and death rates, and the impact of inmigration and outmigration. Also included are age, gender, nationality, religion, education, occupation, and income characteristics of people who live in a geographically defined area. Used to characterize discrete markets. Residential property owners and managers are also interested in such concurrent data as household size, numbers of children and their ages, and levels of homeownership because they relate to requirements for living space in the form of rental apartments.

Department of Housing and Urban Development (HUD) See U.S. Department of Housing and Urban Development.

depreciation Loss of value due to all causes, usually considered to include: (1) physical deterioration (ordinary wear and tear), (2) functional depreciation, and (3) economic obsolescence; see also obsolescence. The tax deduction that allows for exhaustion of property; also called cost recovery.

directors' and officers' liability insurance Protection against financial loss arising out of alleged errors in judgment, breaches of duty, and wrongful acts of a board of directors and/or officers in carrying out their prescribed duties. A recommended coverage for condominium associations.

disability With respect to a person, a physical or mental impairment that substantially limits one or more major life activities, a record of such an impairment, or being regarded as having such an impairment. Further defined as such a condition which is expected to be of long, continued, and indefinite duration.

discrimination Unfair treatment or denial of normal services or privileges to a person or persons because of their skin color, race, national origin, or religion. Sex, disability, and familial status are also protected classes in regard to some types of discrimination. See also Americans with Disabilities Act (ADA); Fair Housing laws.

display classified ad A hybrid type of newspaper ad that is placed in the classified ad section and utilizes artwork, photos, and custom typefaces to distinguish it from the appearance of the standard classified ads.

economic life The number of years during which a building will continue to produce an acceptable yield.

economic vacancy Commonly used in rental housing to mean all vacant units that are not producing income. In addition to physical vacancies, this includes units that are not available for lease (e.g., apartments used as models or offices, staff apartments, cannibalized units) as well as leased units that are not yet occupied and occupied units that are not producing rent (i.e., delinquencies); usually expressed as a percentage of the total number of units.

effective gross income Often called collections. The total amount of income actually collected during a reporting period; the gross receipts of a property. Gross potential rental income less vacancy and collection losses plus miscellaneous or unscheduled income.

efficiency apartment A small, bedroomless apartment usually with a less-than-standard-size kitchen. See also studio apartment.

efficiency factor The percentage of gross building area that is actually rentable.

Net Rentable Area/Gross Building Area = Efficiency Factor

electronic funds transfer (EFT) Movement of funds between banking institutions and between individual accounts via computer transfer of credits rather than using a check or other payment instrument. Direct deposit is commonly handled electronically. Individual consumers can also use computer software to "bank on- line," transferring money from their personal accounts to the accounts of various creditors (e.g., utility, credit card, and rent payments).

e-bike Short for an electric bicycle. An electric motor provides a power-assist from two rechargeable lithium-ion batteries, which can deliver a riding range of 20 to 85 miles on a three-hour charge. It is an expensive, but popular, biking alternative.

e-mail Short for electronic mail. Written communication via the Internet.

e-signature Short for electronic signature. A signature verification technology that permits tenants to sign electronic documents (leases, etc.) online. The process has cleared several legal hurdles and offers speed and convenience in certain circumstances.

eminent domain The right of a government or municipal quasi-public body to acquire private property for public use through a court action called condemnation, in which the court determines that the use is a public use and determines the price or compensation to be paid to the owner.

employee handbook A compilation of a company's employment policies and procedures. It is advisable to include a notice that such handbook does not constitute a set of promises or an employment contract. Depending on state law, it might include a statement that employment is at the will of the company, and that the company or the employee may terminate the employment at any time for any reason. To protect the employer's interests, the contents of such a handbook should be reviewed by an attorney.

employment practices liability A form of liability insurance to protect against employee claims arising from sexual harassment, wrongful discharge, discrimination, and disability suits.

empty-nesters Persons whose children have left home permanently.

endorsement An attachment to an insurance policy that provides or excludes a specific coverage for a specific portion or element of a property; also called a rider.

Environmental Protection Agency (EPA) An independent agency of the U.S. government established in 1970 to enforce laws that preserve and protect the environment.

Equal Employment Opportunity Commission (EEOC) A U.S. governmental body that enforces Title VII of the Civil Rights Act of 1964, which prohibits discrimination in the workplace.

errors and omissions (E&O) insurance Insurance to protect against liabilities resulting from honest mistakes and oversights (no protection is provided in cases of gross negligence).

escalator clause A clause in a contract, lease, or mortgage providing for increases in wages, rent, or interest based on fluctuations in certain economic indexes, costs, or taxes. Also called rent escalator clause.

escrow An agreement that something of value (money, security, a deed) should be held in trust by a third party until certain conditions are met. Upon fulfillment of the specified conditions, the money or other item(s) in escrow is conveyed to the respective parties.

eviction A legal process to reclaim possession of real estate from a tenant who has not performed under the agreed-upon terms. Eviction is a complex undertaking. The tenant may be sent a notice to vacate or notice to quit (i.e., legal notice requiring a tenant to remove himself or herself and all removable possessions from the premises and to surrender the premises to the owner). Action to obtain possession or repossession of real property that had been transferred from one party to another under a contract is referred to as forcible detainer. Failure of a tenant to move out at the end of a tenancy or following lawful eviction is unlawful detainer. Also see constructive eviction.

eviction notice A written notice to a tenant to cure a breach of the lease immediately or vacate the premises within a specified period. Also called demand to pay or quit or demand for compliance or possession.

exclusion A provision in an insurance contract detailing perils that are not covered.

exculpate To free from blame. Hold-harmless clauses are exculpatory.

Fair Credit Reporting Act (FCRA) A federal law that gives people the right to see and correct their credit records at credit reporting bureaus. It also requires property managers to inform applicants if a credit bureau is contracted to investigate their credit and to identify the source of credit information that resulted in their being denied a lease.

Fair Debt Collection Practices Act (FDCPA) A federal law that created a series of guidelines for debt collectors to follow and was designed to prevent collection agencies from harassing debtors. The law was later expanded to include any organization that collects consumer debt (including property managers). The law is governed and regulated by the Federal Trade Commission (FTC).

Fair Housing laws Any law that prohibits discrimination against people seeking housing. There are federal, state, and local Fair Housing laws. Specifically, Title VIII of the Civil Rights Act of 1968 prohibits discrimination in the sale or rental of housing based on race, color, religion, national origin, or sex; the Fair Housing Amendments Act of 1988 further prohibits discrimination on the basis of familial status (children) or physical or mental disability.

Fair Labor Standards Act (FLSA) The federal law that establishes minimum wages per hour and maximum hours of work. It also provides that employees who work in excess of 40 hours per week are to be paid one and one-half times their regular hourly wage. This is frequently referred to as Wage and Hour Law.

familial status The presence in a household of children under age 18 living with parents or guardians, pregnant women, or people seeking custody of children under age 18.

family Most commonly used in referring to a group of persons consisting of parents (father and mother) and their children. A group of blood relatives (extended family). Compare household.

Federal Housing Administration (FHA) An agency—part of the U.S. Department of Housing and Urban Development (HUD)—that administers a variety of housing loan programs.

fidelity bond A casualty insurance guaranteeing one individual against financial loss that might result from dishonest acts of another specific individual.

fiduciary One charged with a relationship of trust and confidence, as between a principal and agent, trustee and beneficiary, or attorney and client.

financing The availability, amount, and terms under which money may be borrowed to assist in the purchase of real property and using the property itself as the security for such borrowing.

fixture An article of personal property attached permanently to a building or to land so that it becomes part of the real estate.

floorplan Drawings showing the floor layout of a building and including room sizes and their interrelationships. The arrangement of the rooms on a single floor of a building, or within a specific apartment, including walls, windows, and doors.

fractional interest properties A coined phrase used to describe real property having varying degrees of ownership. Using the tenants in common (TIC) form of ownership, units are deeded and are traded much the same as most real estate. An IRS ruling permits 1031 Tax Free Exchanges when ownership meets a stringent set of rules.

general partnership The business activity of two or more persons who agree to pool capital, talents, and other assets according to some agreed-to formula, and similarly to divide profits and losses, and to commit the partnership to certain obligations. General partners assume unlimited liability. Compare limited partnership.

gentrification Inmigration of middle- and upper-income people into a deteriorating or recently renewed area so they gradually displace lower-income residents. A form of urban neighborhood renewal.

Global Positioning System (GPS) A constellation of 32 Medium Earth Orbit Satellites that transmit precise microwave signals capable of determining location, speed, and time. Commonly used in the apartment industry to map driving routes, measure distances to work locations, and pinpoint locations of staff personnel.

government-assisted housing Residential rental property in which the lessor (landlord) receives part of the rent payment from a governmental body, either directly from the government on behalf of a resident or indirectly from a grant to a public housing authority, or from the residents in the form of a voucher. Compare subsidized housing.

graduated rent Rent that has two or more levels in the same lease term. gross building area Area equal to length times width of the building(s) times the number of living floors, expressed in square feet.

gross potential rental income (GPI) The sum of the rental rates of all spaces available to be rented in a property, regardless of occupancy. The maximum amount of rent a property can produce. Also called gross possible rental income or scheduled rent.

gross receipts The total cash income from all sources during a specific period of time such as monthly or annually.

group relamping Systematic replacement of all lamps in a building or lighting system after a specific period, based on when the lamps were installed and the rated life for the type of lamp, as opposed to replacing individual lamps as they burn out.

guarantor One who agrees to assume responsibility for a financial obligation of another in the event the other person cannot perform (e.g., payment of rent under a lease).

guest In apartments, a nonresident who stays in a resident's private dwelling (with that resident's consent) for one or more nights. A guest who begins receiving regular mail deliveries looses his/her status as a guest. See also visitor.

habitability A state of being fit for occupancy (e.g., sanitary, safe, in compliance with applicable codes). Under landlord-tenant law, the landlord is bound by an implied warranty of habitability, by which he/she warrants the condition of the leased premises at the time the tenant takes possession and during the period of tenancy.

half-bath A bathroom with a basin and toilet but no bathing facilities such as a tub or shower.

hazardous materials Any of a variety of gaseous, liquid, or solid materials that can pose a potential hazard (e.g., flammability, combustibility, toxicity, corrosivity) to persons who are exposed to them or damage property in the event of a spill. Some types of materials have been declared as specific hazards by federal, state, or local laws.

head rent Rent charged to a person or persons occupying the same premises independently of each other.

heating, ventilating, and air-conditioning (HVAC) system The combination of equipment and ductwork for producing, regulating, and distributing heat, refrigeration, and fresh air throughout a building.

highest and best use That use of real property that will produce the highest property value and develop a site to its fullest economic potential. The four criteria for highest and best use are: physical possibility, legal permissibility, financial feasibility, and maximum profitability.

high-rise apartment building A multiple-unit dwelling that is ten or more stories in height.

hold harmless A declaration that one is not liable for things beyond his/her control. A clause in contracts (e.g., management agreements) through which one party assumes liability inherent in a situation and thereby eliminates the liability of the other party. See also indemnification.

holdover tenancy A situation in which a tenant retains possession of leased premises after the lease has expired, and the landlord, by continuing to accept rent from the tenant, thereby agrees to the tenant's continued occupancy as defined by state law.

host liquor liability insurance Protection against loss arising out of the insured party's legal responsibility as a result of an accident attributed to the use of liquor dispensed (but not sold) on the premises at functions incidental to the insured party's business. Recommended coverage for properties where liquor may be served in the common areas of the premises. May be purchased to cover specific events.

household All persons, related or not, who occupy a housing unit. Compare family.

housekeeping The regular duties involved in keeping a property clean and in good order. Also used in referring to the level of care given to a leased space by the occupant.

Immigration Reform and Control Act (IRCA) Federal law requiring employers to verify an employee's identity and eligibility to work in the United States at the time of employment. Employees must complete Immigration and Naturalization Service (INS) form I-9.

income capitalization approach The process of estimating the value of an income-producing property by capitalization of the annual net income expected to be produced by the property during its remaining useful life. See also capitalization rate.

independent contractor A person who contracts to do work for others by using his/her own methods and without being under the control of the other person(s) regarding how and when the work should be done. Unlike an employee, an independent contractor is responsible for paying all expenses including income and Social Security taxes, receives no employee benefits, and is not covered by workers' compensation.

inflation An economic condition occurring when the money supply increases in relation to the amount of goods available, resulting in substantial and continuing increases in prices. Inflation is associated with increasing wages and costs and decreasing purchasing power.

inspection checklist A printed form used when property managers or other staff members inspect a building and its leased spaces. Usually set up in a grid format with the items to be inspected being listed with space provided to note the condition of the item and identify repair work to be done. Some forms include columns that facilitate scheduling of the work and estimating repair costs.

Institute of Real Estate Management (IREM) A professional association of men and women who meet established standards of experience, education, and ethics with the objective of continually improving their respective managerial skills by mutual education and exchange of ideas and experiences. The Institute is affiliated with the National Association of REALTORS®.

insured The person or other entity for whom insurance is provided. The person whose property, life, or physical well-being is covered by insurance.

interest A share in the ownership of property; a payment for the use of money borrowed.

IRV formula A basic equation in real estate that relates three variables—income, rate, and value—to calculate a property's value. As a formula, its basic form is Income ÷ Rate = Value. The investor's equation—the income-to-value ratio—is the same terms, rearranged (income ÷ value = rate of return).

Integrated Services Digital Network (ISDN) ISDN involves the digitization of the telephone network, which permits voice, data, text, graphics, music, video and other source materials to be transmitted over existing telephone wires.

joint venture An association of two or more persons or businesses to carry out a single business enterprise for profit, for which purpose they combine their assets and agree to share the risks. In real estate, a combination of owners and money partners may be involved in a joint venture.

landlord-tenant law Laws enacted by various jurisdictions (at the state or local level) that regulate the relationship between landlord and tenant.

landscaping The improvements made to and maintenance done on a specific parcel of land. Landscaping may involve contouring the and; planting grass, flowers, trees, and shrubs; and installing items to enhance the appearance or utility of the land (e.g., a fountain or pathway). Regular upkeep (cutting grass, trimming hedges, weeding, picking up litter, etc.) is also considered landscaping.

late fee A fee charged for late payment of rent.

late notice Notification that payment of rent is past due. While sometimes handled informally, such notification may be specifically provided for in a lease. When that is the case, the usual requirement is that notice be presented in writing to a specified address and include a statement of what additional charges (i.e., late fees) apply if the delinquency is not cured immediately (or within a specified time period).

laws of supply and demand In relation to pricing, when demand exceeds supply, prices rise. If supply exceeds demand, prices drop. Prices are stable when supply equals demand. In regard to rental real estate, when demand exceeds supply, absorption of space is favorable (vacancy decreases); when supply exceeds demand, absorption is unfavorable. Stabilization occurs when landlords are able to increase rents in parallel with inflation rates.

lease A contract for the possession of a landowner's land or property for a stipulated period of time in return for the payment of rent or other consideration by the tenant; sometimes called an occupancy agreement.

lease extension agreement A written and executed agreement extending the lease term beyond the expiration date and stating the rental amount for the new term.

lease renewal The process of encouraging qualified residents to renew their leases.

leasing agent The individual in a real estate brokerage firm (or management organization or development company) who is directly responsible for renting space in assigned properties. In some states, leasing agents must have a real estate license unless they are employed directly by the property owner. Residential leasing agents are often called leasing consultants.

legal description The description of real property by metes and bounds, lot and block numbers of a recorded plat, or government survey, including any easement or reservation, used to locate and identify a particular parcel of land in legal instruments (e.g., leases, sale/purchase contracts).

length of stay A phrase to measure a rental resident's stay in the number of days of occupancy. A common goal is to track the length of the average stay and to strive for improvement.

leverage The use of borrowed funds to increase one's purchasing power. It is the expectation of realizing an added financial return when the cost of borrowed funds is less the property's rate of return, which is referred to as positive leverage. Negative leverage occurs when the cost of borrowed funds exceeds the property's return rate.

liability insurance Insurance protection against claims arising out of injury or death of people or physical or financial damage to other people's property that is a consequence of an incident occurring on or about an owner's property.

limited liability company (LLC) Created by state statute, a business ownership form that functions like a corporation (its members are protected from liability) but for income tax purposes is classified as a partnership. Income and expenses flow through to the individual members. The arrangement offers considerable flexibility in its organization and structure.

limited partnership (LP)   A partnership arrangement in which the liability of certain partners is limited to the amount of their investment. Limited partnerships are managed and operated by one or more general partners whose liability is not limited; limited partners have no voice in management. Compare general partnership.

location   Commonly used in real estate to refer to the comparative advantages of one site over another in consideration of such factors as transportation, convenience, social benefits, specific use, and anticipated pattern of change.

low-income household   A household whose annual income is 80 percent or less of median income for the jurisdiction as defined by HUD and adjusted for household size by HUD.

Low Income Housing Tax Credit (LIHTC)   A program developed in conjunction with the Department of the Treasury, Urban Development and Justice to promote greater affordability and a larger number of affordable units than most other housing programs. The two most fundamental LIHTC occupancy requirements relate to household income and maximum rent.

low-rise apartment building   Multiple-unit residential dwelling of four or fewer stories.

majority   The age set by state law at which individuals have the legal right to man- age their own affairs and are responsible for their own actions. The age of majority varies from state to state. See also minor.

management agreement   A contractual arrangement between the owner(s) of a property and the designated managing agent, describing the duties and establishing the authority of the agent and detailing the responsibilities, rights, and obligations of both agent and owner(s).

management company   A real estate organization that specializes in the professional management of real properties for others as a gainful occupation; a management firm.

management fee   The monetary consideration paid monthly or otherwise for the performance of management duties, usually defined in the management agreement as a percentage of the gross receipts (actual collections less security deposits) of the property and/or as a minimum monthly amount.

management plan The fundamental document for the operation of a property that represents a statement of facts, objectives, and policies and details how the property is to be operated during the coming years. Such a plan usually includes the appropriate budgets.

marketing In apartment leasing, methods used to attract new renters and to retain current residents.

market rent Rent that a property is capable of yielding if leased under prevailing market conditions. Also, the amount that comparable space (i.e., an apartment unit of a particular type and size) would command in a competitive market.

mid-rise apartment building A multiple-unit dwelling ranging from five to nine stories tall.

minor One who has not reached the age set by state law to be legally recognized as an adult; therefore, one not legally responsible for contracting debts or signing contracts. See also majority.

miscellaneous income See unscheduled income.

month-to-month tenancy An agreement to rent or lease for consecutive and continuing monthly periods until terminated by proper prior notice by either the landlord or the tenant.

mortgage A pledge of real property conveyed by a written instrument as security for the payment of a debt. Often used in referring to the loan itself, the debt instrument usually creates a lien against the property (i.e., the property becomes security for the debt owed) until the debt has been paid in full. The lender in a mortgage loan transaction is the mortgagee; the borrower is the mortgagor.

mortgage constant The percentage of the original loan amount needed to pay the annual debt service (both principal and interest), usually represented mathematically by a lowercase k. Also referred to as loan constant or, more commonly, just constant. The formula is: annual debt service divided by the original loan amount. Constants are always expressed as an annual percentage.

move-in checklist An inspection checklist used to document the condition of an apartment at the time a new resident moves in. Usual practice is for a member of the management staff to conduct this inspection in the presence of the resident and for both management and resident to sign the completed form acknowledging its accuracy. This will be compared to a move-out checklist to determine if there has been any excessive damage (beyond normal wear and tear) that the resident is responsible for repairing.

move-out checklist An inspection checklist used to document the condition of an apartment at the time a resident moves out. This is compared to a previously used move-in checklist to identify repairs to be made and responsibility for the cost of such repairs. Often combined with the former as a move-in/move-out checklist that facilitates comparison of the before and after condition. Here again, usual practice is to have the management person and the resident sign the completed form and acknowledge responsibility for repair costs to be deducted from the resident's security deposit.

named insured The entity or entities specifically identified in an insurance contract as the insured parties. One of several parties provided coverage, which may include others in addition to the purchaser of the policy. Managing agents are automatically included as a named insured.

negligence Failure to use the level of care a reasonable and prudent person would use under the same circumstances, characterized by inattention and thoughtlessness that results in harm. Failure to exercise reasonable care which, though not accompanied by harmful intent, directly results in an injury to an innocent party or damage to property. A person (e.g., a property manager) or a business entity (e.g., a property management company) can be held liable for negligent acts.

neighborhood An area within which there are common characteristics of population and land use. A district or locality, often defined by referring to its character or inhabitants. In real estate market analysis, a section of a larger region or market area, within which buildings generally compete with one another for residents. The area surrounding and adjacent to a property, especially as it is characterized by similarity of demographic, economic, and other parameters.

net operating income (NOI) Total collections (gross receipts) less operating expenses; may be calculated on an annual or a monthly basis. More broadly, cash available after all operating expenses have been deducted from collected income and before debt service and capital expenses have been deducted.

nonsufficient funds (NSF) Usually used as the acronym in referring to a check drawn on a bank account that does not contain enough cash to cover the draft; an NSF check. Also sometimes called insufficient funds.

non-yield space Space that is essential to the operation of a building but does not produce direct revenue. See also efficiency factor.

obsolescence Generally speaking, a loss of value brought about by a change in design, technology, taste, or demand. Physical obsolescence (deterioration) is a result of aging (wear and tear) or deferred maintenance. Functional obsolescence is a condition of a property related to its design or use. Economic obsolescence is an inability to generate enough income to offset operating expenses, usually due to conditions external to the property (changes in populations and/or land uses, legislation, etc.). Also used in referring to the process by which property loses its economic usefulness to the owner/taxpayer due to causes other than physical deterioration (e.g., technological advancements, changes in public taste); an element of depreciation.

occupancy agreement See lease.

occupancy report A statement of the number of occupied units in a building and, correspondingly, the number of non-revenue-producing units (usually generated every Monday and commonly referred to as the Monday Report). A usual component of the periodic management report to ownership.

Occupational Safety and Health Act (OSHA) A law requiring employers to comply with job safety and health standards issued by the U.S. Department of Labor.

off-site management Management of a property by persons not residing or keeping office hours at the subject property.

onsite manager See resident manager.

operating budget A listing of all anticipated income from and expenses of operating a property, usually projected on an annual basis. While funds for accumulation of reserves would be deducted from net operating income (NOI) in an operating budget, actual expenditures of such reserve funds would be anticipated in a capital budget.

operating expenses In real estate, the expenditures for real estate taxes, salaries, insurance, maintenance, utilities, and similar items paid in connection with the operation of a rental property that are properly charged against income. More broadly, all expenditures made in connection with operating a property with the exception of debt service, capital reserves (and/or capital expenditures), and income taxes.

operating reserves Funds set aside for the payment of a major expense.

operations manual An authoritative collection of information that describes the organization and its goals, explains policies that guide its operations, outlines specific procedures for implementing those policies on a day-to-day basis, assigns responsibility for performing various functions, and contains the various documents (forms) for performing the work; also called standard operating procedures manual. In real estate management, an operations manual is usually developed to guide the management and business operations of a specific property.

option The right to purchase or lease something at a future date for a specified price and terms; the right may or may not be exercised at the option holder's

(optionee's) discretion Options may be received or purchased. In a lease, the right to obtain a specific condition within a specified time (e.g., to renew at the same or a pre-agreed rate when the lease term expires; to cancel the lease under certain circumstances). Options are often incorporated in the lease as an addendum.

owner, landlord, and tenant (OLT) liability Insurance covering claims against a property owner, a landlord, or a tenant arising from personal injury to a person or persons in or about a subject property and including the improvements on the land and any other contiguous areas for which the insured is legally responsible, such as sidewalks. This coverage is generally included in all-risk policies.

party wall This is the wall, made of fire resistant materials, that separates two or more dwelling or commercial units from each other. If the units are individually platted, their deeds will contain a cross-easement provision (party-wall agreement) that identifies the wall's existence and will provide limiting language.

pay for performance As an incentive to use their Internet listing service, firms agree to postpone payment of fees until they actually produce a prospect who becomes a resident.

personal property Movable property belonging to an individual, family, or other entity that is not permanently affixed to real property, such as clothing, fixtures, and furnishings; distinguished from real property. In real estate, the furniture, blinds and drapes, office equipment, appliances, and other items that belong to the property owner apart from the land and the improvements to it. Also, the items owned outright by the tenant in leased premises.

personal time off (PTO) bank A bank of time that employees can use for vacation, personal or sick time, without specifying why they need the time off. The PTO bank provides more privacy and eliminates the guilt of having to make excuses for work absences.

pet agreement A lease addendum that authorizes a tenant to keep a specific pet on the premises as long as certain conditions are met. A pet agreement is actually a separate document that constitutes a license granted by the landlord to the tenant. As such, it can be revoked or canceled without affecting the lease itself.

physical vacancy The number of vacant units in a building or development that are available for rent, usually expressed numerically and/or as a percentage of the total number of units. See also economic vacancy.

price per door This is a phrase sometimes used by condominium managers when making reference to their monthly management fee. This price (fee) is multiplied by the number of dwelling units to arrive at their management fee quote. The phrase is used internally and is rarely mentioned to the customer.

principal In real estate, one who owns property. In real estate management, the property owner who contracts for the services of an agent. In finance, the amount of money that is borrowed in a loan as distinct from the interest on such loan; the original amount or remaining balance of a loan. Also, the original amount of capital invested. In law, the individual being represented in a business transaction by an agent authorized to do so.

professional liability insurance Insurance against a monetary loss caused by failure to meet a professional standard or resulting from negligent actions (e.g., malpractice). Policies that protect directors and officers of corporations are also available. See directors' and officers' liability insurance.

pro forma A projection of gross income, operating expenses, and net operating income of a property; a budget.

property management A professional activity in which someone other than the owner supervises the operation of a property according to the owner's objectives; also referred to as real estate management. The operation of income-producing real estate as a business, including leasing, rent collection, maintenance of the property, and general administration. Usually, this is performed by someone who acts as the owner's agent (i.e., a professional property manager).

property manager A knowledgeable professional who has the experience and skills to operate real estate and understands the fundamentals of business management. The person who supervises the day-to-day operation of a property, making sure it is properly leased, well maintained, competitive with other sites, and otherwise managed according to the owner's objectives.

proprietary lease A document that gives a shareholder in a real estate cooperative the right to occupy a specific unit subject to certain conditions and terms.

protected class A group, usually a minority in the population, specifically protected against discrimination under the U.S. Civil Rights Act of 1964 and later amendments to that law. Protected classes include race, religion, color, national origin, and sex; in regard to housing, familial status and disability are also protected classes.

public adjuster The name commonly used to refer to the individual or company that represents the insured party in an insurance claim. See also adjuster.

Pullman kitchen A small non-walk-in kitchen, with appliances and equipment aligned in a row along a wall or in a small area. Named after the narrow kitchen areas on Pullman train cars.

purchase order (P.O.) Written authorization to an outside vendor to provide certain goods or services in a given amount, at a given price, to be delivered at a certain time and place. Purchase orders are usually preprinted, sequentially numbered forms with multiple copies to ensure that appropriate departments of the company have a record of all such transactions.

quiet enjoyment A lease provision, often only implied, which grants the tenant the right of possession of the leased premises without illegal or unreasonable interference by the landlord or undue disturbance by others; also referred to as peaceful enjoyment.

rate holder A discounted advertising line rate offered by newspapers in return for an agreement to run ads in their paper on a certain frequency.

real estate Land; a portion of the earth's surface extending downward to the center of the earth and upward into space including all things permanently attached to the land by nature or by mankind; also, freehold estates in land.

real estate investment trust (REIT) An entity that sells shares of beneficial interest to investors and uses the funds to invest in real estate or mortgages. Real estate investment trusts must meet certain requirements such as a minimum number of investors and widely dispersed ownership. No corporate taxes need to be paid as long as a series of complex IRS qualifications are met. See also shares of beneficial interest.

recapture An income tax term describing money taken back or forfeited; a kind of tax penalty. For example, if a tax deduction was taken but does not meet all conditions, the deduction will be disallowed and the taxpayer will be required to pay tax on the income that had been offset by the deduction. This money is said to be recaptured by the taxing body.

recurring expenses Operating expenses that recur monthly or periodically, such as those for utilities, supplies, salaries, waste disposal services, insurance, and taxes.

recycling Minimizing the generation of waste by recovering usable materials that might otherwise be disposed. Also, the reprocessing of various materials (e.g., paper, glass, aluminum, and various types of plastic) into usable new products.

rentable area The combined rentable area of all dwelling units. The rentable area of a unit is calculated by multiplying length times width of the apartment, with no discounts for interior partitions, plumbing chases, and other small niches. Balconies, patios, and unheated porches are not included in these measurements. Sometimes called net rentable area.

rent control Laws that regulate rental rates, usually to limit the amount of rent increases and their frequency.

renters by choice People who prefer to rent, either for flexibility, economic advantage, limited commitment, or freedom from home maintenance. Renters by choice include career professionals, senior citizens, and parents of grown children (empty-nesters).

renters by circumstance Persons and households whose current situations require them to rent, at least on a temporary basis; also called renters by necessity. These are people who cannot afford to buy a home or are trying to save enough money for a down-payment, as well as students and people in changing circumstances.

renters' insurance Insurance coverage for tenants' personal possessions, which are not covered by a landlord's insurance policies, including reimbursement of out-of-pocket costs if they cannot live in their rented unit.

rent loss The deficiency increment resulting from vacancies, bad debts, etc., between total projected rental income (for a given period) and the actual rents collected or collectible.

rent roll A list of each rental unit described by size and type and including the following information if the unit is rented: amount of monthly rent, tenant name, and lease expiration date; also called rent schedule. Rent received, date of receipt, period covered, and other related information for each individual tenant is recorded in a rent ledger or tenant ledger.

rent-up budget Projection of income and expenses for a newly developed property; also called *lease-up budget*. Having such a separate budget allows the developer or property manager to account for the wide variances in income and expenses that occur before there is sufficient occupancy to stabilize its financial picture.

replacement cost The estimated cost to replace or restore a building to its preexisting condition and appearance (and in compliance with applicable current building codes); a common method of determining insurance coverage. In insurance, replacement cost coverage reimburses the total cost of rebuilding; no deductions are made for depreciation.

replacement cost coverage Insurance to replace or restore a building or its contents to its pre-existing condition and appearance. Compare actual cash value (ACV).

replacement reserves Funds set aside for future repair and replacement of major building components (e.g., roof, HVAC system).

relaxation garden A defined, somewhat secluded outside garden area that is created with year-round and seasonal plantings and flowers, waterscapes, fountains, seating, and benches. These gardens are popular with residents and are often the source of rent premiums from units that overlook them.

request for proposal (RFP) Written specifications for services to be provided by a bidder, often including the scope of work and details of design and use and asking for specifics regarding materials, labor, pricing, delivery, and payment.

resident One who lives (or resides) in a place. Referring to residential tenants as "residents" is preferred by many real estate professionals.

resident guidebook Minimally, a compilation of house rules and other information apartment occupants need for ready reference; a resident handbook. Ideally, such a guidebook will inform residents of their basic rights and responsibilities, covering basic lease provisions as well as management's policies regarding use of supporting facilities (e.g., swimming pool, exercise room, laundry room), the keeping of pets, and requests for maintenance or other services.

Residential Lead-Based Paint Hazard Reduction Act Federal law enacted in 1992 that requires all owners of residential properties built before 1978 to notify new renters and potential buyers about the presence of lead-based paint. New rules regarding particulars of disclosure came into effect in December 1996. Rental applicants and residents who renew leases must be given a government pamphlet on lead paint hazards, a disclosure form detailing lead paint hazards at the property, and any reports that describe lead paint hazards at the property.

resident manager An employee residing onsite for the purpose of overseeing and administering the day-to-day building affairs in accordance with directions from the manager or owner; also called onsite manager, site manager, and residential manager.

resident organization See tenant organization.

resident profile A study and listing of the similar and dissimilar characteristics of the present occupants of a residential property; used in positioning the property in the market. May also be called tenant profile.

resident retention A defined program that attempts to maintain harmony between tenants and management, often related to sound maintenance procedures; at a residential property, sometimes called tenant retention. In actual practice, a resident retention program includes measurement of tenant satisfaction, often via written surveys, and efforts to encourage lease renewals by providing a superior product and better service. See length of stay.

return on investment (ROI) The ratio of net operating income to the total in- vestment amount, for a given time period, which provides a measure of the financial performance of the investment. A measure of profitability expressed as a percentage and calculated by comparing periodic income to the owner's equity in the property (income ÷ equity = % ROI). It can be calculated either before or after deduction of income tax. ROI measures overall effectiveness of management in generating profits from available assets; however, it does not consider the time value of money.

right of reentry A common lease provision, subject to prevailing landlord-tenant laws, granting the right to inspect, maintain, update, and exhibit the unit for re-renting; sometimes called right of access.

risk management The process of controlling risks and managing losses. There are four methods of risk management: Avoidance is the act or practice of avoiding something or preventing its occurrence. Control involves actions or practices undertaken to reduce the frequency or severity of loss. Retention is acceptance of a certain amount of potential economic loss (rather than pay the cost of insurance premiums). Transfer involves shifting the burden of risk to a third party (i.e., an insurance provider who assumes the risk in return for payment of a premium).

Seasonal Energy Efficiency Rating (SEER) rating A rating and   performance standard developed by the U.S. Government and equipment manufacturers to assist consumers in understanding the energy consumption of air cooling equipment. Its universal formula can be applied to all units and compensates for varying weather conditions. A 12 SEER rating is very common today but some equipment carry ratings of 21.

seasonal rent Rent that is adjusted by season, often used in resort areas. High season is the busiest season at a resort area, when rental rates are highest; low season is an intermediate period (the months just before and after high season) that is differentiated from off season when demand is lowest.

security deposit A preset amount of money advanced by the tenant before occupancy and held by an owner or manager for a specific period to ensure the faithful performance of the lease terms by the tenant; also called lease deposit. (Local or state law may require the landlord to pay the tenant interest on the security deposit during the lease term and/or hold the money in an escrow account.) Part or all of the deposit may be retained to pay for rent owed, miscellaneous charges owed, unpaid utility bills, and damage to the leased space that exceeds normal wear and tear. Limitations on withholding may be imposed by local and state ordinances, which often also stipulate penalties for failing to return the security deposit in a timely manner.

self-service storage facilities A rental property comprising individual storage spaces with individual doors and locks, used for storage of personal property. Sometimes constructed as part of an apartment complex to provide supplementary storage that can be leased to residents or others for a fee.

service contract An agreement to perform certain work, as to maintain specific operating systems (e.g., preventive maintenance of HVAC, elevators) or for general upkeep (e.g., janitorial or custodial maintenance), in exchange for specific compensation. Services may be contracted for a flat fee for a designated period or on a time and materials (T&M) basis (e.g., a rate per hour plus the cost of replacement parts).

service request A form for documenting the specifics of a resident's request for maintenance work; sometimes combined with a work order form. A work order is a written form, letter, or other instrument for authorizing work to be performed. The completed form documents the nature of the work, where it was done, who performed it, and the materials used and time required to complete it.

shares of beneficial interest Shares sold by real estate investment trusts (REITs) and traded on the stock market much like corporate common stock. See also real estate investment trust.

shopper A person who is commissioned to visit a property in the guise of a rental prospect and whose identity is unknown to the property staff. His or her assignment is to accurately report, in a written narrative, the rental experience (both positive and negative) for the purpose of improving future leasing presentations.

signature block Usually the final section of a lease (or other contract) containing a statement that all parties have read and understand the lease (or contract), with space for signatures.

site manager See resident manager.

site plan   A plan, prepared to scale, showing locations of buildings, roadways, parking areas, and other improvements.

special multi-peril (SMP) insurance policy   See all-risk coverage.

specifications   A written description of equipment maintenance or other services that describes the scope of work, materials and methods to be employed, and other specifics used as a basis for estimating project or service costs. Also, a written description of construction work to be done that describes the kind and quality of materials to be used, the mode of construction (type and extent of work), and dimensions and other particulars that define the job as the basis for estimating costs.

spreadsheet   A table of numbers listed in columns and rows and related by formulas. Used in reference to computer software that creates such tables and automatically performs the calculations according to predetermined formulas.

street rent   The rental rate quoted to new prospects; also called market rent.

studio apartment   Commonly used term to describe an efficiency or bedroom- less apartment. In certain areas, the term refers to a small apartment with two levels. See also efficiency apartment.

sublet   The leasing of part or all of the premises by a tenant to a third party for part or all of the tenant's remaining term.

subordination clause   A lease covenant in which the tenant agrees that the landlord may act on the tenant's behalf in certain legal matters, so long as it does not affect the tenant's right to possession.

subsidized housing   Usually privately owned rental property for which a portion of the return on the owner's investment may result from additional tax advantages granted for development, for leasing part of the property to residents who are eligible for housing subsidies, or for leasing to a local housing authority. The National Housing Act, which has been amended substantially over time, includes provisions for subsidies to landlords via low-mortgage-rate loans and for payment of rent on behalf of qualified individuals. Compare government-assisted housing.

sundry income   See unscheduled income.

tenant   One who pays rent to occupy or gain possession of real estate. The estate or interest held is called a tenancy.

tenant organization A group of tenants formed to use their collective powers against an owner to achieve certain goals such as improved conditions, expanded facilities, and lower rent.

term A limited or defined period of time. The duration of a tenant's lease; the duration of a mortgage (e.g., a 30-year term); the duration of a contract for services.

termination The ending of a contract, usually when the conditions of the agreement have been carried out. Ending of an employee's employment; firing. Also used in referring to the process of voluntarily leaving a job.

term rent A type of rent sometimes collected in resort areas for a specified term, usually the high season, and payable in full in advance. Also, the total amount of rent due over the period (term) of the lease.

townhouse A one-, two-, or three-story dwelling with a separate outside entry-way sharing common or partitioning walls with other similar dwellings.

traffic The number of prospects seen by a leasing agent in reference to a particular property or rental space within a given time.

traffic report A record of the number of prospects who visit or make inquiries at a property and the factors that attracted them to it, often used to measure the effectiveness of advertisements and other marketing vehicles.

turnover The number of units vacated during a specific period of time, usually one year. Most turnover rates are expressed as the ratio between the number of move-outs (or the number of new tenancies) and the total number of units in a property.

umbrella liability insurance Extra liability coverage that exceeds the limits of the primary liability policy.

U.S. Department of Housing and Urban Development (HUD) A federal department created to supervise the Federal Housing Administration (FHA) and other government agencies charged with administering various housing programs.

unit mix The combination of apartment types within a property. The number or percentage of the total of each unit size or type contained in a particular property.

unit size A listing of the number of bedrooms and bathrooms an apartment contains; the square footage of an apartment.

universal design The name given to a transition in the design, construction, and utilization of buildings, especially housing, to make use easier for more people with improved access, less bending and stooping, fewer barriers, and increased visual aids. Raising outlets while lowering switches, wider doorways, lever handles set at lower heights, contrasting colors to help delineate transitions, and indexed and pushbutton controls are other design changes that will accommodate an easier and prolonged lifestyle. With the general aging of the population, mobility, flexibility, and visual ability diminish, making these design improvements a welcome change. Most new properties are being outfitted and equipped for easier and safer occupancy.

unscheduled income Property income produced from sources other than rent, such as coin-operated laundry equipment, vending machines, late fees, etc.; also called ancillary, miscellaneous, or sundry income.

useful life The period of time during which a building is expected to yield a competitive return. For purposes of cost recovery under U.S. tax code, useful life is based on property type (e.g., residential or commercial building) and does not necessarily coincide with the building's actual physical or economic life.

vacancy An area in a building that is unoccupied and available for rent.

vacancy rate The ratio of vacant space to total rentable area, expressed as a percentage. On a larger scale, the amount of vacant rental space available in the market expressed as a percentage of the total supply of rental space.

visitor In apartments, a nonresident who spends time at the home of a resident (with that resident's consent) but does not stay overnight. Compare guest.

Wage and Hour Law See Fair Labor Standards Act.

waiting list A list of people who are interested in renting an apartment at a specific property.

walk-up An apartment building of two or more floors in which the only access to the upper floors is by means of stairways.

warranty A form of guarantee, usually in writing, given to a buyer by a seller stating that the goods (or services) purchased are free of defects and will perform as promised for a stated time period, or the seller will repair any defect at no charge or replace the item or refund the purchase price. Warranties are usually effective from the date of purchase.

workers' compensation insurance Insurance which, by law, must be carried by an employer to cover the expenses that arise from employee sicknesses and injuries that occur in the course of employment, usually including medical and disability benefits and lost wages.

working drawings Final drawings (both architectural and mechanical) that contain the information needed to construct a building or a component of a building; sometimes also called construction drawings. See also specifications.

zero-lot-line housing A type of residential development in which individual dwelling units are placed on separately defined lots, but the units are physically attached to one another or share a common wall.

zoning A legal mechanism whereby local (municipal) governments regulate the use of privately owned real property to prevent conflicting land uses, promote orderly development, and regulate such conditions as noise, safety, and density. Zoning regulations are specified in zoning ordinances.

PART I, FINANCE
APPENDIX A: KEY FORMULAS

Gross Potential Income (GPI)
- – Loss to Lease
- – Vacancy and Collection Loss

= Net Rent Revenue
+ Miscellaneous Income
+ Expense Reimbursements

= Effective Gross Income (EGI)
– Operating Expenses

= Net Operating Income (NOI)
– Annual Debt Service (ADS)

– BLANK (CapEx, etc.)

= Before-Tax Cash Flow (BTCF)

IRV

Value (V) = Income (I) ÷ Capitalization Rate (R)

Capitalization Rate (R) = Income (I) ÷ Value (V)

Income (I) = Capitalization Rate (R) x Value (V)

PART II, MAINTENANCE AND RISK MANAGEMENT
APPENDIX B: SAMPLE MATERIAL SAFETY DATA SHEETS (MSDS)

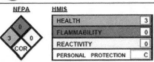

MATERIAL SAFETY DATA SHEET

ACME SPECIAL FLOOR CLEANER - SAMPLE MSDS

NFPA	HMIS	
	HEALTH	3
	FLAMMABILITY	0
	REACTIVITY	0
	PERSONAL PROTECTION	C

1. Product And Company Identification

Supplier
EHS Innovators LLC
203 Main Street
PMB 174
Flemington, NJ 08822-1610 USA

Company Contact: Robert J. Kretvix, CIH, CET
Telephone Number: (877) 392-3474
FAX Number: (908) 782-8082
E-Mail: info@ehsi.com
Web Site: http://www.ehsi.com

Manufacturer
EHS Innovators
P.O. Box 596
St. Marys, PA 15857 USA

Company Contact: J. Fitzgerald
Telephone Number: (814) 781-8566
FAX Number: (814) 814-1488
E-Mail: info@msds-generator.com
Web Site: http://www.msds-generator.com

Supplier Emergency Contacts & Phone Number
CHEMTREC: (800) 424-9300
EHSI CIH Services: (908) 237-9349

Manufacturer Emergency Contacts & Phone Number
CHEMTREC:

Issue Date: 04/11/2000

Product Name: ACME SPECIAL FLOOR CLEANER - SAMPLE MSDS
CAS Number: Not Established
MSDS Number: 2

Product/Material Uses
Industrial floor care

2. Composition/Information On Ingredients

Ingredient Name	CAS Number	Percent Of Total Weight
2-Butoxyethanol	111-76-2	15 - 20
Monoethanolamine	141-43-5	1 - 5
Sodium hydroxide	1310-73-2	1 - 3
Sodium xylene sulfonate	1300-72-7	1 - 5
Water	7732-18-5	<Balance>

EMERGENCY OVERVIEW

DANGER. CORROSIVE. Concentrate may cause eye and skin burns. Avoid contact with skin, eyes and clothing. HARMFUL OR FATAL IF SWALLOWED. Do not taste or swallow. Avoid breathing vapor. KEEP OUT OF REACH OF CHILDREN. FOR INDUSTRIAL USE ONLY.

Source: **www.ehsi.com**. Reprinted with permission.

PART II, MAINTENANCE AND RISK MANAGEMENT
APPENDIX B: SAMPLE MATERIAL SAFETY DATA SHEETS (MSDS)

MATERIAL SAFETY DATA SHEET
ACME SPECIAL FLOOR CLEANER - SAMPLE MSDS

Hazards Identification (Pictograms)

3. Hazards Identification

Primary Routes(s) Of Entry
Eye Contact. Skin Contact.

Eye Hazards
Corrosive to living tissue. May cause blindness.

Skin Hazards
Corrosive to living tissue. Causes severe skin burns.

Ingestion Hazards
Corrosive to living tissue. Harmful or fatal if swallowed. Causes severe digestive tract burns. Aspiration hazard if swallowed. Can enter lungs and cause damage.

Inhalation Hazards
Corrosive. May cause nose, throat, and lung irritation.

Conditions Aggravated By Exposure
None known.

First Aid (Pictograms)

4. First Aid Measures

Eye
In case of contact, hold eyelids apart and immediately flush eyes with plenty of water for at least 15 minutes. Get medical attention immediately.

Skin
Remove contaminated clothing and shoes. In case of contact, immediately flush skin with plenty of water for at least 15 minutes. Get medical attention immediately.

Ingestion
If swallowed, do not induce vomiting. If victim is fully conscious, give water (a cup, a glass, two glasses). Never give anything by mouth to an unconscious victim. Get medical attention immediately.

Inhalation
If inhaled, remove to fresh air. Get medical attention immediately.

Source: **www.ehsi.com**. Reprinted with permission.

PART II, MAINTENANCE AND RISK MANAGEMENT
APPENDIX B: SAMPLE MATERIAL SAFETY DATA SHEETS (MSDS)

MATERIAL SAFETY DATA SHEET

ACME SPECIAL FLOOR CLEANER - SAMPLE MSDS

Fire Fighting (Pictograms)

---

5. Fire Fighting Measures

Flash Point Method: Not applicable
Lower Explosive Limit: Not applicable
Upper Explosive Limit: Not applicable

Fire And Explosion Hazards
Corrosive. Vapors may accumulate in confined spaces (e.g., pits, sumps, sewers) and inadequately ventilated areas.

Extinguishing Media
Use CO2 (Carbon Dioxide), dry chemical, or foam.

Fire Fighting Instructions
Avoid breathing vapors, gases and fumes. Firefighters should wear self-contained breathing apparatus and full protective gear.

---

6. Accidental Release Measures

Wear appropriate PPE. Contain and/or absorb spill with inert material (e.g. sand, vermiculite). Sweep up and remove immediately. Flush spill area with water.

---

7. Handling And Storage

Handling And Storage Precautions
Danger. Corrosive. Keep out of reach of children. Keep containers tightly closed. Use only with adequate ventilation. Wash thoroughly after handling.

Work/Hygienic Practices
Wash thoroughly with soap and water after handling.

Protective Clothing (Pictograms)

---

8. Exposure Controls/Personal Protection

Engineering Controls
Use with adequate general and local exhaust ventilation.

Eye/Face Protection
Safety glasses with side shields or chemical splash goggles.

Skin Protection
Chemical-resistant gloves made of neoprene. Protective footwear. Plastic or rubber apron.

Respiratory Protection
General room ventilation is normally adequate.

PART II, MAINTENANCE AND RISK MANAGEMENT
APPENDIX B: SAMPLE MATERIAL SAFETY DATA SHEETS (MSDS)

MATERIAL SAFETY DATA SHEET
ACME SPECIAL FLOOR CLEANER - SAMPLE MSDS

---

8. Exposure Controls/Personal Protection - Continued

Ingredient(s) - Exposure Limits
  2-Butoxyethanol
    OSHA PEL-TWA: 50 ppm (240 mg/m3), Skin
    ACGIH TLV-TWA: 25 ppm (121 mg/m3), Skin
    NIOSH REL-TWA: 5 ppm (24 mg/m3), Skin
    DFG MAK-TWA: 20 ppm (98 mg/m3)
  Monoethanolamine
    OSHA PEL-TWA: 3 ppm (7.5 mg/m3)
    ACGIH TLV-TWA: 3 ppm (7.5 mg/m3)
    ACGIH TLV-STEL: 6 ppm (15 mg/m3)
    NIOSH REL-TWA: 3 ppm (8 mg/m3)
    NIOSH REL-STEL: 6 ppm (15 mg/m3)
    DFG MAK-TWA: 2 ppm (5.1 mg/m3)
  Sodium hydroxide
    OSHA PEL-TWA: 2 mg/m3
    ACGIH TLV-Ceiling: 2 mg/m3
    NIOSH REL-Ceiling: 2 mg/m3
    DFG MAK-TWA: 2 mg/m3

---

9. Physical And Chemical Properties

Appearance
  Clear, colorless liquid

Odor
  Characteristic odor

Chemical Type: Mixture
Physical State: Liquid
Melting Point: 3 °F -16 °C
Boiling Point: 212 °F 100 °C
Vapor Pressure: Not available
Vapor Density: Not available
pH Factor: >13
Solubility: complete
Evaporation Rate: Not available

---

10. Stability And Reactivity

Stability: Stable
Hazardous Polymerization: Will not occur

Conditions To Avoid (Stability)
  None known.

IncompatibleMaterials
  Strong acids and other materials incompatible with sodium hydroxide (caustics).

Hazardous Decomposition Products
  When exposed to fire, produces normal combustion byproducts.

---

11. Toxicological Information

Acute Studies
  Corrosive

PART II, MAINTENANCE AND RISK MANAGEMENT
APPENDIX B: SAMPLE MATERIAL SAFETY DATA SHEETS (MSDS)

MATERIAL SAFETY DATA SHEET
ACME SPECIAL FLOOR CLEANER - SAMPLE MSDS

11. Toxicological Information - Continued

Chronic/Carcinogenicity
None known.

Ingredient(s) - Toxicological Data
2-Butoxyethanol
  Oral-rat LD50: 560-3,000 mg/kg
  Oral-rat LC50: 500 ppm, 4-hrs
Monoethanolamine
  Oral-rat LD50: 2,050 mg/kg
Sodium hydroxide
  Oral-rat LD50: 140-340 mg/kg
  Inhal-rat LC50: >40 mg/m3
Sodium xylene sulfonate
  Oral-rat LD50: 2000 mg/kg

12. Ecological Information

Other Environmental Information
No information available.

13. Disposal Considerations

Dispose in accordance with applicable federal, state and local government regulations.

RCRA Information
Waste solutions may meet the RCRA Corrosive characteristic.

14. Transport Information

Proper Shipping Name
Corrosive liquids, NOS (sodium hydroxide, monoethanolamine)
8, UN1760, PGIII

Hazard Class
8

DOT Identification Number
UN1760

DOT Shipping Label
Corrosive

Additional Shipping Paper Description
Canadian Shipping Name: Corrosive liquids, NOS (sodium hydroxide, monoethanolamine), 8, UN1760, PGIII

TDG - Canada (Pictograms)

15. Regulatory Information

U.S. Regulatory Information
All ingredients of this product are listed or are excluded from listing under the U.S. Toxic Substances Control Act
(TSCA) Chemical Substance Inventory.

Source: **www.ehsi.com**. Reprinted with permission.

PART II, MAINTENANCE AND RISK MANAGEMENT
APPENDIX B: SAMPLE MATERIAL SAFETY DATA SHEETS (MSDS)

MATERIAL SAFETY DATA SHEET

ACME SPECIAL FLOOR CLEANER - SAMPLE MSDS

---

15. Regulatory Information - Continued

U.S. Regulatory Information - Continued
SARA Hazard Classes
Acute Health Hazard

SARA Section 313 Notification
This product contains ingredients regulated under SARA Title III Form R/TRI for reporting of Toxic Chemicals.

Ingredient(s) - U.S. Regulatory Information
2-Butoxyethanol
SARA Title III - Section 313 Form "R"/TRI Reportable Chemical

Ingredient(s) - State Regulations
2-Butoxyethanol
New Jersey - Workplace Hazard
New Jersey - Environmental Hazard
Pennsylvania - Workplace Hazard
Massachusetts - Hazardous Substance
New York City - Hazardous Substance
Monoethanolamine
New Jersey - Workplace Hazard
New Jersey - Special Hazard
Pennsylvania - Workplace Hazard
Pennsylvania - Special Hazard
Massachusetts - Hazardous Substance
New York City - Hazardous Substance
Sodium hydroxide
New Jersey - Workplace Hazard
New Jersey - Environmental Hazard
Pennsylvania - Workplace Hazard
Pennsylvania - Environmental Hazard
Massachusetts - Hazardous Substance

Canadian Regulatory Information
All ingredients of this product comply with the New Substances Notification requirements of the Canadian Environmental Protection Act (CEPA).

This product contains more than 1% of a known, controlled ingredient regulated under WHMIS.

Class E - Corrosive Material

Ingredient(s) - Canadian Regulatory Information
2-Butoxyethanol
WHMIS - Ingredient Disclosure List
Monoethanolamine
WHMIS - Ingredient Disclosure List
Sodium hydroxide
WHMIS - Ingredient Disclosure List

European Union (EU) Regulatory Information
R20/21/22 - Harmful by inhalation, in contact with skin, and if swallowed
R34 - Causes burns
R36/37/38 - Irritating to eyes, respiratory system and skin
S1/2 - Keep locked up and out of reach of children
S13 - Keep away from food, drink, and animal feeding stuffs

Source: **www.ehsi.com**. Reprinted with permission.

PART II, MAINTENANCE AND RISK MANAGEMENT
APPENDIX B: SAMPLE MATERIAL SAFETY DATA SHEETS (MSDS)

MATERIAL SAFETY DATA SHEET
ACME SPECIAL FLOOR CLEANER - SAMPLE MSDS

---

15. Regulatory Information - Continued

European Union (EU) Regulatory Information - Continued
- S24/25 - Avoid contact with skin and eyes
- S26 - In case of contact with eyes, rinse immediately with plenty of water and seek medical advice
- S28 - After contact with skin, wash immediately with plenty of water
- S36/37 - Wear suitable protective clothing and gloves
- S51 - Use only in well ventilated areas
- S62 - If swallowed, do not induce vomiting; seek medical advice immediately; bring container label
- S7 - Keep container tightly closed

WHMIS - Canada (Pictograms)

DSCL - Europe (Pictograms)

---

16. Other Information

NFPA Rating
Health: 3
Fire: 0
Reactivity: 0
Other: COR

HMIS Rating
Health: 3
Fire: 0
Reactivity: 0
Personal Protection: C

Revision/Preparer Information
MSDS Preparer: Wiley Coyote
MSDS Preparer Phone Number: (908) 237-9348

Reference Documentation
        SAMPLE ONLY!! - DO NOT USE

Disclaimer

Although reasonable care has been taken in the preparation of this document, we extend no warranties and make no representations as to the accuracy or completeness of the information contained therein, and assume no responsibility regarding the suitability of this information for the user's intended purposes or for the consequences of its use. Each individual should make a determination as to the suitability of the information for their particular purposes(s).

EHS Innovators LLC

Printed Using MSDS Generator™ 2003

PART II, MAINTENANCE AND RISK MANAGEMENT
APPENDIX C: ADDITIONAL BIG TICKET MAINTENANCE ITEMS

ELECTRICAL SYSTEMS

Electrical problems have many causes. A comprehensive testing, inspection, analysis, and remedial design program is necessary to diagnose and correct problems. If designed and installed properly, electrical systems should be effective for the life of the building, if they receive proper maintenance.

The design of any electrical system should incorporate buildability and maintainability. *Buildability* means that the system can be assembled and will function. Maintainability means that, after completion, certain components can be accessed for regular inspection and/or removal for normal maintenance. The two features are not always present together.

The malfunctioning of machinery, failure within appliances, improper installation, or lack of adequate maintenance of electrical equipment should not be the cause of an electrical fire, unless some circuit-protection device does not function correctly. Normally all electrical energy used in a building is transformed into some other energy form (thermal, mechanical, etc.) that eventually becomes heat.

Fires and the Proper Installation of Electrical Systems

While heat is expected, sometimes it is created in places where it is not desired and where it can lead to fires. Since the current in the circuit is determined by the load, an increase of temperature comes from a localized increase of resistance along the conductors.

Many places along a circuit, such as splices, fuse clips, wire terminations, and relay or switch contacts, may potentially develop high resistance. Problems at these locations may occur because of improper installation. Even when installation is accurate, oxidation may develop on the conducting medium at various points because of environmental influences. A metal oxide is a less effective conductor than the metal, usually copper or aluminum, which means the resistance is increased and heat develops near oxidation sites. In high-current-carrying conductors, only a small increase in resistance is needed to significantly increase heating.

If left undetected, consequences of the heat development can result. Over a period of time, which may be several years, the temperature can become quite high. Insulation is rated from 75°C to 90°C for normal applications. Since copper is an excellent conductor of heat, insulation adjacent to the problem may melt away. Terminal blocks may carbonize at elevated temperatures and become conductive.

After a time, the heat will usually cause physical deformation of metal circuit components, which will leave a small air gap. The circuit voltage is sufficient to jump this gap, and an arc develops. The arc generates much higher temperatures

PART II, MAINTENANCE AND RISK MANAGEMENT
APPENDIX C: ADDITIONAL BIG TICKET MAINTENANCE ITEMS

and often causes erosion of material at the gap. Because all this happens while normal currents flow in the circuit, protective devices cannot detect an electrical problem.

Once an arc occurs, it may damage the device and the nearby wire to a point that they must be replaced. The arc may actually lead to a break in the conductor, which in turn may swing free and touch something else. Depending on the available fault current from the power source, very high currents may now flow to ground or to another conductor, which can generate heat of almost explosive force.

In less extreme cases, the conductor may simply break, with no adjacent damage. However, if this circuit serves a three-phase motor, loss of a phase will permit the motor to continue to run if lightly loaded. The circuit will overheat rapidly without tripping normal protective devices, destroying the entire motor.

Large-fused disconnect switches cost several hundred dollars, motor controllers approach a thousand dollars, and large motors are several thousand dollars. Obviously the direct cost of an electrical failure is significant, even if no fire results and no consideration is given to the inconvenience of replacing the device or the possible loss of productivity during the outage.

Ensuring Safety
An electrical system should be inspected to uncover areas that may cause harm. In an electrical system inspection, the manager must consider the desire for uninterrupted system operations as well as safety for personnel using the system.

The electrical safety regulations established by the Occupational Safety and Health Administration (OSHA) that became effective in April 1981 are generally quite reasonable. They are intended to avoid unnecessary hazards at the user level. Observing these rules will help reduce liability exposure.

There are two classes of OSHA rules: those that apply to new buildings or major renovations and specific rules that are retroactive to all buildings because of their more serious potential for employee injury. Examples of the latter: All circuit disconnect devices must have permanent labels identifying what they control, and all disconnect devices must be readily accessible. Electrical rooms may not be used to store anything that blocks electric panels, nor may devices be located where a ladder is required to reach them.

Detection Systems
Thermal imaging systems offer a heat picture of the equipment to be inspected, which can help detect problems before the onset of serious damage. These devices

PART II, MAINTENANCE AND RISK MANAGEMENT
APPENDIX C: ADDITIONAL BIG TICKET MAINTENANCE ITEMS

are similar to a portable TV camera and monitor system, except that the camera is sensitive to the infrared (IR) wave portion of the spectrum instead of the visible light spectrum. Viewed on a black-and-white TV set, the hot objects appear white, the cold objects black, and the temperate items as various shades of gray. Color versions of this equipment are also available. Usually however, color is neither needed nor useful for ordinary inspections.

Note that thermal imaging is very different from IR photography. Infrared film is sensitive only to the portion of the infrared spectrum that comes from very high-temperature sources, 400°F or greater. Thus, IR photos (as opposed to thermal images) involve reflected light waves from a high-temperature source, not the waves that are emitted due to the energy or heat of the object itself.

The resolution of thermal imaging systems ranges from 60 to 100 lines for lower-cost units and from 150 to 200 lines for more expensive units. These are significantly less than the 300 to 400 lines one can see on the better-quality broadcast TV monitors. The systems normally can operate continuously for the operator's viewing. If a permanent record is needed when a problem is detected, most units can take a picture of the TV image.

In many cases, IR testing is not excessively expensive and most insurance companies will cover the cost of IR testing on an annual basis.

Inspecting the Electrical System

In traditional electrical system inspections, building owners turn off the power to inspect a system. They then look for discolored items and tighten bolts, terminals, and so forth. This method is inconvenient and not always accurate. The inspector is not likely to disassemble a taped splice at a motor terminal box just to see if it is functioning correctly.

Therefore, a thermal imaging inspection should be conducted under normal operational load, the higher the better. The only inconvenience is that the covers and doors for all panels, breakers, control centers, and so forth must be opened or removed to permit direct viewing of the wire and other conductors.

When a problem appears, the temperature rise is measured and the affected item is identified. Current measurements are often made with a clamp-on-ammeter (instrument for measuring electric current), while direct temperature measurements are made using a digital contact thermometer. These measurements are important in defining whether differences in temperature on different phases are related to an imbalance in phase currents or to a problem on the phase itself.

A temperature rise of less than 5°C is not usually significant if the cause is explainable. Rises of 10°C to 15°C may indicate developing problems and warrant

PART II, MAINTENANCE AND RISK MANAGEMENT
APPENDIX C: ADDITIONAL BIG TICKET MAINTENANCE ITEMS

checking. Rises of 25°C and over 50°C warrant immediate attention. As a reference, most thermoplastic wire insulation is rated at 60°C to 70°C, including ambient conditions. The maximum temperature rise permitted at a terminal block is 50°C.

When performing a thermal inspection, if "hot spots" are detected it is important to shut off the panel and clean all areas. Then re-torque wire connections to obtain the proper tightness between the distribution panel and the wire.

The manager should also conduct visual inspections to detect things that thermal imaging does not reveal. Occasionally, discoloration will be observed at a problem point that is cool.

Sometimes maintenance personnel will replace a breaker that trips regularly with the next larger size, not realizing that the wire size does not permit this. Fused switches have been found with three different sizes of fuses in the three phases. Pieces of copper pipe and birds' nests have also been found in fuse boxes.

Maintainability
In addition to addressing the inspection of existing electrical systems, the manager should address maintainability, or accessibility for regular inspection and/or removal for normal maintenance. Maintainability is the key factor, and access is one of the most critical problems.

Unfortunately, building developers often regard space for electrical equipment as unproductive overhead, and therefore, they make the space as small as possible. Electrical equipment should not be located in areas of extreme temperature and humidity, such as boiler rooms or interior cooling towers. Steam traps should not be located where they can discharge into open drains near electrical equipment. Maintenance of motors involves the ability to clean them, change or lubricate bearings, adjust shaft alignment, lift them for replacement, and so on.

Dependable Emergency Power
Provision for emergency on-site generated power is becoming more essential. Three misconceptions about such power follow:

- The **emergency generator** will protect against everything. In fact, it protects only against the loss of utility power. Beyond its automatic transfer switch (ATS), the power flows through normal electrical switches. There is no further redundancy inside the building.
- **The ATS normally serves circuits that are never turned off, so how can routine preventive maintenance be performed?** Associated devices, called bypass-isolation switches, are now available to remove the ATS from service without disrupting isolation service. Such a device can be as large as the ATS itself, and electrical rooms often have no space for it.

PART II, MAINTENANCE AND RISK MANAGEMENT
APPENDIX C: ADDITIONAL BIG TICKET MAINTENANCE ITEMS

- **The National Electrical Code requires that the generator be tested regularly " under normal load."** In some buildings, the generator may be run regularly, but the transfer switch may not be activated because it disrupts the elevators or sensitive computer equipment. The switch is not tested, and then when needed, the transfer switch may not work properly to transfer power.

Whenever a building needs emergency power, it also needs accessories to ensure that the engine-generator set will function as intended. An alarm should be placed at a security station to indicate when the generator is running or when any malfunction, such as overheating, occurs. These alarm circuits should not rely on normal power to function.

Analysis to Prevent Failure
The electrical engineer, when inspecting an electrical system, should determine not only how the system works but also how the system may fail. Carrying out the latter function requires evaluating failure modes, in particular those that might happen together, and then devising a plan to avoid disaster.

- Are the circuits in the facility adequately documented in one-line drawings, or roadmaps of the electrical system, so that someone on the night crew can find where the faults lie?
- Does the electrical room have battery-powered lighting so that work can be done in the absence of any regular power?
- Does the facility's radio system require normal power to function? That would prevent its use during an emergency.
- Will the telephone system, particularly a computerized one, function without power for several hours?
- In a large electrical system, are there cross-feeds among load centers such that one could be fed from another if its normal feed system required maintenance?

An analysis of potential failure modes and the consequences of a failure may help avoid and/or overcome many future problems, making late-night and weekend emergencies less of a crisis.

Effective Circuit Protection
In large, complicated electrical systems, tests besides thermal imaging should be made. The main and sub-main protective devices have a complicated coordination pattern to ensure that the main breaker will not trip off on a minor branch circuit overload, but will open quickly on a serious fault. Current/time delay curves for these devices are designed to ensure their sequential operation. They should be tested regularly.

PART II, MAINTENANCE AND RISK MANAGEMENT
APPENDIX C: ADDITIONAL BIG TICKET MAINTENANCE ITEMS

Even in smaller systems, the actual tripping calibration of simpler circuit breakers may be in error. This problem can be alleviated somewhat if the important breakers are converted to use electronic sensing, which will eliminate the thermal and dashpot devices (mechanisms to avoid shock) on older units that frequently need maintenance. Systems with high feed or distribution voltages should have the cable and insulator voltage breakdown checked.

Electrical conduit should always be attached to a permanent structural support, such as a wall or beams and columns. Never hang conduit directly from a metal roof deck or directly on roof membrane. Conduit on the roof would be better placed on the outside of the building or routed under the roof.

Importance of Documentation
During inspections, the building owner often has no idea where all the various pieces of electrical equipment that require testing are located. One critical piece of documentation that should be kept up-to-date is the electrical one-line system layout print. A second is an inventory of motors, circuit protection devices, electrical panels, transformers, and so forth. Computer-aided drafting (CAD) systems are available for storing the details of system drawings.

Planning for maintenance of electrical systems is essential if good services are to be maintained. In addition, plan for maintenance when the electrical system is being designed. While most electrical systems are reliable, constant inspection for problems can eliminate serious damage and downtime.

SWIMMING POOLS

A properly maintained swimming pool can be an asset to a property, both as a prestigious amenity for current residents and as a marketable feature. However, if improperly maintained, a pool can become a liability, a health hazard, and an unsightly detraction from the property.

To ensure that a swimming pool remains an asset instead of a liability, the real estate manager should have a thorough understanding of the amenity and its maintenance requirements. The manager should begin by creating a pool maintenance log with one row devoted to each type of service provided including the following items as appropriate:

- Date/month of service
- Tile cleaning
- Changing filters
- Vacuuming

PART II, MAINTENANCE AND RISK MANAGEMENT
APPENDIX C: ADDITIONAL BIG TICKET MAINTENANCE ITEMS

- Brushing walls/floors
- Cleaning pump strainer
- Skimming
- Cleaning skimmer
- Cleaning deck/surrounding area
- Cleaning backwash filters
- Testing chlorine (note reading levels)
- Amount of chlorine added
- Testing acid (note reading levels)
- Amount of acid/alkaline added
- Additional comments
- Name of service person

By including the dates for jobs performed, the log serves as a useful reminder that each maintenance task has been completed on schedule.

Cleaning the Pool
Keeping the property's swimming pool clean involves several steps:

- **Brushing the walls.** Maintenance personnel should brush the walls, steps, benches, etc., all the way to the bottom, using a wide nylon or polypropylene brush on an extension rod. Whenever possible, brush toward the center drain so that the dirt will be pulled into the filter system.

- **Skimming the surface.** Maintenance personnel should skim the water surface with a standard line skimmer to remove leaves and other floating debris. The surrounding area should also be washed down and scrubbed if necessary.

- **Vacuuming the pool.** During the months that it is in use, the bottom of the pool should be vacuumed on a regular basis. Most pool vacuum cleaners plug into a special suction fitting built into the pool, thus getting their suction from the pool's pump. The maintenance worker simply trails the vacuum hose along the bottom of the pool to draw up any debris. Several automatic systems are also available that can be used instead of this manual method.

- **Cleaning the tile.** Regularly clean the tile at or near the water line to help prevent calcium buildup. An acid-based tile cleaner and a stiff-bristled tile brush work well on lighter calcium deposits. On heavier buildup, use a pumice stone.

PART II, MAINTENANCE AND RISK MANAGEMENT
APPENDIX C: ADDITIONAL BIG TICKET MAINTENANCE ITEMS

- **Cleaning equipment and filters.** A self-priming, centrifugal pump requires little care other than cleaning the strainer. The pump motor is factory-lubricated and does not require additional maintenance.
- Keep the air vent at the bottom of the motor free from obstructions that could restrict air flow. In addition, keep the motor clean to prevent rust.
- Remove and clear the pump strainer and skimmer basket of debris on a daily basis. Failure to keep baskets clean will reduce water circulation and permit air to enter the system.
- Clean the filter periodically. When sufficient dirt has been collected in the filter, pressure will rise and the recirculation flow will decrease substantially. In some instances, the filter may be cleaned by back washing (reversing the water flow through the filter). However, consult the manufacturer's operating manual for correct filter cleaning procedures.
- **Algae control.** The problem of algae is serious and ever-present in swimming pools. Even a small amount of algae in a pool will clog filters and impart a disagreeable odor or taste to the water. Furthermore, algae can interfere with the efficiency of chlorine and other common disinfectants. Although algae are not harmful to swimmers, they can create slippery floors and steps that may be hazardous.
- Chlorine is only effective in preventing the growth of some algae. To completely kill algae already present in a pool, an algicide must be added regularly to the pool water.

Cleaning and Testing Pool Water
In addition to cleaning the physical parts of the pool, maintenance involves testing and maintenance of the water to ensure that it is of the best quality for resident use.

- **Chlorine testing.** From the first day a pool is filled, its purity must be guarded and maintained by a chemical disinfectant. This disinfectant, whether chlorine, bromine, or iodine, must be maintained at a level high enough to kill any bacteria brought into the water by swimmers.
  - Chlorine is the most widely used and accepted disinfectant for swimming pools. At least 0.6, and preferably 1.0, parts per million (ppm) of free residual chlorine must be present in pool water at all times to kill bacteria. Obtain a simple test kit from your local pool supply vendor. If, after testing pool water, you find that levels are not at least 0.6 ppm, add more disinfectant.
  - Disinfectant chemicals may be added by hand or with a feeder that floats in the pool or is attached to the side. When liquid disinfectants are manually poured into a pool, begin at the deep end and walk gradually around the pool.

PART II, MAINTENANCE AND RISK MANAGEMENT
APPENDIX C: ADDITIONAL BIG TICKET MAINTENANCE ITEMS

o Also, evenly distribute granular or tablet-form (dry) disinfectant into the pool. Many dry disinfectants will cause pool water to become temporarily cloudy, but the haziness will soon disperse.

o Several factors affect chlorine longevity. These include the number of bathers, the intensity of the sunlight, water temperature (warmer water shortens disinfectant life), pH balance, pool water alkalinity, and winds and rains, which carry elements that overwork pool chemicals.

• **Testing for pH balance.** Improper balance between the acid and alkaline content of pool water can cause discomfort for swimmers, corrosion of metal pool parts, and leeching of plaster pools. Thus, regular testing of pool water for pH balance, using a standard test kit, will assist maintenance personnel in keeping water at its best. Because high chlorine residual affects the water's pH, conduct the pH test when chlorine levels are low.

o Recommended pH levels range between 7.2 and 7.6. If testing indicates that the pool water is too alkaline, muriatic acid or sodium bisulfate may be added in small quantities until pH levels are in balance. Never add more than one pint of acid in a single application, since additional acid may injure swimmers as well as damage pool surfaces or equipment. If additional acid is needed to adjust the pH, add it on successive days.

o Proper alkalinity levels for swimming pool water are usually between 80 and 100 ppm. A rule for adding alkalinity is that 1 1/2 pounds of sodium bicarbonate (baking soda) will raise the level of alkalinity on 10,000 gallons of water by 10 ppm.

General Pool Maintenance
A well-cared-for pool offers an attractive amenity to residents—an amenity that will remain valuable for years to come with regular maintenance. A few simple guidelines:

• Read directions for all chemicals carefully.

• Do not overuse chemicals; measure exactly. Using too many chemicals can cause irritating side effects.

• Do not guess about the amount to use. Take the time to use a test kit. Be sure that testing fluids are replaced annually to ensure accuracy.

• Establish a routine for testing and water treatment. A few minutes every day—or every other day—can assure that your pool is in top shape.

The small amount of time it takes to develop and implement a pool maintenance program will pay off in a more attractive, more leasable property.

PART II, MAINTENANCE AND RISK MANAGEMENT
APPENDIX C: ADDITIONAL BIG TICKET MAINTENANCE ITEMS

Safety Issues
Swimming pools and fountains present special safety concerns to residents and guests. In addition, they can expose employees to particular hazards.

Resident and Guest Safety
Most accidents involving drowning or severe injury occur to children under five years of age who are unsupervised, cannot swim, and fall into a fountain, a pool, or a pool cover with water on top of it. The second largest number of accidents involves teenagers, primarily males. Alcohol is often involved.

Some safety information and interesting statistics from the Association of Pool & Spa Professionals (**www.apsp.org**) follow. These items are worth reviewing with staff and including in on-site inspections. Most municipalities have laws that include rules and require inspections.

- Drowning and swimming accidents are best prevented by
  o Adult supervision
  o Public awareness programs that include water safety training for young children
  o Not drinking alcohol while swimming, diving, or soaking
- Pool and spa areas should have permanent barriers to entry. Local ordinances specify types of fences, fence heights, etc. The gate should be locked when the pool is not in use. Do not place chairs or tables near fences where they can enable a child to climb over and enter the pool area.
- The Association of Pool & Spa Professionals recommends using several approaches to safety and publishes a pamphlet entitled "Layers of Protection." The pamphlet discusses fences, door exit alarms, infrared detectors, security cameras, etc.
- Always have rescue equipment, such as ring buoys and reaching poles as well as a first aid kit, around the pool.
- Always remove a pool or spa cover completely before using the pool or spa. Do not let standing water remain on pool covers.
- A telephone and list of emergency telephone numbers should be near the pool or fountain.
- Make sure lights in pool areas work properly.

PART II, MAINTENANCE AND RISK MANAGEMENT
APPENDIX C: ADDITIONAL BIG TICKET MAINTENANCE ITEMS

LEGAL ISSUE:
The Virginia Graeme Baker Pool and Spa Safety Act went into effect on December 19, 2008. The federal law requires all commercial pools and swim clubs to have new drain covers or a Safety Vacuum Release System (SVRS) installed in all pools to meet the new code to prevent bodily injury and/or death. All covers and SVRS must meet or exceed the ASME/ANSI A112.19.8-2007 National Standards and ASTM G154 for UV Testing. The law is regulated by the U.S. Consumer Product Safety Commission as well as state and local pool inspectors. The bill states that the maximum fine is $1.8 million and for pool closure until it becomes compliant with the law. See **www.poolsafety.gov/vgb.html** for more information.

ELEVATORS

A basic knowledge of elevators can help the building owner and manager properly assess a building's needs and match the capabilities of different elevator companies appropriately.

Service
Building owners are concerned with elevator performance for two related reasons: 1) return on investment and 2) resident satisfaction. While return on investment is a standard concern for property owners, resident satisfaction is less tangible but equally important. Dissatisfaction can negatively affect building profitability by discouraging potential residents and angering current residents.

Residents may become dissatisfied with a building's elevator system because it has too few elevators. However, because architects and builders generally consult the leading elevator companies and independent contractors when deciding on the number, speed, and capacity of elevators to be installed, residents are more likely to become dissatisfied with the operation and performance of the elevators than with the quantity or speed.

An elevator system has electrical, mechanical, and often, hydraulic subsystems. Approximately 60 percent to 70 percent, of an elevator system's parts are subject to wear. When properly maintained and serviced, the average life expectancy of major parts is about 20 to 22 years. Many smaller parts will wear out much sooner, resulting in lowered performance and possibly causing a major subsystem to fail

PART II, MAINTENANCE AND RISK MANAGEMENT
APPENDIX C: ADDITIONAL BIG TICKET MAINTENANCE ITEMS

if they are not serviced promptly. For example, a worn selector device can affect brake-to-brake time, and make it difficult for the elevator to hold the floor. This poses a potential hazard.

The large number of elevator companies and independent elevator service organizations available can make choosing the right elevator service company a confusing process. A basic understanding of elevator functions and performance is required to select the proper maintenance contract.

Service Organization Evaluation Criteria
Use the following criteria to evaluate an elevator manufacturer's service capabilities and measure them against those of an independent service company.

- **Service organization expertise.** The company's service personnel should be highly trained technicians who work as a team to ensure the adequate handling of all types of routine and problem servicing. Back-up support should be available at all times.

- **Communication.** The company's frontline management team should serve as agent and representative for the building owner or manager when problems or questions arise.

- **Equipment.** The maintenance organization should have a full complement of equipment for basic repair. This includes sophisticated precision measuring and testing instruments.

- **Elevator usage and performance monitoring.** The company should have measuring devices to monitor building traffic and flow on a regular basis. Using these devices, performance criteria can be adjusted if elevators are experiencing unexpectedly high or low usage. When elevators are used more frequently than initially anticipated, adjustments must be made to reflect higher usage.

- **Parts availability.** Immediate access to required parts is critical to continuing performance. Frequently used parts should be stocked on-site or in a local office. Major spare parts should be available on a lending basis in an emergency.

- **Regularly scheduled maintenance.** Frequent routine examination of elevators should be included as part of the company's basic service. The company should also have back-up service personnel who can respond quickly if a routine call turns up a problem that requires immediate attention and additional expertise.

- **Equipment testing.** The company should also provide scheduled testing of equipment for compliance with the latest local and American National Standards Institute (ANSI) codes.

PART II, MAINTENANCE AND RISK MANAGEMENT
APPENDIX C: ADDITIONAL BIG TICKET MAINTENANCE ITEMS

• **Emergency service.** The service organization should respond quickly in an emergency situation. They must have the parts and personnel on hand to keep the elevators running. A good service organization will be able to obtain expertise, up to and including that of its chief engineer, to service an emergency situation.

If a maintenance contractor fails to provide these minimum requirements and allows equipment to deteriorate, the cost of repairing the neglect may far exceed the cost of properly preventing it.

Elevator Maintenance Contracts

The suggested minimum term of an elevator maintenance contract is five years, with the option to renew automatically for additional five-year periods, and the ability to terminate with 30 days advance notice. An advantage of this arrangement is that a five-year or longer contract forces the company performing the maintenance to commit itself to preventive maintenance and to forecast major replacements properly. Short-term contracts do not offer this protection.

An elevator maintenance company should also be able to keep the elevators running in like-new condition with minimum interruption of service. The company performing maintenance should keep the building owner and/or manager informed of the latest technological innovations to improve elevator service, maintain the integrity of the equipment, and enhance building values. The company should offer regular suggestions for ways to improve performance through adjustments or ongoing equipment modernization. This will help minimize the cost of future modernization.

Software programs operate many elevator systems. Larger companies will often include software upgrades to the system as a part of the standard maintenance contract. This should be considered when agreeing to a contract. Smaller independent companies have a much more difficult time keeping up with technological changes.

Modernization

Before any modernization work is performed, first determine if the real problem is actually maintenance-related. If it is, focusing on improved maintenance may save a substantial amount of money.

Buildings 10 to 20 years old may require second-generation elevator modernization, with an emphasis on operational updating to better respond to passenger demand.

Three questions should guide all modernization efforts:

PART II, MAINTENANCE AND RISK MANAGEMENT
APPENDIX C: ADDITIONAL BIG TICKET MAINTENANCE ITEMS

1. Was the original elevator system designed properly?
2. If so, what are the reasons for the current dissatisfaction?
3. How can the problem best be solved?

The focus is on performance and on understanding whether it can be adequately improved through repair or replacement of parts, or if innovations are required. Only after the system is at its peak operating condition can the need for and extent of modernization be decided.

Elevator systems 10 to 20 years old may require both control and operational updating. However, if the system initially installed was the most sophisticated available at the time, the problem is most likely an operational one, and the system will probably be less costly to modernize.

Although some very sophisticated control devices that provide fine service are on the market, not all buildings require them. For example, direct drive is a very energy-efficient control system—an excellent choice for a new installation and for some modernizations. However, a false conception exists about the total amount of power elevator systems use. When kilowatt costs in a given area are evaluated, the installation of a new form of control to conserve energy doesn't necessarily provide an adequate return on investment.

Other control modifications include incorporating new, sophisticated computer techniques. These control devices can provide some very dramatic operational improvements. Again, they must be weighed carefully for their necessity and value to the building, since major equipment might have to be replaced at substantial cost.

A series of modernizations that are performed in a relatively short span of time and that involve a gradual addition of features may create a costly chain effect. Each time an improvement is made, equipment that has already been modernized might again have to be changed to accommodate the new feature. This can add up to a time-consuming, costly procedure. With modernization of elevators, performing all necessary work once costs less than spreading the work out over time.

Accessibility
Because of the increased focus on building accessibility for the disabled, individual state and local codes have been enacted in an attempt to fill the gaps created by the American National Standards Institute (ANSI) standard. However, these codes sometimes conflict, and that, along with the large number of codes, can make compliance difficult and costly. A reliable elevator service company, acting

PART II, MAINTENANCE AND RISK MANAGEMENT
APPENDIX C: ADDITIONAL BIG TICKET MAINTENANCE ITEMS

as a consultant, can help ease the confusion and ensure that all necessary code requirements are met.

The decision to place an elevator on the outside of a building should be based on several factors, such as minimum disruption of operations, building construction, restricted access, and loss of usable area. Inside elevators are best in buildings where the facade would be marred by the addition of an exterior hoistway and in buildings where the elevator can be centrally located to provide the maximum convenience for all users.

If a building is located on a problem site, such as where there is hidden rock, subsoil water, or unstable or electrolyte conditions, a hydraulic elevator that does not require drilling can cut costs associated with geophysical problems. A "holeless" hydraulic, suitable for either interior or exterior installation, has several advantages. It does not disturb building footings, it requires a minimum of structural changes, and it reduces major remodeling costs.

Elevator Safety and Security

Analyzing a building's usage, resident needs, code requirements, and other factors, can help a professional elevator representative determine the building's safety and security needs with regard to its elevators. Safety and security packages can be tailored to meet the needs of almost any building. Three benefits of addressing safety and security in elevators follow:

1. Resident safety increased

2. Owner liability minimized

3. Loss and damage to the building and physical property lessened or eliminated

Emergency Service

At a minimal cost, elevators can be equipped with an emergency service that provides immediate access to specific holding areas to help prevent an emergency from becoming a disaster. In some areas, this feature is required totally, or in part, by code.

Emergency service operates in two phases:

PART II, MAINTENANCE AND RISK MANAGEMENT
APPENDIX C: ADDITIONAL BIG TICKET MAINTENANCE ITEMS

Phase 1	• All cars are brought to one location that prevents public use. • Automatic passenger cars return to the lobby (or another floor designated by local codes). • Cars already at the lobby remain parked with doors open. • Cars leaving the lobby reverse and return nonstop to the lobby. • The system is usually activated automatically by a sprinkler system or by heat and smoke sensors. • The system can be activated manually by a key switch in the lobby.
Phase 2	• Firefighters, paramedics, medical professionals, police, or other designated persons can use the elevators. • The system is initiated only with a key-operated switch in, or adjacent to, the car-operating panel. • Elevator functions are controlled directly from the car. • When appropriate, normal operating conditions can be restored quickly by bringing all cars to the lobby and by returning the two key switches to their normal positions.

Emergency service was designed to meet fire safety requirements, but it can also be used for medical emergencies, security threats, and other problems. Consult the elevator safety codes to determine which elevator safety features are needed.

Optional Packages

Optional emergency service packages include the following:

- **Riot control.** This system is designed to prevent unauthorized persons from gaining access to the upper floors of a building. A key switch is activated to remove all elevators from the lobby. Travel is limited between the second and top floors until normal operation is resumed. This feature is useful in government buildings, large corporate headquarters, or other buildings with high security priorities and the need for restricted access

- **Disaster protection.** This system is designed to minimize serious accidents and damage due to earthquakes or tremors. The force of an earthquake can overturn or shift elevator equipment, including guide rails, without necessarily shutting down the elevator car. Machinery tie-down and reinforced guide rails and supports are available for earthquake protection.

- **Safety features for explosions.** Elevators can be equipped with a system that detects any displacement and immediately sends a signal that hails the elevator.

PART II, MAINTENANCE AND RISK MANAGEMENT
APPENDIX C: ADDITIONAL BIG TICKET MAINTENANCE ITEMS

LIFE SAFETY SYSTEMS

Fire Sprinkler Systems

Many areas of the country have local fire codes that apply to sprinkler systems. The system must comply with local codes, so the real estate manager must remain aware of any changes to the code. Some code changes may require that the property be retrofitted with current systems.

Fire Sprinkler Types

Wet pipe sprinkler systems are the most common. As the name implies, a wet pipe system is one in which water is constantly maintained within the sprinkler piping. When a sprinkler activates, the water is immediately discharged onto the fire. The main disadvantage of these systems is that they are not suited for subfreezing environments. Another concern is in locations where piping is subject to severe impact damage and could consequently leak, e.g., warehouses.

A *dry pipe sprinkler* system is one in which pipes are filled with pressurized air or nitrogen, rather than water. The air or nitrogen holds a remote valve, known as a dry pipe valve, in a closed position. Located in a heated space, the dry pipe valve prevents water from entering the pipe until a fire causes one or more sprinklers to operate. Once that happens, the air escapes and the dry pipe valve releases. Water then enters the pipe, flowing through open sprinklers onto the fire. The main advantage of dry pipe sprinkler systems is their ability to provide automatic protection in spaces where freezing is possible. Typical dry pipe installations include unheated warehouses and attics, parking garages, outside exposed loading docks, and inside commercial freezers.

A *pre-action sprinkler* system employs the basic concept of a dry pipe system in that water is not normally contained within the pipes. The difference, however, is that water is held from the piping by an electrically operated valve, known as a pre-action valve. Valve operation is controlled by independent flame, heat, or smoke detection.

Two separate events must happen to initiate sprinkler discharge. First, the detection system must identify a developing fire and then open the pre-action valve. This allows water to flow into the system's piping, which effectively creates a wet pipe sprinkler system. Second, individual sprinkler heads must release to permit water to flow onto the fire. This feature provides an added level of protection against inadvertent discharge. For this reason, pre-action systems are frequently employed in water-sensitive environments such as archival vaults, fine art storage rooms, rare book libraries, and computer centers.

PART II, MAINTENANCE AND RISK MANAGEMENT
APPENDIX C: ADDITIONAL BIG TICKET MAINTENANCE ITEMS

Fire sprinkler heads have two types of activation devices:

- One device is a filament that melts when the temperature reaches a certain level. The sprinkler head is then activated.
- The second device has a small solder link or a glass tube. Heat melts the solder or the liquid expands causing the glass tube to shatter and the sprinkler head is activated.

Fire Sprinkler Concerns

In the past 10 years, corrosion-related failures have increased in fire sprinkler systems. Systems installed before the 1970s commonly used thicker wall, extra strong schedule 80 piping. Since then, thinner wall schedule 40 piping has been used, and over the last 20 years, the schedule 40 piping has been replaced with an even thinner wall schedule 10 piping. The problem with using thinner wall piping is that very little pipe wall is available to corrode before the pipe reaches minimal acceptable thickness limits.

Schedule 10 piping has less than half the wall thickness of schedule 80 piping. It can provide from 10 to 20 years of service. However, depending on the system and corrosion, failure can occur in as little as 5 years or less.

For high-pressure applications, schedule 10 piping will only provide acceptable service if there is no corrosion, which is almost an impossibility. Carbon black piping is traditionally used for fire sprinkler systems, and the water used in the systems is not chemically treated. Corrosion, then, is a real and serious condition that affects sprinkler systems.

Other factors that influence a system's operation are pipe location, material, age, and the frequency with which the pipe is drained and refilled. Systems that are frequently drained, extended, or modified suffer greater corrosion than systems in which water is left standing. In standing water, the oxygen level depletes and corrosion stops. A fire sprinkler system should never have a constant flow of water running through it.

A frequently running *jockey pump* (the jockey pump keeps a high positive pressure on the discharge side of fire pumps) or a cold, sweaty fire sprinkler pipe is a sign of a leak somewhere in the system. The worst situation is when an underground water leak goes undetected and continues for years.

PART II, MAINTENANCE AND RISK MANAGEMENT
APPENDIX C: ADDITIONAL BIG TICKET MAINTENANCE ITEMS

If a pipe is cold, water is likely to be entering the system. A stagnant pipe will have an ambient temperature. Rust and moisture condensation are also indications that water is entering the system.

Microbiologically influenced corrosion (MIC) can destroy a fire sprinkler system in just a few years. MIC is difficult to identify and requires metallurgical and microbiological testing. The cause and prevention of MIC are also not known at this time. MIC is a serious problem for clamped joint piping systems because microbes tend to flourish in small gaps between pipe ends. Systems should always be cleaned and sterilized when installed. Water flow should be minimized. Once MIC is firmly established in a system, most corrosion authorities consider it impossible to correct.

Buildup of iron oxide deposits is another serious threat to fire sprinkler systems. These deposits are created by corrosion, which can add thousands of pounds of moveable rust debris. The debris can dislodge and move through the system to control and actuating valves and eventually to sprinkler heads.

There are new concerns for fire sprinkler systems that did not exist previously. Managers must inspect sprinkler systems and carefully plan for maintenance and annual testing.

Fire Extinguishers
Fire extinguishers must be inspected frequently (usually annually or semiannually). To inspect a fire extinguisher:

- Ensure that access to the extinguisher is not blocked and that the cabinet door, if any, opens easily.
- Check that the pressure is within the recommended level on extinguishers equipped with a gauge. The needle should be in the green zone. If the needle is not in the green zone, the extinguisher requires professional maintenance. This should be noted on the inspection report.
- Verify that the locking pin is intact and the tamper seal is not broken.
- Visually inspect the hose and nozzle to ensure they are in good condition.
- Visually inspect the extinguisher for dents, leaks, rust, chemical deposits, or other signs of abuse or wear and note any findings on the inspection report. If the extinguisher is damaged or needs recharging, remove it from service and note this on the inspection report.
- Ensure that fire extinguishers are pressure tested (a process called hydrostatic testing) every six years to verify that the cylinder is safe to use. The inspection sheet should note all hydrostatic testing dates. If an extinguisher requires this service, this should be noted in the comments.

PART II, MAINTENANCE AND RISK MANAGEMENT
APPENDIX C: ADDITIONAL BIG TICKET MAINTENANCE ITEMS

Fire Hoses

The manager or maintenance supervisor must ensure the following:

- Fire hoses are free of debris.
- Fire hoses have no evidence of mildew, rot, or damage by chemicals, burns, cuts, abrasions, or vermin.
- Fire cabinets are not obstructed and the latches work.
- Nozzles are not damaged.
- No parts are missing.
- Shutoff valve works.
- Fire hoses are not for resident or building personnel use (for safety reasons).

Fire Alarm Systems

Fire alarm system maintenance typically requires a manufacturer's service technician because facility maintenance personnel usually do not possess the level of experience and knowledge necessary. A factory service agreement can range from a basic on-call agreement to regularly scheduled service visits. Most service agreements offer optional 24-hour-a-day emergency service with four- and eight-hour response times. This service usually provides response within the specified time, along with repair and replacement of the equipment.

Before signing a maintenance agreement, the manager must ensure that technicians are certified by the National Institute for the Certification of Engineering Technologies (NICET), and that they specialize in life safety.

Most system manufacturers recommend at least one full annual test and inspection after initial installation and acceptance. Various agencies, organizations, and local authorities recommend, and in some cases, mandate, testing intervals. The National Fire Protection Association (NFPA) provides the National Fire Alarm Code, NFPA 72. This standard covers the application, installation, performance, and maintenance of protective signaling systems and their components.

The local authority having jurisdiction (AHJ) and insurance companies also influence, recommend, or set forth standards they deem necessary for the proper operation of life safety systems. AHJs may establish guidelines that exceed NFPA guidelines.

PART II, MAINTENANCE AND RISK MANAGEMENT
APPENDIX C: ADDITIONAL BIG TICKET MAINTENANCE ITEMS

Fire Alarm System Test

A test of the alarm system should include the following:

1. Test and calibrate alarm sensors, such as flame and smoke detectors, per manufacturer specifications. This requires knowledge about the different sensors and their testing requirements, failure modes, and reinstallation requirements.

2. Simulate inputs and test the annunciators (electronically controlled signal boards). This requires specific knowledge of the system under test.

3. Set sensitivity. This requires an understanding of the particular system, the specific application, and fire detection theory.

4. Coordinate with the fire department to test the input to their system

5. Check the battery for corrosion and expiration date, and take appropriate action.

Smoke Evacuation Systems

Just as with fire alarm systems, smoke evacuation systems should be maintained and tested by certified technicians on a scheduled basis.

Smoke-Proof Towers

Smoke-proof towers are used in high-rise buildings and are designed to allow people to leave a floor without smoke following them and filling up the stairway. This is accomplished because the smoke-proof stairway has an intermediate vestibule, open to the outside atmosphere. Any smoke that follows people exiting the building will rise into the atmosphere instead of following people into the fire stairway.

Fire Drills

Fire drills are an important part of an overall fire safety plan. They should be conducted on an annual basis in conjunction with the fire department. The main purpose of a fire drill is to help residents understand how they should respond in the event of an emergency. Fire drills also allow residents to hear what the fire alarm sounds like, to hear the public address system (where provided), and to learn where the exits/stairs are located.

Security Systems

Whether the security system in a building consists of a card access system, a closed-circuit television system, or biometric access, this system needs to work perfectly every day. To maintain a security system properly, two considerations are very important—scheduled testing of the system and scheduled maintenance of

PART II, MAINTENANCE AND RISK MANAGEMENT
APPENDIX C: ADDITIONAL BIG TICKET MAINTENANCE ITEMS

the system. Testing and maintenance programs can minimize equipment failures, forecast impending operational problems, identify functional weaknesses, and help in future upgrades and improvements. Depending on the technical nature of the security system, contracting with a vendor to regularly service and repair the system may be necessary.

Depending on the type, location, and size of the building, talking with a security consulting firm may be helpful to a real estate manager. A security consulting firm can provide the following services:

- Physical risk assessment of the building and areas inside the building
- Perimeter control
- Access control
- Life safety issues
- Crisis management
- Evacuation protocol
- Emergency response planning
- Executive protection
- Business continuity

PART II, MAINTENANCE AND RISK MANAGEMENT
APPENDIX D: ADDITIONAL ENVIRONMENTAL ISSUES

Abestos

What is asbestos?	• *Asbestos* is the generic name for a group of natural minerals that separate into fibers that are incombustible and offer high tensile strength, good thermal and electrical insulating properties, and moderate-to-good chemical resistance.
Where is asbestos found?	• Asbestos can be found in pipe wrapping, acoustical ceilings, floor tile, caulking in joint and spackling compounds, etc.
Why is it a problem?	• It is a problem only when it is friable (crumbling into small particles or fibers). Asbestos fibers, individually invisible to the naked eye, cannot be destroyed or degraded easily and, due to their size and shape, remain airborne for long periods. Thus, building inhabitants can easily inhale them. Most fibers will not remain in the lungs, but those that remain do so indefinitely. • Airborne asbestos fibers can cause *asbestosis*, which contributes to the development of lung cancer.
What is the site manager's responsibility?	• Identify asbestos-containing materials before suspected material is disturbed by renovation or other work. (Conduct a building-wide inspection for asbestos-containing materials.) • Educate employees and residents to recognize problems.
What actions should be taken?	• Ensure that employees always wear proper respiratory protection, use special wet cloths when cleaning up around ACMs, and do not dry-brush or dry-sweep where asbestos dust or debris may be present. • Inform both employees and residents that they should not touch any possible asbestos-containing material, hang anything (i.e., decorative items) from such material, or bump into the material or push furniture against it. • Ensure that work done under a required permit includes proof that the space was tested for asbestos. This should be done regardless of building age. • Instead of requiring removal of asbestos, OSHA regulations focus on improving the management of existing asbestos through inspections, notifications, and employee training • The regulations also define four classifications of work practices that must be followed, regardless of anticipated asbestos levels

PART II, MAINTENANCE AND RISK MANAGEMENT
APPENDIX D: ADDITIONAL ENVIRONMENTAL ISSUES

Freon/Chlorofluorocarbons (CFCs)

What are CFCs?	• These manufactured molecules have chlorine (Cl) and fluorine (F) atoms replacing hydrogen atoms in hydrocarbon structures. Because they do not occur naturally, natural processes in the lower atmosphere do not destroy CFCs. They are generally used as liquids. In the gaseous form, CFCs rise into the upper atmosphere where they destroy ozone molecules.
Where are CFCs found?	• CFCs are used as refrigerants in air conditioners, refrigerators, and freezers, where they remain in liquid form in enclosed systems. (They are readily vaporized to gaseous form in the environment, however.) Check HVAC equipment and household appliances for leaks. • Although new products are not made with CFCs, old refrigerators and fire extinguishers still contain them.
Why are CFCs a problem?	• CFCs have been implicated in global warming and ozone depletion. Freon represents several different CFCs
What is the site manager's responsibility?	• Be aware of products containing CFCs and take responsibility for disposing of them appropriately.
Action items	• Choose less-damaging refrigerants, although this may require modification or replacement of some equipment. • Opt for products that do not include CFC aerosol propellants. • Train maintenance personnel on the proper procedures for reclamation, evacuation, and recycling, if necessary. • Require contractors to be certified (by state) for the recovery of Freon, and any work performed should be noted on a service ticket or job invoice.

PART II, MAINTENANCE AND RISK MANAGEMENT
APPENDIX D: ADDITIONAL ENVIRONMENTAL ISSUES

INDOOR AIR QUALITY (IAQ)

What is IAQ?

Most properties have acceptable air quality, and few real estate managers will ever have to handle IAQ problems. However, managers must be aware that certain human symptoms have been related to poor IAQ. When a number of people in a building exhibit symptoms related to poor IAQ, the building may be "sick." *Sick-building syndrome* (SBS) is a label used for buildings with poor IAQ. Symptoms of a sick building may include watery eyes, shortness of breath, nasal irritations, rashes, headaches, fatigue, dizziness, and flu-like symptoms.

What to Look for

IAQ is affected by a building's structure as well as its internal systems, occupancy, and location. The EPA defines four major contributors to IAQ:

Outside Sources

The 1990 *Clean Air Act* (CAA) and some earlier local ordinances instituted requirements concerning ambient air ("fresh" air from the outside surroundings). These regulations stipulate that a certain percentage of the air in a building has to be ambient air. Such regulations are worthwhile in most areas of the country, but in some *central business districts* (CBDs) the pollution from traffic and general operations may render outside air more polluted than the air recycled through the buildings.

Heating, Ventilation, and Air Conditioning (HVAC) Systems

HVAC systems not only control temperature (which affects the growth of a variety of organisms, including microscopic ones), they also regulate air supply (inflow and return). Too much inflow or return air in certain areas of the building can lead to a buildup of dust and other residues, cause drafts that may increase human exposure to certain substances, or create "cold spots" and "hot spots" in the building. Ventilation equipment must be properly maintained.

Building Occupants

Day-to-day activities of building occupants have an impact. From the perspective of IAQ, the most detrimental human activity is smoking. This "secondhand smoke" gets into the air-return system and leaves a residue in ducts and other HVAC system components.

Construction Materials

Every building is made up of a different combination of materials, each of which has a unique impact on IAQ (e.g., formaldehyde gas emitted by building materials and asbestos). Some caulks and sealants release *volatile organic compounds* (VOCs) that have an adverse effect on IAQ (e.g., paints, refrigerants, disinfectants, etc.).

PART II, MAINTENANCE AND RISK MANAGEMENT
APPENDIX D: ADDITIONAL ENVIRONMENTAL ISSUES

Action Items

Although real estate professionals do not need highly technical knowledge regarding IAQ, it is wise to have a basic understanding of typical IAQ problems, their origins, and possible solutions. The issue of IAQ becomes more important every day as public awareness of sick-building syndrome increases.

CARBON MONOXIDE (CO)

What is CO?

Carbon monoxide (CO) is a colorless, odorless, and toxic gas that is produced by the burning of solid, liquid, and gaseous fuels.

What to Look for

At lower levels of exposure, CO causes symptoms similar to the flu such as fatigue, nausea, headaches, and dizziness. However, because CO is impossible to see, taste, or smell it can be difficult to detect, and may cause death before its presence is even known.

Depending on the person, the effects of CO poisoning can vary greatly. Factors include age, overall health and the concentration and length of exposure.

Action Items

Carbon monoxide alarms are designed to alarm before potentially life-threatening levels of CO are reached. The U.S. Consumer Product Safety Commission (CPSC) recommends that one CO alarm be installed in the hallway outside the bedrooms in each separate sleeping area of the home. States and municipalities have passed laws requiring the installation of CO alarms.

An important step to reducing exposure to carbon monoxide is to ensure combustion equipment is maintained and properly adjusted. Additional steps include:
- Keep gas appliances properly adjusted
- Consider purchasing a vented space heater when replacing an unvented one
- Use proper fuel in kerosene space heaters
- Install and use an exhaust fan vented to outdoors over gas stoves
- Open flues when fireplaces are in use
- Choose properly sized wood stoves that are certified to meet EPA emission standards. Make certain that doors on all wood stoves fit tightly.
- Have a trained professional inspect, clean, and tune-up central heating system (furnaces, flues, and chimneys) annually. Repair any leaks promptly.
- Do not idle the car inside garage
- Never burn charcoal inside a home, garage, vehicle, or tent.

PART II, MAINTENANCE AND RISK MANAGEMENT
APPENDIX D: ADDITIONAL ENVIRONMENTAL ISSUES

CARBON DIOXIDE (CO_2)

What is CO_2?

Carbon dioxide (CO_2) is a colorless, odorless gas that occurs naturally in the environment. Although it comprises a very small percentage of our atmosphere, it is vital for nearly all forms of life. Animals exhale carbon dioxide and plants use photosynthesis to convert it to sugars and other forms of energy.

Carbon dioxide is also generated artificially and has many commercial applications. For example, carbonation in beverages and fire suppression since it does not support combustion.

Although it is naturally present in the atmosphere, carbon dioxide is considered a "greenhouse gas." Many activities, such as the combustion of fossil fuels, have drastically increased the concentration of CO_2 in the atmosphere and contributed to global warming.

What to Look for

Because we breathe out carbon dioxide, the highest concentrations of this gas can be found in rooms where most people spend the most time. Animals, cooking appliances, and cigarette smoking can also increase the carbon dioxide content within these areas.

Working in a building with poor ventilation, may cause a buildup of CO_2 which can lead to adverse health effects. Common complaints from increases in CO_2 levels include difficulty in breathing, increase in the breathing rate and/or pulse rate, headaches, sweating, shortness of breath, abnormal fatigue and a feeling of "stuffiness."

At extremely high levels the symptoms can include nausea, dizziness, mental depression, shaking, visual disturbances, vomiting, and loss of consciousness. The seriousness of the symptoms is dependent on the concentration of carbon dioxide and the length of time the individual is exposed.

Action Items

The use of a well-designed, properly operated, mechanical ventilation system is the most effective way to reduce indoor carbon dioxide levels.

Additional measures to prevent the concentration of carbon dioxide include:

- Adding fresh air to a room periodically by opening doors and windows
- Ensuring that all gas burning appliances are properly vented
- Turning on exhaust fans over cooking equipment and in bathrooms.

PART II, MAINTENANCE AND RISK MANAGEMENT
APPENDIX D: ADDITIONAL ENVIRONMENTAL ISSUES

Finally, Carbon Dioxide detectors are an easy way to continuously check CO_2 levels and provide data to maintenance personnel in order to adjust HVAC ventilation rates and ensure resident safety and comfort.

The Occupational Safety and Health Administration (OSHA) has set a standard for the maximum allowable concentration of carbon dioxide in the air of 0.5 percent (5000 ppm) for eight continuous hours of exposure.

RADON

What Is Radon?
Radon is a colorless, odorless gas that occurs naturally as a by-product of the radioactive decay of radium and uranium. It collects in the lower levels of energy-efficient buildings (insulation limits air flow from inside to outside), more often in buildings with slab foundations than in those with basements.

What to Look for
Radon enters the building in many ways—through the soil, via underground water, and in natural gas. It seeps through all but the most airtight substances and infiltrates a structure along water lines, gas lines, and walls. As we become more energy efficient and dwellings are made more airtight, radon cannot dissipate as easily.

Lung cancer is the health risk most frequently associated with the inhalation of radon. Even though the life span of radon is only about three days, it can damage lungs in a short time. Radon testing is a good business practice, and it is very inexpensive.

Action Items
The EPA recommends a variety of methods to mediate radon entry into residential structures. An effective radon reduction system includes a combination of seal s on foundations, basement floors, walls, and other areas of the structure that come into direct contact with the ground and ventilation systems (e.g., fans, piping) to help diffuse and dissipate radon.

One ventilation method that has met with some success is the installation of a series of underground pipes beneath the foundation and/or around the basement walls; these pipes vent above ground. This method actually provides an alternative route for radon, preventing it from entering the building in the first place. Sometimes piping and fans are placed in critical areas. An attic fan is another effective tool for removing radon. See **www.epa.gov/radon/ index.html** for more information.

PART II, MAINTENANCE AND RISK MANAGEMENT
APPENDIX D: ADDITIONAL ENVIRONMENTAL ISSUES

LEAKING UNDERGROUND STORAGE TANKS (USTS)

What Are USTs?

Underground fuel storage tanks can cause contamination of groundwater due to leakage. Such leaking *underground storage tanks* (USTs) have spurred regulations that require inspection, testing of tanks still in use, and repair or replacement of tanks that are leaking.

Some state and local regulatory authorities, however, may include these tank types in their UST regulations—the property owner and the manager must check with those authorities if they have questions about the requirements for their tank type. Some states require USTs to be registered and periodically inspected by a state-approved vendor. The following Web site has information regarding procedures for dealing with these types of concerns: **www.epa.gov/swerust1/states/statcon1.htm**. Note that state and local environmental laws may be more stringent than the federal regulations, in which case the former prevail.

What to Look for

If underground storage tanks are on a property, the manager should watch for the following signs of possible leaking:

- An odor or an oily sheen on water near the facility
- Residents or neighbors complaining about vapors in their basements or water that tastes or smells of petroleum
- Equipment that does not operate correctly, for example, erratic behavior of the dispensing pump
- Monitoring devices indicate a leak

If a leak is suspected, state and local agencies must be notified within 24 hours or other period specified by the state or local agency. Take action to stop the leak and make sure there is no safety threat to the vicinity. Spills or overfills of 25 gallons or less, or an amount specified by state or local authorities, don't have to be reported if they can be contained and cleaned up within 24 hours.

Based on the information provided about a leak, the governing agency will decide if further action must be taken at the site. The manager may need to develop and submit a corrective action plan that explains how requirements for the site will be met.

PART II, MAINTENANCE AND RISK MANAGEMENT
APPENDIX D: ADDITIONAL ENVIRONMENTAL ISSUES

 Single Family Home Impact: Leaking USTs are a significant issue with single family houses. If single family houses are a part of your portfolio, you should be aware of any underground storage tanks on the property and routinely inspect for signs of leakage

POLYCHLORINATED BIPHENYLS (PCBS)

What are PCBs?

PCBs are used as heat transfer agents in electrical transformers. They are essentially harmless if undisturbed. However if a transformer leaks, burns, or explodes, lethal dioxin gas may be released.

The Environmental Protection Agency (EPA) has classified PCBs as human carcinogens, hazardous materials, and priority toxic pollutants. When PCBs are introduced into the environment, they contaminate soil, water, plants, and animals and can eventually contaminate the entire food chain. Contamination from PCBs affects the eyes, throat, liver, and skin. Children are especially sensitive to exposure. Physical side effects in humans include skin cancer, liver cancer, cirrhosis of the liver, anorexia, and permanent eye damage.

What to Look for

The presence of PCBs may complicate the sale or purchase of a property. PCB-containing electrical transformers have been around for many years; some of them are still in use and have presented no threat to the environment. However, when PCBs are discovered on a property, it is crucial to take the time to determine the best, safest, and most cost-effective plan of action regarding them.

Action Items

Consult with the local utility and have electrical transformers on the property checked out, especially if the transformers were installed before 1976. The utility can identify PCB-containing transformers, which should be inspected regularly to make sure they are not leaking. Also keep in mind the following:

- Only authorized waste handlers may dispose of leaking transformers, and they must dispose of them in licensed locations.

- Property owners are liable for any PCB contamination, even after a leaking transformer has been removed.

- Transformers may be owned by the electrical utility that is responsible for their maintenance.

PART II, MAINTENANCE AND RISK MANAGEMENT
APPENDIX D: ADDITIONAL ENVIRONMENTAL ISSUES

FIBERGLASS

What is Fiberglass?

Fiberglass, sometimes called fibrous glass, is a man-made fiber in which the fiber-forming substance is glass. Fiberglass is an extremely useful manufactured product. It has numerous commercial applications, such as reinforcing plastic materials and serving as insulation in buildings, stoves, refrigerators, and furnaces. Its physical properties make it ideal for structural building materials because it is inert, lightweight, and heat resistant, and it is a very strong fiber. These same properties are also responsible for some of the hazards it produces in the workplace.

What to Look for

Building construction and maintenance workers who use fiberglass may be exposed to airborne fibers from the fiberglass itself and to various chemicals associated with its use.

- Direct contact with fiberglass materials or exposure to airborne fiberglass dust may irritate the skin, eyes, nose, and throat. These fibers may cause permanent damage to the lungs or airways or may increase the likelihood of developing lung cancer. Inhaling the fibers may irritate the airways, resulting in cough and production of excess mucus.

- *Resins* are chemicals used in lacquers, varnishes, and plastics or in combination with other components to form plastics. They are also used to strengthen, harden, or give flexibility to fiberglass. Breathing epoxy resins may cause chest tightness, shortness of breath, or wheezing. Skin contact can cause a rash.

- *Styrene* is part of the polyester resin used with fiberglass. It is extremely irritating to the eyes and nose at low concentrations; at higher concentrations it causes headache, dizziness, and sometimes nausea.

- *Acetone and MEK* (Methyl Ethyl Ketone) are commonly used solvents in fiberglass lay-up and spray-up. They are irritating to the eyes, nose, and throat. Inhaling the vapors may cause drowsiness, breathing difficulties, and serious damage to the lungs and nervous system.

Action Items

There are several ways to reduce risks of exposure to fiberglass and the toxic substances often used with it.

- Adhere to Occupational Safety and Health Administration (OSHA) Hazard Communication Standards to protect workers from hazards and risks.

- Adequately ventilate fiberglass work areas.

- Provide protective clothing and equipment (e.g., gloves, goggles, dust masks, booties) to help prevent skin problems by reducing direct contact

PART II, MAINTENANCE AND RISK MANAGEMENT
APPENDIX D: ADDITIONAL ENVIRONMENTAL ISSUES

with glass fibers.

• Ensure that fibers don't spread to the HVAC system or clothing because that can cause further contamination.

HAZARDOUS WASTE

Hazardous waste presents immediate and long-term risks to humans, animals, plants, and the environment. It requires special handling for detoxification or safe disposal.

In the United States, *hazardous waste* is legally defined as any discarded solid or liquid that contains one or more of 39 carcinogenic, mutagenic, or teratogenic (causing developmental malformations) compounds at levels that exceed established limits (including many solvents, pesticides, and paint strippers) and that (1) catches fire easily, (2) is reactive or unstable enough to explode or release toxic fumes, or (3) is capable of corroding metal containers such as tanks, drums, and barrels.

Examples include:

• Automotive products, such as gasoline, antifreeze, and batteries

• Oil-based paints and thinners

• Pool chemicals

• Pesticides, herbicides, and other garden products

• Household cleaning products (acids, ammonia, chlorine bleach, oven and drain cleaners)

Proper disposal of hazardous waste is imperative for the health and safety of residents and the environment. Check state and local listings for specific rules and regulations regarding disposal procedures.

In addition to the identification and disposal of hazardous maintenance items, the real estate manager should establish procedures for handling situations involving potentially harmful substances. The primary concern is the protection and safety of residents and maintenance personnel. Trained personnel who have the proper protective equipment and/or, when required, experts who have the proper certification, should perform maintenance and clean-up when one of the following is present:

PART II, MAINTENANCE AND RISK MANAGEMENT
APPENDIX D: ADDITIONAL ENVIRONMENTAL ISSUES

- Toilet overflow
- Sewage backup
- Bodily fluid
- Crime scene
- Syringe

RESOURCES:
www.learner.org/exhibits/garbage/hazardous.html

Page numbers followed by "f," such as 320f, indicate figures.

T

"Tag and tear" inventory system, 187
Tankless hot water heaters, 215
Tap Inspect (app), 152
Tar-and-gravel roofs, 206f, 207f
Tardiness, 67
Target market, 268
Taxes, 129, 227, 343
Teams, 12, 177, 180, 282–283
Technology, responding to, 12
Telephone, 53
Tenancy:
    holdover, 321, 355
    month-to-month, 360
Tenant organizations, 371
Tenants. *See also* Residents
    defined, 370
    duties, 316
    Hispanic, 299
    rights, 316–317
Term, 371
Termination:
    of employment, 69, 72–73, 371
    of occupancy, 319f, 324, 371
Term rent, 371
Territorial reinforcement, 163f
Testing:
    chlorine, 389–390
    drug, 47
    elevator equipment, 393
    fire alarm system, 402
    infrared, 384
    job applicant, 44
    pH balance, 390
    pool water, 389–390
Themes:
    property, 269, 270
    site management, 5–7
Theory X, 8
Theory Y, 9
Theory Z, 9–10
Thermal imaging systems, 383–385
Tile roofs, 207f
Time management, 17
Time off, 50
Title VII (Civil Rights Act), 27, 29–32
Title X, 242
Total Quality Management (TQM), 10–11
Townhouses, 371
Toxic Substances and Control Act, 242
Traditionalists (generation), 13
Traffic, 371
Traffic reports, 278, 279f, 371
Training and development, 19, 66, 336

Transfer (risk management method), 159f
Transfer clause, 323
Truth, moments of, 333
Tumblr, 276
Turnover, 70–73, 371
Twitter, 275, 276

U

Umbrella liability insurance, 371
Underground storage tanks (USTs), 410–411
Unfavorable budget variance, 98–99, 99f,
    100, 101, 102f
Unions, 61, 70
Unit air conditioners, 215
Unit files, 142–143
Unit mix, 371
Unit size, 371
Universal design, 372
Unlawful detainer, 326
Unscheduled income, 108, 372
Upheaval, 221
Urgency, 53, 294
U.S. Bureau of Economic Analysis, 257
U.S. Department of Energy, 225, 225f
U.S. Department of Housing and Urban
    Development (HUD):
    citizenship/immigration status
        inquiries, 306–307
    defined, 349
    discrimination, 299
    "Fair Housing Accessibility Guidelines,"
        305
    Fair Housing App, 297
    fair housing assessment, 308
    familial status, 300–301
    Housing Choice Voucher program, 306
    occupancy guidelines, 300–301, 311
    reserve plans, 128
    service animals, 304–305
U.S. Department of Justice, 300, 302, 304, 309
U.S. Department of Labor, 22
Useful life, 372
Use of premise clause, 171
USTs (underground storage tanks), 410–411
Utilities and services clause, 319f, 321

V

Vacancy:
    defined, 372
    economic, 106, 350
    physical, 106, 364
Vacancy and collection loss, 106–107
Vacancy rate, 255, 256, 372
Vacancy reports, 114, 114f
Vacant apartments, showing, 290–291